THE RUSSIAN COLD

The Environment in History: International Perspectives
Series Editors: Stefania Barca, *University of Coimbra*; Kieko Matteson, *University of Hawai'i at Mānoa*; Christof Mauch, *LMU Munich*; Helmuth Trischler, *Deutsches Museum, Munich*

Recent volumes:

Volume 22
The Russian Cold: Histories of Ice, Frost, and Snow
Edited by Julia Herzberg, Andreas Renner, and Ingrid Schierle

Volume 21
Risk on the Table: Food Production, Health, and the Environment
Edited by Angela N. H. Creager and Jean-Paul Gaudillière

Volume 20
The Meanings of a Disaster: Chernobyl and Its Afterlives in Britain and France
Karena Kalmbach

Volume 19
Conservation's Roots: Managing for Sustainability in Preindustrial Europe, 1100–1800
Edited by Abigail P. Dowling and Richard Keyser

Volume 18
Colonial Seeds in African Soil: A Critical History of Forest Conservation in Sierra Leone
Paul Munro

Volume 17
Hazardous Chemicals: Agents of Risk and Change, 1800–2000
Edited by Ernst Homburg and Elisabeth Vaupel

Volume 16
Planning for the Planet: Environmental Expertise and the International Union for Conservation of Nature and Natural Resources, 1960–1980
Simone Schleper

Volume 15
Changes in the Air: Hurricanes in New Orleans from 1718 to the Present
Eleonora Rohland

Volume 14
Ice and Snow in the Cold War: Histories of Extreme Climatic Environments
Edited by Julia Herzberg, Christian Kehrt, and Franziska Torma

Volume 13
A Living Past: Environmental Histories of Modern Latin America
Edited by John Soluri, Claudia Leal, and José Augusto Pádua

For a full volume listing, please see the series page on our website: http://berghahnbooks.com/series/environment-in-history

The Russian Cold
Histories of Ice, Frost, and Snow

Edited by
Julia Herzberg, Andreas Renner, and Ingrid Schierle

First published in 2021 by
Berghahn Books
www.berghahnbooks.com

© 2021, 2025 Julia Herzberg, Andreas Renner, and Ingrid Schierle
First paperback edition published in 2025

All rights reserved. Except for the quotation of short passages for the purposes of criticism and review, no part of this book may be reproduced in any form or by any means, electronic or mechanical, including photocopying, recording, or any information storage and retrieval system now known or to be invented, without written permission of the publisher.

Library of Congress Cataloging-in-Publication Data

A C.I.P. cataloging record is available
from the Library of Congress
Library of Congress Cataloging in
Publication Control Number: 2021031573

British Library Cataloguing in Publication Data

A catalogue record for this book is available from the British Library

ISBN 978-1-80073-127-1 hardback
ISBN 978-1-80539-750-2 paperback
ISBN 978-1-80539-928-5 epub
ISBN 978-1-80073-128-8 web pdf

https://doi.org/10.3167/9781800731271

Contents

List of Illustrations   vii

PART I. FOUNDATIONS

Introduction. The Russian Cold   3
    Julia Herzberg, Andreas Renner, and Ingrid Schierle

Chapter 1. Climate Ideas and the Cold in Russia   19
    Julia Herzberg

PART II. SCIENCE AND POLITICS

Chapter 2. The Nature of Cold: Russia's Climate and the Academy of Sciences in the Eighteenth Century   47
    Julia Herzberg

Chapter 3. The Russian South Pole Expedition in the Context of Political Interests of the Soviet Union during the Cold War Era   74
    Erki Tammiksaar

Chapter 4. *The Subarctic*: A Classic Soviet Study of the Tundra   95
    Denis J. B. Shaw

PART III. IMAGES AND NARRATIVES

Chapter 5. From a "Country of Cold and Gloom" to a "Welcoming Land": Climate and the Image of Siberia in the Russian Periodical Press, 1860s to the Early 1900s   113
    Nataliia Rodigina

Chapter 6. Local Warming: Cold, Ice, and Snow in Russian and
    Soviet Cinema   134
    Appendix: Filmography   154
      Oksana Bulgakowa

Chapter 7. The Aesthetics of Cold: Narrating National Trauma
    in Film   169
      Roman Mauer

PART IV. PAIN AND PLEASURE

Chapter 8. The Wehrmacht and the Russian Winter: The Impact
    of Climate at the Front and in Soviet Captivity   187
      Aleksandr Kuzminykh

Chapter 9. Winter Tourism and Skiing in the Soviet Union: School
    of Courage, Source of Health, National Pastime   204
      Aleksei Popov

Chapter 10. Heroes of the Ice: The Polar Explorer and the Ice Hockey
    Player as Two Masculine Identity Scripts of the Soviet Era   226
      Alexander Ananyev

Conclusion   249
    Julia Herzberg, Andreas Renner, and Ingrid Schierle

Index   255

Illustrations

Figures

8.1. Average monthly air temperature in Moscow in 1941–42 and "normal" (mean annual) temperature values (second curve). — 189

Maps

3.1. Islands in the southern hemisphere discovered by the Russian Antarctic expedition (Bellinsgauzen 1831). — 77

3.2. Map no. 61 from *Atlas of Bellingshausen*, the route of the Russian Antarctic expedition near the coast of Alexander I Land on 17/29 January 1821. — 78

3.3. The map of the voyage of the Russian Antarctic expedition around Antarctica compiled by Soviet geographers and published first in 1949. — 81

Tables

4.1. Geographic zonality. — 102

9.1. Winter tourist routes across the Soviet Union involving active means of travel (1980). — 213

 PART I

Foundations

Introduction
The Russian Cold

Julia Herzberg, Andreas Renner, and Ingrid Schierle

"In general, the country lacks heat."[1] With this statement Paul E. Lydolph opens his introduction to climatology in the Soviet Union. Like its vast expanses of land, Russia's cold was one of the characteristic features that travelers in Russia expected to experience—even if the actual temperatures, particularly in the European part of Russia, were in fact nearly not as extreme as they were portrayed in the persistent narratives about Russia's legendary frosts. The explorer Alexander von Humboldt, who traveled through Russia in the early nineteenth century, noted in his report that the cold seldom reached the point that the mercury in his thermometer froze: "Even cold of -25°R is rarer in Petersburg than travelers claim."[2]

Yet even though the frigid temperatures failed to live up to Humboldt's expectations, Russia's continental position means that the country was and is shaped by cold: a cold that has left its mark on the living environments of its residents, as well as on external perceptions and the self-image of Russia. The annually repeating cycle of cold, long winters, frost, ice, and snow is a pattern that can be interpreted as strongly influencing the social world. Connections have been frequently drawn between the development of serfdom, in particular the specific form it assumed in Russia, and the climatic conditions of the sixteenth and seventeenth centuries. Other key events in Russian history—above all wartime victories, from the Battle on the Ice, fought on the frozen Lake Peipus in 1242, to the victory over the Grande Armée in 1812 and the German forces in World War II—are similarly linked to narratives of cold. There is no doubt that these historic events reinforced the view of snow, ice, and cold as close allies of the Russians, but even more than that, as a central element of local, national, and imperial identity. The glorification of cold that flourished particularly during the Cold War era has led to Russia's harsh climate being seen as a constant, while the climatic diversity of the country has often tended to be neglected both in popular accounts and in historical studies.[3]

At present, however, the idea of harsh winters and extreme cold as unchanging features of the Russian world is beginning to be threatened. As a result of climate change, which has a particularly visible impact on Arctic regions, global warming has become a source of both hope and concern for the residents of Russia and for politicians and economists. On the one hand, warmer temperatures may make it possible to grow crops in regions that have until now been unsuitable for agriculture, and they may spur on economic growth and open up the Northeast Passage for regular shipping traffic.[4] Popular science writers like A. P. Nikonov write enthusiastically about how the thawing of the permafrost regions could extend the territory of Russia.[5] With every degree of warming, optimists suggest, Russia could enjoy an annual savings of 120 million tons of fuel.[6] "We are terribly lucky: Russia is the center of global warming, which means that warming has a tendency to be magnified: A 2°C increase in global temperature will in Russia result in 4–5°C, and in some places 10°C!"[7] Soon, so goes the prediction, it will be possible to harvest grapes in Moscow.[8] Again and again, it is suggested that Russia is one of the few countries that will profit from climate change.[9] The yearning for an end of the cold as a consequence of global warming recalls utopias of the Cold War era in which Soviet scientists hoped that an "improvement" of the world climate would also strengthen Russia's position in the struggle between the world powers.[10] Again and again, Russia's poor economy, its difficulties providing supplies, and its food shortages have been connected to its northern position. For example, Russia is described as disadvantaged in comparison with the United States because more than 80 percent of its farmland is located "within the least productive thermal zone,"[11] while in the United States this is the case for only 19 percent of the farmland.[12] A few years before the collapse of the Soviet Union, it was even claimed that "climactic limitations" were the reason why Russia had fallen behind the United States.[13]

However, there are others, particularly from within the world of science and academia, who warn that the consequences of global warming will likely not be quite so positive: Russia, they note, is extremely vulnerable.[14] In their studies, researchers point out negative ways that climate change will affect the regions like the north, which are already seeing the thawing of the permafrost layer and an increase in extreme weather and droughts.[15] This is felt particularly in the northern cities where the infrastructure breaks down and once-solid ground turns into marsh.[16] But the greatest concern is that the thawing of the permafrost will release large quantities of methane that will in turn further accelerate climate change processes. These new insights have led to increasing skepticism among the general population of Russia about the supposed advantages of climate change, even while the topic of global warming is still a low-key problem in official and public discourses.[17]

The debates about climate change have also strengthened discussions about the economic and geostrategic potential of the northern, climatically poorly situated regions. For the governments of Gorbachev and Yeltsin, these regions were of little political importance; today, however, Vladimir Putin and Dmitrii Medvedev have directed the focus of Russian politics northward again. The melting polar ice has launched a new "race for the Arctic" that is reminiscent, both in terms of its political direction and in terms of the narratives and imagery it employs, of the myth of the Arctic during the 1930s and the Cold War. Once again, the Arctic regions are being valued as fundamental for Russia's position and power as a world player and for its national security; once again the costs of living in the cold are a topic of much discussion.[18] Russia dominates the Arctic region geographically, with its territory encompassing half of the Arctic coastline and 40 percent of land within the Arctic Circle. Three-quarters of the Arctic population live in Russia.[19] While the major cities of the far North in Alaska, Canada, and Greenland have around 10,000 residents, Russia's northern cities often contain more than 100,000 residents. With spectacular initiatives that have gained the support not just of the general population but also of representatives of science and industry, Russian political leaders are determined to stake their claim as masters of the Arctic and the cold. In 2007, the three-person crew of a Russian submersible descended to the sea floor below the geographic North Pole and planted a titanium Russian flag at a depth of 4,261 meters.

In an era in which the future of cold as a fixture of Russian identity has become uncertain and, simultaneously, climate awareness in Russia is growing in part due to the significance of the country for the global climate and weather system, this volume looks into the past to take stock of the historical research on Russia's cold climate. The contributors work in a variety of scholarly traditions and offer a variety of different perspectives on how to "read" cold in Russian culture and history. Through this work, we have sought to understand and emphasize the multiplicity and ambiguity of meaning and values given to "cold" and to explore the relevance of environmental-historical research questions for writing a climate-based history of Russia. There are a number of goals connected with this interdisciplinary venture.

First, it picks up on new trends in environmental history that seek to decouple climate from its primary associations with climatology as a natural science.[20] Climate science, like most natural sciences, is not historically contextualized. The volume contributes both to the cultural history of climate and to historical studies into the effects of climate. It reveals moments in which the perception of climate changed in tsarist and Soviet Russia, but it will also provide insights into the ecological, social, and political circumstances that sought to promote climate stability or climate change. The volume will complement extant studies of historical perceptions of weather, climate, and climate change, which for the most part ignore tsarist Russia and the Soviet Union and which are mostly limited to the "Little Ice Age" and the twenty-first century.[21]

While in earlier historical studies the reconstruction of climate was a central concern, our volume turns instead to the topic of climate-impact research and the history of climate knowledge. In particular, we show that it was experiences of extreme cold in particular that awakened scholarly interest in understanding weather and climate. Furthermore, the wide range of variation within Russia, which encompasses multiple and diverse climate zones, created conditions that were particularly favorable to studying weather and climatic patterns. Here the volume connects with studies that trace the emergence of Russian environmental knowledge.[22]

Societies interact with the climate and its fluctuations in a wide variety of ways, from their architectural styles and construction materials to their crop choices. But they also interact with the climate and weather through cognitive constructs, through their ideas about what causes it and whether it can be influenced by human efforts. This volume discusses the ways in which Russians have adapted to cold climate in history. It shows how they have coped with the disastrous effects of cold weather conditions, and how they have instrumentalized cold, frost, and snow for their political, imperial, and scientific ambitions. The volume demonstrates that ideas about climate and weather, as well as the ways societies deal with them, have their own histories.

Second, we hope to bring about a shift in focus within the environmental history of Russia and Eastern Europe. A large proportion of environmental history studies of the Russian Empire and the Soviet Union consider nature and the environment only as a target of human activity. Therefore, they typically focus on pollution or, approaching the problem from the other direction, on conservation. Much more strongly than for other countries, the environmental history of Russia and the Soviet Union concentrates on political and economic factors.[23] But "nature" is itself a social construct that does not exist independently of us and our perceptions. This volume offers readers a chance to understand the relationship between nature and society as truly mutual, with the environment and nature playing an active role. Frost, ice, and snow are perennial phenomena. They are both the cause of events and a circumstance that has shaped daily life, science, and culture. The ways that people perceive and deal with cold reminds us that human history has always been influenced by natural factors. This volume thus also argues for including the active role of the environment and nature when considering historical causalities.[24]

But this volume also assigns human actors more scope for action than has previously been (and often still is) the case in discussions of the significance of the environment and the climate in Russian history. We wish to counter views that hold that alterations in the climate take place in the context of immutable social realities. Climate and weather are causal factors that can trigger action, but ultimately do not determine it. Here the volume joins other studies that have argued for a new way of looking at the environment in Russian history. For a long time, discussions were dominated by the environmental deterministic views of scholars like Sergei Solov'ev and Vasilii Kliuchevskii, which also influenced the interpretation of Russian history in the West and which enjoyed renewed popularity in the 1990s through the work of scholars like Leonid Milov.[25] In popular scientific discourses in particular, climate determinism remained alive and well—not just in Russia but also in Western Europe.

The environmental history scholarship on Russia and the Soviet Union is still strongly focused on catastrophes and ways of dealing with them.[26] Frost, ice, and snow are not one-time events like earthquakes, nuclear disasters, or industrial accidents but are recurrent in seasonal cycles. Although cold and frost had a central importance for Russian history, there are only a few studies that have systematically explored how people reacted to adverse climatic conditions in Muscovite and tsarist Russia, or in the Soviet Union. This volume investigates the practices with which people in Russia reacted to freezing temperatures. The focus here is on the adaptive achievements that emerged or were negotiated politically, socially, aesthetically, and economically. We have examined how knowledge and technology have restructured human ecological relations and shaped the ways uncertainty is dealt with.

By considering the preparatory and adaptive measures undertaken in Russia to deal with such recurring events and the ways these measures shape everyday life, we can also gain insights into possible ways of dealing with the consequences of climate change. Solutions meant to avert global warming must, if they are to be successful, also take into account established historical and cultural configurations. The environmental humanities can help us to better understand the social and cultural roots of our relationship to nature and the environment, and this, in turn, can help us to find and implement political solutions in the struggle against climate change, as well as against other challenges like environmental destruction and pollution.

Third, the volume adds the category of climate to the category of space. Space plays an important role in the history of Eastern Europe. Likewise, the current interest in the Arctic can also be located in this research area. The rapidly growing number of studies on the history of the Arctic usually have a spatial approach and are also frequently limited to the Soviet period.[27] But it is not just the vast physical space that has shaped human history in Russia; Russians have also located themselves poorly in "thermal spaces." While political and economic decisions have stood at the center of the acquisition of northern regions as Russian territory, it is seldom asked what role the cultural and scientific mastery of the climate and the weather played in the colonization of the country. Why has the category of space determined the historical perception of Russia, while climate has played only a subordinate role in the historical representations of the nineteenth and twentieth centuries? What would it look like to write a history of Russia in which climate is a central factor?

Fourth, this volume complements studies that investigate the "North" both as a region and as an idea and mental image and that increasingly emphasize the ways that the meanings associated with the North vary over time and in different societies.[28] Up until the eighteenth century, Russia was considered a northern region in accordance with interpretive schemata of the world and the character of its peoples that dated back to antiquity.[29] The ancient theory of climate was both simple and vastly influential: one-sided and extreme climates, such as that believed to be the case in the North, gave rise to one-sided people, while the peoples of variable and temperate climates had a complex character. The boundaries of this northern region were rather nebulous and extended from Greenland, the British Isles, and Scandinavia to Russia and Asia. With the emergence of the idea of Eastern Europe as a region, the geographic extent of the North shrank accordingly. During the course of the nineteenth century, Russia, which until that time had been considered a northern nation, gradually came to be perceived as an eastern one.[30] In literary scholarship in particular, Russia has been treated as part of the North.[31] Literary scholar Otto Boele, who has studied the motif of the North in literature of the Romantic period, notes that in the first half of the nineteenth century the North became increasingly "internalized." He has shown that ice, snow, and winter as manifestations of a northern climate were regarded as typically Russian phenomena. During this period, they lost their specifically "northern" aura and became a distinctive part of Russianness.[32] The victory over Napoleon's freezing troops, in particular, contributed to the understanding of winter as the nation's savior and a central part of the national self-image. Foreign correspondents who reported on the events of 1812 also emphasized Russia's acquaintance with the cold.[33] So far no systematic study has attempted to analyze the association of cold with the national character, both in the self-understanding of the Russians and in the perceptions of foreigners, and how it changed before and after the nineteenth century. The contributions to this volume take some first steps in this direction by looking at various facets of Russia's nature and environment—for example, the steppes, the nation's orientation in relation to the points of the compass, its harsh conditions, or the vastness of its territories—and their significance for Russia's national and imperial self-image.[34] Such approaches make it possible to identify the epistemological, social, and cultural impulses that stimulated and strengthened the engagement with the physical environment.

Finally, a global perspective plays an important role both in the book project as a whole and in the individual contributions. The majority of the contributions are interested not only in Russia's efforts to cope with the cold but also in Russia's adaptation strategies and how they differ from other "cold" countries. The volume shows how Russia's approach to the cold has changed as a result of the actions, politics, and scientific activities of other international actors. As several of the contributions demonstrate, Russia's relationship to the environment is not determined just by its climate and weather but also by the perception and study of climate and the scientific discussions taking place internationally. Furthermore, by looking at external perceptions of the region and its self-image as Europe's "cold realm," the book maintains a global perspective.

The contributors to this volume represent a diverse spectrum of disciplines, scholarly traditions, and countries, and they present a kaleidoscope of perspectives on the ways that cold can be interpreted in Russian history and culture. The chapters reflect the inclusiveness and rich diversity of approaches found in the field of environmental history.

Part I: Foundations

Following this introduction, chapter 1 by Julia Herzberg outlines how scholarly research has approached the question of the connection between Russia's harsh climate and its national character and what role Russia has played in international discourses about climate. The remaining contributions are divided into three additional sections.

Part II: Science and Politics

The second section explores the connection between adverse climatic conditions, science, and politics. It contributes to the history of climate knowledge and climate science—topics that, unlike climate reconstruction and research on the effects of climate, have only recently begun to receive increased attention.[35] What ideas about climate guided the efforts to "temper" regional and imperial weather conditions? What scientific fields took an interest in the cold, and what did scientists believe was worthy of investigation? How did scientists develop and advance their scientific disciplines by speaking about climate and cold? In contrast to the countless studies that focus mainly on polar and Arctic research during the Soviet era, this collection also looks at the period before 1917. One central theme of the volume is the Enlightenment era and the importance of the Russian Academy of Sciences for the investigation of cold and frost. The chapter by Julia Herzberg shows how the individual and collective experiences of scholars in Russia motivated them to turn their attention to the phenomenon of cold. This led them to test the various theories of the time regarding the causes of extreme cold. Herzberg's study makes it clear that, in terms of the development of the disciplines of meteorology and climatology, as well as physics, Russia was part of European knowledge networks. Alongside literature and art, the natural sciences also contributed to cold becoming a symbol of Russia.

The conflicts that were generated as a result of the new knowledge about cold regions is the topic of the chapter by Erki Tammiksaar, who shows how the Russian South Pole expedition led by Fabian Gottlieb von Bellingshausen in 1820 later came to be used as an argument during the Cold War struggle to determine who had a right to make territorial claims on Antarctica. An important issue under dispute was the question of whether the ice shelf counted as part of the continent and whether therefore the sighting of it constituted the first discovery of Antarctica.

The chapter by Denis J. B. Shaw also examines the emergence of new knowledge. Through the example of Andrei Aleksandrovich Grigor'ev's study *Subarctic* and its reception, he shows how Russian scientists contributed to global knowledge about the environment and influenced our contemporary understanding of climate and environmental change. At the same time, Grigor'ev's scientific career reveals how political considerations facilitated these insights, for the conceptualization of these geographic ideas as dynamic processes was congruent with the political dictates of historical materialism.

Part III: Images and Narratives

The third section examines cold as an aesthetic phenomenon and a cultural construct. It is concerned with the narratives and media that have conveyed communication about climatic conditions in Russia and shows how communication about cold helped shape individual and collective identities; it also illuminates the significance these representations of harsh climate possessed for external perceptions and the country's self-image. This section supplements literary investigations that have examined the motif of the North in Russian literature, as well as comparative studies of how ice, snow, and cold are portrayed in literature across national boundaries.[36] The chapters show the importance of considering not just the literature of the nineteenth century but also visual media in order to understand how Russia became the land of cold. These studies reveal the degree to which perceptions of Russia and Russian identity were shaped by the association with extreme cold. Nataliia Rodigina examines discourses about the climate in the press in the years leading up to the Russian Revolution. She shows that, on the one hand, the references to Siberia's legendary cold diminished in the course of efforts to integrate the region into the communicative space of the empire. On the other hand, the revolutionary opposition characterized their experiences of extreme cold while in Siberian exile as the punishment of an inhumane regime.

Oksana Bulgakowa considers the difficulties of translating temperature into visual media in her chapter on the iconography of cold. She looks at the ways snow and ice are integrated into the language of the cinema and why the "screen temperature" changed during the Soviet period. Her study shows that in film and the visual arts the cold is not a physical or meteorological phenomenon but rather an *image* that can be linked to specific symbols, narratives, myths, and metaphors.

Roman Mauer turns to the external perspective on Russia and shows that the image of cold also played an important role in Germans' view of the country. Much like the Russian exiles of the revolutionary era, German prisoners of war in the Soviet Union experienced cold as a punishment imposed upon them for the failed megalomaniac fantasies of the National Socialist regime. The chapter focuses on portrayals of Russian coldness within German popular film culture as a symbolic mechanism to compensate for traumatic experiences during the war. This section furthers another important goal of this volume, namely to critically examine national and imperial stereotypes about climate and at the same time to consider what made these narratives so powerful. Looking at media and discourses, can the Russian winter and the Siberian cold be understood as Russian or even European sites of memory?

Part IV: Pain and Pleasure

Although cold and frost had a central importance for Russian history, there are only a few studies that have systematically explored how people reacted to the adverse climatic conditions in tsarist Russia and the Soviet Union. The final section of this volume looks at cold and snow both as a threat and as a focal point for building a common identity, as well as their recreational function. It investigates the practices with which people in Russia reacted to cold temperatures. The focus here is on the adaptive practices that manifested themselves or were negotiated politically, socially, aesthetically, and economically. In this section, the contributors analyze the adaptive strategies that were implemented or reconstituted as a result of military conflict.

Aleksandr Kuzminykh's chapter continues the investigation of the role of Russian cold during World War II. He examines the influence of weather and climate on the progression of the war. It becomes clear that the symbolic associations with cold seen in Mauer's study of the film genre were fed both by real experiences as well as by Soviet propaganda, which endeavored to further weaken the fighting power of the German Wehrmacht by awakening their fears of a "white death" (*belaia smert'*) awaiting them in Russia.

The contributions in this section contrast long-term adaptive practices with short-term efforts to overcome, mitigate, or utilize the cold. Here we build on the work of Fiona Hill and Clifford G. Gaddy, whose study *The Siberian Curse: How Communist Planners Left Russia Out in the Cold* offered one of the first counternarratives to the Soviet glorification of the Arctic and cold.[37] At the same time, this section shows that in regions dominated by frost, ice, and snow, the climate was a source not just of struggle and suffering but also of recreation and opportunity. The chapter by Aleksei Popov, which focuses on winter tourism in the Soviet Union, examines the discourses that surround skiing and shows that during the political thaw of the 1950s and 1960s the heroization of the ability to endure snow and cold also tapered off. But during other periods, this association remained prominent: in his chapter Alexander Ananyev traces the importance of two types of heroic figures in the Soviet Union, the polar explorer and the ice hockey player, who were closely connected with the ability to master the cold. It also sheds light on why and how these discourses have undergone an update and revitalization in contemporary Russia, where the polar explorers and ice hockey players both serve as role models and identification figures. As Ananyev shows, as do all the other contributors to this volume, it is not enough to focus only on the various costs and challenges that come with the adaptation to cold in Russia;[38] rather, it is essential to also map out the rationales, dreams, and utopias that shape life in the cold and motivate the efforts to extend human presence ever further into extreme climatic environments.

We are grateful to the German Historical Institute in Moscow and the Rachel Carson Center for Environment and Society for their support.

Julia Herzberg is professor for the history of East Central Europe and Russia in early modern times at LMU Munich. Her recent research has focused on, among other topics, the environmental history of Central Eastern Europe and Russia. She coedited *Ice and Snow in the Cold War: Histories of Extreme Climatic Environments* (2019) with Christian Kehrt and Franziska Torma, and *Umweltgeschichte(n): Ostmitteleuropa von der Industrialisierung bis zum Postsozialismus* (2013) with Martin Zückert and Horst Förster. She is currently working on an environmental history of "frost" in Russia that examines various social and cultural aspects of Russia's harsh climate.

Andreas Renner is a historian of Russia and professor of Russian-Asian studies at LMU Munich. His interest in the Russian cold stems from his research on the Northern Sea Route.

Ingrid Schierle is a lecturer at the University of Tübingen. Her research interests include the history of concepts, the Russian language in the eighteenth century, and provincial life in the Russian empire. She coedited *Dvorianstvo, vlast' and obshchestvo v provincial'noi Rossii XVIII veka* (2012) with Olga Glagoleva, and *"Poniatiia o Rossii": K istoricheskoi semantike imperskogo perioda* (2012) with Aleksei Miller and Denis Sdvizhkov.

Notes

1. Paul E. Lydolph, *Climates of the Soviet Union*, World Survey of Climatology 7 (Amsterdam, 1977), 1.
2. Alexander v. Humboldt, *Central-Asien: Untersuchungen über die Gebirgsketten und die Vergleichende Klimatologie* (Berlin, 1844), Bd. 1, 30.
3. John Thompson and Christopher J. Ward, *Russia: A Historical Introduction from Kievan Rus' to the Present*, 8th ed. (Milton, 2018).
4. The opening of the Northeast Passage as a navigable sea route is a particular focus in predictions about the positive economic effects of global warming. Oliver T. Ried, *The Impact of a Warming Arctic on International Shipping: Transit Traffic along Arctic Routes; Developments, Opportunities and Imponderables* (Göttingen, 2015).
5. A. P. Nikonov, *Istoriia Otmorozhennykh v Kontekste Global'nogo Potepleniia* (Moscow, 2010), 381.
6. Ibid., 374.
7. Ibid., 378.
8. Ibid.
9. A nuanced analysis of the positive and negative consequences of climate change can be found in Marlène Laruelle, *Russia's Arctic Strategies and the Future of the Far North* (Armonk, NY, 2014), 68–93.
10. James R. Fleming, *Historical Perspectives on Climate Change* (New York, 1998); Boris Belge and Klaus Gestwa, "Wetterkrieg und Klimawandel: Meteorologie im Kalten Krieg," *Osteuropa* 59, no. 10 (2009); Julia Herzberg, Christian Kehrt, and Franziska Torma, eds., *Ice and Snow in the Cold War: Histories of Extreme Climatic Environments*, The Environment in History (New York, 2018).
11. Nikolai M. Dronin and Edward G. Bellinger, *Climate Dependence and Food Problems in Russia 1900–1990: The Interaction of Climate and Agricultural Policy and Their Effect on Food Problems* (Budapest, 2005), 2.
12. Ibid., 1–2.
13. Colin M. White, *Russia and America: The Roots of Economic Divergence* (London, 1987), 52–53.
14. Maria Rakklolainen and Monica Tennberg, "Adaptation in Russian Climate Governance," in *Governing the Uncertain: Adaptation and Climate in Russia and Finland*, ed. Monica Tennberg (Dordrecht, 2012), 39–54.
15. Vanda Ignat'eva, "Sakha Republic (Iakutia): Local Projections of Climate Changes and Adaptation Problems of Indigenous Peoples," in *Global Warming and Human–Nature Dimension in Northern Eurasia*, ed. Tetsuya Hiyama and Hiroki Takakura, Global Environmental Studies (Singapore, 2018), 11–28.
16. Colin Reisser, "Russia's Arctic Cities: Recent Evolution and Drivers of Change," in *Sustaining Russia's Arctic Cities: Resource Politics, Migration, and Climate Change*, ed. Robert W. Orttung, Studies in the Circumpolar North 2 (New York, 2016), 1–22.
17. Marianna Poberezhskaya, "Traditional Media and Climate Change in Russia: A Case Study of Izvestiia," in *Climate Change Discourse in Russia: Past and Present*, ed. Marianna Poberezhskaya and Teresa Ashe, Routledge Focus on Environment and Sustainability (London, New York, 2019), 64–79.
18. Laruelle, *Russia's Arctic Strategies*; Elana Wilson Rowe, Marlène Laruelle, and Dmitry Gotenburg, "Russian Policy Options in the Arctic," *Russian Analytical Digest* 96

(Bremen, Zürich, 2011); Marlène Laruelle, *Russia's Arctic Ambitions: Transforming the "Cost of Cold,"* Policy Brief 7 (Stockholm, 2009).

19. Laruelle, *Russia's Arctic Strategies*, xxi.
20. Examples of such studies include: James R. Fleming and Vladimir Janković, "Revisiting Klima," *Osiris* 26 (2011); Jan de Vries, "Measuring the Impact of Climate on History: The Search for Appropriate Methodologies," *Journal of Interdisciplinary History* 10, no. 4 (1980); John L. Brooke, *Climate Change and the Course of Global History: A Rough Journey*, Studies in Environment and History (Cambridge, 2014); Wolfgang Behringer, "Weather, Hunger and Fear: Origins of the European Witch-Hunts in Climate, Society and Mentality," *German History* 13 (1995); Mike Hulme, "Reducing the Future to Climate: A Story of Climate Determinism and Reductionism," *Osiris* 26, no. 1 (2011).
21. An exception is the volume by Marianna Poberezhskaya and Teresa Ashe, which investigates discourses about climate change in both the Soviet Union and post-Soviet Russia. Marianna Poberezhskaya and Teresa Ashe, eds., *Climate Change Discourse in Russia: Past and Present*, Routledge Focus on Environment and Sustainability (New York, 2019).
22. Jonathan D. Oldfield, *Russian Nature: Exploring the Environmental Consequences of Societal Change* (Burlington, VT, 2006); Katja Doose and Jonathan Oldfield, "Natural and Anthropogenic Climate Change Understanding in the Soviet Union, 1960s–1980s," in *Climate Change Discourse in Russia: Past and Present*, eds. Marianna Poberezhskaya and Teresa Ashe, Routledge Focus on Environment and Sustainability (New York, 2019), 17–31.
23. This tendency is particularly evident in introductions to the environmental history of Russia. Paul R. Josephson, ed., *An Environmental History of Russia*, Studies in Environment and History (New York, 2013).
24. Nicholas Breyfogle also recently made this point in his excellent introduction to a volume on Russian environmental history: Nicholas B. Breyfogle, "Toward an Environmental History of Tsarist Russia and the Soviet Union," in *Eurasian Environments: Nature and Ecology in Imperial Russian and Soviet History*, ed. Nicholas B. Breyfogle, Pitt Series in Russian and East European Studies (Pittsburgh, PA, 2018), 14–15.
25. L. V. Milov, "Natural and Climate Factor and Peculiarities of Russian Historic Process," *Historical Social Research* 16, no. 2 (1991); L. V. Milov, *Velikorusskii pakhar' i osobennosti rossiiskogo istoricheskogo protsessa* (Moscow, 1998).
26. Nigel Raab, *All Shook Up: The Shifting Soviet Response to Catastrophes, 1917–1991* (Chicago, 2017).
27. Linda Trautman, "Modernisation of Russia's Last Frontier: The Arctic and the Northern Sea Route from the 1930s to the 1990s," in *Modernisation in Russia since 1900*, ed. Markku Kangaspuro, Studia Fennica Historica 12 (Helsinki, 2006), 252–66; Laruelle, *Russia's Arctic Strategies*; Richard Vaughan, *The Arctic: A History*, rev. and updated ed. (Stroud, 2007); Paul R. Josephson, "Technology and the Conquest of the Soviet Arctic," *Russian Review* 70, no. 3 (2011); Paul R. Josephson, *The Conquest of the Russian Arctic* (Harvard, 2014); John McCannon, "Positive Heroes at the Pole: Celebrity Status, Socialist-Realist Ideals and the Soviet Myth of the Arctic, 1932–39," *Russian Review* 56, no. 3 (1997); John McCannon, *Red Arctic: Polar Exploration and the Myth of the North*

in the Soviet Union, 1932–1939 (New York, 1998); John McCannon, *A History of the Arctic: Nature, Exploration and Exploitation* (London, 2012); Manfred Sapper, ed., *Logbuch Arktis: Der Raum, Die Interessen Und Das Recht*, Osteuropa Jg. 61, H. 2/3 (Berlin, 2011); Roger D. Launius, James R. Fleming and David H. DeVorkin, eds., *Globalizing Polar Science* (New York, 2010); Gail Osherenko and Oran R. Young, eds., *The Age of the Arctic: Hot Conflicts and Cold Realities*, Studies in Polar Research (New York, 1989).

28. Numerous studies emphasize the importance of "northernness" as a part of national identity, as, for example, the work of Sverker Sörlin on Swedish nationality and culture: Sverker Sörlin, "Rituals and Resources of Natural History," in *Narrating the Arctic: A Cultural History of Nordic Scientific Practices*, ed. Michael Bravo (Canton, MA, 2002), 73–122; Dolly Jørgensen and Sverker Sörlin, eds., *Northscapes: History, Technology, and the Making of Northern Environments* (Vancouver, 2013); Dolly Jørgensen and Virginia Langum, eds., *Visions of North in Premodern Europe*, Cursor Mundi 31 (Turnhout, 2018); Astrid Arndt, ed., *Imagologie des Nordens*, Imaginatio borealis 7 (Frankfurt/Main, 2004); Gonthier-Louis Fink, "Diskriminierung und Rehabilitierung des Nordens im Spiegel der Klimatheorie," in *Imagologie des Nordens*, ed. Astrid Arndt, Imaginatio borealis 7 (Frankfurt/Main, 2004), 44–107; Dennis Hormuth and Maike Schmidt, eds., *Norden und Nördlichkeit: Darstellung vom Eigenen und Fremden*, Imaginatio borealis 21 (Frankfurt/Main, 2010); Hendriette Kliemann, *Koordinaten des Nordens: Wissenschaftliche Konstruktionen einer europäischen Region 1770–1850*, Nordeuropäische Studien 19 (Berlin, 2005).

29. Hans Lemberg, "Zur Entstehung des Osteuropabegriffs im 19. Jahrhundert: Vom Norden zum Osten Europas," *Jahrbücher für Geschichte Osteuropas* 33, no. 1 (1985); Andreas Fülberth, "Herbersteins Rerum Moscoviticarum Commentarii als Zeugnis der frühneuzeittypischen Lokalisierung Russlands im 'Norden,'" in Hormuth and Schmidt, *Norden und Nördlichkeit*, 31–40.

30. Hendriette Kliemann, *Koordinaten des Nordens: Wissenschaftliche Konstruktionen einer europäischen Region 1770–1850*, Nordeuropäische Studien 19 (Berlin, 2005), 13–14; Lemberg, "Zur Entstehung des Osteuropabegriffs im 19. Jahrhundert."

31. Andreas Fülberth, "Herbersteins Rerum Moscoviticarum Commentarii als Zeugnis der frühneuzeittypischen Lokalisierung Russlands im 'Norden,'" in Hormuth and Schmidt, *Norden und Nördlichkeit*; Ludwig Steindorff, "Bilder vom Norden in der Geschichte Altrusslands," in Hormuth and Schmidt, *Norden und Nördlichkeit*, 13–30.

32. Otto F. Boele, *The North in Russian Romantic Literature* (Amsterdam, 1996), 11.

33. Ibid., 71–77.

34. David Moon, *The Plough That Broke the Steppes: Agriculture and Environment on Russia's Grasslands, 1700–1914*, Oxford studies in modern European history (Oxford, 2014); Christopher D. Ely, *This Meager Nature: Landscape and National Identity in Imperial Russia* (DeKalb, 2002).

35. Matthias Heymann, "The Evolution of Climate Ideas and Knowledge," *Wiley Interdisciplinary Reviews: Climate Change* 1, no. 4 (2010); Spencer R. Weart, "The Idea of Anthropogenic Global Climate Change in the 20th Century," *Wiley Interdisciplinary Reviews: Climate Change* 1, no. 1 (2010); Poberezhskaya and Ashe, *Climate Change Discourse in Russia*; Fleming, *Historical Perspectives on Climate Change*.

36. Boele, *North in Russian Romantic Literature*; Andrea Dortmann, *Winter Facets: Traces and Tropes of the Cold* (Bern, Oxford, 2007); Heidi Hansson and Cathrine Norberg,

eds., *Cold Matters: Cultural Perceptions of Snow, Ice and Cold* (Umeå, 2009); Susi K. Frank, "City of the Sun on Ice: The Soviet (Counter-)Discourse of the Arctic in the 1930s," in *Arctic Discourses*, ed. Anka Ryall, Johan Schimanski, and Henning H. Waerp, 106–31 (Cambridge, 2010).
37. Fiona Hill and Clifford G. Gaddy, *The Siberian Curse: How Communist Planners Left Russia Out in the Cold* (Washington, DC, 2003).
38. Laruelle, *Russia's Arctic Ambitions*; Hill and Gaddy, *Siberian Curse*.

Bibliography

Arndt, Astrid, ed. *Imagologie des Nordens*. Imaginatio borealis 7. Frankfurt/Main, 2004.
Behringer, Wolfgang. "Weather, Hunger and Fear: Origins of the European Witch-Hunts in Climate, Society and Mentality." *German History* 13 (1995): 1–27.
Belge, Boris, and Klaus Gestwa. "Wetterkrieg und Klimawandel: Meteorologie im Kalten Krieg." *Osteuropa* 59, no. 10 (2009): 15–42.
Boele, Otto F. *The North in Russian Romantic Literature*. Amsterdam, 1996.
Breyfogle, Nicholas B. "Toward an Environmental History of Tsarist Russia and the Soviet Union." In *Eurasian Environments: Nature and Ecology in Imperial Russian and Soviet History*, edited by Nicholas B. Breyfogle, 3–19. Pitt Series in Russian and East European Studies. Pittsburgh, PA, 2018.
Brooke, John L. *Climate Change and the Course of Global History: A Rough Journey*. Studies in Environment and History. Cambridge, 2014.
Doose, Katja, and Jonathan Oldfield. "Natural and Anthropogenic Climate Change Understanding in the Soviet Union, 1960s–1980s." In *Climate Change Discourse in Russia: Past and Present*, edited by Marianna Poberezhskaya and Teresa Ashe, 17–31. Routledge Focus on Environment and Sustainability. New York, 2019.
Dortmann, Andrea. *Winter Facets: Traces and Tropes of the Cold*. Oxford, 2007.
Dronin, Nikolai M., and Edward G. Bellinger. *Climate Dependence and Food Problems in Russia 1900–1990: The Interaction of Climate and Agricultural Policy and Their Effect on Food Problems*. Budapest, 2005.
Ely, Christopher D. *This Meager Nature: Landscape and National Identity in Imperial Russia*. DeKalb, 2002.
Fink, Gonthier-Louis. "Diskriminierung und Rehabilitierung des Nordens im Spiegel der Klimatheorie." In *Imagologie des Nordens*, edited by Astrid Arndt, 45–108. Imaginatio borealis 7. Frankfurt/Main, 2004.
Fleming, James R. *Historical Perspectives on Climate Change*. New York, 1998.
Fleming, James R., and Vladimir Janković. "Revisiting Klima." *Osiris* 26 (2011): 1–15.
Frank, Susi K. "City of the Sun on Ice: The Soviet (Counter-)Discourse of the Arctic in the 1930s." In *Arctic Discourses*, edited by Anka Ryall, Johan Schimanski, and Henning H. Waerp, 106–31. Cambridge, 2010.
Fülberth, Andreas. "Herbersteins Rerum Moscoviticarum Commentarii als Zeugnis der frühneuzeittypischen Lokalisierung Russlands im 'Norden.'" In *Norden und Nördlichkeit: Darstellung vom Eigenen und Fremden*, edited by Dennis Hormuth and Maike Schmidt, 31–40. Imaginatio borealis 21. Frankfurt/Main, 2010.
Hansson, Heidi, and Cathrine Norberg, eds. *Cold Matters: Cultural Perceptions of Snow, Ice and Cold*. Umeå, 2009.

Herzberg, Julia, Christian Kehrt, and Franziska Torma, eds. *Ice and Snow in the Cold War: Histories of Extreme Climatic Environments*. The Environment in History. New York, 2018.

Heymann, Matthias. "The Evolution of Climate Ideas and Knowledge." *Wiley Interdisciplinary Reviews: Climate Change* 1, no. 4 (2010): 581–97.

Hill, Fiona, and Clifford G. Gaddy. *The Siberian Curse: How Communist Planners Left Russia Out in the Cold*. Washington, DC, 2003.

Hormuth, Dennis, and Maike Schmidt, eds. *Norden und Nördlichkeit: Darstellung vom Eigenen und Fremden*. Imaginatio borealis 21. Frankfurt/Main, 2010.

Hulme, Mike. "Reducing the Future to Climate: A Story of Climate Determinism and Reductionism." *Osiris* 26, no. 1 (2011): 245–66.

Humboldt, Alexander v. *Central-Asien: Untersuchungen über die Gebirgsketten und die Vergleichende Klimatologie*. Bd. 1. Berlin, 1844.

Ignat'eva, Vanda. "Sakha Republic (Iakutia): Local Projections of Climate Changes and Adaptation Problems of Indigenous Peoples." In *Global Warming and Human–Nature Dimension in Northern Eurasia*, edited by Tetsuya Hiyama and Hiroki Takakura, 11–28. Global Environmental Studies. Singapore, 2018.

Jørgensen, Dolly, and Virginia Langum, eds. *Visions of North in Premodern Europe*. Cursor Mundi 31. Turnhout, 2018.

Jørgensen, Dolly, and Sverker Sörlin, eds. *Northscapes: History, Technology, and the Making of Northern Environments*. Vancouver, 2013.

Josephson, Paul R., ed. *An Environmental History of Russia*. Studies in Environment and History. Cambridge, New York, 2013.

———. *The Conquest of the Russian Arctic*. Harvard, 2014.

———. "Technology and the Conquest of the Soviet Arctic." *Russian Review* 70, no. 3 (2011): 419–39.

Kliemann, Hendriette. *Koordinaten des Nordens: Wissenschaftliche Konstruktionen einer europäischen Region 1770–1850*. Nordeuropäische Studien 19. Berlin, 2005.

Laruelle, Marlène. *Russia's Arctic Ambitions: Transforming the "Cost of Cold."* Policy Brief 7. Stockholm, 2009.

———. *Russia's Arctic Strategies and the Future of the Far North*. Armonk, NY, 2014.

Launius, Roger D., James R. Fleming, and David H. DeVorkin, eds. *Globalizing Polar Science*. New York, 2010.

Lemberg, Hans. "Zur Entstehung des Osteuropabegriffs im 19. Jahrhundert: Vom Norden zum Osten Europas." *Jahrbücher für Geschichte Osteuropas* 33, no. 1 (1985): 48–91.

Lydolph, Paul E. *Climates of the Soviet Union*. World Survey of Climatology 7. Amsterdam, 1977.

McCannon, John. *A History of the Arctic: Nature, Exploration and Exploitation*. London, 2012.

———. "Positive Heroes at the Pole: Celebrity Status, Socialist-Realist Ideals and the Soviet Myth of the Arctic, 1932–39." *Russian Review* 56, no. 3 (1997): 346–65.

———. *Red Arctic: Polar Exploration and the Myth of the North in the Soviet Union, 1932–1939*. New York, 1998.

Milov, L. V. "Natural and Climate Factor and Peculiarities of Russian Historic Process." *Historical Social Research* 16, no. 2 (1991): 40–59.

———. *Velikorusskii pakhar' i osobennosti rossiiskogo istoricheskogo protsessa*. Moscow, 1998.

Moon, David. *The Plough That Broke the Steppes: Agriculture and Environment on Russia's Grasslands, 1700–1914*. Oxford Studies in Modern European History. Oxford, 2014.
Nikonov, A. P. *Istoriia Otmorozhennykh v Kontekste Global'nogo Potepleniia*. Moscow, 2010.
Oldfield, Jonathan D. *Russian Nature: Exploring the Environmental Consequences of Societal Change*. Burlington, VT, 2006.
Osherenko, Gail, and Oran R. Young, eds. *The Age of the Arctic: Hot Conflicts and Cold Realities*. Studies in Polar Research. New York, 1989.
Poberezhskaya, Marianna. "Traditional Media and Climate Change in Russia: A Case Study of Izvestiia." In *Climate Change Discourse in Russia: Past and Present*, edited by Marianna Poberezhskaya and Teresa Ashe, 64–79. Routledge Focus on Environment and Sustainability. New York, 2019.
Poberezhskaya, Marianna, and Teresa Ashe, eds. *Climate Change Discourse in Russia: Past and Present*. Routledge Focus on Environment and Sustainability. New York, 2019.
Raab, Nigel. *All Shook Up: The Shifting Soviet Response to Catastrophes, 1917–1991*. Chicago, 2017.
Rakklolainen, Maria, and Monica Tennberg. "Adaptation in Russian Climate Governance." In *Governing the Uncertain: Adaptation and Climate in Russia and Finland*, edited by Monica Tennberg, 39–54. Dordrecht, 2012.
Reisser, Colin. "Russia's Arctic Cities: Recent Evolution and Drivers of Change." In *Sustaining Russia's Arctic Cities: Resource Politics, Migration, and Climate Change*, edited by Robert W. Orttung, 1–22. Studies in the Circumpolar North 2. New York, 2016.
Ried, Oliver T. *The Impact of a Warming Arctic on International Shipping: Transit Traffic along Arctic Routes; Developments, Opportunities and Imponderables*. Göttingen, 2015.
Rowe, Elana Wilson, Marlène Laruelle, and Dmitry Gotenburg. "Russian Policy Options in the Arctic." *Russian Analytical Digest* 96. Bremen, Zürich, 2011.
Sapper, Manfred, ed. *Logbuch Arktis: Der Raum, die Interessen und das Recht*, Osteuropa Jg. 61, H. 2/3. Berlin, 2011.
Sörlin, Sverker. "Rituals and Resources of Natural History." In *Narrating the Arctic: A Cultural History of Nordic Scientific Practices*, edited by Michael Bravo, 73–122. Canton, MA, 2002.
Steindorff, Ludwig. "Bilder vom Norden in der Geschichte Altrusslands." In *Norden und Nördlichkeit: Darstellung vom Eigenen und Fremden*, edited by Dennis Hormuth and Maike Schmidt, 13–30. Imaginatio borealis 21. Frankfurt/Main, 2010.
Thompson, John, and Christopher J. Ward. *Russia: A Historical Introduction from Kievan Rus' to the Present*. 8th ed. Milton, 2018.
Trautman, Linda. "Modernisation of Russia's Last Frontier: The Arctic and the Northern Sea Route from the 1930s to the 1990s." In *Modernisation in Russia since 1900*, edited by Markku Kangaspuro, 252–66. Studia Fennica Historica 12. Helsinki, 2006.
Vaughan, Richard. *The Arctic: A History*. Rev. and updated ed. Stroud, 2007.
Vries, Jan de. "Measuring the Impact of Climate on History: The Search for Appropriate Methodologies." *Journal of Interdisciplinary History* 10, no. 4 (1980): 599–630.
Wert, Spencer R. "The Idea of Anthropogenic Global Climate Change in the 20th Century." *Wiley Interdisciplinary Reviews: Climate Change* 1, no. 1 (2010): 67–81.
White, Colin M. *Russia and America: The Roots of Economic Divergence*. London, 1987.

CHAPTER 1

Climate Ideas and the Cold in Russia

Julia Herzberg

In tsarist Russia and the Soviet Union, the cold was a constant challenge, a phenomenon that influenced actions, everyday experiences, and mentalities and determined both external perceptions of the region and the region's self-image. According to the climate categories of geographer Wladimir Köppen, 31 percent of the area covered by the former Soviet Union belongs to the category "humid, continental," with cool summers and long winters. While farmers in the United States can plant crops during a growing season that averages 130 to 150 days, farmers in Russia must make do with 125 to 130. After that, winter arrives.[1]

Cold is connected with key episodes in Russian history. It has helped Russians emerge victorious in military confrontations with their neighbors, but it has also been a factor in some of their defeats. Major sites of memory in Russian history are associated with cold, with frost, ice, and snow: frozen rivers facilitated the Mongol invasion of Russia in the thirteenth century; Aleksander Nevskii's defeat of the Teutonic Knights took place on the ice-covered Lake Peipus; and Napoleon's troops succumbed in 1812 to the cold Russian winter. During the Siege of Leningrad, urgently needed provisions reached the cold and starving population via the "Road of Life," a transport route across the frozen Lake Ladoga.

These Russian sites of memory show how the phenomenon of cold can be seen in quite varied ways, both positively and negatively. But attitudes toward cold also depend on their historical, cultural, and social contexts. Three areas of scholarship in particular have served as arenas in which to discuss the effects of climate and weather on the Russian people: (1) climate theories; (2) meteorology and climatology (two disciplines that developed in the nineteenth century); and (3) history. These arenas served as spaces to debate not only the ways that people could respond to and cope with frost and cold but also the question of whether experiences with cold had produced a specifically "Russian" national character and whether it promoted or hindered the country's prosperity. At the same time, the discussion in Russia did not take place in isolation: it was part of larger European and global debates in which Russia was a popular example cited in deliberations about climate and its effects.

Climate Theories

Climate and weather—specifically, the effects of climate on humans, both as individuals and as a group—have long been a subject of interest. Particular attention has been given to the connections between climate, weather, and health. As far back as ancient Greece, climate has been seen as an explanation for the differences between peoples and as a basis for demonstrating one's own superiority.[2] A key text in the development of climate theory was Hippocrates's *De aere aquis et locis*, in which the various peoples inhabiting the world are classified according to the meteorological and atmospheric characteristics of their environment.[3] This treatise is one of the first studies of the effects of climate on the human constitution. Building on these premises, Aristotle considered climate a reason why the Greeks were superior to the "barbarians." Even the characteristics of phenomena such as language have been explained using climate: in 1733 Scottish doctor John Arbuthnot wrote in *An Essay Concerning the Effects of Air on Human Bodies* that northern peoples avoid vowels so that they do not have to open their mouths so widely in the cold air.[4]

As Europeans expanded their settlements into the Americas and Siberia, the climate theories developed between the sixteenth and nineteenth centuries were an attempt to deal with the experience of a new diversity of humankind by reducing it to a few general principles. European scientists, explorers, and colonists used climate as a descriptor to classify and explain the differences between the newly discovered peoples and "races" in Asia, Africa, and the Americas. Climate was understood as more than just a meteorological phenomenon, and it was typically interpreted from a Eurocentric perspective, with the result that a temperate climate such as that of western Europe was seen as most favorable and considered ideal for social progress and prosperity.[5]

In the eighteenth century, however, a substantial change took place. As Russia's status and influence grew and Siberia became the subject of scientific study, the value assigned to cold also changed. The extreme temperatures that German, French, and later Russian scientists recorded on their expeditions into Siberia in the eighteenth century were a sensation in the learned circles of Europe. The foreign scientists encountered temperatures unlike anything they had experienced, and the study and measurement of this region raised a new question that was debated in scientific academies and journals, namely how temperatures are distributed across the Russian empire and the rest of the world. It led to an enthusiasm for weather that was fed by new meteorological instruments and the promise of soon being able to make predictions about future weather.

It is difficult to say what factors were decisive in the new value given to cold in climate theories of the mid-eighteenth century. Russia's rise to become a major power, Peter I's radical politics of modernization that was followed with great interest abroad, and the growing importance of Saint Petersburg as a hub of the Enlightenment all contributed to a revaluation of cold and a rehabilitation of the North. Countries that had previously been considered cold, northern, and barbaric were no longer treated as an entirely alien other. Through climate theories, Russia became a country that was strongly associated with a different kind of cold, one that was no longer only a devastating force on humans and the environment. During this period the geographical categorization of Russia also began to change: Russia was increasingly considered part of Eastern Europe and less frequently as a truly northern European nation.[6]

The new, positive assessment of cold and the North is most strongly associated with Montesquieu, although he is not the only one who contributed to the transformation. His *The Spirit of the Laws* (1748) drew upon theses from Hippocrates, Herodotus, and Arbuthnot that attributed weakness and laziness to fertile, warm regions and saw less fruitful, cold lands as bringing forth "heroic" individuals.[7] Even the resistance of the Russian nobility to autocratic rule had, according to his theory, its roots in the harsh climate: "The Russian nobility have indeed been reduced to slavery by the ambition of one of their princes; but they have always discovered those marks of impatience and discontent which are never to be seen in the southern climates."[8] Climate, for Montesquieu, was a central explanatory model for understanding differences in social and cultural phenomena such as political institutions, family structures, and social orders.[9] But unlike his predecessors, Montesquieu did not give preference to the temperate regions above all others. Rather, he saw the various climates of the world as presenting particular challenges for the lawgiver in each region, whose task was to make rational use of the advantages of the climatically determined national character and simultaneously mitigate its limitations.[10] In the Russian tsar Peter I he saw a ruler who had overcome the disadvantages of a climate by means of clever modernization policies. Nor was Montesquieu the only one who held this opinion. In 1718, during the tsar's lifetime, the English poet Aaron Hill praised Peter I as a "giant-genius" who had healed Russia from the curse of "frozen Climes" with his "intensest Heat."[11] Catherine II, in turn, adopted this discourse in 1767. Directly referring to Montesquieu, she described Russia as a European country, for Peter I had overcome the climate by introducing European customs.[12]

In spite of the criticism that deterministic climate theories attracted in the second half of the eighteenth century, a belief persisted—particularly in popular representations of science—that climate had an essential and defining influence on humans and their civilizations.[13] The rise and fall of civilizations were explained with the help of climate and climate fluctuations.[14] Montesquieu's idea that forms of government could be adapted to the climate was gradually lost in these treatises.[15] These European climate theories with their ethnocentric perspectives that offered the possibility of elevating one's own people and demoting others are, in a way, an early component of the anthropology and racial theories of the modern era. In an announcement for a lecture *On the Different Races of Man*, Immanuel Kant, for example, associated the "first race" not only with blonde hair but also with "damp cold."[16] It was not difficult to connect climate and weather with ideas about health or ethnic and racial differences. Looking ahead to the early twentieth century, the political instrumentalization of these theories becomes particularly evident: Ellsworth Huntington, the best-known exponent of climatic determinism, connected prosperity and domination over other countries with a temperate climate, or more precisely, 18°C.[17] He, too, considered Russia one of the "strongest nations of the world," which were able to assume their primacy thanks to an "optimal" climate.[18] Even the narratives by former exiles whom the autocratic tsarist government had banned to Siberia did not shake Huntington's conviction. He was rather astonished by their reports of how the bitter cold extinguished enthusiasm for work, but it did not cause him to doubt his basic theory that cold is correlated with efficiency.[19]

Huntington's praise of cold was also picked up by other authors, such as meteorologist Wladimir Köppen from Saint Petersburg, who stated in 1918 that "the hotspots of culture ... have shifted noticeably polewards" and that this movement was facilitated by the "world traffic" (*Weltverkehr*) that favored the "enterprising Northerners."[20] Similar arguments were expressed by US sociologist Seabury Colum GilFillan. In 1920 GilFillan put forward the theory that civilizations advance toward the north, toward colder regions, and in fact it was the cold that allowed for more "thinking" and "self-control." Although civilizations had their origins in warm regions, he thought, increasing prosperity would make it possible to expand into cold regions, while civilizations that were on the decline would withdraw back into warmer areas. GilFillan predicted that Scandinavia, thanks to its harsh climate, was on its way to becoming the leader of the world in the near future, and Russia, too, was "rousing herself from sleep of ages."[21]

This revaluing of cold that had begun with Montesquieu was not just a reaction to the fascination with polar regions, it was also connected to the "romanticization of ice-ages" that spread around the world in the early twentieth century, starting with Europe. However, this new attitude was not without ambivalence: at the beginning of the twentieth century, cold also evoked fear—even if this fear was sometimes experienced as more of a thrill. The discovery of ice ages, the causes of which were not known, led to renewed beliefs that the end of days was approaching.[22] The fear of a worldwide winter and visions of glaciers suddenly covering the land became a "fashionable malaise" everywhere.[23] Russian popular periodicals also discussed the question of whether a previously unknown cooling of the world was imminent and could wipe out humanity.[24] The link between cold and progress, as presented by Huntington and GilFillan, stripped this type of doomsday prediction of some of its terror, or at least made the dark scenario seem a little bit lighter.

While the apocalyptic visions of a coming ice age were based on a premise of terrifying changes, according to climate-determinist conceptions of the world, major changes of this sort were impossible: climate always had the same effect across space and time. According to Hippocrates, Herodotus, Montesquieu, and Huntington, a constant, unchanging climate created stable living environments, which due to this lack of change could then become inscribed in the "essence" of the people, in their constitutions, habits, and customs. The connection between climate and its consequences was so strong that climate was the decisive variable in nearly every historical process. It defined the framework in which social action could develop.[25] In these conceptions, there was no possibility for people, either individually or collectively, to emancipate themselves from the climate; nor was it possible for people to alter the climate. Humankind was seen as the plaything of the climate system, dominated by both the laws of nature and by a social and political order that was itself shaped by the climate.

This failure to allow for change in either climate or in the humans subject to the effects of climate and weather phenomena drew criticism of climate-determinist theories. Nearly simultaneously with the publication of Montesquieu's *The Spirit of the Laws*, other voices challenged the simple correlation between climate and the "most delicate functions of the human mind" and the "most accidental ordinances of society."[26] Criticism focused on three main arguments: first, the denial of humans' abilities to adapt; second, the recognition that climate does, in fact, change; and third, the possibility that humans can influence the climate themselves. In a reaction to Montesquieu, Scottish philosopher David Hume offered a refutation of the thesis that climate directly determines the character of a nation, citing various historical examples to demonstrate this. Hume listed religion and language as the reason why these two peoples had developed "a distinct and even opposite set of manners." He likewise rejected the thesis, propagated since antiquity and frequently applied to the Russians, that people living in cold regions are especially courageous; economic reasons were the primary motivation for the tendency of northern peoples to wage wars in the south.[27] The only weather- and climate-related difference that Hume was willing to concede was "that people in the northern regions have a greater inclination to strong liquors, and those in the southern to love and women."[28]

The interest in how peoples differ from one another was also applied to the inner reaches of Russia. Scientists such as Gerhard Friedrich Müller, who traveled to Siberia on behalf of the Academy of Sciences in Saint Petersburg, not only recorded the various ways that the indigenous peoples adapted to the cold but also pondered the degree to which their differences could be ascribed to the specific climate zones they lived in. Sometimes, to the scientists' astonishment, the climate did not give rise to the effects they expected. For example, in spite of the "cold and pure climate," the peoples of Siberia did not display a greater fecundity than peoples elsewhere. This, too, Müller thought, was a sign that "nature does not always act according to the same rules in all matters."[29]

Müller's field research led him to insights similar to those suggested by Johann Gottfried Herder, whose 1784 treatise *What Is Climate? And What Effect Has It in Forming the Body and Mind of Man?* attempted to moderate Montesquieu's theses with the help of examples from history, concluding that "climate does not force, but incline."[30] Rather, it is merely one variable that cannot exhaustively explain either the character of people or historical processes: "It is true, we are ductile clay in the hand of Climate; but her fingers mould so variously, and the laws, that counteract them, are so numerous, that perhaps the genius of mankind alone is capable of combining the relations of all these powers in one whole."[31] Furthermore, he argued against a unidirectional, deterministic view of the relationship between humans and the climate by pointing out that humans, like "diminutive giants," could not only adapt to the climate, they could also overcome its constraints by modifying it.[32] The idea that humans were capable of altering the climate was not unique to Herder, as Eva Horn has recently shown. It can also be found among the European colonists in the Americas, who hoped to induce a warmer climate in their new homeland by cutting down the forests.[33]

The charge that climatic determinist theories failed to acknowledge the social dynamics that were quite capable of overriding geographic and climatic factors continued to be made in the twentieth century. For example, in 1928 Russian-American social scientist Pitirim A. Sorokin criticized Huntington for suppressing all other possible interpretations, as well as for basing his conclusions on insufficient data.[34] Sorokin did not see any unequivocal or uniform influence of climatic factors on work efficiency: "Prosperity is not something static, but rather something that by its very nature changes according to the social circumstances."[35] But it was not just methodological concerns that spurred increasing doubt about the thesis of a direct connection between climate and culture. A fundamental shift in the underlying premises was also occurring. One decisive factor in this was the professionalization of meteorology and the development of climatology as a field of natural science in the nineteenth century, as well as the temporalization of climate and weather that came with this.[36]

Climatology and Meteorology

How did the young disciplines of meteorology and climatology approach the interrelationships between climate/weather and humans? Two main tendencies can be identified. In one approach, humans were considered only incidentally. Starting at the end of the nineteenth century, scholars who pursued meteorology and climatology as natural-science disciplines withdrew into investigations limited to purely physical, quantitative observation of the weather and the climate.[37] They considered climate to be simply "the sum of meteorological phenomena that characterize the average state of the atmosphere at a particular location on the surface of the globe."[38] Meteorologists like Julius Hann and Heinrich Wild, director of the Central Physical Observatory in Saint Petersburg, avoided any discussion about the influence of climate on human societies. Physical, psychological, and societal effects of weather and climate featured only rarely in their studies—a departure from previous definitions of climate. While in 1845 Alexander von Humboldt had made the influence of climate "on the feelings and mental condition of men" into a central component of his climate typology, Hann and Wild were primarily interested in explaining weather phenomena such as hail or cold spells as physical phenomena.[39] This narrowed understanding of climate was not only the result of technological innovations that shaped the development of meteorology and climatology during this period. Another determining factor was the increasing professionalization of these disciplines, which relied less and less on capable amateurs—literate Cossacks, peasants, or exiles—for the measurement of temperature, atmospheric pressure, and precipitation and the documentation of unusual weather occurrences. The training of experts and the increasingly professionalized meteorological networks thus correlated with a distancing of the discipline from everyday life.[40]

Weather anomalies—the cause of crop failures and famines—were the main reason for scientists to put the social and economic consequences of climate and weather on their agenda. Following several particularly hard winters and cool summers, such as those that struck Russia and the rest of Europe in 1709 and 1739, scholars began to raise the question of whether the climate had become cooler.[41] The concern that the climate was worsening had not disappeared in the late nineteenth century, when meteorologists increasingly were confronted by the perception of the general population that the past had been better: "When one listens to the forefathers, most of them say that in the good old days not only were people more valiant, the climate was better, too."[42]

By the nineteenth century, there was more and more evidence that the earth's climate was anything but constant. In 1837 Louis Agassiz interpreted a mammoth found frozen in the ice in Siberia as an indication that the world's climate was characterized by dramatic shifts and that there had been periods of pronounced cooling—ice ages.[43] Eduard Brückner, by contrast, was interested in less drastic changes in his study on *Climate Fluctuations since 1700*, in which he surmised that the changing water level of the Caspian Sea was caused by fluctuations in the climate and occurred every thirty-five years. Brückner's theses were considered particularly relevant for Russia, where, due to the continental climate, climate changes would be manifested much more distinctly than in maritime Western Europe.[44] Also highly discussed was Rudolf Wolf's theory from 1849 that suggested the fluctuations in sunspots were responsible for cool periods that followed an eleven-year cycle.[45]

Agassiz's and Brückner's studies gave climate and weather a history. This had not existed in deterministic climate theories, for these perceived the climate as constant, with the exception perhaps of very gradual changes. In Russia, too, there were fierce debates about whether the climatic anomalies were merely fluctuations in accordance with Brückner's theory or the heralds of a profound shift, a new ice age. Renowned Russian meteorologists like Alexander Voeikov argued that they were fluctuations, and thus that there was less reason for alarm and prophecies of doom: "There is certainly a great variation in this respect in single years, and even in periods from ten and twenty years. But nothing indicates a permanent change of climate. Cold years are followed by warm ones, and vice versa."[46]

Even after harsh winters and cool summers in 1891 and 1892 brought famine and cholera epidemics to Russia, Voeikov continued to disagree with the theories that interpreted several cool years in the 1880s as a "return of the ice age,"[47] pointing out that in spite of the very cold winters, the average temperature had not noticeably decreased. If one looked at when and how long the rivers had frozen over in the last 180 years, he suggested, it was clear that Saint Petersburg was actually in a warm period.[48] This view that the events of 1891 were the result of normal—and thus temporary—variations motivated meteorologists to act in support of those left hungry by the famine. Ferdinand Vrangel, for example, ended a public lecture on the topic at the Alexander Lyceum with the call "to support the victims of the climate fluctuations with all our efforts."[49]

In the early twentieth century, an increasing number of scholars in Russia began to express the position that the earth was not merely undergoing fluctuations but was instead in the grip of a more substantial climatic shift. Soviet oceanologist Nikolai Knipovich had determined that the water in the Barents Sea had become warmer. Elsewhere, too, scientists identified an "Arctic warming" that had resulted in the permafrost receding in the north of Russia.[50] But in the 1940s it became clear that the predicted warming of the climate had only been a fluctuation: with the return of colder temperatures, fur-lined shoes came into fashion again.[51]

The temporalization of weather and climate also directed attention to the possibility of emancipation from their effects. The theories that posited various periodic weather and climate cycles also created an expectation that meteorologists might be able to make predictions that would benefit agriculture and the economy.[52] Cycles such as those described by Brückner and Wolf were based on the assumption not only that the periodic alterations observed in the past would continue to occur in the future but also that the social and economic effects would remain constant. Thus, according to Brückner, climate fluctuations—manifested, for example, in changes in how long the rivers remained covered with ice each year—also meant "fluctuations in transport activities."[53] He did not recognize that the railroad was increasingly replacing rivers as a mode of transport.

Critics complained that Brückner's cycle was too imprecise to be of any practical use.[54] Especially since the famines in 1891 and 1892, meteorology was called upon to meet the challenge of being able to predict frosts and droughts and explore the available options for engaging in agriculture even in the cold north. In the Soviet Union, the disciplines of meteorology and climatology were subjected to even greater pressure under Stalin in the 1940s. Like other scientific disciplines such as genetics, meteorology had to comply with the demand to distance itself from purely theorizing and provide evidence of its applicability in practice.[55] And just as in the fields of genetics or plant breeding, theoreticians like Wild and applied scientists like Voeikov were pitted against one another: "For Wild, theory had precedence. And if nature did not adhere to the theory, then it was nature that was at fault."[56] The temporalization of climate did not just raise questions about the predictability of weather, it also revived the question about whether humans could alter climate and weather to suit their needs. The question was not new: draining swamps and planting trees had been seen as a way to alter the local climate as far back as antiquity. In Russia, the famines of 1891 and 1892 gave the possibility of altering the climate a new urgency. Scientists and the public disputed whether and to what degree humans could alter climate and the weather to benefit themselves. Opinions were greatly divided. While some were convinced that it was possible "to transform even the Sahara into a fertile land," others denied that humans could influence the climate in any way.[57] Renowned meteorologists like Voeikov argued that, although humans were not capable of altering the basic conditions that determined the climate, some amount of anthropogenic alteration to the lower levels of the atmosphere was possible.[58] Ultimately, however, human agency remained quite limited in Voeikov's deliberations.

Stalin's *Great Plan for the Transformation of Nature* in 1948 was inspired by these debates, although little remains of the modest claims of people like Voeikov. The plan included the ambitious goal of improving the climate in the Soviet Union by planting six million hectares of forest.[59] Through this afforestation over the course of fifteen years, a climate leveling would take place between the north, with its rich forests and waterways, and the steppes of the south, resulting in the opening up of new areas of agricultural land. The plan, which was promoted by extensive propaganda measures, was a response to the drought of 1946 that had resulted in major crop failures. It was a continuation of plans from the mid-nineteenth century, as Stephen Brain has shown.[60]

Pre-revolutionary nature transformation projects had been much less ambitious. Unlike the Stalin Plan of 1948, they did not aim to alter the entire climate of Russia, but only transform the steppe regions of the south into fertile land. Although the Stalin Plan was abandoned within just a few years, it was not the end of utopian ambitions to improve the climate. In the 1950s, the Davydov Plan called for diverting the rivers of northern Russia and Siberia toward the south in order to stimulate cotton cultivation in Central Asia by providing water for irrigation.[61] And finally, in the 1960s, Petr Borisov proposed a plan to regulate the world's climate by building a dam across the Bering Strait between Alaska and Russia. The idea was to pump cold Arctic water into the Pacific; in return, warm water would flow northward from the Atlantic.[62] According to Borisov's calculations, Atlantic water would reach the Arctic within three years. The increased water temperature would cause the Arctic ice to melt, and this, in turn, would reduce the albedo of the earth and thereby reduce solar radiation loss due to reflection. In the United States, too, scientists began to conduct their own research regarding this proposal under President Nixon, and at a summit in Vladivostok in 1974 US president Gerald Ford and Soviet general secretary Leonid Brezhnev discussed the possibility of implementing the plan.[63]

The Cold War increased the demand for meteorology to move from predicting the weather to controlling it—and even to controlling the climate more generally. Triggered by a series of harsh winters and cool summers, and later by the oil crises in the 1960s and 1970s, the fears of global cooling that had recurred since the eighteenth century were awoken once again.[64] But the scale had changed significantly: instead of merely hoping to improve the climate of a single region or country, people had started to think on a global scale. The Cold War competition with the United States included Soviet efforts to reshape the climate of the planet. Russian scientists like Mikhail Budyko were convinced that the Soviet Union would benefit from milder temperatures in the Arctic. He proposed to melt the polar ice caps by coating their surface with soot, thereby reducing their reflectivity.[65] Another, no less ambitious plan was to create an artificial planetary ring around the earth: 2.4 million tons of dust particles would be sent into orbit at a distance of 1,000 kilometers from the surface and distributed along the earth's north-south axis. The dust particles were to function as reflectors to bring warmth and light into the polar regions and thereby improve the earth's overall balance of warmth.⁶⁶ The sense of necessity that motivated the development of these plans was intensified by the nuclear arms race between the two superpowers and fears of a nuclear winter caused by the use of atomic weapons.

These utopian climate plans were meant to have an impact both domestically and internationally. They were a means of internal colonization and annexation of new natural spaces and simultaneously an attempt to express the triumph of World War II victory in the everyday life of postwar society. Instead of mourning the victims and losses of the war, these Promethean visions celebrated a humanity empowered to conquer not only military opponents but also nature itself. Looking outward, these plans were a way to impress other world powers, both competitors and allies. However, these plans to improve nature were defeated by the misgivings of experts and on occasion also by the opposition of the people.⁶⁷

Then, in the 1970s, another change in perspective occurred when scientists recognized that they had been basing their ideas on false premises. Rather than an overall cooling of the climate, anthropogenic global warming was well underway. Instead of making plans for a deliberate artificial warming of the climate in order to improve conditions for living and expand the range of agriculture northward, Soviet experts now began, along with the international scientific community, to warn about the effects—such as droughts and floods—of this unintentional climate change.

History and Climate History

Today, the question of whether we are living in the Anthropocene, a geological era characterized by the influence of humans, has become a subject of intense debate. The Anthropocene thesis has brought with it a change in our understanding of climate that has had repercussions in extending into the social sciences and humanities. As a result of such reflection on the effects of climate change and our options for protecting ourselves from it or even slowing or preventing it, renewed attention has been directed to the question of human agency and the social effects of climate and weather. Historians, too, have rediscovered a forgotten interest in the role of weather and climate in human history.

In the nineteenth century the connections between humans and nature were still given an important place in the study of history, as can be seen, for example, in the works of Russian historians Sergei Solov'ev and Vasilii Kliuchevskii. Kliuchevskii saw nature—alongside human personalities and human society—as one of the most important historical forces.⁶⁸ Russia's wide expanses were considered an important factor that explained the development of autocratic forms of government. Moreover, in the late nineteenth century, Russian historians associated climate with the progress of civilization: civilizations, they thought, could only develop in climates that were not too harsh or extreme.[69]

Just as in the disciplines of meteorology and climatology, the famine of 1891 and 1892 marked a caesura in Russian historiography. It not only put the question of what the climate had been like in the past on the agenda of historical research, it also resulted in historians writing studies of how humans had protected themselves from the vagaries of nature. In 1892, historian Dmitrii Bagalei looked back into the past to argue for improving contemporary precautions and preparations: in the early eighteenth century Peter I had mitigated the negative effects of climate-related crop failures by creating state grain stores and improving medical care. Consequently, since the eighteenth century Russia had "not experienced any more famine years such as were common previously."[70] In these studies, climate, and the summer frosts and hard winters that accompanied it, played an important role, but at the same time the historians emphasized that social dynamics, not just climatic factors, were what caused the famines.

Like the meteorologists and climatologists, historians became interested in explaining whether the climatic anomalies that had caused the famines were the result of a profound shift in the climate or only temporary fluctuations. Here historians considered themselves primarily the handmaidens of the natural sciences who could use their specialized knowledge of historical sources to help reconstruct the climate of the past. Methodologically, the scientists were breaking new ground. In 1930, for example, biophysicist Alexander Chizhevskii published an interdisciplinary study that attempted to draw connections between major epidemics of the past and fluctuations in climate. He hoped that by looking into the past it would become possible to make predictions about the future.[71]

This development came to an abrupt end in Stalin's Soviet Union. Starting in the mid-1930s, geography became a problematic category for explaining causal connections between climate and the social world. After the publication in 1935 of the *History of the All-Union Communist Party (Bolsheviks): Short Course*, which rejected the possibility that geographic environment could affect society, discussions became increasingly dogmatic.[72] Even the writings of the "Eurasianists," a movement based largely among émigré Russians that took the position that Eurasia should be considered a single geographic entity, could not be published in the Soviet Union.[73] Partly in distinction to the Eurasianist movement growing abroad, the discussions taking place in the Soviet Union about the relationship between humans and nature began to follow different theoretical and methodological premises than in Western Europe; radical limitations were placed on the influence of geographical and thereby also climatic factors. The gap between the natural sciences on the one hand and the social sciences and humanities on the other deepened, and a sociological Marxism arose that influenced the understanding of historical change.[74]

In particular, in the confrontation with Russia's "backwardness" and the reasons for it, the possibility of geographical conditions influencing history was no longer considered a valid line of argument. This was illustrated vividly in the defamation of the young historian M. V. Nechkina following a 1941 lecture at the Institute of History of the Soviet Academy of Sciences in which she asked why Russia had embarked on the path of capitalism so much later than other countries.[75] Her thesis was that geographic factors could accelerate or delay historical processes. This contradicted the position of Stalin and the *Short Course*, which stated in 1935 that the geographic setting could not have any "determinative influence" because "the changes and development of society occur incomparably faster than the changes and development of the geographic milieu."[76] Leaving aside sudden chance events such as volcanic eruptions and summer frosts, Stalin and his ideologues considered that the development of society was determined solely by humans.[77] Chizhevskii, too, found himself on the wrong side of the ideological debate about how historical change occurs. When he was unwilling to retract his research on the *Physical Factors of the Historical Process* in 1942, he was arrested and sent to a prison camp for eight years.[78] In criticizing Nechkina and Chizhevskii, Stalin and his followers cited in particular the work of Georgii Plekhanov, whose theories came to assume a central role in Soviet Marxism. The geographic setting, according to Plekhanov's 1896 volume *Essays on the History of Materialism*, only has an effect on history through the medium of productive forces,[79] and neither summer frost nor crop failure could interrupt the historical laws that determine the development of humanity.[80]

The effect of climate on human history could only be discussed in terms of an indirect influence. For example, historians traced the strengthening of the system of serfdom or the collective character of agriculture back to the harsh climate and the short growing season.[81] Only works that limited themselves to reconstructing the climate of the past could be published during this period, so long as they refrained from discussing the social and economic consequences of climatic anomalies. Vasilii Betin and Iurii Preobrazhenskii, for example, made no mention of the effects on people in their 1962 list of the most extreme winters dating back to 1760.[82] In historiographical theory, discussions of the interrelations between humans and nature or the climate remained largely absent until the 1980s, when the ecological crisis of the late Soviet Union brought with it a sense of living in a fragile world. At this time, glasnost and perestroika also made it easier to talk openly about ecological questions.

Although the rationale behind these developments in the discipline of history was specifically Soviet, there are a number of obvious parallels with developments in Western European historiography. In countries like France and Germany, the separation between social sciences and humanities contributed to a tendency to ignore the social and economic consequences of climate in historical discussions. Historians for whom history was a social science discipline felt that social phenomena could only be explained in terms of the social. Despite major differences, this approach had close affinities to the *Outline of the Principles of History* by Johann Gustav Droysen, for whom nature had no place in the study of history and the only sources that could be elevated to the status of historical evidence were those that bore the trace of "human spirit and human hand."[83] Even historians such as Emmanuel Le Roy Ladurie, who considered themselves scholars of climate history, saw their role as primarily assisting the work of climatologists and meteorologists. The data that they compiled were not, in their view, usable as an "explanation of human history." Only a tiny portion of it might prove of value for a "chronology of famines and possibly of pestilences."[84] Following from these premises, the effects of climate and weather on humans played only a minimal role in history, and studies that thematized this subject were often dismissed as being climate determinist.

While many historical studies treated weather and climate as universal, timeless, and without influence—in other words, as phenomena that were subject to very little change—the discussions happening elsewhere in society about environmental damage, pollution, and anthropogenic climate change put the historical nature of climate and weather back on the agenda of scholars, in the Soviet Union as in Western Europe. Starting in the 1970s and 1980s, Soviet historians increasingly began to ask how weather and climate play out within social and political contexts. The diminishing importance of Marxism as the guiding philosophy in the 1980s undoubtedly contributed to this. It is notable that these new historical studies focused exclusively on the tsarist period when discussing the interrelations between humans and nature. By restricting themselves to the period before the October Revolution, historians like A. V. Dulov could thematize the exploitation of nature during the transition from feudalism to capitalism without having to address the sins committed by the Soviet regime.[85] In spite of this reluctance to broach the topic directly, Dulov did not fail to remark that "the use of nature in the past could be useful for contemporary practices."[86] The contemporary ecological crises were also reflected in the work of historian V. A. Anuchin, who in 1982 revived the discussion of whether geographic factors should be considered a historical category. He emphasized that dependence on the geographic environment was growing rather than waning. Humankind, Anuchin argued, is not only subject to nature, it is also part of nature.[87] This assertion contradicted not only the view that history was determined entirely by humans but also the Promethean visions that had long dominated the Soviet treatment of the natural world.

Another sign of the substantial change that had taken place in the late Soviet Union and post-Soviet Russia was the fact that works of members of the "Eurasian movement" began to be published again in the 1980s. One of the first of these was Lev Gumilev's study *Ethnogenesis and the Biosphere of Earth* in 1979, which moved beyond the original geographic determinism of the early Eurasianists.[88] In addition to geographic factors, Gumilev saw biochemical processes in the earth's atmosphere and the laws of thermodynamics as contributing to ethnogenesis and the course of history.[89] And he connected this with the doubts raised by pollution and low standards of living about whether Russia might perhaps be too large and too cold to survive at all in such a radically changing world.[90]

This brief overview has shown how the relation between humans and climate has been an important question in various scholarly disciplines. In today's debates about phenomena such as global warming, it is clear that they pose important questions not just for the natural sciences but also for the social sciences and humanities. Looking at the work of writers such as Brückner, Wolf, and Bogolepov reveals that the issues being raised as a result of climate change today are not new but part of a long tradition. Philosophers, meteorologists, climatologists, and historians have all, in various ways, grappled with the significance and effects of climate fluctuations, and this continues to be a source of political disagreement today. The history of climate theories also demonstrates how the desire to examine the past is closely connected with the hope of making predictions and thereby better preparing ourselves for the future.

Yet there is another aspect that seems even more important. Indian historian Dipesh Chakrabarty recently suggested that climate change forces us to reconsider the role of humans in history. As a result of fossil fuel consumption, humans are leaving ever more substantial traces in all of the earth's systems. We must ask ourselves how we think about humans and humanity as actors in the Anthropocene. Even the history of the most remote regions of the planet can no longer be written without humans. While historians were debating whether nature could be an actor in human history, humanity itself became a geophysical force—an actor in the planet's geological history. Although this question has acquired a new quality in the Anthropocene, this overview of the history of climate theories through to the development of climate history shows that human agency has long been a topic in the investigation of the relations between humans and climate. Phenomena such as summer frosts and crop failures gave rise to discussions about what drives historical change. These were not and are not idle questions, as the ideological discussions in the Soviet Union clearly show: here a possible influence of the geographic environment was rejected and a Promethean image of humanity was promoted. What is agency and to whom do we attribute this power? To whom do we deny it? How and using what sources do we write a history in which nature is not merely an object of human activity? This volume asks these questions through the exploration of the interrelations between humans, weather, and climate as expressed in the phenomena of cold.

Julia Herzberg is professor for the history of East Central Europe and Russia in early modern times at LMU Munich. Her recent research has focused on, among other topics, the environmental history of Central Eastern Europe and Russia. She coedited *Ice and Snow in the Cold War: Histories of Extreme Climatic Environments* (2019) with Christian Kehrt and Franziska Torma, and *Umweltgeschichte(n): Ostmitteleuropa von der Industrialisierung bis zum Postsozialismus* (2013) with Martin Zückert and Horst Förster. She is currently working on an environmental history of "frost" in Russia that examines various social and cultural aspects of Russia's harsh climate.

Notes

1. Nikolai M. Dronin and Edward G. Bellinger, *Climate Dependence and Food Problems in Russia 1900–1990: The Interaction of Climate and Agricultural Policy and their Effect on Food Problems* (Budapest, 2005), 1–5.
2. Lucian Boia, *The Weather in the Imagination* (London, 2005), 11.
3. Waldemar Zacharasiewicz, *Die Klimatheorie in der englischen Literatur und Literaturkritik: Von der Mitte des 16. bis zum frühen 18. Jahrhundert*, Wiener Beiträge zur englischen Philologie 77 (Vienna, 1977), 24; Evan Hayes, Stephen Nimis, and Hippocrates, *Hippocrates' On Airs, Waters, and Places and the Hippocratic Oath: An Intermediate Greek Reader; Greek Text with Running Vocabulary and Commentary* (Oxford, 2013).
4. John Arbuthnot, *An Essay Concerning the Effects of Air on Human Bodies*, 3rd ed. (London, 1751), 153–54.
5. Gonthier-Louis Fink, "Diskriminierung und Rehabilitierung des Nordens im Spiegel der Klimatheorie," in *Imagologie des Nordens*, ed. Astrid Arndt, Imaginatio borealis 7 (Frankfurt/Main [i.a.], 2004), 45–46; Manfred Beller, "Johann Gottfried Herders Völkerbilder und die Tradition der Klimatheorie," in *Eingebildete Nationalcharaktere: Vorträge und Aufsätze zur literarischen Imagologie*, ed. Manfred Beller, Elena Agazzi, and Raul Calzoni (Göttingen, 2006), 240–41.
6. Hans Lemberg, "Zur Entstehung des Osteuropabegriffs im 19. Jahrhundert: Vom Norden zum Osten Europas," *Jahrbücher für Geschichte Osteuropas* 33, no. 1 (1985).
7. Charles Montesquieu, *Vom Geist der Gesetze: Bd. 1*, with the assistance of Ernst Forsthoff, 2nd ed., 2 vols. (Tübingen, 1992), 311, English translation: http://www.constitution.org/cm/sol_14.htm; Also: Hippocrates, *De aere aquis locis*, with the assistance of Hans Diller, Corpus medicorum Graecorum 1,1,2 (Berlin, 1970), publ. and trans. by Hans Diller, 63.
8. Montesquieu, *Vom Geist der Gesetze*, 370.
9. Frederick Sargent II, *Hippocratic Heritage: A History of Ideas about Weather and Human Health* (New York, 1982).

10. Fink, "Diskriminierung," 82.
11. Aaron Hill, *The Northern Star: A Poem; Originally Publish'd in the Life-time of Peter Alexiovitz, Great Czar of Russia*, 5th ed., rev., and corrected, by the author (London, 1739), http://find.galegroup.com/ecco/infomark.do?contentSet=ECCOArticles&docType=ECCOArticles&bookId=0110902500&type=getFullCitation&tabID=T001&prodId=ECCO&docLevel=TEXT_GRAPHICS&version=1.0&source=library, 7.
12. William F. Reddaway, ed., *Documents of Catherine the Great: The Correspondence with Voltaire and the Instruction of 1767 in the English Text of 1768* (Cambridge, 2011), 216.
13. Nico Stehr and Hans von Storch, *Klima, Wetter, Mensch* (Munich, 1999), 45–47.
14. For example, Edward Gibbon and Henry Hart Milman, *The History of the Decline and Fall of the Roman Empire*, vols. 1–4, new ed. (New York, 1844–51). Today the idea that specific types of natural environment define human life still continues to enjoy some popularity. See Jared M. Diamond, *Collapse: How Societies Choose to Fail or Succeed* (New York, 2005), http://www.loc.gov/catdir/enhancements/fy0719/2004057152-b.html; Reinhard Falter, *Natur prägt Kultur: Der Einfluß von Landschaft und Klima auf den Menschen. Zur Geschichte der Geophilosophie* (Munich, 2006).
15. Eva Horn, "Klimatologie um 1800: Zur Genealogie des Anthropozäns," *ZFK. Zeitschrift für Kulturwissenschaft* 10, no. 1 (2016).
16. Beller, "Johann Gottfried Herders Völkerbilder," 254; Immanuel Kant, *Von den verschiedenen Racen der Menschen: Zur Ankündigung der Vorlesungen der physischen Geographie im Sommerhalbenjahre 1775* (Königsberg, 1775), http://resolver.staatsbibliothek-berlin.de/SBB000200DD00000000.
17. James Rodger Fleming, *Historical Perspectives on Climate Change* (New York, 1998), 95–107.
18. Ellsworth Huntington, *The Pulse of Asia: A Journey in Central Asia Illustrating the Geographic Basis of History* (London, 1907), 384–85. Similarly, S. F. Markham, *Climate and the Energy of Nations*, 2nd ed. (London, 1944), 21, 31.
19. Ellsworth Huntington, *Civilization and Climate*, 3rd ed. (New Haven, CT, 1924), 235–38.
20. Wladimir Köppen, *Klimakunde*, 2nd rev. ed., repr. 1918 (Leipzig, 1918), 122–23.
21. S. C. GilFillan, "The Coldward Course of Progress," *Political Science Quarterly* 35, no. 3 (1920): 409.
22. Tobias Krüger, *Die Entdeckung der Eiszeiten* (Basel, Bern, 2006); Doug Macdougall, *Frozen Earth: The Once and Future Story of Ice Ages* (Berkeley, CA, 2004).
23. Helmut Lethen, "Lob der Kälte: Ein Motiv der historischen Avantgarden," in *Unheimliche Nachbarschaften: Essays zum Kälte-Kult und der Schlaflosigkeit der Philosophischen Anthropologie im 20. Jahrhundert* (Freiburg i. Br., 2009), 62.
24. "Potukhnet li solntse?," *Niva*, no. 36 (1884); "Okhlazhdenie solntsa i zemli," *Vestnik znaniia*, no. 4 (1905).
25. Fleming, *Historical Perspectives on Climate Change*, 11–18.
26. Johann Gottfried Herder, *Ideen zur Philosophie der Geschichte der Menschheit*, with the assistance of Martin Bollacher (Frankfurt/Main, 1989), 265; Johann Gottfried Herder, *Outlines of a Philosophy of the History of Man: Translated from the German of John Godfrey Herder, by T. Churchill* (London, 1800), http://find.galegroup.com/ecco/infomark.do?contentSet=ECCOArticles&docType=ECCOArticles&

bookId=0004300300&type=getFullCitation&tabID=T001&prodId=ECCO &docLevel=TEXT_GRAPHICS&version=1.0&source=library, 311.
27. David Hume, "Of National Characters (1748)," in *Political Essays*, ed. David Hume (Cambridge, 1994), 84–89.
28. Ibid., 90; Montesquieu and Kant also brought up this argument: Montesquieu, *Vom Geist der Gesetze*, 314; Immanuel Kant and Friedrich Theodor Rink, *Immanuel Kant's physische Geographie: Bd. 2* (Königsberg, 1802), 13.
29. Gerhard Friedrich Müller and Aleksandr Élert, eds., *Ethnographische Schriften I*, Quellen zur Geschichte Sibiriens und Alaskas aus russischen Archiven 8 (Halle, 2010), 561.
30. Herder, *Outlines of a Philosophy of the History of Man*, 317.
31. Ibid., 311.
32. Ibid., 316–17.
33. Horn, "Klimatologie um 1800," 95.
34. Sorokin's criticism of Huntington was shared by his Soviet colleagues: K. Bruks, *Klimaty proshlogo: Perevod s angliiskogo V. G. Levinsona* (Moscow, 1952), 5–6.
35. Pitirim Sorokin, *Soziologische Theorien im 19. und 20. Jahrhundert* (Munich, 1931), 33.
36. Wolf Lepenies, *Das Ende der Naturgeschichte: Wandel kultureller Selbstverständlichkeiten in den Wissenschaften des 18. und 19. Jahrhunderts* (Munich, Vienna, 1976).
37. Stehr and Storch, *Klima, Wetter, Mensch*, 10.
38. Julius von Hann, *Handbuch der Klimatologie* (Stuttgart, 1883), 1.
39. Alexander von Humboldt and Eduard Buschmann, *Kosmos: Entwurf einer physischen Weltbeschreibung. Bd. 1*, 2 vols. (Stuttgart, Tübingen, 1845), 340.
40. R. Bergmann, "Über die Vertheilung und Thätigkeit der meteorologischen Stationen in Russland: Von den ersten Anfängen bis zum Jahre 1889 inclusive," *Repertorium für Meteorologie* 15, Nr. 11 (Saint Petersburg, 1892); A. I. Berdickii et al., *Ocherki po istorii gidrometeorologicheskoi sluzhby Rossii: T. 1* (Saint Petersburg, 1997).
41. "Primechanie o klimatakh [Kholodnee li stali nashi klimatyy, nezheli prezhde?]," *Mesiacoslov s nastavleniiami* (1779).
42. F. F. Vrangel', *Kolebaniia klimata: Lektsii v Imperatorskom Aleksandrovskom Litsee* (Saint Petersburg, 1891), 3.
43. Macdougall, *Frozen Earth*, 36–37; Krüger, *Die Entdeckung der Eiszeiten*, 225–27; Louis Agassiz, *Geological Sketches* (London, 1866).
44. M. Bogolepov, *O kolebaniiakh klimata Evropeiskoi Rossii v istoricheskuiu èpokhu: S prilozheniem materialov, izvlechennykh iz russkikh letopisei* (Moscow, 1908), 4.
45. M. A. Bogolepov, *Periodicheskie vozmushcheniia klimata*, 2nd ed. (Moscow, 1928), 9; Mikhail Aleksandrovich Bogolepov, *Vozmushcheniia klimata i zhizn' zemli i narodov* (Berlin, 1923), 23.
46. A. Woeikof, *Meteorology in Russia* (Washington, DC, 1874), 5.
47. A. I. Voeikov, *O temperature poslednikh 9-ti let (1882–90): Otdel'nyi ottisk iz Meteorologicheskago vestnika, 1891, Nr. 4* (Saint Petersburg, 1891), 1.
48. D. N. A[nuchin], "K voprosu ob izmenenii klimata," *Russkie vedomosti*, no. 70 (1891).
49. Vrangel', *Kolebaniia klimata*, 18.
50. L. S. Berg, "Poteplenie severa," *Vestnik znaniia*, no. 10 (1935); E. I. Tikhomirov, "Kolebanie klimata ili ego izmenenie?" *Meteorologicheskii vestnik* 7/8 (1935).
51. K. S. Losev, *Klimat: Vchera, segodnia ... i zavtra?* (Leningrad, 1985), 129.

52. M. Spasskii, *Ob uspekhakh meteorologii: Rech', proiznesennaia v torzhestvennom sobranii Imperatorskogo Moskovkago Universiteta* (Moscow, 1831), 27.
53. Eduard Brückner, *Klimaschwankungen seit 1700 nebst Bemerkungen über die Klimaschwankungen der Diluvialzeit,* Geographische Abhandlungen IV,2 (Vienna, Olomouc, 1890), 276.
54. B. P. Alisov et al., *Kurs klimatologii* (Leningrad, Moscow, 1940), 304.
55. Julia Herzberg, "Lenken und Erziehen: Mensch und Natur in der Debatte um die sowjetische Genetik," in *Projektion Natur: Grüne Gentechnik im Fokus der Wissenschaften,* ed. Annette Meyer and Stephan Schleissing (Göttingen, 2014).
56. Tverskoi, P. N. *Razvitie Meteorologii V SSSR* (Leningrad, 1949), 23–24; M. Il'in, *Preobrzovanie planety: Rasskazy o pokorenii prirody* (Moscow, 1951), 93.
57. "Rev.: A. Voeikov, Vozdeistvie cheloveka na prirodu," *Meteorologicheskii vestnik,* no. 1 (1896): 19.
58. A. I. Voeikov, "Sposoby vozdeistviia cheloveka na prirodu," *Russkoe obozrenie,* no. 4 (1892).
59. Stephen Brain, "The Great Stalin Plan for the Transformation of Nature," *Environmental History* 15 (2010); Kh. P. Pogosian, *Izmenenie klimata v sviazi s planom preobrazovaniia prirody zaslushlivykh raionov SSSR* (Leningrad, 1952).
60. Brain, "Great Stalin Plan," 670–700.
61. M. Dawydov, "Flüsse werden rückwärts fließen," *Die Presse der Sowjetunion,* no. 83 (1956).
62. P. M. Borisov, *Mozhet li chelovek izmenit' klimat,* Nauchno-popularnaia seriia / Akademiia Nauk SSSR (Moscow, 1970).
63. E. N. Kuzovkova, "Tol'ko fakty," in *Socializm i priroda: Sbornik statei* (Moscow, 1976), 41–42, 46; Wolfgang Behringer, *Kulturgeschichte des Klimas: Von der Eiszeit bis zur globalen Erwärmung* (Munich, 2007), 251.
64. Reid A. Bryson and Thomas J. Murray, *Climates of Hunger: Mankind and the World's Changing Weather* (Madison, WI, 1977), 131; Kuzovkova, "Tol'ko fakty," 41–42.
65. Fleming, *Historical Perspectives on Climate Change,* 134.
66. Boris Belge and Klaus Gestwa, "Wetterkrieg und Klimawandel: Die Meteorologie im Kalten Krieg," *Osteuropa* 59, no. 10 (2009): 32; Fleming, *Historical Perspectives on Climate Change,* 134.
67. Werner Leimbach, "Der Dawydow-Plan der Sowjetunion," *Zeitschrift für Raumforschung* 1/2 (1950).
68. V. I. Tkachev, *Rol' geograficheskogo faktora v istorii Rossii: Uchebnoe posobie* (Saratov, 2000), 3.
69. L. I. Mechnikov, *Tsivilizatsiia i velikiia istoricheskiia reki: Geograficheskaia teoriia razvitiia sovremennych obshchestv* (SPb, 1898); Perevod s francuzskagi M. D. Grodekkago, 36–40.
70. D. I. Bagalei, "Stikhiinyia bedstviia i bor'ba s nimi V Rossii v starinu," *Istoricheskii vestnik* 47 (1892): 195.
71. A. L. Chizhevskii, *Épidemicheskie katastrofy i periodicheskaia deiatel'nost' solntsa,* Izdanie vserossiiskogo Obshchestva vrachei-gomeopatov (Moscow, 1930).
72. I. L. Belen'kii, *Rol' geograficheskogo faktora v otechestvennom istoricheskom protsesse: Analiticheskii obzor* (Moscow, 2000), 7–8; M. A. Bogolepov, *Nastupaiushchie vozmu-*

shcheniia klimata: Po istoricheskim dannym (Moscow, 1921); M. A. Bogolepov, Prichiny neurozhaev i goloda v Rossii v istoricheskoe vremia (Moscow, 1922); M. A. Bogolepov, Princip rastiazheniia litosfery i o periodicheskich izmeneniiakh klimata (Moscow, 1925); Bogolepov, Periodicheskie vozmushcheniia klimata; Bogolepov, Vozmushcheniia klimata i zhizn' zemli i narodov; L. S. Berg, "Klimaty geologicheskago proshlago," Priroda, no. 1 (1918); L. S. Berg, Klimat i zhizn', 2nd ed. (Moscow, 1947).

73. Otto Böss, Die Lehre der Eurasier: Ein Beitrag zur russischen Ideengeschichte der 20. Jahrhunderts, Veröffentlichungen des Osteuropa-Institutes, München 15 (Wiesbaden, 1961); Assen Ignatow, Der "Eurasismus" und die Suche nach einer neuen russischen Kulturidentität: Die Neubelebung des "Evraziistvo"-Mythos, Berichte des Bundesinstituts für Ostwissenschaftliche und Internationale Studien 1992, 15 (Cologne, 1992); Stefan Wiederkehr, Die eurasische Bewegung: Wissenschaft und Politik in der russischen Emigration der Zwischenkriegszeit und im postsowjetischen Russland, Beiträge zur Geschichte Osteuropas 39 (Weimar, 2007).

74. Rolf Löther, "Bemerkungen zum Verhältnis von Natur, Mensch und Gesellschaft in der Geschichte der marxistischen Philosophie," in Umweltschutz in der DDR: Analysen und Zeitzeugenberichte, ed. Hermann Behrens (Munich, 2007), 195–96

75. M. V. Nechkina, "O prichinakh otstalosti Rossii: Doklad i itogi diskussii 1941," Istoricheskii vestnik, no. 3 (1993); M. V. Nechkina, "O prichinakh otstalosti Rossii: Doklad i itogi diskussii 1941," Istoricheskii Arkhiv, no. 2 (1993).

76. Löther, "Bemerkungen zum Verhältnis von Natur," 196.

77. Iosif V. Stalin, Über dialektischen und historischen Materialismus, Grundschriften des wissenschaftlichen Kommunismus 6 (Offenbach, 1997).

78. A. L. Chizhevskii, Fizicheskie faktory istoricheskogo protsessa (Kaluga, 1924); Viktor Nikolaevich Iagodinskii, Aleksandr Leonidovich Chizhevskii: 1897–1964, Izd. vtoroe, pererabot. i dop, Seriia "Nauchno-biograficheskaia literatura" (Moscow, 2004), 280.

79. Carsten Goehrke, Russland: Eine Strukturgeschichte (Paderborn, Munich, Vienna, Zürich, 2010), 27.

80. Georgii V. Plechanov, "Beiträge zur Geschichte des Materialismus: Holbach, Helvetius, Marx," in Internationale Bibliothek 29 (Stuttgart, 1896), 199.

81. Tkachev, Rol' geograficheskogo faktora v istorii Rossii, 14–16, 19.

82. V. V. Betin and Iu. V. Preobrazhenskii, Surovost' zim v Evrope i ledovitost' Baltiki (Leningrad, 1962).

83. Johann G. Droysen, "Natur und Geschichte," in Historik. Vorlesungen über Enzyklopädie und Methodologie der Geschichte, ed. Rudolf Hübner, 5th ed. (Munich, 1967).

84. Emmanuel Le Roy Ladurie, "Die Geschichte von Sonnenschein und Regenwetter," in Schrift und Materie der Geschichte, ed. Claudia Honegger (Frankfurt/Main, 1977), 222.

85. A. V. Dulov, Geograficheskaia sreda i istoriia Rossii: Konec XV—seredina XIX v. (Moscow, 1983), 163.

86. Dulov, Gograficheskaia Sreda i istoriia Rossii, 3.

87. V. A. Anuchin, Geograficheskii faktor v razvitii obshchestva (Moscow, 1982), 323.

88. L. N. Gumilëv, Ėtnogenez i biosfera zemli (Moscow, 1979). For a critical assessment of his work, see Marlène Laruelle and Mischa Gabovich, Russian Eurasianism: An Ideology of Empire (Washington, DC, 2008), 81–82.

89. Wiederkehr, Die eurasische Bewegung, 196–99.

90. V. S. Myglan, "Vliianie klimaticheskikh izmenenii na sotsial'nye i prirodnye protsessy v Sibiri v XVII—pervoi polovine XIX vv. po istoricheskim i dendrokhronologicheskim dannym (Avtoreferat)" (Krasnodar, 2005), 5.

Bibliography

Agassiz, Louis. *Geological Sketches*. London, 1866.
Alisov, B. P., et al. *Kurs klimatologii*. Leningrad, Moscow, 1940.
Anuchin, V. A. *Geograficheskii faktor v razvitii obshchestva*. Moscow, 1982.
A[nuchin], D. N. "K voprosu ob izmenenii klimata." *Russkie vedomosti*, no. 70 (1891): 3.
Arbuthnot, John. *An Essay Concerning the Effects of Air on Human Bodies*. 3rd ed. London, 1751.
Bagalei, D. I. "Stikhiinyia bedstviia i bor'ba s nimi V Rossii v starinu." *Istoricheskii vestnik* 47 (1892): 177–95.
Behringer, Wolfgang. *Kulturgeschichte des Klimas: Von der Eiszeit bis zur globalen Erwärmung*. Munich, 2007.
Belen'kii, I. L. *Rol' geograficheskogo faktora v otechestvennom istoricheskom protsesse: Analiticheskii obzor*. Moscow, 2000.
Belge, Boris, and Klaus Gestwa. "Wetterkrieg und Klimawandel: Die Meteorologie im Kalten Krieg." *Osteuropa* 59, no. 10 (2009): 15–42.
Beller, Manfred. "Johann Gottfried Herders Völkerbilder und die Tradition der Klimatheorie." In *Eingebildete Nationalcharaktere: Vorträge und Aufsätze zur literarischen Imagologie*, edited by Manfred Beller, Elena Agazzi, and Raul Calzoni, 239–60. Göttingen, 2006.
Berdickii, A. I. et al. *Ocherki po istorii gidrometeorologicheskoi sluzhby Rossii: T. 1*. Saint Petersburg, 1997.
Berg, L. S. *Klimat i zhizn'*. 2nd ed. Moscow, 1947.
———. "Klimaty geologicheskago proshlago." *Priroda*, no. 1 (1918): 3–27.
———. "Poteplenie severa." *Vestnik znaniia*, no. 10 (1935): 749–50.
Bergmann, R. "Über die Vertheilung und Thätigkeit der meteorologischen Stationen in Russland: Von den ersten Anfängen bis zum Jahre 1889 inclusive." *Repertorium für Meteorologie* 15, no. 11. Saint Petersburg, 1892.
Betin, V. V., and Iu. V. Preobrazhenskii. *Surovost' zim v Evrope i ledovitost' Baltiki*. Leningrad, 1962.
Bogolepov, M. A. *Nastupaiushchie vozmushcheniia klimata: Po istoricheskim dannym*. Moscow, 1921.
———. *O kolebaniiakh klimata Evropeiskoi Rossii v istoricheskuiu ėpokhu: S prilozheniem materialov, izvlechennykh iz russkikh letopisei*. Moscow, 1908.
———. *Periodicheskie vozmushcheniia klimata*. 2nd ed. Moscow, 1928.
———. *Prichiny neurozhaev i goloda v Rossii v istoricheskoe vremia*. Moscow, 1922.
———. *Princip rastiazheniia litosfery i o periodicheskich izmeneniiakh klimata*. Moscow, 1925.
———. *Vozmushcheniia klimata i zhizn' zemli i narodov*. Berlin, 1923.
Boia, Lucian. *The Weather in the Imagination*. London, 2005.
Borisov, P. M. *Mozhet li chelovek izmenit' klimat*. Nauchno-popularnaia seriia / Akademiia Nauk SSSR. Moscow, 1970.

Böss, Otto. *Die Lehre der Eurasier: Ein Beitrag zur russischen Ideengeschichte der 20. Jahrhunderts*. Veröffentlichungen des Osteuropa-Institutes, München 15. Wiesbaden, 1961.
Brain, Stephen. "The Great Stalin Plan for the Transformation of Nature." *Environmental History* 15 (2010): 670–700.
Brückner, Eduard. *Klimaschwankungen seit 1700 nebst Bemerkungen über die Klimaschwankungen der Diluvialzeit*. Geographische Abhandlungen IV, 2. Vienna, Olomouc, 1890.
Bruks, K. *Klimaty proshlogo: Perevod s angliiskogo V. G. Levinsona*. Moscow, 1952.
Bryson, Reid A., and Thomas J. Murray. *Climates of Hunger: Mankind and the World's Changing Weather*. Madison, WI, 1977.
Chizhevskii, A. L. *Ėpidemicheskie katastrofy i periodicheskaia deiatel'nost' solntsa*. Izdanie vserossiiskogo Obshchestva vrachei-gomeopatov. Moscow, 1930.
———. *Fizicheskie faktory istoricheskogo protsessa*. Kaluga, 1924.
Dawydov, M. "Flüsse werden rückwärts fließen." *Die Presse der Sowjetunion*, no. 83 (1956): 1913–14.
Diamond, Jared M. *Collapse: How Societies Choose to Fail or Succeed*. New York, 2005. http://www.loc.gov/catdir/enhancements/fy0719/2004057152-b.html.
Dronin, Nikolai M., and Edward G. Bellinger. *Climate Dependence and Food Problems in Russia 1900–1990: The Interaction of Climate and Agricultural Policy and their Effect on Food Problems*. Budapest, 2005.
Droysen, Johann G. "Natur und Geschichte." In *Historik: Vorlesungen über Enzyklopädie und Methodologie der Geschichte*, edited by Rudolf Hübner, 406–15. 5th ed. Munich, 1967.
Dulov, A. V. *Geograficheskaia sreda i istoriia Rossii: Konec XV—seredina XIX v.* Moscow, 1983.
Falter, Reinhard. *Natur prägt Kultur: Der Einfluß von Landschaft und Klima auf den Menschen. Zur Geschichte der Geophilosophie*. Munich, 2006.
Fink, Gonthier-Louis. "Diskriminierung und Rehabilitierung des Nordens im Spiegel der Klimatheorie." In *Imagologie des Nordens*, edited by Astrid Arndt, 45–108. Imaginatio borealis 7. Frankfurt/Main [i.a.], 2004.
Fleming, James Rodger. *Historical Perspectives on Climate Change*. New York, 1998.
Gibbon, Edward, and Henry Hart Milman. *The History of the Decline and Fall of the Roman Empire*. Vols. 1–4. New ed. New York, 1844–51.
GilFillan, S. C. "The Coldward Course of Progress." *Political Science Quarterly* 35, no. 3 (1920): 393–410.
Goehrke, Carsten. *Russland: Eine Strukturgeschichte*. Paderborn, Munich, Vienna, Zürich, 2010.
Gumilëv, L. N. *Ėtnogenez i biosfera zemli*. Moscow, 1979.
Hann, Julius von. *Handbuch der Klimatologie*. Stuttgart, 1883.
Hayes, Evan, Stephen Nimis, and Hippocrates. *Hippocrates' On Airs, Waters, and Places and the Hippocratic Oath: An Intermediate Greek Reader; Greek Text with Running Vocabulary and Commentary*. Oxford, 2013.
Herder, Johann Gottfried. *Ideen zur Philosophie der Geschichte der Menschheit*. With the assistance of Martin Bollacher. Frankfurt/Main, 1989.
———. *Outlines of a Philosophy of the History of Man: Translated from the German of John Godfrey Herder, by T. Churchill*. London, 1800. http://find.galegroup.com/ecco/

infomark.do?contentSet=ECCOArticles&docType=ECCOArticles&bookId=0004300300&type=getFullCitation&tabID=T001&prodId=ECCO&docLevel=TEXT_GRAPHICS&version=1.0&source=library.

Herzberg, Julia. "Lenken und Erziehen: Mensch und Natur in der Debatte um die sowjetische Genetik." In *Projektion Natur: Grüne Gentechnik im Fokus der Wissenschaften*, edited by Annette Meyer and Stephan Schleissing, 106–31. Göttingen, 2014.

Hill, Aaron. *The Northern Star: A Poem; Originally Publish'd in the Life-time of Peter Alexiovitz, Great Czar of Russia*. 5th ed. Revised, and corrected, by the author. London, 1739. http://find.galegroup.com/ecco/infomark.do?contentSet=ECCOArticles&docType=ECCOArticles&bookId=0110902500&type=getFullCitation&tabID=T001&prodId=ECCO&docLevel=TEXT_GRAPHICS&version=1.0&source=library.

Hippocrates. *De aere aquis locis*. With the assistance of Hans Diller, Corpus medicorum Graecorum 1,1,2. Published and translated by Hans Diller. Berlin, 1970.

Horn, Eva. "Klimatologie um 1800: Zur Genealogie des Anthropozäns." *ZFK: Zeitschrift für Kulturwissenschaft* 10, no. 1 (2016): 87–100.

Humboldt, Alexander von, and Eduard Buschmann. *Kosmos: Entwurf einer physischen Weltbeschreibung: Bd. 1*. 2 vols. Stuttgart, Tübingen, 1845.

Hume, David. "Of National Characters (1748)." In *Political Essays*, edited by David Hume, 78–92. Cambridge, 1994.

Huntington, Ellsworth. *Civilization and Climate*. 3rd ed. New Haven, CT, 1924.

———. *The Pulse of Asia: A Journey in Central Asia Illustrating the Geographic Basis of History*. London, 1907.

Iagodinskii, V. N. *Aleksandr Leonidovich Chizhevskii: 1897–1964*, Izd. vtoroe, pererabot. i dop, Seriia "Nauchno-biograficheskaia literatura." Moscow, 2004.

Ignatow, Assen. *Der "Eurasismus" und die Suche nach einer neuen russischen Kulturidentität: Die Neubelebung des "Evraziistvo"-Mythos*. Berichte des Bundesinstituts für Ostwissenschaftliche und Internationale Studien 1992, 15. Cologne, 1992.

Il'in, M. *Preobrzovanie planety: Rasskazy o pokorenii prirody*. Moscow, 1951.

Kant, Immanuel. *Von den verschiedenen Racen der Menschen: Zur Ankündigung der Vorlesungen der physischen Geographie im Sommerhalbenjahre 1775*. Königsberg, 1775. http://resolver.staatsbibliothek-berlin.de/SBB000200DD00000000.

Kant, Immanuel, and Friedrich Theodor Rink. *Immanuel Kant's physische Geographie: Bd. 2*. Königsberg, 1802.

Köppen, Wladimir. *Klimakunde*. 2nd rev. ed., repr. 1918. Leipzig, 1918.

Krüger, Tobias. *Die Entdeckung der Eiszeiten*. Basel, Bern, 2006.

Kuzovkova, E. N. "Tol'ko fakty." In *Socializm i priroda: Sbornik statei*, 38–47. Moscow, 1976.

Laruelle, Marlène, and Mischa Gabovich. *Russian Eurasianism: An Ideology of Empire*. Washington, DC, 2008.

Ladurie, Emmanuel Le Roy. "Die Geschichte von Sonnenschein und Regenwetter." In *Schrift und Materie der Geschichte*, edited by Claudia Honegger, 220–46. Frankfurt/Main, 1977.

Leimbach, Werner. "Der Dawydow-Plan der Sowjetunion." *Zeitschrift für Raumforschung* 1/2 (1950): 57–61.

Lemberg, Hans. "Zur Entstehung des Osteuropabegriffs im 19. Jahrhundert: Vom Norden zum Osten Europas." *Jahrbücher für Geschichte Osteuropas* 33, no. 1 (1985): 48–91.

Lepenies, Wolf. *Das Ende der Naturgeschichte: Wandel kultureller Selbstverständlichkeiten in den Wissenschaften des 18. und 19. Jahrhunderts*. Munich, Vienna, 1976.
Lethen, Helmut. "Lob der Kälte: Ein Motiv der historischen Avantgarden." In *Unheimliche Nachbarschaften. Essays zum Kälte-Kult und der Schlaflosigkeit der Philosophischen Anthropologie im 20. Jahrhundert*, 59–97. Freiburg i. Br., 2009.
Losev, K. S. *Klimat: Vchera, segodnia … i zavtra?* Leningrad, 1985.
Löther, Rolf. "Bemerkungen zum Verhältnis von Natur, Mensch und Gesellschaft in der Geschichte der marxistischen Philosophie." In *Umweltschutz in der DDR: Analysen und Zeitzeugenberichte*, edited by Hermann Behrens, 191–99. Munich, 2007.
Macdougall, Doug. *Frozen Earth: The Once and Future Story of Ice Ages*. Berkeley, CA, 2004.
Markham, S. F. *Climate and the Energy of Nations*. 2nd ed. London, 1944.
Mechnikov, L. I. *Tsivilizatsiia i velikiia istoricheskiia reki: Geograficheskaia teoriia razvitiia sovremennych obshchestv*. SPb, 1898.
Montesquieu, Charles. *Vom Geist der Gesetze: Bd. 1*. With the assistance of Ernst Forsthoff. 2nd ed. 2 vols. Tübingen, 1992. English translation: http://www.constitution.org/cm/sol_14.htm.
Müller, Gerhard Friedrich, and Aleksandr Èlert, eds. *Ethnographische Schriften I. Quellen zur Geschichte Sibiriens und Alaskas aus russischen Archiven 8*. Halle, 2010.
Myglan, V. S. "Vliianie klimaticheskikh izmenenii na sotsial'nye i prirodnye protsessy v Sibiri v XVII—pervoi polovine XIX vv. po istoricheskim i dendrokhronologicheskim dannym (Avtoreferat)." Krasnodar, 2005.
Nechkina, M. V. "O prichinakh otstalosti Rossii: Doklad i itogi diskussii 1941." *Istoricheskii Arkhiv*, no. 2 (1993): 210–16.
———. "O prichinakh otstalosti Rossii: Doklad i itogi diskussii 1941." *Istoricheskii vestnik*, no. 3 (1993): 176–208.
"Okhlazhdenie solntsa i zemli," *Vestnik znaniia*, no. 4 (1905): 197.
Plechanov, Georgii V. *Beiträge zur Geschichte des Materialismus: Holbach, Helvetius, Marx*. Stuttgart, 1896.
Pogosian, Kh. P. *Izmenenie klimata v sviazi s planom preobrazovaniia prirody zaslushlivykh raionov SSSR*. Leningrad, 1952.
"Potukhnet li solntse?" *Niva*, no. 36 (1884): 862.
"Primechanie o klimatakh [Kholodnee li stali nashi klimaty, nezheli prezhde?]." *Mesiacoslov s nastavleniiami*, 1779.
Reddaway, William F., ed. *Documents of Catherine the Great: The Correspondence with Voltaire and the Instruction of 1767 in the English Text of 1768*. Cambridge, 2011.
"Rev.: A. Voeikov, Vozdeistvie cheloveka na prirodu." *Meteorologicheskii vestnik*, no. 1 (1896): 18–19.
Sargent II, Frederick. *Hippocratic Heritage: A History of Ideas about Weather and Human Health*. New York, 1982.
Sorokin, Pitirim. *Soziologische Theorien im 19. und 20. Jahrhundert*. Munich, 1931.
Spasskii, M. *Ob uspekhakh meteorologii: Rech', proiznesennaia v torzhestvennom sobranii Imperatorskogo Moskovkago Universiteta*. Moscow, 1831.
Stalin, Iosif V. *Über dialektischen und historischen Materialismus*. Grundschriften des wissenschaftlichen Kommunismus 6. Offenbach, 1997.
Stehr, Nico, and Hans von Storch. *Klima, Wetter, Mensch*. Munich, 1999.

Tikhomirov, E. I. "Kolebanie klimata ili ego izmenenie?" *Meteorologicheskii vestnik* 7/8 (1935): 41–42.
Tkachev, V. I. *Rol' geograficheskogo faktora v istorii Rossii: Uchebnoe posobie*. Saratov, 2000.
Tverskoi, P. N. *Razvitie Meteorologii V SSSR*. Leningrad, 1949.
Voeikov, A. I. *O temperature poslednikh 9-ti let (1882–90): Otdel'nyi ottisk iz Meteorologicheskago vestnika, 1891, Nr. 4*. Saint Petersburg, 1891.
———. "Sposoby vozdeistviia cheloveka na prirodu." *Russkoe obozrenie*, no. 4 (1892): 530–60.
Vrangel', F. F. *Kolebaniia klimata: Lektsii v Imperatorskom Aleksandrovskom Litsee*. Saint Petersburg, 1891.
Wiederkehr, Stefan. *Die eurasische Bewegung: Wissenschaft und Politik in der russischen Emigration der Zwischenkriegszeit und im postsowjetischen Russland*. Beiträge zur Geschichte Osteuropas 39. Weimar, 2007.
Woeikof, A. *Meteorology in Russia*. Washington, DC, 1874.
Zacharasiewicz, Waldemar. *Die Klimatheorie in der englischen Literatur und Literaturkritik: Von der Mitte des 16. bis zum frühen 18. Jahrhundert*. Wiener Beiträge zur englischen Philologie 77. Vienna, 1977.

 PART II

Science and Politics

 CHAPTER 2

The Nature of Cold
Russia's Climate and the Academy of Sciences in the Eighteenth Century

Julia Herzberg

Frost, ice, and snow: for the foreign scholars of the Saint Petersburg Academy of Sciences established in 1725, this was the first impression of their new, "cold" homeland. The drift ice on the Neva made their travel to and from work difficult, they were constantly freezing, and they were amazed by the "interesting contrast" presented by the Saint Petersburg palaces, seemingly built for "an Italian climate" but located in "a Siberian region with a Siberian climate."[1]

But these scholars' readjustment of their internal thermometers went far beyond just the temperature differences between their homelands and their place of residence. It was also connected with a perceptible "cooling off" of the entire Russian empire; in addition to climatic anomalies and fringe effects of the Little Ice Age, the territory was also expanding to the north and east. The temperature of the empire "sank" in the first half of the eighteenth century for three reasons. First, the capital was relocated from Moscow to Saint Petersburg—from the heart of Russia to the inhospitable North. As Hans Lemberg, Larry Wolff, and Otto Boele have shown, it led to a northward shift in the way the Russian empire was thought about in the mental maps of the time.[2] Another source of an even more dramatic drop in the overall temperature of the empire was, second, the exploration and conquest of Siberia starting in the sixteenth century. The *temperature per capita*, the average temperature experienced by a subject of the tsar, sunk substantially as the territory encompassed more and more of Siberia.[3] The expeditions sent out by the Academy of Sciences to explore these mostly unknown regions exposed their participants to temperatures unlike anything the foreign scholars in particular had ever experienced in Basel, Tübingen, or Paris. And third, the individual and collective thermoregulation was further upset by several unusually cold winters at the beginning of the eighteenth century. The winter of 1709 was still very much a part of the communicative memory when another harsh winter left Europe groaning again under the burden of cold. The winter of 1739/40 provoked scientists to ask new questions: Had the climate become cooler? How long would it be before the next winter of such bitter cold? What were the causes and effects of extreme cold? Saint Petersburg scholars such as Georg Wolfgang Krafft began to ponder "what made the air cold."[4]

This chapter looks at how the members of the academy interpreted these shocks to individual and collective temperature expectations and thereby demystified the phenomenon. It will show how they radically reconceptualized their knowledge about cold, its causes, its nature, and its consequences. While in the 1730s scholars such as Georg Wolfgang Krafft still believed that cold was a substance, the research of the Academy of Sciences played an important role in developing a new understanding of extreme cold as an atmospheric phenomenon.

This process will be examined using three examples that represent the different theories about how cold originated and functioned. They are not only organized chronologically, but they also show a spatial progression, tracing the path of cold from the vast expanses of Siberia to the studies and laboratories in Saint Petersburg. The first example particularly illustrates the interplay between center and periphery in the empire. The meteorological observations stimulated by the Academy of Sciences in the provinces were not just a means to measure climate and weather. They also carried new epistemologies and civilization practices to the farthest reaches of the empire. At the same time, the temperatures and effects of cold observed in the provinces posed new questions for the research agenda of the Academy of Sciences in Saint Petersburg.

The second episode centers on the winter of 1739/40, which, both in the empire and beyond, deeply challenged ideas about climate being something constant. This example will examine how the Saint Petersburg scholars viewed the new capital and the Ice Palace built on the frozen Neva as part of the festivities celebrating the victory over the Ottomans; for them, it was the site of a large-scale "experimentum physicum."[5] The spectacle, which was engineered by the scientists of the academy, was well suited to portray the domestication of the cold and vast expanses of the empire using science—a vivid demonstration intended for both the empire's subjects as well as the educated elite in Europe.

The third example looks at the Saint Petersburg scientists at work in the laboratory. It shows how they took the phenomena observed on their expeditions—for example, mercury freezing in their thermometers—and translated them into research questions, which scholars such as Joseph Adam Braun then investigated in controlled laboratory conditions. The recognition that Siberian temperatures could be artificially created using salts and saltpeter deepened the distinction between "natural" and "artificial" cold and showed that even extreme cold had become a reproducible physical and chemical phenomenon.

By asking what effect the shift in felt temperature had on the history of science, this chapter broadens our view of the cultural history of climate, since existing studies have primarily investigated the social, political, and religious consequences of the so-called Little Ice Age that started in the fifteenth century.[6] At the same time, it shows that the sciences, not only literature and art, contributed to "cold" becoming a symbol of Russia.

In Search of Cold:
Meteorological Observations at the Center and Periphery

Everyone talks about the weather! At any rate, this might be the impression of a reader studying the academic journals of the eighteenth century, regardless of whether they were printed in London, Paris, or Saint Petersburg. New meteorological instruments such as the barometer, thermometer, and hygrometer offered more than just the possibility of gathering information about weather phenomena more systematically. They also led to a shift away from the Aristotelian categories of *meteora*—hail, lightning, and thunder—which had heretofore been the focus of attention. Instead, scientists dedicated themselves to measuring everyday weather.

The establishment of the academy in Saint Petersburg came at a time when meteorological questions were high on the agenda of academies and universities throughout Europe. In Paris, London, Edinburgh, and, after 1725, Saint Petersburg, scientists set themselves the goal of understanding and predicting weather and its various manifestations. Inspired by the field of astronomy, considered the observational science par excellence, they hoped to make meteorology predictive and find the natural rules that determine when the sun shines or when it is rainy or windy. At the same time, their efforts to explain the fundamental causes and implications of weather phenomena were connected with questions that today are no longer closely linked with the discipline of meteorology.[7] As they collected data about heat waves and cold spells, the scholars were in fact looking at chemical and physical processes and trying to determine the biological, medical, and cultural consequences of the phenomena they observed. Weather and climate were considered to be responsible for causing various sicknesses; in this, the scientists were following ideas handed down from ancient authors such as Hippocrates.[8] Thanks to this additional focus, which aimed at once to explain the causes of both mud and melancholy, the new weather science found its way out of the laboratory and into drawing rooms and salons. Like the educated elite in Paris and London, the Saint Petersburg nobility purchased almanacs, calendars, and journals with essays on meteorology that explained the workings of instruments such as thermometers and barometers, provided guides for do-it-yourself weather observation, and published predictions for the coming seasons. As a result of such publications, readers began to form increasingly precise ideas about the different climate zones of the world. As the Academy of Sciences began to preoccupy itself increasingly with the question of how temperature was distributed around the world, another result of their investigations was the cultivation and growth of a Europe-wide network of experts with Saint Petersburg as its hub.

The growing conviction of European men of letters that it was impossible to form a comprehensive picture of the Earth's temperature patterns and thermal regulation without observational data from Russia started with responses to an appeal by the physicist James Jurin in 1723.[9] In his "Invitatio" in the *Philosophical Transactions* of the Royal Society of London, Jurin provided his future correspondents with detailed instructions: to record barometer and thermometer readings at least once a day, to measure wind speed and direction, to record precipitation and the appearance of the sky. Countless correspondents in England, central Europe, and North America answered his appeal. From Saint Petersburg, too, a letter arrived in London. A certain Rev. Thomas Consett, who presumably was working as a minister for the English church in Saint Petersburg, carried out weather observations between 24 November 1724 and 23 July 1725 in response to Jurin's appeal.[10] He had adhered strictly to Jurin's instructions, recording thermometer and barometer measurements three times daily, indicated wind speed and direction, and noted the days in which the annual minimum and maximum temperatures had occurred. Eight years later, William Derham, the secretary of the Royal Society, published these notations together with meteorological observations taken over the same period in Lund, Sweden. As justification for this way of presenting the data, Derham claimed that it would have been too "tedious" to present the data during a meeting of the Royal Society.[11] At the same time, Derham complained about the lack of comparability. He was forced to admit that "I scarce understand the Divisions of his Thermometer."[12] Because Jurin's correspondents had not used instruments calibrated to the same scales, it was very difficult to make comparisons among the collected data. Nevertheless, Consett's observations were the beginning of a qualitative shift in the historical weather data available from Russia. There was a turn toward measurement with instruments on location. Although records of weather observations in Russia are available going back to the sixteenth century, before this period they had been carried out without instruments and were mostly concerned with recording the freezing and thawing of river waters.

In December 1725, just a few months after the establishment of the Academy of Sciences, F. C. Meier began to carry out meteorological observations in Saint Petersburg, although these were still quite basic.[13] A transition to more continuity, precision, and theoretical grounding was established with the arrival of Georg Wolfgang Krafft, an adjunct from Tübingen, who, starting on 7 February 1726, not only observed weather events in Saint Petersburg but also regularly published them in the *Commentarii* of the Academy of Sciences.[14] He noted the temperatures in Saint Petersburg and indicated the rise and fall of river waters. Like their English colleagues, the scholars of the Saint Petersburg Academy were very aware of the use that could be gained from a systematically and rationally pursued weather science, since the weather "has a great influence, not only on the bodies of people, and their health and sickness, but also in many of their affairs and activities."[15]

But the scholars also had doubts about whether they had the means necessary for achieving certainty about the future using scientific methods. The instruments were far from adequate, some suggested; predictions were possible only for a very short period in advance, and even then, they were uncertain.[16] No wonder the annual prognoses were rarely reliable! In the early 1730s, Georg Wolfgang Krafft expressed his displeasure with the instructions given to the members of the Academy of Sciences to express their weather predictions as ambiguously as possible: the annual calendars, Krafft wrote, "secretly announce the weather in such a way that one cannot rely on anything for certain."[17] However, he believed that this "imperfection of weather science (*Witterungs-Wissenschaft*), which has until now predominated," should not "prevent [the scientists] from continuing to observe the weather, but rather incite them to work all the more assiduously."[18]

Krafft's introduction to the discussion of the meteorological observations gathered between 1726 and 1736 in Saint Petersburg makes clear that he considered information collected at a single location to be of little use. Nevertheless, he did not abandon hope that even isolated observations could lead to insight into the natural laws that govern the weather. However—and here one hears the echo of James Jurin's appeal—he suggests that it would be much more sensible to commission a worldwide network of "capable people" for the purpose of "continuous observation of the air and its changes," even if this would be "nearly too great an undertaking." These cooperative efforts would be able to demonstrate that each country "has its own individual and particular history of changes in the air and weather."[19] But dreaming of a network of correspondents was not enough for the James Jurin–inspired ambitions of these scholars. In 1727 his colleague Georg Bernhard Bilfinger, also from Tübingen, wrote to the secretary of the Royal Society that the Saint Petersburg scholars were in the process of setting up a network of meteorological observation stations throughout the city.[20] In addition, the Academy of Sciences planned to arrange for observations at as many locations throughout the Russian empire as possible. Krafft himself used an article on his ten years of weather observation in Russia to urge for the establishment of twelve new meteorological stations.[21] The expeditions initiated by the Academy of Sciences to Siberia in the first half of the eighteenth century finally offered an opportunity to implement this plan.

Even though the dimensions of the Russian network of correspondents were quite modest in comparison with others that followed their lead, such as the Societas Meteorologica Palatina, the contacts nonetheless played an important role in enabling communication between the center and the periphery. The expectations of the European-educated scholars for their provincial correspondents not only provided these specially chosen assistants with new scientific knowledge but also transmitted ideals of the Enlightenment. The academicians suggested that everyone, regardless of their education or rank, could be useful for science if only they showed enough discipline and zeal. Initiative, modesty, and the willingness to value the task at hand over one's own affairs were the criteria according to which the correspondents were selected and awarded praise. "Open minds"[22] were necessary, not self-important learnedness. Thus, for example, Johann Georg Gmelin, sent on a research expedition by the academy, chose the Cossack Petr Salamatov as his correspondent in Tomsk due to his love of science, although he could barely read and write.[23]

Meteorological observation required a high degree of discipline. Gmelin's instructions for Petr Salamatov in 1734, for example, called for temperature and air pressure, as well as wind direction and speed, to be measured four times a day, along with descriptions of atmospheric phenomena such as hail or the characteristics of the snow.[24] The instructions addressed to the observers also carried values extolled by the Academy of Sciences—precision, diligence, objectivity, curiosity—to the farthest reaches of the empire. The correspondents, who strove to present themselves in their writings as credible observers, thus had to submit to both a new temporal discipline as well as new scientific forms of notation if they wished to receive attention and recognition for their work. The directives imparted knowledge; they explained how the instruments were to be read and urged the observers to comply with these methods.[25] But they also granted even those with little education the possibility of being able to make an important contribution to science. The idea that the natural order could be comprehended and that human living conditions could be improved—central characteristics of the Age of Enlightenment—are unmistakable components of the Saint Petersburg scholars' appeals.[26]

The meteorological observations offered the "lovers of science" in the provinces the possibility of establishing contact with the academy. Weather science was a participatory science. For Lutheran pastor Erich Laxmann, for example, who used self-built instruments to observe the weather in the Altai Mountains and even established a small local network of his own, the letters and the interaction with the academy members was like manna: "If you lived in the desert, as I do, then you would know how pleasant it is to receive letters from friends in the educated realm. It would make me very happy if you would write to me once more."[27]

For the Academy of Sciences, the network of correspondents was also a way of making itself visible to the European scientific world as the center of science in the empire, even if the successes they expected to gain from the meteorological research did not materialize at first. The correspondents sent their observations to the academy, which, much like the Royal Society in London, functioned as a "clearing-house for natural knowledge."[28] It evaluated the quality of the documents and judged the likelihood of the observed phenomena. This process also reinforced social hierarchies and made visible the difference in knowledge between the center and the periphery. At the same time, the observations made on the periphery had an effect on the interests of the scientists in the capital. The effects triggered by phenomena such as severe frosts, which were systematically described for the first time, provoked new questions and required new designs for experiments. The Siberian cold, which the newly recruited correspondents far from the capital measured with instruments for the first time, became a factor for scientific attention.

The Saint Petersburg scholars successfully established a reputation as experts on cold. The observations of unprecedented low temperatures inspired Krafft to develop a minimum thermometer in 1738, while his teacher Bilfinger devised improved thermometers and barometers. Among the weather experts of the day, the meteorological instruments designed by the scholars of the academy were considered extremely accurate. Joseph Nicolas Delisle in particular became a well-known name in European history of meteorology. Not only did he invent a "machine" to provide quantified measurements of precipitation, his temperature scale was as widely used during his time as those of René-Antoine Ferchault de Réaumur, Daniel Fahrenheit, and Anders Celsius.

But no treatise about the different temperatures within the empire was able to convey the scientific accomplishments of the Academy of Sciences so effectively to the public as the Ice Palace built in the winter of 1740 in Saint Petersburg as part of the festivities celebrating the peace treaty with the Ottoman Empire. The Ice Palace proclaimed to Europe the power of the empress of Russia, Anna Ivanovna, as well the cultural and climatic diversity of the empire. The Academy of Sciences used the festivities as an opportunity to display their successes in measuring, understanding, and mastering the weather.

Mastering the Cold:
The Ice Palace of 1740 as an "Experimentum Physicum"

The winter of 1739/40 was unusually severe, causing all of Europe to shiver beneath its icy hand. In the Russian empire, too, its impact was no less extreme. It is not surprising that this harsh winter has left traces in the accounts of contemporaries. But it is striking that authors writing about their experiences in Saint Petersburg during this time make little mention of problems or anxieties about the cold. They report neither precautionary measures nor difficulties with the supply of provisions. At the center of their descriptions is the Ice Palace glittering on the frozen Neva River from January to March 1740. This palace—which required neither stones nor mortar for its construction but merely water, both solid and liquid—was built, as noted by Georg Wolfgang Krafft, "according to all the rules of the most current architecture."[29] Blocks of pure ice were stacked upon one another and decorated with all manner of icy ornaments. Everyone in Saint Petersburg was eager to see this marvel constructed of ice with their own eyes.[30]

The Ice Palace was the centerpiece of the festivities organized by Empress Anna to celebrate the victory over the Ottoman Empire. The location became the setting of a most unusual event in which Prince Mikhail Golitsyn was forced to play the leading role. Anna, who, like Peter the Great before her, maintained a number of court jesters, had degraded the prince to the rank of jester as a punishment. Golitsyn had fallen into disfavor because he had married an Italian woman during his travels abroad and converted to Catholicism. Upon his return, the empress demanded that he remarry. She was prepared to pay for the wedding, but she had chosen a Kalmyk woman to be his wife. Some historians claim that she was old and ugly.[31]

The preparations for this wedding were elaborate and were not limited to the construction of the Ice Palace. The empress required each of the provinces of her realm to send for the wedding procession a couple dressed in the traditional costume of the region. In the end, a colorful wedding procession with representatives from some three hundred tribes accompanied the bride and groom through the streets of Saint Petersburg. The exoticness of these peoples was emphasized by the fact that their representatives rode in sleds pulled by pigs, wild boars, and moose. The bridal couple themselves were carried through the city in a cage strapped to the back of an elephant. The wedding procession ended at the Ice Palace, where the newlyweds were taken to a bed made of ice in which to spend their first night together. Guards were posted in front of the doors, so that the newlyweds could not attempt to flee prematurely from the pleasures of their wedding night.

Especially those contemporaries who did not witness the proceedings in person have described the Ice Palace and the wedding as particular events that blatantly reflect the sadistic tendencies of the empress and the corruption of autocracy. Historians, too, have used the story of the Ice Palace to demonstrate the character of Anna as someone who heedlessly gave in to her cruel whims and desires. Only Simon Werrett and Elena Pogosian have suggested interpretations that contradict this view. Werrett reads the Ice Palace as an event through which the scholars of the Academy of Sciences sought to gain attention for their research. Pogosian provides a summary of the plans that preceded the wedding. Through the ethnological exposition, Pogosian suggests, Anna aimed to demonstrate the vastness of her empire.[32] Neither the construction material used for the palace nor the unusual cold of that winter have played an important role in interpretations to date.

The empress and the Academy of Sciences used the Ice Palace to pursue very different goals; at the same time, the palace offered a mutual platform for them to demonstrate their accomplishments. While for Anna, the scientifically conceived festival was a chance to present herself as an enlightened ruler, the academy pointed out the fruitfulness of the alliance between autocratic rule and science. Anna used the Ice Palace and the research of the academy to display her power and assert the legitimacy of her right to rule.[33] First, the nobility, who at the beginning of Anna's reign had attempted to overpower her, was put in its place. The public reprimand of the nobility was carried out by making an example of Prince Mikhail Golitsyn, who, with his conversion to the Catholic faith, had stained the reputation of the empire as a haven for Orthodox belief. He was ridiculed before the eyes of all without any way to hide his shame.

But the festival depicted more than just the rebellious nobility as opponents who could only be brought into submission by a powerful ruler such as Anna. In addition, the winter, and ultimately the climate as well, also underwent a metamorphosis from an indomitable danger to a risk that could be controlled by human effort. The festivities surrounding the Ice Palace also made the cold itself something that could be laughed at, as art, reason, and science caused it to lose more and more of its terror. At least, this was what the dramaturgy and symbolism of the festival promised. In order to effectively demonstrate to the public the successful taming of the cold, the organizers of the festival played with the contrast between fire and ice, winter and summer, and thus also with the seemingly impossible contemporaneousness of the uncontemporary: next to the Ice Palace was a *bania*, a steam bath, likewise built of ice, which was fired up on several occasions. The dolphins carved of ice also combined cold with heat: they breathed fire from their frozen mouths.[34]

The academy also used the celebration to demonstrate their importance to a wider public. The festival especially reflected the research agenda of the institution, with its focus on physics, meteorology, geography, and ethnography, and it presented new knowledge acquired during the scientific expeditions. It demonstrated the difference between observation and experiment and showed how chance experiences could be turned into planned recognition. In spite of the spectacular backdrop, as Krafft had emphasized in a treatise on experiments in physics in 1738, the true goal of these tests was not pleasurable amazement.[35] If the incredible scenes of the festivities caused many a spectator's jaw to drop in astonishment, their amazement was soon reined in again. The festival presented the cool instruments of enlightened scientists, who were able, thanks to observation and experiment, to "dissolve the astonishment."[36]

The festival was an occasion for the scholars to show how reason and knowledge could make it possible to tame the cold, whose strength seemed particularly overpowering that winter. The physics professor Georg Wolfgang Krafft, who in his *True and Detailed Description [...] of the Remarkable House of Ice*, published in 1741, had ensured the fame of the Ice Palace for years to come, used the attention created by the festival to discuss various theories about the causes and effects of extreme cold.[37] His pamphlet can be read as a consolidation of all the research on cold conducted at the Saint Petersburg Academy until that date. The text, which was accompanied by a multitude of copper engravings, was published in German, Russian, and French and widely distributed. While it mentions some of the more curious elements of the festivities, it more closely resembles the treatises published in the *Philosophical Transactions* about experiments with cold, which had also been inspired by extremely severe winters. Just as Robert Boyle and William Derham were motivated by the harsh winters of 1662 and 1708/9 to reflect upon the causes and effects of cold, Krafft also wrote about experiments carried out in the snow and ice.[38] He emphasizes that the current severe cold not only made it possible to enact "harmless amusements"[39] but also provided the conditions necessary for art and science to try their hand at applying their skills to ice. He himself had carried out systematic experiments on the ice of the Neva since his appointment as successor to the mathematician Leonhard Euler in 1733.

In his treatise Krafft emphasizes that the Ice Palace was not an object of meaningless merrymaking but must be understood instead as a "true experimentum physicum," the scientific value of which was all the greater because of the large scale on which it was conceived.[40] The urban space that served as Krafft's laboratory thus assumed an intermediate position between the tests undertaken in the far reaches of Siberia and those undertaken in the controlled conditions of a laboratory. At the same time, it guaranteed the reliability of the accounts, for according to Krafft, thousands of people had witnessed the experiments connected with the Ice Palace.

Krafft emphasizes that the usefulness of solid water had not yet been recognized, although nobody would question the importance of liquid water. In its frozen state, he notes, water has many positive characteristics. On the basis of the experiments carried out at the Academy of Sciences, the physics professor attributes many vital qualities to cold, which in the Russian empire, as elsewhere, was associated with misfortune and death. Like Boyle and Derham before him, he points out the different freezing points of various liquids such as water, beer, and saltwater, as well as the preservative effects of low temperatures.[41] Even fire can be kindled using frozen water if the ice is polished like glass into a lens.[42] He mentions this as an additional indication that the compatibility of ice and fire demonstrated in various ways during the festivities was not merely cheap entertainment. Even frozen water could be turned into a resource. For Krafft, the Ice Palace showed that ice is excellently suited as a construction material.[43] The ice house propagated the observations made by Gmelin in Siberia that ice can be used in the construction of dwellings, for example, as a replacement for glass. The palace carried back to the center the insights gained in the Siberian periphery about the qualities of ice and snow, which Gmelin had reported on to the academy in his essay *De frigore et calore glaciei, nivis et aquae* in 1739.[44]

But scholars such as Krafft found the Ice Palace useful for exploring more than just practical questions. They also used it as an opportunity to debate the theories of matter, which had been the focus of scientific attention since the seventeenth century, in particular the corpuscular theory and the aggregate states associated with various temperatures. What determines the characteristics of a piece of material? Does cold or heat arise in something by adding another material? Aristotle, Descartes, Pierre Gassendi, or Robert Boyle—whose theory of matter was correct?

Krafft's treatises on the Ice Palace posed the question of whether the quality and composition of a material changes when it is frozen. While metals contracted under the influence of cold, water expanded. Krafft, who even before the construction of the Ice Palace had carried out experiments regarding the expansion of water during the crystallization process, had discussed in his writings in the 1730s whether the "freezing of water" and the "hardening of metals" had the same cause, and whether cold or the process of freezing was decisive for the different processes.[45] Related to this was the question of whether there was a *primum frigidum*, that is, a substance that causes cold.[46] While Gmelin on his travels pondered the question of whether tea boiled from frozen water tasted better, Krafft interpreted the "particular flavor" of tea or coffee prepared using frozen water as a sign of the presence of "a new material."[47] The fact that melted snow cools off further when salt is added since it lowers the melting point seemed to confirm his hypothesis that salts and saltpeter were the materials out of which cold is made. In 1740, he thought, the unusual cold was caused by "salts floating about in the air." Salt and saltpeter fumes from "great Tartary and Armenia," his theory went, had covered all of Europe with cold.[48]

Krafft's hypothesis was consistent with the teachings of Aristotle and Pierre Gassendi, who believed that the temperature of an object was the result of the involvement of another element. While Aristotle thought that the addition of water caused cold, Gassendi had argued that sharp-pointed atoms in the form of tetrahedrons produced cold.[49] Although Robert Boyle had already declared in 1665 that the *primum frigidum* was a fictional substance, the winter of 1740 gave Georg Wolfgang Krafft a reason to look once again for a material substance as the cause of cold.[50] His accounts of the causes of the unusually severe winter of 1739/40 show that the trigger for cold had not yet been definitively found.

Even after the melting of the Ice Palace, the scientists in Saint Petersburg continued to be preoccupied with the question of the nature of cold and the difficulty of reconciling the different explanations for it. In addition to the theory that cold could be considered a substance comparable to the substance of heat (*caloricum*), the researchers also expressed other conjectures about the nature of cold in which the boundaries between meteorology, chemistry, and physics were not clearly drawn. The scientists disputed the role of the moon and the location of the sun as causes of cold spells. Their modest-sized meteorological network and the insight that temperatures did not cool off equally "on their way to Russia" led to the conclusion that the topography of a location is important for its climatic characteristics. Finally, in 1745 Mikhail Lomonosov proposed that heat is motion—a theory that was at first rejected by the assembly of the Saint Petersburg academics as being inadequately developed. The scholars found the idea that cold is caused by a reduction in the motion of particles interesting in principle, but they criticized the young adjunct—justly so—of having stolen the idea from Robert Boyle.[51]

The fluidity of the boundaries between chemistry, physics, and weather science is also evident in the fact that Krafft used his treatises on the Ice Palace as an occasion to sketch how a "history of the air" might be written. He described the merits of the new meteorological instruments and showed his readers which weather events it was necessary to record in order to track down the causes of cold spells.[52] Krafft exchanged temperature data with famous colleagues such as Professor Anders Celsius in Uppsala, and he compiled chronicles that listed the most severe winters since the year 177 BC

For Krafft, preparing for cold meant above all predicting it. Based on his observations, he arrived at the conjecture that Europe should prepare itself for a cold spell every thirty-one years. The time span between 1709 and 1740 served as a reference value, and he thought that he could discern it as a reoccurring pattern over longer temporal periods. For example, this thirty-one-year period fit exactly twenty times between 177 BC and 443 AD, two dates that had been marked by especially extreme cold. This attempt to predict cold periods and not just record them was one major characteristic that set Krafft's text apart from William Derham's report of the severe cold of 1709.

This shows a change at two different levels: first, it makes evident how much the two winters in 1709 and 1740 had shaken the belief that climate was unchanging. In the years that followed, the scholars repeatedly questioned whether the temperatures at their line of latitude had become colder.[53] Second, one can see the process that Wolf Lepenies has referred to as the "temporalization" of scientific thought, the gradual replacement of natural history, in which the natural world was seen as having a fixed, unchanging order, with a developmental perspective of history.[54] In Krafft's view, the observations and experiments made in connection with the Ice Palace were a particularly powerful demonstration of the possibility of domesticating winter through art and science, and not just temporarily. By looking at much longer time periods and thus at the climate as the totality of weather phenomena, the winter of 1739/40 no longer appeared to be such an anomaly, and thus it lost some of its terror. In this view, the winter of 1739/40 was only a sensation for those who did not yet have the means to discern the weather cycles and the natural laws that governed them. Art and science, progress and civilization—the visible presence of the Ice Palace proclaimed—could also thrive in the colder regions of the world. Russia's scientific achievements showed that it did not in any way need to hide in the shadow of the other European nations in spite of its particularly cold climate.

Demystifying Cold: Frozen Mercury—A Wonder of Nature?

The expeditions to Siberia brought with them new experiences: things that had never been seen before and seemed, indeed, most unbelievable. This was not limited to new spaces and the discovery of unknown peoples, animals, and plants. The climates of these regions were also entirely new. In many of Gmelin's reports for the academy, he described the legendary Siberian cold that could scarcely be compared with anything the scholars were familiar with. In December 1734 in Eniseisk, not only did "sparrows and jays" fall dead from the air, the mercury in the thermometers also "contracted from the cold to a level far lower than had previously been seen in nature."[55] Gmelin also reported that a "certain man" had informed him of something quite unheard of: the mercury in his barometer had frozen. Gmelin described how he hurried over—the man whose name Gmelin avoids mentioning was, in fact, the astronomer Louis de l'Isle de la Croyère—in order to witness for himself this "wonder of nature." But even on the way it seemed to him that the cold was not unusually bitter.[56] The mercury, too, seemed "rather suspicious" to him: "It occurred to me immediately that this mercury, in order to purify it, had perhaps been washed with vinegar and salt but not allowed to dry sufficiently."[57]

Mercury that had solidified because it was impure was not a sensation for Gmelin: "I am thus far from considering presenting this frozen mercury as evidence of the cold of the local regions."[58] In the winter of 1736/37, this "wonder of nature" reoccurred in Iakutsk,[59] where Gmelin recorded that mercury, which had allegedly always been liquid before, had become solid as a result of natural cold. Other correspondents of the academy also dispatched news to Saint Petersburg, telling how they had witnessed mercury transforming from a liquid state into a solid one.[60]

But due to circumstances and the lack of witnesses, there was no definite certainty of whether there existed, in fact, a cold capable of bringing mercury from a liquid into a solid state. Nor could the scientists provide any verifiable statements regarding precisely what conditions or what temperatures caused mercury to become solid. These objections to conclusions drawn in the course of incidental everyday experiences were quelled for the first time by the experiments of Joseph Adam Braun. In 1759 Braun managed to cool a mixture of snow and saltpeter so much that the mercury in his thermometer froze. He had succeeded in producing evidence for the unimaginable under controlled laboratory conditions. In his Saint Petersburg laboratory he was able to demonstrate, repeatedly and before witnesses, that it was possible to produce such an extreme cold that even mercury could be made to freeze.

The circumstances of the experiment are known in detail. Not only Braun but also his followers and critics, whether they replicated his experiment or doubted its believability, have always described the conditions in detail.[61] Not only did Braun give a talk for the empress in which he explained his method of creating such an extreme "artificial cold," but readers in Saint Petersburg were also informed about the experiments in the academy's journal *Sanktpeterburgskiia Vedomosti*.[62] Braun's goal was to remove all doubt for the "scholars of other nations," for whom the freezing of mercury seemed "unbelievable," and to make it possible for "natural scientists in other places to replicate this remarkable experiment."[63]

It was the extreme cold in December 1759 that prompted Braun to prove his experiences with frozen mercury during the Siberian expeditions as scientific fact. He poured saltpeter into a beaker filled with snow and succeeded in reducing the temperature of the frigorific mixture to 470 degrees on the Delisle scale,[64] after which the mercury no longer moved.[65] But Braun did not break open the expensive thermometer in order to examine the mercury more closely. Three days later a renewed cold spell broke over Saint Petersburg, allowing Braun to successfully replicate the experiment and announce his discovery at an assembly of the academy.[66] The repeated results were not, however, considered sufficient evidence; only after the experiment had been witnessed and reproduced by others did his claims become credible. On 25 December the temperature dropped significantly once again, and both Braun and his colleague Franz Ulrich Theodor Æpinus busied themselves with repeating the experiment. This time they broke open the thermometer: the mercury had not solidified completely; the ball still had a liquid core. Æpinus reduced the temperature further to 500 degrees on the Delisle scale and determined that "the mercury was frozen through."[67] The normally liquid material could be hammered and shaped. In its frozen state it behaved in all respects "like any other metal."[68] Lomonosov, Zeiher, and the apothecary Johann Georg Model, who repeated the experiment during the cold days in December 1759, arrived at similar results.[69] The "unanimous testimony of so many natural scientists" was suited to "absolutely confirm the truth of the matter."[70]

But who was in fact the first person to have observed mercury freezing? Was it actually Braun, or rather de l'Isle de la Croyère, whose report of having seen frozen mercury in 1734 in Eniseisk was denounced as an exaggeration? On the basis of the experimental results, the academy members came to the conclusion that the Frenchman had evidently been deceived as a result of using contaminated mercury. At the temperatures that had been measured at the time of 195 to 200 degrees on the Delisle scale, the experiments had clearly shown that "pure mercury does not freeze, otherwise its solidification would not be an unusual matter here, since cold of this degree is not unusual."[71] In order to prevent similar charges from being made against themselves, the scientists of the academy emphasized that they had used pure mercury in their experiments in 1759. But the Saint Petersburg scholars, who judged their colleague so harshly, made mistakes of their own: because the mercury contracted significantly under the influence of cold, they had interpreted their thermometers as indicating that they had achieved the astonishing temperature of 1,500 degrees on the Delisle scale.[72] Æpinus, who repeated the experiment on 28 December, was able to cause mercury to transform from liquid to solid at a temperature of only 300 degrees Delisle, according to his alcohol thermometer. Thus he wondered whether it might not be possible to reproduce the experiment with similar results even in regions of Europe with more mild climates.[73]

In the days that followed there were quarrels and resentment about the degree of cold that had been reached during the experiments. The temperature necessary to cause mercury to freeze was also hotly disputed. Æpinus in particular, who had been the second person to repeat the experiment, was reluctant to let Braun get all the credit for the discovery. He published his opinion about the experiment in foreign journals and described Braun's experiment as a product of chance.[74] And yet as demonstrated by a speech given in the presence of Empress Anna in September 1760 titled "On the Incredible Artificially Created Cold," Braun considered his experiment—in spite of the enmities—as an important discovery, one comparable with the invention of the thermometer.[75]

Today it is harder for us to grasp why the Saint Petersburg scientists' frozen mercury was the object of so much attention that even foreign journals reported about it and countless others were inspired to attempt—under various conditions of both natural and artificial cold—to create frozen mercury. Undoubtedly the symbolic meaning of mercury played a role: in alchemy it was considered an essential ingredient for the transmutation of base metals into gold.[76] My thesis is that the experiments with mercury attracted so much attention because they were part of a process of negotiating fundamental theories about matter and physics. Braun's experiment reopened the question of the causes and effects of extreme cold and thus issues that had preoccupied scholars since Aristotle. Braun's experiment revealed that adequate answers to these questions had still not been found.

The discussions called forth by Braun's experiment show that even in 1759 there was still no consensus about what caused cold. Was there a *primum frigidum*, a substance that could generate cold? And was saltpeter—as the means by which the snow could be cooled so far that the supposedly always liquid mercury froze—in fact this substance? Or, on the contrary, was heat—and thus its inverse, cold—actually movement, as Robert Boyle and Lomonosov had conjectured? Why did mixing snow with saltpeter cause it to cool off so dramatically? How was it possible, with the help of saltpeter and aluminum chloride, to achieve such low temperatures that mercury could be frozen even in Göttingen, with a comparatively mild outside temperature of -10°F (-23.3°C), as reported in 1774 by the physics student Johann Friedrich Blumenbach in the *Göttingischen Anzeigen von gelehrten Sachen*?[77] To what degree were natural and artificially created cold different phenomena? Braun's followers discussed, based on the experiment, whether the solidified mercury created using artificial cold was different than mercury that had frozen in naturally cold conditions, and whether some substance had been added to the mercury that made it cold. Traveling scientists and correspondents like Peter Simon Pallas and Laxmann sent their reports, in which they discussed the characteristics of the frozen mercury, to Saint Petersburg, where the scholars of the academy compared these descriptions with treatises from abroad that also discussed experiments with mercury in laboratory conditions and in conditions of extreme cold weather.[78]

The search for a substance that caused cold was also connected with the question of whether there could be an absolute absence of heat. Daniel Fahrenheit, who had begun to experiment with frigorific solutions in 1724 and whose experiences Braun had drawn on for his own work, had proclaimed that he could produce a greater degree of cold by using purer chemicals. The experiments with saltpeter, Fahrenheit concluded, had shown that "we know as little about the beginning of heat as we do about its extreme end."[79] Braun's interpretation of the significant and irregular contraction of mercury after its freezing point had been reached, which he took as a sign of temperatures lower than anything ever previously measured, also raised the question of an absolute zero point.[80] In 1745 Lomonosov had already rejected the hypothesis of an absolute zero temperature on earth. Substances such as air would always be fluid and in motion and thus contain heat.[81] But if heat were really movement, how might it be possible to bring the particles to an absolute standstill and thereby achieve "the absolute degree of cold"?[82]

The mercury experiment was a sensation because it provided insight into the material properties of substances. Thus Leonhard Euler, for example, responded enthusiastically to the experiment: "Herr Prof. Braun's discovery is of the greatest importance and in particular awakened for me the greatest delight, for I had always believed that heat is the true cause of liquidity."[83] Prior to Braun's experiment, European scholars had operated on the assumption that there were substances that never became solid, even in the greatest cold. Lomonosov, who repeated the mercury experiment, had conjectured a few years earlier that air, highly purified alcohol, and the sap of certain plants, in addition to mercury, always remained liquid even at extremely cold temperatures.[84] Still unclear was the question of whether the temperature at which the shift in state from liquid to solid occurred was always the same. The difficulty of determining the precise freezing point of mercury during the progression of the experiment meant that this question remained unanswered.

The experiment—and this was one of the reasons for the enormous interest in it—problematized how the degree of cold could be determined at all. The human senses, as Lomonosov had complained a few years before Braun's mercury experiment, were not reliable: "Everything that seems cold to us is merely less warm than our sensory organs."[85] Thermometers, which permitted comparison and thus should make it possible to make statements about the distribution of heat around the world, seemed to promise more clarity; however, they had also created misunderstandings. The confusion was considerable, and not just because of a lack of agreement about the temperature scales. The various thermometer liquids—water, linseed oil, ethyl alcohol, mercury—made this more difficult. The expansion coefficient of the different fluids, which was highly affected by impurities such as the percentage of water, had not been taken into account when fixed temperature points on thermometers were established, which resulted in incomprehensible deviations. While Gmelin had referred to the mercury thermometer as "not being subject to the deceptions of the senses," Braun's experiment raised the question of whether mercury was even a suitable thermometer liquid.[86] In his *Guide to the Production of Consistent Thermometers*, Ernst August Strohmeyer disagreed, based on Braun's experiments, with the Swiss merchant and meteorologist Jean André de Luc, who had described mercury as the ideal thermometer liquid.[87] For measuring extremely low temperatures, he argued, ethyl alcohol was more suitable than mercury.[88]

Because of the questions raised by the experiment, the Academy of Sciences succeeded in laying claim to a scientific sensation, which, unlike the experiments connected with the Ice Palace, did not require the staging of an amazing spectacle in order to attract attention. The academy used the mercury experiments to show that they were conducting first-rate research that satisfied the most demanding scientific criteria of the age. With the experiments, they demonstrated how, using the scientific process—the careful recording of observations and the accompanying circumstances, confirmation by witnesses, and reproduction of results—they were able to derive scientific facts from incidental observations.

Braun's experimental setup and his descriptions and results became authoritative for the countless experiments with mercury under conditions of both natural and artificial cold that were carried out in the years that followed. These mercury experiments deepened the distinction between natural and artificial cold and raised questions about what the determining factors were. Thanks to the observations of de l'Isle de la Croyère and Gmelin, as well as Braun's experiments, Russia's reputation as a land of cold where even mercury could freeze under natural conditions traveled to Europe and America. The attention given to frozen mercury as a benchmark for extreme cold and the numerous reports of it from the Russian empire contributed to the creation of a mental map of the coldest regions of the world. Most commonly included on this map were locations in Siberia and in the northern regions of European Russia such as Krasnoiarsk, Irkutsk, Iakutsk, and Velikii Ustiug. As a result of this, doubts began to increase about the theory positing that the degree of cold increased uniformly the further north one went. This eventually led to the development of the concept of Poles of Cold, and with it the search for the coldest location on earth.

Conclusion

The new environments that the European scholars and explorers found in Saint Petersburg and on their travels through the empire influenced the questions they asked and the topics that interested them. The discovery of these new regions, which seemed so foreign due to their particular climate, not only instigated the creation of new maps but also structured and expanded existing knowledge, leading to new insights into the workings of nature. The Saint Petersburg scholars pursued popular questions of their age when they attempted to fathom the nature of cold. In so doing—as shown by the three examples examined here—they succeeded in presenting themselves as successful investigators of cold. The network of meteorologists, the experiments connected with the Ice Palace, and the experiments with frozen mercury demonstrated to European scholars not only that cold had become measurable, understandable, predictable, and a material for artwork but also that it could be produced artificially. Thus extremely harsh winters and sudden cold spells were revealed to be subject to natural laws rather than random, unpredictable occurrences or a punishment from God against which humans are defenseless. And thus cold lost some of its terror.

The newly formed Academy of Sciences was able to establish a reputation as a respected research institution through its members' work in the fields of meteorology and physics, as they distinguished themselves as experts on cold. By translating chance observations into verifiable and reproducible experiments certified by witnesses, the Saint Petersburg scientists demonstrated that scientific norms and conventions were still being upheld even at the edges of the enlightened world and that, thanks to its research and teaching, its network of correspondents, and its scientific expeditions, the Russian empire was an important hub in the communicative space of the Enlightenment.

The participation of Russia in scientific debates and information flows showed European scholars that without the research from Russia, it would not be possible to draw conclusions about how the climate is distributed around the world and to what degree climate and weather affect culture and social structures. Through their research, scholars such as Krafft, Gmelin, Braun, Æpinus, and Lomonosov contributed to the spread of the popular Enlightenment idea that although culture is strongly influenced by climate, it is possible for culture and science to thrive even in zones with a less temperate climate. The message from Saint Petersburg and Siberia suggested that while Russia was indeed a cold country, in matters of culture and science it was definitely a European power.

The scientific investigations of frost, ice, and snow, which demonstrated that cold could be understood, predicted, and even artificially produced, also supported those theories of climate positing that cold could have a positive influence on the character of individuals and societies. The effects of this increase in knowledge were apparent when Montesquieu's *De l'esprit des lois* appeared in 1748, after the Siberian expeditions of the Saint Petersburg Academy had drastically expanded the extent of cold regions in the world that had been studied scientifically. The French philosopher, whose influential text was one of the first to consider connections between climate, the nature of the people, and their customs and traditions, as well as their community and governance structures, mentioned Russia repeatedly, characterizing it as a cold land. He was hopeful that as a consequence of this cold, which he believed provided vigor and courage, and because laws were "the necessary relations arising from the nature of things,"[89] that Russia would eventually take the path to a bright future. Through the research of the Academy of Sciences, too, Russia became an empire of cold whose potential, singularity, and size were the result not only of spatial and geographic factors but of climatic ones as well.

Julia Herzberg is professor for the history of East Central Europe and Russia in early modern times at LMU Munich. Her recent research has focused on, among other topics, the environmental history of Central Eastern Europe and Russia. She coedited *Ice and Snow in the Cold War: Histories of Extreme Climatic Environments* (2019) with Christian Kehrt and Franziska Torma, and *Umweltgeschichte(n): Ostmitteleuropa von der Industrialisierung bis zum Postsozialismus* (2013) with Martin Zückert and Horst Förster. She is currently working on an environmental history of "frost" in Russia that examines various social and cultural aspects of Russia's harsh climate.

Notes

1. Alexander Kaplunovskiy, ed., 'Auch in Moskwa habe ich Ursache zufrieden zu sein': Christian von Schlözers Privatkorrespondenz mit der Familie (Berlin, 2014), 103.
2. Hans Lemberg, "Zur Entstehung des Osteuropabegriffs im 19. Jahrhundert: Vom Norden zum Osten Europas," *Jahrbücher für Geschichte Osteuropas* 33 (1985), 48–91; Otto Floris Boele, *The North in Russian Romantic Literature* (Amsterdam, 1996); Larry Wolff, *Inventing Eastern Europe: The Map of Civilization on the Mind of the Enlightenment* (Stanford, 1994).
3. The category of *temperature per capita* goes back to Hill and Gaddy: Fiona Hill and Clifford G. Gaddy, *The Siberian Curse: How Communist Planners Left Russia out in the Cold* (Washington, DC, 2003).
4. "Von der ungewöhnlichen Kälte des nächst vergangenen Winters in gantz Europa," *Anmerkungen bey den Zeitungen*, 11 November 1740, 361–64.
5. Georg Wolffgang Krafft, *Wahrhaffte und Umständliche Beschreibung und Abbildung des im Monath Januarius 1740 in St. Petersburg aufgerichteten merckwürdigen Hauses von Eiß* (Saint Petersburg, 1741), 17.
6. Wolfgang Behringer, ed., *Kulturelle Konsequenzen der 'Kleinen Eiszeit'* (Göttingen, 2005); Wolfgang Behringer, *Kulturgeschichte des Klimas: Von der Eiszeit bis zur globalen Erwärmung* (Munich, 2007); Brian Fagan, *The Little Ice Age: How Climate Made History, 1300–1850* (New York, 2000).
7. Lucian Boia, *The Weather in the Imagination* (London, 2005).
8. John Arbuthnot, *An Essay Concerning the Effects of Air on Human Bodies* (London, 1733).
9. Jacobo Jurin, "Invitatio ad Observationes Meteorologicas Communi Consilio Instituendas," *Philosophical Transactions of the Royal Society of London* 32 (1722–23), 422–27.
10. Gustav Hellmann, "Die Entwicklung der meteorologischen Beobachtungen bis zum Ende des XVIII. Jahrhunderts: Teil 2," *Abhandlungen der Preussischen Akademie der Wissenschaften* (1927): 1–48.
11. Wm. Derham and Tho. Consett, "An Abstract of the Meteorological Diaries," *Philosophical Transactions of the Royal Society of London* 38 (1733): 101–9.
12. Ibid., 106.
13. A. I. Berditskii, E. P. Borisenkov, A. S. Korovchenko, V. M. Pasetskii, *Ocherki po istorii gidrometeorologicheskoi sluzhby Rossii* (Saint Petersburg, 1997), 1:18.
14. *Materialy dlia istorii Imperatorskoi Akademii nauk, 1716-1730* (Saint Petersburg, 1885), 1:600; Georg Wolfgang Krafft, "Observationum meteorologicum, 1726–1736," *Commentarii Academiae Imperialis Scientiarum Petropolitanae* 9 ([1737] 1744): 316–44, 344–57.
15. "Kurtze Beschreibung der merckwürdigsten Witterungs-Geschichten allhier in St. Petersburg," *Anmerkungen über die Zeitungen*, 31 August 1738, 277–80.
16. Ibid., 278.
17. *Protokoly zasedanii konferentsii Imperatorskoi akademii nauk s 1725 po 1803 goda*, vol. 1: *1725–1743* (Saint Petersburg, 1897), 420.
18. "Kurtze Beschreibung der merckwürdigsten Witterungs-Geschichten," 278.
19. Ibid., 278–79.
20. *Istoriia Akademii Nauk SSSR*, vol. 1: *1724–1803* (Moscow, Leningrad, 1958), 91–93.

21. Berditskii et al., *Ocherki po istorii gidrometeorologicheskoi sluzhby Rossii*, 18; *Istoriia Akademii Nauk SSSR*, 93n92.
22. *Materialy dlja istorii Imperatorskoi Akademii nauk, 1725–1743*, 364.
23. Ibid., 363.
24. Berditskii et al., *Ocherki po istorii gidrometeorologicheskoi sluzhby Rossii*, 21; RAN f. 21 op. 5 d. 66.
25. Archive of the Russian *Academy* of Sciences in Saint Petersburg, RAN f. 3 op. 23 d. 2b.
26. Andreas Renner, "Russland: Die Autokratie der Aufklärung," in *Orte eigener Vernunft: Europäische Aufklärung jenseits der Zentren*, edited by Alexander Kraus and Andreas Renner (New York, 2008), 134.
27. Erich Laxmann, *Erich Laxmann's Sibirische Briefe* (Göttingen, 1769), 57.
28. Andrea A. Rusnock, "Correspondence Networks and the Royal Society, 1700–1750," *British Journal for the History of Science* 32 (1999): 155.
29. Krafft, *Wahrhaffte und Umständliche Beschreibung*, 9.
30. Georg Wolfgang Krafft provides the most detailed description of the Ice Palace: ibid. Less extensive reports can be found in V. I. Nashchokin, *Zapiski. S 1712-go po 5-e Sentiabria 1759 goda* (Saint Petersburg, 1842), 62–65; Christoph Hermann von Mannstein, *Historische, politische und militärische Nachrichten von Rußland von dem Jahre 1727 bis 1744* (Leipzig, 1771), 343–44; Christoph Hermann von Manstein, *Beytrag zur Geschichte Rußlands vom Jahre 1727 bis 1744* (Hamburg, Bremen, 1771), 403–5; Markiz de-la-Shetardi, "Pis'mo Markiza de-la-Shetardi iz Peterburga 1-go Marta/19-go fevralia 1740 g.," in *Markiz de-la-Shetardi v Rossii 1740–1742 godov: Perevod rukopisnykh depesh francuzskago posol'stva v Peterburge*, ed. P. Pekarskii (Saint Petersburg, 1862), 55–57; C. N. Shubinskii, *Istoricheskiie ocherki i razskazy* (Saint Petersburg, 1869), 25–39.
31. James Hadley Billington, *The Icon and the Axe: An Interpretive History of Russian Culture* (London, 1966), 187.
32. Simon Werrett, *An Odd Sort of Exhibition: The St. Petersburg Academy of Sciences in Enlightened Russia* (Cambridge, 2000), 166–78; E. Pogosian, "'I nevozmozhnoe vozmozhno': Svad'ba shutov v ledianom dome kak fakt ofitsial'noi kul'tury," *Trudy po russkoi i slavianskoi filologii: Literaturovedenie* 4 (2001): 80–109.
33. For more on the symbolism of the peace treaty celebration, see Julia Herzberg, "The Domestication of Ice and Cold: The Ice Palace in Saint Petersburg 1740," in "On Water: Perceptions, Politics, Perils," ed. Agnes Kneitz and Marc Landry, *RCC Perspectives*, no. 2 (2012): 53–62.
34. "Fortsetzung der Friedens-Festivitäten-Beschreibung," *Anmerkungen bey den Zeitungen*, 13 June 1740, 189–96.
35. Georg Wolfgang Krafft, *Experimentorum physicorum praecipuorum brevis descriptio* (Saint Petersburg, 1738), 8. Quote: V. P. Zubov, "Lomonosovs Übersetzung der Wolffschen Experimentalphysik," in *Lomonosov, Schlözer, Pallas: Deutsch-russische Wissenschaftsbeziehungen im 18. Jahrhundert*, ed. Eduard Winter (Berlin, 1962), 12:48.
36. Denis Diderot, *Gedanken zur Interpretation der Natur: Philosophische Grundsätze über Materie und Bewegung*, 3rd ed. (Leipzig, 1976), 34–35; Wolf Lepenies, *Das Ende der Naturgeschichte: Wandel kultureller Selbstverständlichkeiten in den Wissenschaften des 18. und 19. Jahrhunderts* (Munich, Vienna, 1976), 208.
37. "Beschreibung des aus Eiß gemachten Hauses," *Anmerkungen bey den Zeitungen*, 9 December 1740, 393–96; Krafft, *Wahrhaffte und Umständliche Beschreibung*.

38. "An Experimental History of Cold," *Philosophical Transactions of the Royal Society of London* 1 (1665–66), 8–9; W. Derham, "The History of the Great Frost in the Last Winter 1703 and 1708/9," *Philosophical Transactions of the Royal Society of London* 26 (1708–9), 454–78; Tom Shachtman, *Minusgrade—Auf Der Suche nach dem Absoluten Nullpunkt: Eine Chronik Der Kälte* (Reinbek, 2001), 39.
39. Krafft, *Wahrhaffte und Umständliche Beschreibung*, 9.
40. Ibid., 17.
41. Derham, "History of the Great Frost," 463; Christiana Christopoulou, "Early Modern History of Cold: Robert Boyle and the Emergence of a New Experimental Field in Seventeenth Century Experimental Philosophy," in *History of Artificial Cold, Scientific, Technological and Cultural Issues*, ed. Kostas Gavroglu (New York, 2013), 25.
42. Krafft, *Wahrhaffte und Umständliche Beschreibung*, 4.
43. Ibid., 17.
44. *Istoriia Akademii Nauk SSSR*, 91.
45. "Von dem Eiße," *Anmerkungen über die Zeitungen*, 21 January 1733, 23.
46. Gmelin, *Johann Georg Gmelins Reise durch Sibirien von dem Jahr 1733–1743*, 407.
47. "Von der ungewöhnlichen Kälte," 364.
48. Ibid., 364.
49. Christopoulou, "Early Modern History of Cold," 21–24; Shachtman, *Minusgrade*, 40.
50. Jaime Wisniak, "Development of the Concept of Absolute Zero Temperature," *Educación Química* 16 (2005): 104–13.
51. M. V. Lomonosov, "1 Meditationes de caloris et frigoris causa auctore Michaele Lomonosow," in M. V. Lomonosov, *Polnoe sobranie sochinenii*, vol. 2, *Trudy po fizike i khimii, 1747–1752 gg.* (Moscow, Leningrad, 1951); *Protokoly zasedanii konferentsii Imperatorskoi akademii nauk s 1725 po 1803 goda*, vol. 2: *1744–1770*, (Saint Petersburg, 1899), 48–49; Loren R. Graham, *Science in Russia and the Soviet Union. A Short History* (New York, 1993), 23.
52. Krafft, *Wahrhaffte und Umständliche Beschreibung*, 26.
53. "Primechanie o klimatakh [Kholodnee li stali nashi klimatyy, nezheli prezhde?]," *Mesiatsoslov s nastavleniiami* (1779), 106–19.
54. Lepenies, *Das Ende der Naturgeschichte*.
55. Gmelin, *Reise durch Sibirien*, 356.
56. C. Blagden, "History of the Congelation of Quicksilver," *Philosophical Transactions of the Royal Society of London* 73 (1783), 329–97.
57. Gmelin, *Reise durch Sibirien*, 452.
58. Ibid., 452.
59. Ibid., 451.
60. K. A. Kielmann and J. R. Meyer, *Systematische Darstellung aller Erfahrungen über die einzelnen Metalle in zwei Bänden* (Arau, 1807), 1:200.
61. Braun himself published a precise description of the experiment: Iosif-Adam Braun, *O udivitel'noi stuzhe, isskusstvom proizvedennoi, ot kotoroi rtut' zamerzla* (Saint Petersburg, 1760).
62. "V Sanktpeterburge dekabria 20 dnia," *Sanktpeterburgskiia Vedomosti*, 21 December 1759, 809–11; "V Sanktpeterburge dekabria 27 dnia," *Sanktpeterburgskiia Vedomosti*, 28 December 1759, 825–26.

63. RAN f. 21 op. 1 Nr. 58, l. 177.
64. Like the Celsius scale, the Delisle scale was defined based on the temperatures at which water changes state, with the boiling point as 0 degrees and the melting (or freezing) point as 150 degrees. The numbering of the scale was the opposite of those of Celsius, Réamur, or Fahrenheit, with larger numbers indicating increasingly cold temperatures.
65. RAN f. 21 op. 1 Nr. 58, l. 165ob.
66. RAN f. 21 op. 1 Nr. 58, l. 166.
67. RAN f. 21 op. 1 Nr. 58, l. 177.
68. RAN f. 21 op. 1 Nr. 58, l. 166ob.
69. RAN f. 21 op. 1 Nr. 58, l. 166ob; Braun, *O udivitel'noi stuzhe*, 26; M. V. Lomonosov, "19 Meditationes de solido et fluido," in M. V. Lomonosov, *Polnoe sobranie sochinenii*, vol. 3: *Trudy po fizike, 1753-1765 gg.* (Moscow, Leningrad, 1952), 401–9.
70. RAN f. 21 op. 1 Nr. 58, l. 168.
71. RAN f. 21 op. 1 Nr. 58, l. 168 ob; l. 178.
72. Braun, *O udivitel'noi stuzhe*, 9.
73. RAN f. 21 op. 1 Nr. 58, l. 175.
74. M. V. Lomonosov, "21 [Zapiska ob opytakh po zamorazhivaniiu rtuti]," in M. V. Lomonosov, *Polnoe sobranie sochinenii*, vol. 3: *Trudy po fizike, 1753–1765 gg* (Moscow, Leningrad, 1952), notes: S. 567. Quote: RAN f. 21 op. 1 Nr. 58, l. 181.
75. Braun, *O udivitel'noi stuzhe*, 1.
76. Friedrich Hildebrandt, *Chemische und mineralogische Geschichte des Quecksilbers* (Braunschweig, München, 1793), 3.
77. Kielmann and Meyer, *Systematische Darstellung*, 201; Blagden, "History of the Congelation of Quicksilver," 336; Johann Friedrich Blumenbach, "Göttingen," *Göttingische Anzeigen von gelehrten Sachen*, 29 January 1774, 105–7.
78. Blagden, "History of the Congelation of Quicksilver," 340, 378–80.
79. Cited from Shachtman, *Minusgrade*, 68.
80. Ibid., 63–64. Jean André de Luc, *Untersuchungen über die Atmosphäre und die zu Abmessung ihrer Veränderungen dienlichen Werkzeuge* (Leipzig, 1776), 413.
81. Lomonosov, "1 Meditationes de caloris et frigoris causa auctore Michaele Lomonosow," 37–39; M. V. Lomonosov, "3 Meditationes de caloris et frigoris meditationes physicae," in M. V. Lomonosov, *Polnoe sobranie sochinenii*, vol. 2: *Trudy po fizike i khimii, 1747–1752 gg.* (Moscow, Leningrad, 1951), 91. Cited from Károly Simonyi, *Kulturgeschichte der Physik: Von den Anfängen bis heute*. 3rd ed. (Frankfurt/Main, 2004), 307.
82. Lomonosov, "1 Meditationes de caloris et frigoris causa auctore Michaele Lomonosow," 11.
83. Leonhard Euler and Gerard Friedrich Müller, *Die Berliner und Petersburger Akademie der Wissenschaften im Briefwechsel Leonhard Eulers: Der Briefwechsel L. Eulers mit G. F. Müller*, part 1, vol. 3,1 ([East] Berlin, 1959), 149.
84. Lomonosov, "3 Meditationes de caloris et frigoris meditationes physicae," 91.
85. Lomonosov, "1 Meditationes de caloris et frigoris causa auctore Michaele Lomonosow," 39.
86. Gmelin, *Reise durch Sibirien*, 356.

87. de Luc, *Untersuchungen über die Atmosphäre*, 455–512.
88. Ernst August Strohmeyer, *Anleitung übereinstimmende Thermometer zu verfertigen* (Göttingen, 1775), 11; W. E. Knowles Middleton, *A History of the Thermometer and Its Use in Meteorology* (Baltimore, 1966), 123.
89. Charles Louis de Secondat de Montesquieu, *Vom Geist der Gesetze* (Munich, 1967), 57.

Bibliography

"An Experimental History of Cold." *Philosophical Transactions of the Royal Society of London* 1 (1665–66): 8–9.

Arbuthnot, John. *An Essay Concerning the Effects of Air on Human Bodies*. London, 1733.

Behringer, Wolfgang, ed. *Kulturelle Konsequenzen der "Kleinen Eiszeit."* Göttingen, 2005.

———. *Kulturgeschichte des Klimas: Von der Eiszeit bis zur globalen Erwärmung*. Munich, 2007.

Berditskii, A. I., E. P. Borisenkov, A. S. Korovchenko, and V. M. Pasetskii. *Ocherki po istorii gidrometeorologicheskoi sluzhby Rossii*. Vol. 1. Saint Petersburg, 1997.

"Beschreibung des aus Eiß gemachten Hauses." *Anmerkungen bey den Zeitungen*, 9 December 1740, 393–96.

Billington, James Hadley. *The Icon and the Axe: An Interpretive History of Russian Culture*. London, 1966.

Blagden, C. "History of the Congelation of Quicksilver." *Philosophical Transactions of the Royal Society of London* 73 (1783): 329–97.

Blumenbach, Johann Friedrich. "Göttingen." *Göttingische Anzeigen von gelehrten Sachen*, 29 January 1774, 105–7.

Boele, Otto Floris. *The North in Russian Romantic Literature*. Amsterdam, 1996.

Boia, Lucian. *The Weather in the Imagination*. London, 2005.

Braun, Iosif-Adam. *O udivitel'noi stuzhe, isskusstvom proizvedennoi, ot kotoroi rtut' zamerzla*. Saint Petersburg, 1760.

Christopoulou, Christiana. "Early Modern History of Cold: Robert Boyle and the Emergence of a New Experimental Field in Seventeenth Century Experimental Philosophy." In *History of Artificial Cold, Scientific, Technological and Cultural Issues*, edited by Kostas Gavroglu, 21–51. New York, 2013.

Derham, W. "The History of the Great Frost in the Last Winter 1703 and 1708/9." *Philosophical Transactions of the Royal Society of London* 26 (1708-9): 454–78.

Derham, Wm., and Tho. Consett. "An Abstract of the Meteorological Diaries." *Philosophical Transactions of the Royal Society of London* 38 (1733): 101–9.

Diderot, Denis. *Gedanken zur Interpretation der Natur: Philosophische Grundsätze über Materie und Bewegung*. 3rd ed. Leipzig, 1976.

Euler, Leonhard, and Gerard Friedrich Müller. *Die Berliner und Petersburger Akademie der Wissenschaften im Briefwechsel Leonhard Eulers: Der Briefwechsel L. Eulers mit G. F. Müller*, part 1. Vol. 3,1. [East] Berlin, 1959.

Fagan, Brian. *The Little Ice Age: How Climate Made History, 1300–1850*. New York, 2000.

"Fortsetzung der Friedens-Festivitäten-Beschreibung." *Anmerkungen bey den Zeitungen*, 13 June 1740, 189–96.

Graham, Loren R. *Science in Russia and the Soviet Union: A Short History*. New York, 1993.

Hellmann, Gustav. "Die Entwicklung der meteorologischen Beobachtungen bis zum Ende des XVIII. Jahrhunderts: Teil 2." *Abhandlungen der Preussischen Akademie der Wissenschaften* (1927): 1–48.

Herzberg, Julia. "The Domestication of Ice and Cold: The Ice Palace in Saint Petersburg 1740." In "On Water: Perceptions, Politics, Perils," edited by Agnes Kneitz and Marc Landry, *RCC Perspectives*, no. 2 (2012): 53–62.

Hildebrandt, Friedrich. *Chemische und mineralogische Geschichte des Quecksilbers*. Braunschweig, München, 1793.

Hill, Fiona, and Clifford G. Gaddy. *The Siberian Curse: How Communist Planners Left Russia out in the Cold*. Washington, DC, 2003.

Istoriia Akademii Nauk SSSR. Vol. 1: *1724–1803*. Moscow, Leningrad, 1958.

Jurin, Jacobo [James]. "Invitatio ad Observationes Meteorologicas Communi Consilio Instituendas." *Philosophical Transactions of the Royal Society of London* 32 (1722–23): 422–27.

Kaplunovskiy, Alexander, ed. *"Auch in Moskwa habe ich Ursache zufrieden zu sein": Christian von Schlözers Privatkorrespondenz mit der Familie*. Berlin, 2014.

Kielmann, K. A., and J. R. Meyer. *Systematische Darstellung aller Erfahrungen über die einzelnen Metalle in zwei Bänden*. Vol. 1. Arau, 1807.

Krafft, Georg Wolfgang. *Experimentorum physicorum praecipuorum brevis description*. Saint Petersburg, 1738.

———. "Observationum meteorologicum, *1726–1736*." *Commentarii Academiae Imperialis Scientiarum Petropolitanae* 9 ([1737] 1744): 316–44, 344–57.

———. *Wahrhaffte und Umständliche Beschreibung und Abbildung des im Monath Januarius 1740 in St. Petersburg aufgerichteten merckwürdigen Hauses von Eiß*. Saint Petersburg, 1741.

"Kurtze Beschreibung der merckwürdigsten Witterungs-Geschichten allhier in St. Petersburg." *Anmerkungen über die Zeitungen*, 31 August 1738, 277–80.

Laxmann, Erich. *Erich Laxmann's Sibirische Briefe*. Göttingen, 1769.

Lemberg, Hans. "Zur Entstehung des Osteuropabegriffs im 19. Jahrhundert. Vom Norden zum Osten Europas." *Jahrbücher für Geschichte Osteuropas* 33 (1985): 48–91.

Lepenies, Wolf. *Das Ende der Naturgeschichte: Wandel kultureller Selbstverständlichkeiten in den Wissenschaften des 18. und 19. Jahrhunderts*. Munich, Vienna, 1976.

Lomonosov, M. V. "1 Meditationes de caloris et frigoris causa auctore Michaele Lomonosow." In M. V. Lomonosov, *Polnoe sobranie sochinenii*. Vol. 2: *Trudy po fizike i khimii, 1747–1752 gg.*, 8–55, 647–48. Moscow, Leningrad, 1951.

———. "3 Meditationes de caloris et frigoris meditationes physicae." In M. V. Lomonosov, *Polnoe sobranie sochinenii*. Vol. 2: *Trudy po fizike i khimii, 1747–1752 gg.*, 64–103. Moscow, Leningrad, 1951.

———. "19 Meditationes de solido et fluido." In M. V. Lomonosov, *Polnoe sobranie sochinenii*. Vol. 3: *Trudy po fizike, 1753–1765 gg.*, 378–409. Moscow, Leningrad, 1952.

———. "21 [Zapiska ob opytakh po zamorazhivaniiu rtuti]." In M. V. Lomonosov, *Polnoe sobranie sochinenii*. Vol. 3: *Trudy po fizike, 1753–1765 gg*, 422–27. Moscow, Leningrad, 1952.

Luc, Jean André de. *Untersuchungen über die Atmosphäre und die zu Abmessung ihrer Veränderungen dienlichen Werkzeuge*. Leipzig, 1776.

Manstein, Christoph Hermann von. *Beytrag zur Geschichte Rußlands vom Jahre 1727 bis 1744.* Hamburg, Bremen, 1771.

———. *Historische, politische und militärische Nachrichten von Rußland von dem Jahre 1727 bis 1744.* Leipzig, 1771.

Materialy dlia istorii Imperatorskoi Akademii nauk, 1716–1730. Vol. 1. Saint Petersburg, 1885.

Knowles Middleton, W. E. *A History of the Thermometer and Its Use in Meteorology.* Baltimore, 1966.

Montesquieu, Charles Louis de Secondat de. *Vom Geist der Gesetze.* Munich, 1967.

Nashchokin, V. I. *Zapiski. S 1712-go po 5-e Sentiabria 1759 goda.* Saint Petersburg, 1842.

Pogosian, E. "'I nevozmozhnoe vozmozhno': Svad'ba shutov v ledianom dome kak fakt ofitsial'noi kul'tury." *Trudy po russkoi i slavianskoi filologii: Literaturovedenie* 4 (2001): 80–109.

"Primechanie o klimatakh [Kholodnee li stali nashi klimatyy, nezheli prezhde?]." *Mesiatsoslov s nastavleniiami* (1779): 106–19.

Protokoly zasedanii konferentsii Imperatorskoi akademii nauk s 1725 po 1803 goda. Vol. 1: *1725–1743.* Saint Petersburg, 1897.

Protokoly zasedanii konferentsii Imperatorskoi akademii nauk s 1725 po 1803 goda. Vol. 2: *1744–1770.* Saint Petersburg, 1899.

Renner, Andreas. "Russland: Die Autokratie der Aufklärung." In *Orte eigener Vernunft: Europäische Aufklärung jenseits der Zentren*, edited by Alexander Kraus and Andreas Renner, 125–42. New York, 2008.

Rusnock, Andrea A. "Correspondence Networks and the Royal Society, 1700–1750." *British Journal for the History of Science* 32 (1999): 155–69.

Shachtman, Tom. *Minusgrade—Auf Der Suche nach dem Absoluten Nullpunkt: Eine Chronik Der Kälte.* Reinbek, 2001.

de-la-Shetardi, Markiz. "Pis'mo Markiza de-la-Shetardi iz Peterburga 1-go Marta/19-go fevralia 1740 g." In *Markiz de-la-Shetardi v Rossii 1740–1742 godov: Perevod rukopisnykh depesh francuzskago posol'stva v Peterburge*, edited by P. Pekarskii, 55–64. Saint Petersburg, 1862.

Shubinskii, C. N. *Istoricheskiie ocherki i razskazy.* Saint Petersburg, 1869.

Simonyi, Károly. *Kulturgeschichte der Physik: Von den Anfängen bis heute.* 3rd ed. Frankfurt/Main, 2004.

Strohmeyer, Ernst August. *Anleitung übereinstimmende Thermometer zu verfertigen.* Göttingen, 1775.

"Von dem Eiße." *Anmerkungen über die Zeitungen*, 21 January 1733, 21–24.

"Von der ungewöhnlichen Kälte des nächst vergangenen Winters in gantz Europa." *Anmerkungen bey den Zeitungen*, 11 November 1740, 361–64.

"V Sanktpeterburge dekabria 20 dnia." *Sanktpeterburgskiia Vedomosti*, 21 December 1759, 809–11.

"V Sanktpeterburge dekabria 27 dnia." *Sanktpeterburgskiia Vedomosti*, 28 December 1759, 825–26.

Werrett, Simon. *An Odd Sort of Exhibition: The St. Petersburg Academy of Sciences in Enlightened Russia.* Cambridge, 2000.

Wisniak, Jaime. "Development of the Concept of Absolute Zero Temperature." *Educación Quimica* 16 (2005): 104–13.

Wolff, Larry. *Inventing Eastern Europe: The Map of Civilization on the Mind of the Enlightenment*. Stanford, 1994.

Zubov, V. P. "Lomonosovs Übersetzung der Wolffschen Experimentalphysik." in *Lomonosov, Schlözer, Pallas: Deutsch-russische Wissenschaftsbeziehungen im 18. Jahrhundert*, edited by Eduard Winter, 12:42–51. Berlin, 1962.

CHAPTER 3

The Russian South Pole Expedition in the Context of Political Interests of the Soviet Union during the Cold War Era

Erki Tammiksaar

Introduction

Julia Herzberg, editor of this volume, starts chapter 1 with an influential sentence: "In tsarist Russia and the Soviet Union, the cold was a constant challenge, a phenomenon that influenced actions, everyday experiences, and mentalities and determined both external perceptions of the region and the region's self-image." The term "cold" is describing, however, not only the low temperatures prevailing in the atmosphere or in the solid ground but also relations in or between the human societies. The *Cold* War between capitalist West and communist East after World War II was a brilliant example of this tendency. In this chapter, I will analyze the political and scientific ambitions of Soviets, Americans, and Brits during the Cold War era to gain the title of the discoverer of the extremely cold "Ice Continent," as Antarctica was often called in the Soviet press. Being "the first" was an important political tool in proving one's supremacy in the world.

The Sovietization of Russian science began in the early 1930s and was almost concluded before World War II. Repression and several campaigns against scientists created an atmosphere of fear to make scientists loyal to the Soviet regime.[1] The next ideological step was to rewrite the history of world science on the basis of materials from the Soviet archives, in order to emphasize the prominence of Russian science in numerous scientific discoveries as well as in geographical studies. The Academy of Sciences of the Soviet Union took responsibility for this, such as in 1947 when the Soviet Union took part in an international discussion on the invention of radio. This debate had an important ideological aspect[2]: the academy general assembly, devoted to the questions of science history, took place in January 1949, two hundred years after the founding of the first chemical laboratory in Russia, and provided an opportunity to illuminate the achievements of Soviet science. Such an undertaking had to be coordinated with the secretariat of the Central Committee of the Communist Party of the Soviet Union (CPSU).[3] On 11 January 1949, the general meeting of the academy accepted the Central Committee's "suggestions for ideological activities and Joseph Stalin's instructions concerning the revision of science history in the Marxist-Leninist [context]," emphasizing the "urgent need for improving and extending the activities in the fields of science history and technology."[4]

In writing the "true history" of science, the Russian expedition to the Antarctic in the nineteenth century (its official name was the Russian South Pole expedition) under the leadership of Fabian Gottlieb von Bellingshausen became one of the first ideological battlefields for Soviet researchers. On 9 August 1948, the United States of America called upon seven states that had made colonial claims to Antarctica (Argentina, Australia, Chile, France, New Zealand, Norway, and the United Kingdom) to give up their demands and together establish "an eight power condominium to assume collective sovereignty over Antarctica";[5] the Soviet Union was to be excluded from this collective. Such a proposal could not be met without contest. On 29 January 1949, the CPSU decided that, at first, it would be inappropriate to use official methods to draw attention to the rights of the Soviet Union to the Antarctic.[6] This suggestion was included in the resolution of the meeting of the Russian Geographical Society, convened especially for this purpose on the initiative of the CPSU on 10 February 1949.[7] The Soviet Union's right to participate in political discussions about Antarctica was due primarily to the Bellingshausen expedition. This fact on its own, however, was not sufficient to assert Soviet interests—a new version of the "exploration" of the Antarctic continent, starting with the Russian Antarctic expedition, had to be planned.

This chapter analyzes the reception of nineteenth- and twentieth-century exploration of Antarctica in Russian and Soviet scientific literature, based on written sources of the Russian Antarctic expedition. The analysis focuses on the arguments put forward by Soviet scientists between 1945 and 1970 that the ice shelf (verge of the Antarctic continent) was first sighted and thus discovered namely by the Russian expedition. In this context, whether Bellingshausen and his contemporaries interpreted the nature of continental ice the same way scientists of the twentieth century did is the decisive question. The answer would indicate whether it is correct to ascribe present-day knowledge to people from the nineteenth century—in this context, that a continent can also consist of ice. Even today, a definitive claim over the "first exploration" of the Antarctic continent depends on the answer to this question, which is political in nature. From a scientific and historical point of view, it would perhaps not be correct to give one definite answer. The article tries to contribute to the depoliticization of the history of Antarctic exploration and Russian science.

Antarctic Expeditions from the 1820s to 1920s

The course and results of the Bellingshausen expedition on the sloops *Mirnyi* and *Vostok* (July 1819–August 1821) are generally known today.[8] The members of the Russian South Pole expedition, Bellingshausen, and the astronomer Ivan M. Simonov completely accepted the opinion of James Cook (who had made the first serious attempt to find a southern continent from 1772-75) that it was impossible to determine whether the Antarctic continent existed.[9] But, unlike Cook, the Russians discovered patches of terrestrial land—Peter I Island and Alexander I Coast—south of the Antarctic Circle in January 1821 (cf. maps 3.1, 3.2).

After Bellingshausen's voyage, expeditions to the region of the South Pole continued. In 1821-24, the British sealer Benjamin Morrell sailed in the southern polar waters; in 1822-24, there was the British sealer James Weddell; in 1830-33, the British sealer John Biscoe; in 1837-40, the British sealer John Balleny; in 1838-41, the French circumnavigator Jules Sebastién César Dumont d'Urville; in 1838-39, the American captain Charles Wilkes; and in 1839-41, the British explorer and scientist James Clark Ross. Discoveries made during these expeditions were similar to the Bellingshausen expedition; new separate patches of terrestrial land were added to the maps of the region in the southern hemisphere. The Ross expedition in 1841, however, discovered a large landmass—Victoria Land—and high ice shelves that were more numerous than the patches of terrestrial land discovered during previous expeditions. Numerous discoveries changed the general situation, and more people began speculating on whether there was a continent, sea, or archipelago behind the ice barriers in the region of the South Pole. Those who were more cautiously inclined left questions open about the existence of a continent or a sea. The fact that most of the seafarers saw ice in the south made the problem even more complicated, as they did not find a logical explanation for the origin of such high ice masses—whether they had been formed on the continent, in the sea, or between islands. Each explorer put forward his own argument; in terms of today's knowledge, their assumptions were not accurate.

But shortly before new expeditions in the early 1840s were sent to the South Pole area, Swiss scholars Jean de Charpentier and Louis Agassiz proposed their ingenious theory of the glacial era, a theory that was only partly based on field observations.[10] Their studies had proven that the glaciers in the Alps had previously been considerably larger and thicker, and that they would have covered the entire territory from the North Pole to the Mediterranean and Caspian Seas. Agassiz called this Pleistocene epoch the "ice age."[11] However, Antarctic explorers could not provide new information to prove the existence of the ice age, since difficult ice conditions did not enable them to land and obtain information about the Inner Antarctic and its ice shelves. Debates about the

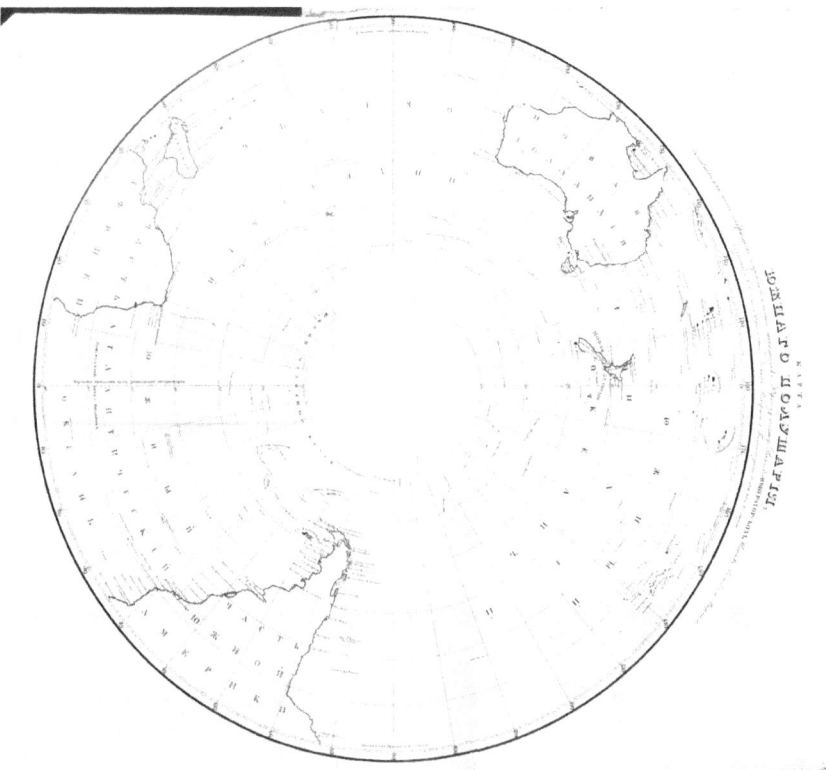

Map 3.1. Islands in the southern hemisphere discovered by the Russian Antarctic expedition (Bellinsgauzen 1831). Reprinted with permission from the Russian Academy of Sciences library at Saint Petersburg.

validity of the ice age theory lasted until the 1880s and thus were not helpful in answering questions on the Antarctic continent: Could a continent be made of ice, with a permanently changing coastline?

For Russian scientists, as well as their European colleagues, it was difficult to establish what was there in the South Pole region. However, although reliable knowledge of the physical geography of the South Pole region was scant, this did not bother those who believed in the existence of a continent there, and, depending on their nationality, people considered Wilkes, d'Urville, or Ross as the first explorer of Antarctica. Among them, Ross was considered to have contributed the most to the exploration of the Antarctic.[12] Pavel M. Novosil'skii, an officer on the *Mirnyi*, was reportedly disappointed that his contribution to the discovery of the Antarctic continent was not mentioned in the obituaries for Bellingshausen, who died in 1852.[13] He published two

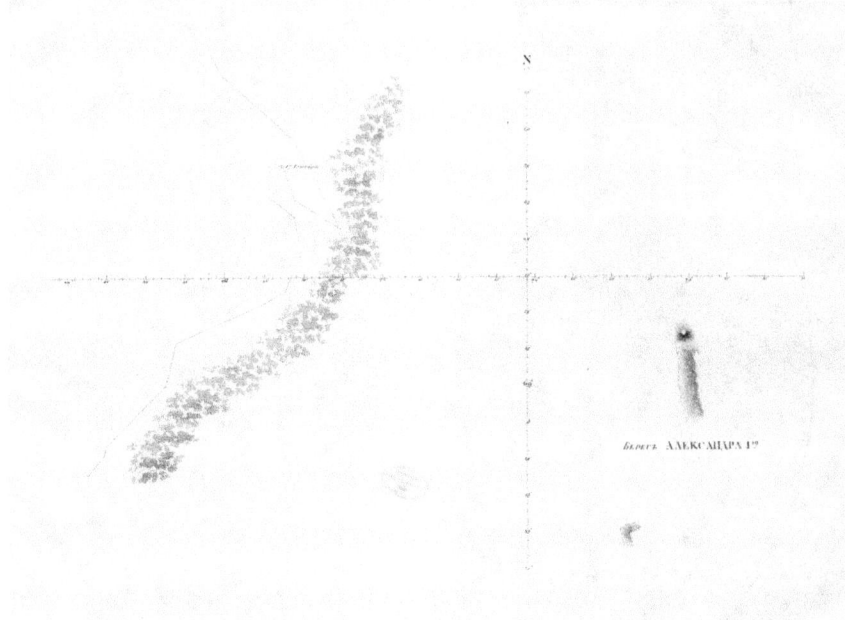

Map 3.2. Map no. 61 from *Atlas of Bellingshausen*, the route of the Russian Antarctic expedition near the coast of Alexander I Land on 17/29 January 1821. Reprinted with permission from the Russian Academy of Sciences library at Saint Petersburg.

pamphlets, *The Sixth Continent, or, a Brief Account of Voyages to the South from Cook to Ross*[14] and a diary titled *South Pole* (written under influence of Bellingshausen's travelogue), claiming publicly, for the first time in Russia, that Russians, who discovered the Alexander I Coast in January 1821, should be considered the pioneers of the Antarctic continent. He wrote: "Until the present day, neither in Russian nor in foreign languages, has there appeared any special study on the southern continent [which I have compiled] and the first discovery of it rightly belongs to Russian navigators."[15]

The Russian government had not considered the question of who discovered Antarctica important. Thus, Novosil'skii's publications had been forgotten in Russia by the beginning of the twentieth century. However, the claim that the Russian expedition had discovered the Antarctic continent upon the discovery of the Alexander I Coast attracted more attention after expeditions by Belgian (Adrien de Gerlache de Gomery, 1897–99), British (Carsten Borchgrevink, 1898–1900; Robert Falcon Scott, 1901–3; Ernest Shackleton, 1908), German (Erich von Drygalski, 1901–3), Swedish (Otto von Nordenskiöld, 1901–3), and French (Jean-Baptiste Charcot, 1904–7) explorers yielded evidence of the existence of an Antarctic continent consisting mainly of continental ice. This was supported by the famous Russian geographer Lev Berg[16] as well as other Russian authors.[17]

Such an approach was still not dominant in Russia in the first half of the twentieth century. Bellingshausen's expedition did not *result* in the discovery of Antarctica, but it was considered very important in the exploration of southern polar areas in the 1840s, although this expedition was not the immediate trigger for the understanding of Antarctica as a continent.[18] The most important supporter of this view was another Russian geographer, Iulii Shokal'skiji.[19]

Soviets Declare Themselves the Discoverers of Antarctica

By the beginning of the 1920s, when the existence of the Ice Continent had been already proven, Wilkes, Ross, and d'Urville were no longer considered to have discovered the Antarctic continent. In 1902, Edwin Swift Balch had pointed out that American sealer Nathaniel Palmer could have discovered Antarctica on 17 November 1820.[20] However, according to an article published by Lieutenant Rupert Thomas Gould in 1925, British sealer Edward Bransfield, rather than Palmer, saw Antarctica first.[21] Russell Owen wrote in 1941: "The argument as to who [Palmer or Bransfield] saw it [Antarctic mainland] first has been for many years, particularly in the twentieth century, a matter of acrimonious debate between American and British scientists."[22] Meanwhile, Soviet Russia was mainly interested in preparations for the Second International Polar Year (1932–33) and was drifting stations in the North Polar Sea to guarantee its geopolitical interests in international scientific collaboration in northern polar areas.[23] It is not surprising, then, that when the Antarctic coastline Crown Princess Martha Land, to which the Bellingshausen expedition had been quite close on 28 January 1820 (all the dates according to the Gregorian calendar), was discovered by the Hjalmar Riiser-Larsen expedition in 1930, the Russians did not ascribe much official attention to it.

The English translation of Bellingshausen's entire voyage narrative was first published in 1945. The preface and commentaries of the book were written by Frank Debenham, the director of the Scott Polar Research Institute. He proposed, based on available knowledge of the physical geography of the Antarctic continent in 1945, that the key to who truly discovered Antarctica does not lie in the discovery of Alexander I Coast in January 1821 but rather in the date 28 January 1820, when the Russian expedition had made the first attempt to approach the South Pole through ice. Debenham described that as follows: "This day must be considered an unfortunate one for the Russian expedition, for we know now that they must have been within a few miles, not more than twenty at most, of the coast of what is now called Princess Martha Land, discovered in 1929–30 by the Norwegian expedition. It is even possible that the 'solid stretch of ice running from east through south to west' was indeed the land ice which, everywhere along this coast, marks the edge of the continent. In any case, a few hours of clear weather on this day would have certainly antedated the discovery of land here by 110 years."[24] The fact that Bransfield discovered the extreme northern portion of the Antarctic Peninsula, as proven by the British, later named Trinity Land, on 30 January 1820 made the situation even more complicated. In 1947, Rear Admiral Evgenii E. Shvede published a review of this book in the journal of the Russian Geographical Society, in which he did not dispute Debenham's statements.[25]

A great political game had not yet started as the Americans undertook their démarche in 1948. As a result, Bellingshausen's expedition, the discoveries made, and writings and other issues became very important to political authorities. Due to that, the Palmer-Bransfield discussion and the book by Debenham were studied more thoroughly by Soviet geographers at the beginning of 1949. A hasty study of Russian-language archival documents and literature provided plenty of material proving that it was certainly the Russian South Pole expedition that discovered the Antarctic continent.[26]

On 10 February 1949, a general assembly of the Geographical Society took place. Berg, president of the society, relayed the main report. To strengthen the political message, he spoke about the view of James Cook (that is, that it was impossible to see a continent/land in the Antarctic because of complicated ice conditions), which had hindered further exploration in the Antarctic, and how brave Russian seafarers had refuted such a misleading view. After this report, it became very important to Soviet researchers to prove that Cook's expedition had disproved the existence of a continent in the south. Such political allegations were explicitly expressed in the publisher's preface to the 1949 book *The Voyage of the Sloops* Vostok *and* Mirnyi *to the Antarctic in the Years 1819–1821*. It reads: "Russian explorers sailed to the southern hemisphere with a special aim to discover lands in the vicinity of the South Pole after it had been completely assumed in the West [by Cook] that the South continent did not exist. The discovery [did] take place."[27] In this way, the communist Soviet Union brought discredit upon the capitalist West.

It was also important to prove that the honor of discovering the Antarctic continent first belonged to Russia. In his report, Berg stated that, as proven by Debenham, the rough ice that Bellingshausen described on 28 January 1820 was actually the verge of the Antarctic continent (map 3.3).[28]

However, Berg did not declare that Bellingshausen had assumed that he had discovered the Antarctic continent on that day; as an experienced historian of geography and a researcher-practitioner, Berg knew that in such circumstances it would be too provocative to assume so. Some other distinguished Soviet geographers, such as Andrei A. Grigor'ev,[29] Aleksandr I. Andreev,[30] and Stan-

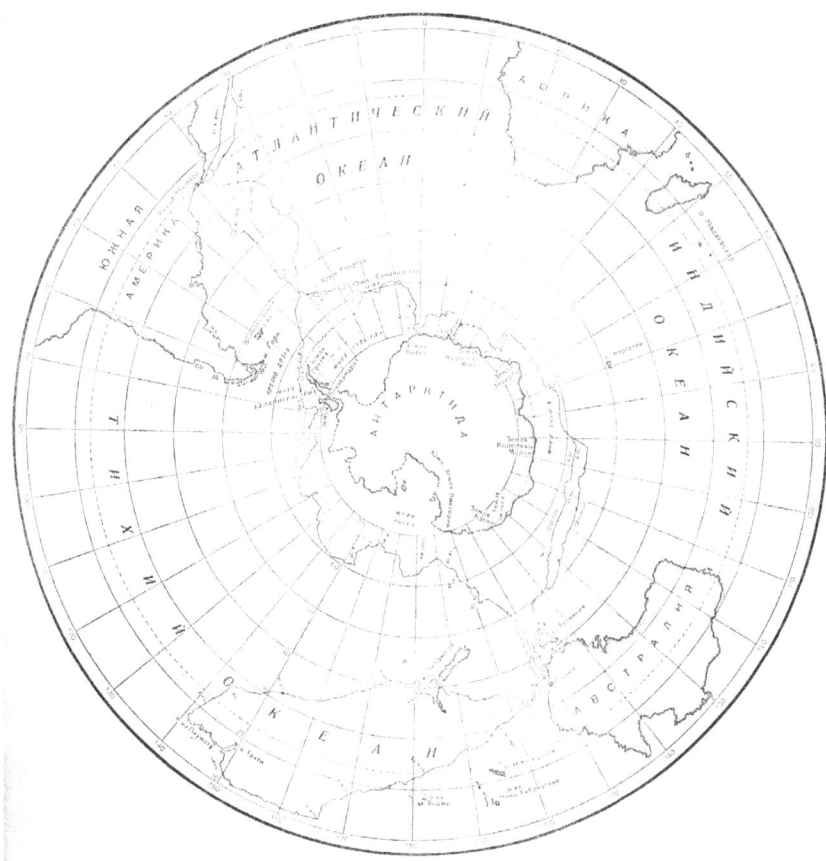

Map 3.3. The map of the voyage of the Russian Antarctic expedition around Antarctica compiled by Soviet geographers and published first in 1949. It is remarkable that the boundaries of the Antarctic continent have been indicated in the map, due to which it was accepted as proof of the discovery of the continent by the expedition. Reprinted with permission from the Baer House library, Tartu.

islav V. Kalesnik,[31] also used the data by Debenham in their articles. Admiral Shvede also participated in the general assembly and, relying on Debenham, noted that the discoveries of the Bellingshausen expedition should not be limited to the officially recognized discoveries of Peter I Island and Alexander I Coast in 1821. Specifically, it should be acknowledged that the expedition repeatedly approached the Antarctic continent and, judging by the descriptions presented by Bellingshausen, he had certainly seen Antarctica considerably earlier than what was assumed.[32] In this way, Shvede recognized that there was a problem for Soviet geographers and encouraged finding proof that it was just the Russian South Pole expedition that discovered the Antarctic continent.

Since prominent Russian geographers Berg, Grigor'ev, Andreev, and Kalesnik were not completely successful in solving the problem, Shvede tried to do it himself by creating a different account of the Russian South Pole expedition. In 1949, on his initiative, the second edition of Bellingshausen's narrative was published in Russian. A critical analysis of the available archival documents and published materials in the introduction to the book indicated that he was convinced that Bellingshausen could not see the Antarctic continent on 28 January 1820 due to bad weather. He compared the observation data of the second Soviet whale flotilla *Slava*[33] of 20 March 1948 in clear weather with those from the Bellingshausen expedition on 2 February 1820 and deemed them similar. Thus, Shvede wrote: "If the visibility had not been bad, Bellingshausen and Lazarev would have presented data on the Antarctic continent on 28 January 1820 already."[34] Furthermore, in order to highlight the Russian explorers' integrity, Shvede said: "It was only because of extraordinary fairness and strictness to the reliability of the discovery that the Russian navigators did not allow the declaration that [on 28 January 1820] they had actually seen the low part of the continent, rather than the coastal ice."[35] Shvede tried to show that "extraordinary fairness and strictness to the reliability of the discovery" indicated that Russian navigators had known the ice age theory (which was not founded until the second half of 1830s).[36]

Shvede's declaration, in one version or another, was later often used in the publications of Russian authors. However, Shvede knew well that this was false because he used in his introduction Bellingshausen's report of 20 April 1819 to the minister of the navy,[37] in which Bellingshausen admits that "I found no evidence anywhere of a great Southern land [from the Sandwich Islands to New Holland], although I held most of my course inside or near the polar circle, as much as the winds allowed. If such a land does exist, it must lie far within the ice and be covered by it, and there would be no way to recognize it."[38] This statement was the only one by Bellingshausen that refuted the whole notion that Antarctica, mostly made up of continental ice, was sighted first by Russians in 1820. A similar opinion was also expressed in the writings by Simonov.[39] Berg and Andreev had also used Bellingshausen's report as a source.[40]

Nevertheless, Soviet authors tried to portray the Russian South Pole expedition as having discovered the Antarctic continent on 28 January 1820, although the publications of the materials about the expedition[41] containing notes by Egor Kiselev, a sailor aboard the ship *Vostok* under the command of Bellingshausen,[42] and the diary by Pavel Novosil'skii, sailing as an officer on the *Mirnyi*, proved well that the navigators had not seen anything special on that day.[43] This was also well known in the West.[44] To maintain the prominence of the Russian expedition over the American (Palmer) and British (Bransfield) expeditions, the Soviet researchers had to find a source that differed from the notes of other expedition members on the same date.

Lazarev: The Discoverer of the Ice Continent?

Such a source already existed: from Mikhail P. Lazarev, captain of the *Mirnyi*. Lazarev's letter to a friend from 15 September 1821 was published in the Russian navy journal in 1918,[45] describing the course of the voyage as follows: "It was a wonderful evening on 28 January 1820 when we encountered an extremely high ice slope [*ледяный материк*], and a sight from the crosstrees indicated that it extended as far as the reach of sight. But we could not enjoy this surprising sight for long, as very soon the air became thick and ordinary snow began to fall."[46]

The sights described by Bellingshausen, Kiselev, and Novosil'skii on 28 January were similar; only the one by Lazarev was different. Comparing their descriptions of 17 February 1820, when they approached the verge of the continental ice of Antarctica, there is no doubt that just on that day Bellingshausen[47] and Kiselev on the *Vostok*[48] and Novosil'skii[49] on the *Mirnyi* had seen the verge of the continental ice of Antarctica, which made a strong impression on them. According to written sources, Lazarev was the only one who did not see this; at least, he did not write about that in his letter. This letter was used by geographers Berg, Grigor'ev, Andreev, and Kalesnik in their writings, but because Lazarev was not aware of understanding the nature of continental ice and did not state anything about discovering the Antarctic continent at the end of the letter, it was probably not used as proof that the Russian expedition had seen the Antarctic continent on 28 January.[50] In spite of that, in 1957 Vladimir Lebedev (a member of the Russian Antarctic Commission organizing the International Geophysical Year) declared the letter by Lazarev as the most important proof of the discovery of Antarctica.[51] Subsequently several Soviet authors credited the discovery of Antarctica to Lazarev.[52] Shvede also relied on Lazarev's letter in 1958 to defend the importance of the discovery by Russians, but he accepted that the data presented by Bellingshausen were more reliable than Lazarev's letter.[53] This means that Lazarev's letter as the only proof of the involvement of Russians in the discovery of Antarctica was of little value to several Soviet scientists.

In 1962 and 1963, Russian navy historian Mikhail I. Belov published two important studies in which he analyzed unsigned navigation charts of the Russian South Pole expedition. According to his analysis, the compilers of the maps were officers of the Russian Antarctic expedition. On the basis of the navigation charts and the colors used on it, Belov tried to prove that the verge of the continental ice Lazarev had seen on 28 January had been depicted on the navigation chart.[54] But on the chart, a note on that day reads "solid stretch of ice was seen," rather than "continental ice" as written by Lazarev. "Solid stretch of ice" was that day seen from the ships by Bellingshausen[55] as well as by Novosil'skii.[56] Thus, the navigation chart confirms what was written by Bellingshausen and Novosil'skii, not the information in Lazarev's letter.

The question is why Bellingshausen had considered it necessary to indicate on the navigation chart with his own hand a "solid stretch of ice." Aside from this note, Bellingshausen wrote six other important notes on the map, which denoted the sighting of previous known islands, and the discovery of Peter I Island and Alexander I Coast as "saw the land"[57]—this is understandable. The note on "solid stretch of ice" extending south, however, marks the end of Bellingshausen's first attempt at approaching the South Pole, since according to the instruction by Marquis de Traversay, the minister of the navy, he had to sail as far as possible to discover new lands (South Continent).[58] The corresponding dark blue color on the map denoted impenetrable ice, not the verge of continental ice.[59] Later, as the "solid stretch of ice" or continental ice seen on 17 February blocked their way to the south, and with the contours of ice depicted in the navigation chart found in the Bellingshausen map coinciding with the ice contours published in the uncolored maps of Peter I Island and Alexander I Coast (see map 3.2),[60] there is no reason to doubt that the ice colored dark blue in the navigation charts simply indicated the limit from which the ships could not move farther, nothing else.

Thus it is not surprising that Bellingshausen, as a good cartographer who had compiled maps of the first Russian voyage around the world (1803–6), had omitted the navigation charts from his atlas. He did not consider the sighting of continental ice a discovery, and the position of ice could be described in his narrative, as indeed it was.[61]

Thus the navigation chart of the Russian South Pole expedition proves the validity of the texts by Bellingshausen, not those by Lazarev. But how is it possible that these two dates—28 January and 17 February 1820—which appeared to be so important from the point of view of later Antarctic exploration, were described completely differently by Lazarev? The only explanation is that Lazarev wrote the letter to his friend without consulting the navigation map and travel notes (which have not been found up to the present day). He probably made the simple human mistake of exchanging the dates 28 January and 17 February in his letter. This was not important at the time. According to some Soviet authors, it was just Lazarev's letter that proved that he, not Bellingshausen, had discovered the Antarctic continent and had known the nature of continental ice in Antarctica.[62] But Lazarev, at the same time, resolutely disproved the existence of the Antarctic continent at the end of his letter.[63] Neither Lazarev nor other participants in the expedition paid much attention to the sight of the verge of continental ice and associated it with land, as can be concluded from the articles by Simonov and the writing by Bellingshausen. But there was one thing in his writing accepted by every member of the expedition—lands discovered within the Antarctic Circle in January 1821 were the southernmost as compared to those discovered up to that time. This was an important result that should be accepted.

Conclusion

According to the instructions of Minister of the Navy de Traversay, the aim of the Russian South Pole expedition (1819–21) was to find the fabled South Continent, the existence of which Cook assumed but considered impossible to discover. As opposed to Cook, the Russian South Pole expedition under the command of Bellingshausen and Lazarev discovered terrestrial land within the Antarctic Circle in January 1821. However, like Cook, they could not prove the presence of a continent. In this context, Bellingshausen and Simonov, who wrote about the Russian South Pole expedition in detail, agreed that it was impossible to discover the continent. The view that the Russian South Pole expedition had not sighted the Antarctic continent dominated in Russia until the beginning of the twentieth century.

The expeditions launched by Great Britain, the United States, and France discovered several new patches of land in the region of the South Pole at the end of 1830s and the beginning of the 1840s. As a result, several scientists, cartographers, and navigators began to speak openly about the presence of a continent in the South Pole region, although the point of view that there was no continent was just as popular. Specific geographical conditions of the Antarctic continent—the hard-to-define icy coastline, difficulties in approaching it, and severe natural conditions—prevented any clear answers until the first decade of the twentieth century. The few expeditions to the southern polar areas that provided some data of scientific importance in the nineteenth century were searching for land rather than ice. Little, however, was discovered during these voyages. No expedition or explorer of the nineteenth century was able to solve the main problem of the southern polar areas: i.e., the existence of extensive and large icebergs, and the presence of ice shelves (continental ice) in this region. Let us remember that Christopher Columbus reaching America and Wilhelm Janszoon sighting Australia were not accepted by the public as the European "discoveries" of America and Australia. Later exploration established these continents, and it is important that they were not sighted several times as the case is with Antarctica. The peculiarity of Antarctica lies in the fact that it is not mainland but a land of ice—totally different from terrestrial land. The idea that a continent can also be made up of ice is only feasible through the ice age theory, a perspective developed only from the end of the nineteenth century.

In the 1840s, after the results of the Wilkes and Ross expeditions had been published, discussions about who discovered the Antarctic continent first arose. According to some American researchers, it was Wilkes; for the British, it was Ross; for the French, it was d'Urville; and in Russia, some authors stressed that the discovery of Alexander I Coast could be regarded as the discovery of the entire Antarctic continent. As there were very few empirical data about the (non)presence of the continent, these discussions could not be resolved. As a result of the "Heroic Age" in the 1900s in the exploration of Antarctica and attempts to prove the existence of the continent theoretically as well as empirically, the question of who discovered Antarctica continued into the twentieth century. To secure status in that discovery, new names were included in the list of discoverers. The Americans stressed the services of Nathaniel Palmer and the British those of Edward Bransfield. Both were navigators whose scientific contributions to the exploration of Antarctica were little known in the nineteenth century, even to specialists. The supporters of Palmer and Bransfield showed little interest in the views of Palmer and Bransfield themselves and their contemporaries.

At the beginning of the twentieth century and in the 1930s, several Russian authors concluded on the basis of most recent investigations in the Antarctic that the sighting of Alexander I Coast could be classified as the discovery of the Antarctic continent by Russians. This view, however, was not popular and thus not presented as the political view of state officials. In August 1948, after the démarche of the United States of America, the Soviet Union also began to take political interest. The United States and its allies could not deny that the Russian South Pole expedition under the command of Bellingshausen and Lazarev had taken place. The Soviet Union decided not to confine itself to being a participant in determining the status of Antarctica, but was instead eager to prove that Russians under the lead of Bellingshausen and Lazarev had discovered the Antarctic continent. To reach that aim, texts by James Cook, Bellingshausen, and his traveling companions were altered to an extent that their content was in accordance with the interests of the Soviet authorities. This patriotic step, given rise to by the Cold War, made the history of Antarctic exploration political, in which little room was left for scientific argumentation. Soviet researchers relying on scientific investigations of the most recent period took little interest in how Bellingshausen and Lazarev had estimated their observation results. Partly under political pressure and partly on their own patriotic initiative, they considered it a priority to prove, at any rate, that Bellingshausen and Lazarev knew the nature of the continental ice and discovered the Antarctic continent in January 1820, not in January 1821 when they first sighted terrestrial land within the Antarctic Circle.

It is regrettable that Bellingshausen, Bransfield, and Palmer were drawn into Cold War agendas and that scientific integrity was almost forgotten. Bellingshausen, Lazarev, Ross, Wilkes, d'Urville, and others did not know as much about Antarctica as we know today. Antarctica (in this case) should be analyzed with consideration to what was known about it at the time (e.g., ice theory, doubts about the existence of continents that are not terrestrial). This has been the main problem of the history of Antarctic exploration, given its complicated physical geography.

Proceeding from today's knowledge, we could consider either Bellingshausen, Lazarev, Palmer, or Bransfield as discoverers of Antarctica, but we should not deliberately ascribe modern aspects of scientific knowledge to them or other Antarctic explorers. It would be more correct to accept that our knowledge of the complicated physical geography of southern polar areas has changed slowly but completely, and for that reason, it is not justified to point out the first pioneer of Antarctica. The Antarctic Treaty concluded in 1959 was a reasonable compromise in solving the claims to Antarctica in a neutral way. Such a neutral attitude should be used in solving the question of the discovery of Antarctica too. In my opinion, the treatment of the exploration of southern polar areas should be based on the general level of scientific knowledge characteristic of certain periods. The following voyagers can be considered pioneers of Antarctica (not considering their actual contribution to the exploration of southern polar areas):

1. 1830–1930s: Biscoe, Bellingshausen, Ross, Wilkes, D'Urville.

2. Beginning in the 1940s: Bellingshausen, Bransfield, and Palmer.

There is no sense in trying to establish who discovered Antarctica first, since it is not within anyone's power to solve this problem.

Acknowledgments

This chapter was supported by Estonian Ministry of Education Grants No IUT 02-16 and from the Grant of European Union KESTA No 3.2.0801.12-0044. Many thanks to my good friends Natal'ya Sukhova, Vello Paatsi, and Rip Bulkeley for valuable comments and help with literature sources.

Erki Tammiksaar is director of the Centre for Science Studies of the Estonian University of Life Sciences and a senior research fellow in the Department of Geography of the University of Tartu. His scholarly interests include the scientific activities of Karl Ernst von Baer, the history of science in Estonia in the nineteenth and twentieth centuries, the role of Baltic German scientists in the scientific and political activities of the Russian Empire in the nineteenth century, and the history of the oil shale industry in Estonia.

Notes

1. Cf. Nikolai Krementsov, *Stalinist Science* (Princeton, NJ, 1996); Ethan Pollock, *Stalin and the Soviet Science Wars* (Princeton, NJ, 2006).
2. Anatolii S. Sonin, *Bor'ba s kosmopolitizmom v sovetskoi nauke* (Moscow, 2011), 411-16, 433.
3. Vladimir D. Esakov, *Akademiia nauk v resheniiakh po politbiuro CK RKP(b)-VKP(b) 1922-1952* (Moscow, 2000), 391.
4. "Postanovlenie obshchego sobraniia Akademii Nauk SSSR 11 ianvaria 1949 goda," in *Voprosy istorii otechestvennoi nauki: Obshchee sobranie Akademi nauk SSSR posviashchennoe istorii otechestvennoi nauki 5-11 ianvaria 1949 g.*, ed. Sergei I. Vavilov (Moscow, Leningrad, 1949), 881.
5. Rip Bulkeley, "Bellingshausen's First Accounts of his Antarctic Voyage of 1819-1821," *Polar Record* 49, no. 248 (2013): 10.
6. *Dokladnaia zapiska ministra inostrannykh del SSSR A. Ia. Vyshinskogo I. V. Stalinu po voprosu o memorandume riadu pravitel'stv o rezhime Antarktike, 20.02.1950*, http://www.alexanderyakovlev.org/fond/issues-doc/71711.
7. Lev S. Berg, *Russkie otkrytiia v Antarktike i sovremennyi interes k nei* (Moscow, 1949), 31-32.
8. Rip Bulkeley, "Cold War Whaling: Bellingshausen and the *Slava* Flotilla," *Polar Record* 47, no. 241 (2011): 135-55; Bulkeley, "Bellingshausen's First Accounts," 9-25; Frank Debenham, "Introduction," in *The Voyage of Captain Bellingshausen to the Antarctic Seas, 1819-1821*, ed. Frank Debenham, no. 1 (91) (London, 1945), xi-xxx; Erki Tammiksaar and Tarmo Kiik, "Origins of the Russian Antarctic Expedition: 1819-1821," *Polar Record* 49, no. 249 (2013): 180-92.
9. *The Voyage of Captain Bellingshausen to the Antarctic Seas, 1819-1821*, ed. Frank Debenham, Hakluyt Society 2nd Series, nos. 1-2 (91-92) (London, 1945); Faddei F. Bellinsgauzen, "Donesenie kapitana 2 ranga Billingsauzena iz Porta Zhaksona o svoem plavanii [...]," *Zapiski, izdavaemyia gosudarstvennym admiral'teiskim departamentom otnosiashchiiasia k moreplavaniiu, naukam i slovestnosti* 5 (1823): 201-19; Ivan M. Simonov, *Beschreibung einer neuen Entdeckungsreise in das südliche Eismeer*, trans. M. Banyi (Vienna, 1824).
10. Jean de Charpentier, *Sur la cause probable du transport des blocs erratiques de la Suisse* (Paris, 1835); Louis Agassiz, "Des glaciers, des moraines, et des blocs erratiques," *Bibliothèque universelle de Genève* 12 (1837): 369-94.
11. Louis Agassiz, "Discours prononcé à l'ouverture des séances de la Société Helvétique des Sciences naturelles," *Actes de la Société Helvétique des Sciences naturelles* II (1837): v-xxxii.
12. "Otkrytie novogo materika v Iuzhnom polusharii," *Zhurnal ministerstva narodnogo prosveshcheniia* 35, no. 7 (1842): 48-52; Karl Ernst von Baer, "Materialien zur Kenntniss des unvergänglichen Boden-Eises in Sibirien," in *Berichte und Arbeiten aus der Universitätsbibliothek und dem Universitätsarchiv Giessen*, ed. Lorenz King, no. 51 (Giessen, 2001), 45; Valentin G. Smirnov, "Proekt M. F. Mori ob issledovanii iuzhnykh poliarnykh stran," *Izvestiia Russkogo geograficheskogo obshchestva* 130, no. 5 (1998): 46-54.
13. "Admiral Faddei Faddeevich Bellinsgauzen," *Morskoi sbornik* 19, no. 7 (1852): 26-32; "Zhizneopisanie sostavliavshago pri osobe ego Imperatorskogo Velichestva admirala

Faddeia Faddeevicha Bellinsgauzena," *Severnaia Pchela*, nos. 91–92 (1853): 363–64, 367–68.
14. [Pavel Novosil'skii,] *Shestoi kontinent ili kratkoe obozrenie plavanii k iugu ot Kuka do Rossa* (Saint Petersburg, 1854).
15. Ibid., 17.
16. Lev S. Berg, "Ocherk istorii russkoi geograficheskoi nauki," *Trudy komissii po istorii znanii* (Leningrad, 1929), 4:47; Lev S. Berg, *Ocherki po istorii russkikh geograficheskikh otkrytii* (Moscow, Leningrad, 1946), 109.
17. Ivan O. Rabinovich, *Shestaia chast' sveta (Vopros ob Antarkticheskom materike)* (Saint Petersburg, 1908), 5; Nikolai Vvedenskii, *V poiskakh Iuzhnogo materika* (Leningrad, Moscow, 1940), 46; Nikolai Vvedenskii, "K voprosu o russkikh otkrytiiakh v Antarktike v 1819–1821 godakh, v svete noveishikh geograficheskikh issledovanii," *Izvestiia Russkogo geograficheskogo obshchestva* 73, no. 1 (1941), 121; Evgenii L. Shister, *V Antarktiku za kitami* (Moscow, 1948), 9.
18. Sergei G. Grigor'ev, *Vokrug iuzhnogo poliusa* (Moscow, 1937), 15.
19. Iulii M. Shokal'skii, "Poliarnyia strany Iuzhnogo polushariia," in *Entsiklopedicheskii slovar'*, ed. K. K. Arsen'ev and F. F. Petrushevskii (Saint Petersburg, 1898), XXIVⒶ, 492–94; Iulii M. Shokalskii, "Stoletie so vremeni otpravleniia Russkoi antarkticheskoi ekspeditsii pod komandoiu F. Bellinsgauzena i M. Lazareva 4 iiuliia 1819 g. iz Kronshstadta," *Izvestiia Russkogo geograficheskogo obshchestva* 60, no. 2 (1928): 191.
20. Edwin S. Balch, *Antarctica* (Philadelphia, 1902), 91.
21. Rupert T. Gould, "The First Sighting of the Antarctic Continent," *Geographical Journal* 65, no. 3 (1925): 220–25; R. J. Campbell, ed., *The Discovery of the South Shetland Islands: The Voyages of the Brig Williams 1819–1820 as Recorded in Contemporary Documents and the Journal of Midshipman C. W. Poynter* (London, 2000), 132–33.
22. Russell Owen, *The Antarctic Ocean* (New York, 1941), 41.
23. Leonid Breitfuß, "The Most Important Voyages and Events in the Arctic since the Beginning of Our History," in *The Arctic*, ed. Leonid Breitfuß (Berlin, 1939), 126–83; Cornelia Lüdecke and Julia Lajus, "The Second International Polar Year 1932–1933," in *The History of the International Polar Years (IPYs)*, ed. Susan Barr and Cornelia Lüdecke (Heidelberg, 2010), 135–73.
24. Debenham, *Voyage of Captain Bellingshausen,* 117n2.
25. Evgenii E. Shvede, "Puteshestvie kapitana Bellinsgauzena v antarkticheskie moria 1819–1821: Perevod s russkogo pod redakciei Franka Dibenkhema (The voyage of Captain Bellingshausen to the Antarctic Seas 1819–1821. Edited by Frank Debenham, London, issued by the Haklyut Society)," *Izvestiia Russkogo geograficheskogo obshchestva* 79, no. 3 (1947): 357–58.
26. Berg, *Russkie otkrytiia*, n17.
27. "Vvedenie," in *Plavaniia shliupov 'Vostok' i 'Mirnyi' v Antarktiku v 1819, 1820 i 1821 godakh*, ed. Aleksandr I. Andreev (Moscow, 1949), 3.
28. Berg, *Russkie otkrytiia*, 12.
29. Andrei A. Grigor'ev and Dmitrii M. Lebedev, "Otkrytie Antarkticheskogo materika russkoi ekspeditsiei Bellinsgauzena-Lazareva 1819–1821 gg.," *Izvestiia Akademii nauk SSSR, seriia geograficheskaia i geofizicheskaia* 13, no. 3 (1949): 118–93.
30. Aleksandr I. Andreev, "Ekspeditsiia F. F. Bellinsgauzena—M. P. Lazareva v Iuzhnyi Ledovityi okean v 1819–1821 gg. i otkrytie russkimi moriakami Antarktidy," in *Plavaniia*

shliupov 'Vostok' i 'Mirnyi' v Antarktiku v 1819, 1820 i 1821 godakh, ed. Aleksandr I. Andreev (Moscow, 1949), 5–16.
31. Stanislav V. Kalesnik, "Russkie otkrytiia v Antarktike," *Slaviane* 4 (1949): 19–21.
32. Berg, *Russkie otkrytiia*, 24.
33. Books about the first (1946–47) and the third (1948–49) trips of the first Soviet Antarctic whale-hunting flotilla have been written by Evgenii L. Shister, each with a different approach regarding Bellingshausen and his discoveries: in the first book, the author pointed out Bellingshausen's discoveries in January 1821 (Shishter, *V Antarktiku*, 39–40), while the second book described the approach to Antarctica on 28 January 1820 (Evgenii L. Shister, *Pod sozvezdiem iuzhnogo kresta: Plavanie sovetskikh kitoboev v Antarktike* [Moscow, Leningrad, 1949], 35–36). The author had used Berg's report of February 1949, not the observations of the members of the second expedition of the *Slava* flotilla (October 1947–June 1948). It is important to note that no publications have appeared about the second *Slava* expedition, even though this was very important to the Russians in the debate of the discovery of Antarctica. There exists only Georgii M. Tauber's report (Georgii M. Tauber, "Plavanie v Antarktike v 1947–1948," *Izvestiia Russkogo geograficheskogo obshchestva* 81, no. 4 [1949]: 369–85), which was presented at the state institute of oceanography on 12 and 19 November 1948. From the printed version of the report, it is evident that the abstract (not appropriate to the text) describing the approach to the Antarctic continent by the *Slava* on 20 March 1948 in 69°10′ southern latitude and 0°52′ western longitude, in the region (69°25′sl and 1°11′wl) where the Russian South Pole expedition had been on 2 February 1820, was added later. According to Tauber, since the conditions were perfect, the Antarctic continent was clearly seen from the *Slava* (Georgii M. Tauber, "Plavanie," 370). It is not known whose idea it was to include that paragraph in the text. But the fact that in March 1948 the question of the discovery of the Antarctic continent on 28 January 1820 was not on the agenda (otherwise the *Slava* would have been sent straight to that position) can provide an answer. It is more probable that it was pure chance that the *Slava* reached the region of Princess Martha Land.
34. Evgenii E. Shvede, "Pervaia russkaia antarkticheskaia ekspeditsiia 1819–1821 gg.," in *Faddei Faddeevich Bellinsgauzen: Dvukratnye izyskaniia v Iuzhnom Ledovitom okeane i plavanie vokrug sveta v prodolzhenie 1819, 1820, i 1821 godov, sovershennye na shliupakh "Vostoke" i "Mirnom,"* ed. Evgenii E. Shvede (Moscow, 1949), 7–30.
35. Berg, *Russkie otkrytiia*, 24; Shvede, "Pervaia russkaia," 27.
36. On the development of ice age theory in the world and especially in the polar regions, see Thomas Krüger, *Discovering the Ice Ages: International Reception and Consequences for a Historical Understanding of Climate* (Boston, 2013); Erki Tammiksaar, "The Russian Antarctic Expedition under the Command of Fabian Gottlieb von Bellingshausen and Its Reception in Russia and the World," *Polar Record* 52, no. 266 (2016): 582–83.
37. Shvede, "Pervaia russkaia," 25, 26.
38. Quoted in Bulkeley, "Bellingshausen's First Accounts," 15.
39. Simonow, *Beschreibung*, 11.
40. Berg, *Russkie otkrytiia*, 17; Andreev, "'Ekspeditsiia F. F. Bellinsgauzena," 170n16.
41. *Plavaniia shliupov 'Vostok' i 'Mirnyi' v Antarktiku v 1819, 1820 i 1821 godakh*, ed. Aleksandr I. Andreev (Moscow, 1949).

42. Ia. Tarnopol'skii, "Dnevnik matrosa Egora Kiseleva," *Vokrug sveta* 4 (1941): 40-43.
43. Debenham, *Voyage of Captain Bellingshausen,* 117; Tarnopol'skii, "Dnevnik matrosa," 41; [Pavel Novosil'skii,] *Iuzhnyi polius': Iz zapisok byvshago morskogo otsicera* (Saint Petersburg, 1853), 28-29.
44. Terry Armstrong, "Four Eye-Witness Accounts of Bellingshausen's Antarctic Voyage of 1819-21," *Polar Record* 6, no. 41 (1951): 85-87.
45. This letter would be published in English in a book by Rip Bulkeley, *Bellingshausen and the Russian Antarctic Expedition, 1819-21* (Basingstoke, 2014).
46. "Pis'ma Mikhaila Petrovicha Lazareva k Alekseiu Antonovichu Shestakovu v g. Krasnyi Smolenskoi gubernii," *Morskoi sbornik* CDIII, no. 1 (1918): 55.

   According to the first *Explanatory Dictionary of the Russian Language* by Vladimir Dal', in a geographical context, the word материк was used in the nineteenth century as a general term for solid ground (from island to continent), but it also denoted a *slope* of a coast, a river, or a mountain, as opposed to level relief (Vladimir Dal', *Tol'kovyi slovar' zhivogo velikorusskogo iazyka*, 2nd ed. [Saint Petersburg, Moscow, 1880], 1:311), for example, to sea level. From the texts by Lazarev and Bellingshausen it follows that they both used the word материк, in the first place, to denote the slope seen, i.e., to describe the relief, not a mainland/continent, which is different from what Soviet scientists have tried to prove with contemporary Russian terminology. Certainly, it is very difficult to interpret what Bellingshausen had meant. The fact is that in the first translation of Bellingshausen's narrative into German in 1842, the translator had not translated the description of the sight on 17 February by Bellingshausen at all (F. Löwe, "Bellingshausens Reise nach der Südsee und Entdeckungen im südlichen Eismeer," *Archiv für wissenschaftliche Kunde von Russland* 2 (1842): 139.
47. Debenham, *Voyage of Captain Bellingshausen,* 127-28.
48. Tarnopol'skii, "Dnevnik matrosa," 41.
49. [Novosil'skii,] *Iuzhnyi polius'*, 30.
50. Berg, *Russkie otkrytiia*, 17-18; Andreev, "'Ekspeditsiia F. F. Bellinsgauzena," 21, 168n4.
51. Vladimir L. Lebedev, *Antarktika* (Moscow, 1957), 20-21; Vladimir L. Lebedev, *Antarctica* (Moscow, 1959), 22.
52. Ivan I. Firsov, *Pervootkryvatel' golubogo kontinenta* (Vladimir, 1963); A. A. Trapeznikov, *Velikie russkie: Russkie puteshestvenniki* (Moscow, 2003), 128-39.
53. Evgenii E. Shvede, "Otkrytie Antarktidy russkimi moreplavateliami v 1819-1821 gg.," in *Antarktika: Materialy po istorii issledovaniia i po fizicheskoi geografii,* ed. E. N. Pavlovskii and Stanislav V. Kalesnik (Moscow, 1958), 50.
54. Mikhail I. Belov, "Shestaia chast' sveta otkryta russkimi moriakami," *Izvestiia Russkogo geograficheskogo obshchestva* 94, no. 2 (1962): 111. Relying mainly on the analysis put forward by Belov, the polar historian A. C. E. Jones accepted that the Russian expedition had discovered the Antarctic continent (A. C. E. Jones, *Antarctica Observed: Who Discovered the Antarctic Continent?* (Caedmon of Whitby, 1982).
55. Debenham, *Voyage of Captain Bellingshausen,* 117.
56. [Novosil'skii,] *Iuzhnyi polius'*, 29.
57. Belov, "Shestaia chast," 110.
58. Tammiksaar and Kiik, "Origin," 186.
59. The point of view of Bellingshausen is also confirmed by what Simonov had seen on 28 January 1820. Simonov has written, "At last we approached 69°30′ S, where impen-

etrable eternal ice set limits to the power of man in moving on [to south]" (Simonow, *Beschreibung*, 11).
60. Faddei F. Bellinsgauzen, *Atlas k puteshestviiu Kapitana Bellinsgauzena v Iuzhnom Ledovitom more i vo krug sveta v prodolzhenii 1819, 1820 i 1820 godov* (Saint Petersburg, 1831).
61. Debenham, *Voyage of Captain Bellingshausen*.
62. Trapeznikov, *Velikie russkie*, 128–39.
63. "Pis'ma Mikhaila Petrovicha Lazareva," 59.

Bibliography

"Admiral Faddei Faddeevich Bellinsgauzen," *Morskoi sbornik* 19, no. 7 (1852): 26–32.
Agassiz, Louis. "Des glaciers, des moraines, et des blocs erratiques." *Bibliothèque universelle de Genève* 12 (1837): 369–94.
———. "Discours prononcé à l'ouverture des séances de la Société Helvétique des Sciences naturelles." *Actes de la Société Helvétique des Sciences naturelles* II (1837): v–xxxii.
Andreev, Aleksandr I. "Ekspeditsiia F. F. Bellingauzena—M. P. Lazareva v Iuzhnyi Ledovityi okean v 1819–1821 gg. i otkrytie russkimi moriakami Antarktidy." In *Plavaniia shliupov 'Vostok' i 'Mirnyi' v Antarktiku v 1819, 1820 i 1821 godakh*, edited by Aleksandr I. Andreev, 5–16. Moscow, 1949.
Armstrong, Terry. "Four Eye-Witness Accounts of Bellingshausen's Antarctic Voyage of 1819–21." *Polar Record* 6, no. 41 (1951): 85–87.
Baer, Karl Ernst von. "Materialien zur Kenntniss des unvergänglichen Boden-Eises in Sibirien." *Berichte und Arbeiten aus der Universitätsbibliothek und dem Universitätsarchiv Giessen*, no. 51, edited by Lorenz King. Giessen, 2001.
Balch, Edwin S. *Antarctica*. Philadelphia, 1902.
Bellinsgauzen, Faddei F. *Atlas k puteshestviiu Kapitana Bellinsgauzena v Iuzhnom Ledovitom more i vokrug sveta v prodolzhenii 1819, 1820 i 1820 godov*. Saint Petersburg, 1831.
———. "Donesenie kapitana 2 ranga Billingauzena iz Porta Zhaksona o svoem plavanii [...]." *Zapiski, izdavaemyia gosudarstvennym admiral'teiskim departamentom otnosiashchiiasia k moreplavaniiu, naukam i slovesnosti* 5 (1823): 201–19.
Belov, Mikhail I. "Shestaia chast' sveta otkryta russkimi moriakami." *Izvestiia Russkogo geograficheskogo obshchestva* 94, no. 2 (1962): 105–14.
Berg, Lev S. "Ocherk istorii russkoi geograficheskoi nauki." *Trudy komissii po istorii znanii*. Vol. 4. Leningrad, 1929.
———. *Ocherki po istorii russkikh geograficheskikh otkrytii*. Moscow, Leningrad, 1946.
———. *Russkie otkrytiia v Antarktike i sovremennyi interes k nei*. Moscow, 1949.
Beritfuß, Leonid. "The Most Important Voyages and Events in the Arctic since the Beginning of our History." In *The Arctic*, edited by Leonid Breitfuß, 126–83. Berlin, 1939.
Bulkeley, Rip. *Bellingshausen and the Russian Antarctic Expedition, 1819–21*. Basingstoke, 2014.
———. "Bellingshausen's First Accounts of His Antarctic Voyage of 1819–1821." *Polar Record* 49, no. 248 (2013): 9–25.
———. "Cold War Whaling: Bellingshausen and the *Slava* Flotilla." *Polar Record* 47, no. 241 (2011): 135–55.
Campbell, R. J., ed. *The Discovery of the South Shetland Islands: The Voyages of the Brig Williams 1819–1820 as Recorded in Contemporary Documents and the Journal of Midshipman C. W. Poynter*. London, 2000.

Charpentier, Jean de. *Sur la cause probable du transport des blocs erratiques de la Suisse.* Paris, 1835.
Dal', Vladimir. *Tol'kovyi slovar' zhivogo velikorusskogo iazyka.* Vol 1. 2nd ed. Saint Petersburg, Moscow, 1880.
Debenham, Frank. "Introduction." In *The Voyage of Captain Bellingshausen to the Antarctic Seas, 1819–1821,* edited by Frank Debenham, no. 1 (91), xi–xxx. London, 1945.
Dokladnaia zapiska ministra inostrannykh del SSSR A. Ia. Vyshinskogo I. V. Stalinu po voprosu o memorandume riadu pravitel'stv o rezhime Antarktike, 20.02.1950. http://www.alexanderyakovlev.org/fond/issues-doc/71711.
Esakov, Vladimir D. *Akademiia nauk v resheniiakh po politbiuro CK RKP(b)-VKP(b) 1922–1952.* Moscow, 2000.
Firsov, Ivan I. *Pervootkryvatel' golubogo kontinenta.* Vladimir, 1963.
Gould, Rupert T. "The First Sighting of the Antarctic Continent." *Geographical Journal* 65, no. 3 (1925): 220–25.
Grigor'ev, Andrei A., and Dmitrii M. Lebedev. "Otkrytie Antarkticheskogo materika russkoi ekspeditsiei Bellinsgauzena-Lazareva 1819–1821 gg." *Izvestiia Akademii nauk SSSR, seriia geograficheskaia i geofizicheskaia* 13, no. 3 (1949): 118–93.
Grigor'ev, Sergei G. *Vokrug iuzhnogo poliusa.* Moscow, 1937.
Jones, A. C. E. *Antarctica Observed: Who Discovered the Antarctic Continent?* Caedmon of Whitby, 1982.
Krementsov, Cf. Nikolai. *Stalinist Science.* Princeton, NJ, 1996.
Krüger, Thomas. *Discovering the Ice Ages: International Reception and Consequences for a Historical Understanding of Climate.* Leiden, Boston, 2013.
Lebedev, Vladimir L. *Antarctica.* Moscow, 1959.
———. *Antarktika.* Moscow, 1957.
Löwe, F. "Bellingshausens Reise nach der Südsee und Entdeckungen im südlichen Eismeer." *Archiv für wissenschaftliche Kunde von Russland* 2 (1842): 125–74.
Lüdecke, Cornelia, and Julia Lajus. "The Second International Polar Year 1932–1933." In *The History of the International Polar Years (IPYs),* edited by Susan Barr and Cornelia Lüdecke, 135–73. Heidelberg, 2010.
[Novosil'skii, Pavel.] *Shestoi kontinent ili kratkoe obozrenie plavanii k iugu ot Kuka do Rossa.* Saint Petersburg, 1854.
———. *Iuzhnyi polius': Iz zapisok byvshago morskogo ofitsera.* Saint Petersburg, 1853.
"Otkrytie novogo materika v Iuzhnom polusharii." *Zhurnal ministerstva narodnogo prosveshcheniia* 35, no. 7 (1842): 48–52.
Owen, Russell. *The Antarctic Ocean.* New York, 1941.
"Pis'ma Mikhaila Petrovicha Lazareva k Alekseiu Antonovichu Shestakovu v g. Krasnyi Smolenskoi gubernii." *Morskoi sbornik* CDIII, no. 1 (1918): 51–66.
Plavaniia shliupov 'Vostok' i 'Mirnyi' v Antarktiku v 1819, 1820 i 1821 godakh, ed. Aleksandr I. Andreev. Moscow, 1949.
Pollock, Ethan. *Stalin and the Soviet Science Wars.* Princeton, NJ, 2006.
"Postanovlenie obshchego sobraniia Akademii Nauk SSSR 11 ianvaria 1949 goda." In *Voprosy istorii otechestvennoi nauki: Obshchee sobranie Akademi nauk SSSR posviashchennoe istorii otechestvennoi nauki 5–11 ianvaria 1949 g.,* edited by Sergei I. Vavilov, 880–84. Moscow, Leningrad, 1949.
Rabinovich, Ivan O. *Shestaia chast' sveta (Vopros ob Antarkticheskom materike).* Saint Petersburg, 1908.

Shister, Evgenii L. *Pod sozvezdiem iuzhnogo kresta: Plavanie sovetskikh kitoboev v Antarktike.* Moscow, Leningrad, 1949.

———. *V Antarktiku za kitami.* Moscow, 1948.

Shokal'skii, Iulii M. "Poliarnyia strany Iuzhnogo polushariia." In *Entsiklopedicheskii slovar'*, edited by K. K. Arsen'ev and F. F. Petrushevskii, XXIV[a], 492–94. Saint Petersburg, 1898.

———. "Stoletie so vremeni otpravleniia Russkoi antarkticheskoi ekspeditsii pod komandoiu F. Bellingauzena i M. Lazareva 4 iiuliia 1819 g. iz Kronshtadta." *Izvestiia Russkogo geograficheskogo obshchestva* 60, no. 2 (1928): 176–212.

Shvede, Evgenii E. "Otkrytie Antarktidy russkimi moreplavateliami v 1819–1821 gg." In *Antarktika: Materialy po istorii issledovaniia i po fizicheskoi geografii*, edited by E. N. Pavlovskii and Stanislav V. Kalesnik, 6–53. Moscow, 1958.

———. "Pervaia russkaia antarkticheskaia ekspeditsiia 1819–1821 gg." In *Faddei Faddeevich Bellinsgauzen: Dvukratnye izyskaniia v Iuzhnom Ledovitom okeane i plavanie vokrug sveta v prodolzhenie 1819, 1820, i 1821 godov, sovershennye na shliupakh "Vostoke" i "Mirnom,"* edited by Evgenii E. Shvede, 7–30. Moscow, 1949.

———. "Puteshestvie kapitana Bellingsgauzena v antarkticheskie moria 1819–1821: Perevod s russkogo pod redakciei Franka Dibenkhema (The voyage of Captain Bellingshausen to the Antarctic Seas 1819–1821. Edited by Frank Debenham, London, issued by the Haklyut Society)." *Izvestiia Russkogo geograficheskogo obshchestva* 79, no. 3 (1947): 357–58.

Simonow, Ivan M. *Beschreibung einer neuen Entdeckungsreise in das südliche Eismeer.* Translated by M. Banyi. Vienna, 1824.

Smirnov, Valentin G. "Proekt M. F. Mori ob issledovanii iuzhnykh poliarnykh stran." *Izvestiia Russkogo geograficheskogo obshchestva* 130, no. 5 (1998): 46–54.

Sonin, Anatolii S. *Bor'ba s kosmopolitizmom v sovetskoi nauke.* Moscow, 2011.

Tammiksaar, Erki. "The Russian Antarctic Expedition under the Command of Fabian Gottlieb von Bellingshausen and Its Reception in Russia and the World." *Polar Record* 52, no. 266 (2016): 578–600.

Tammiksaar, Erki, and Tarmo Kiik. "Origins of the Russian Antarctic Expedition: 1819–1821." *Polar Record* 49, no. 249 (2013): 180–92.

Tarnopol'skii, Ya. "Dnevnik matrosa Egora Kiseleva." *Vokrug sveta* 4 (1941): 40–43.

Tauber, Georgii M. "Plavanie v Antarktike v 1947–1948." *Izvestiia Russkogo geograficheskogo obshchestva* 81, no. 4 (1949): 369–85.

The Voyage of Captain Bellingshausen to the Antarctic Seas, 1819–1821. Edited by Frank Debenham, Hakluyt Society 2nd Series, nos. 1–2 (91–92). London, 1945.

Trapeznikov, A. A. *Velikie russkie: Russkie puteshestvenniki.* Moscow, 2003.

"Vvedenie." In *Plavaniia shliupov 'Vostok' i 'Mirnyi' v Antarktiku v 1819, 1820 i 1821 godakh*, edited by Aleksandr I. Andreev, 3. Moscow, 1949.

Vvedenskii, Nikolai. "K voprosu o russkikh otkrytiiakh v Antarktike v 1819–1821 godakh, v svete noveishikh geograficheskikh issledovanii." *Izvestiia Russkogo geograficheskogo obshchestva* 73, no. 1 (1941), 118–22.

———. *V poiskakh Iuzhnogo materika.* Leningrad, Moscow, 1940.

"Zhizneopisanie sostavliavshago pri osobe ego Imperatorskogo Velichestva admirala Faddeia Faddeevicha Bellinsgauzena." *Severnaia Pchela*, nos. 91–92 (1853): 363–64, 367–68.

 CHAPTER 4

The Subarctic
A Classic Soviet Study of the Tundra

Denis J. B. Shaw

A. A. Grigor'ev's classic study, *The Subarctic*,[1] published in 1946, was part of a series of works by the author titled Essays on the Characteristics of the Basic Types of Physical-Geographical Environment. As the author states in the introduction to his book, work for the first three studies, on the equatorial, tropical, and arctic belts, and the introductory parts of the studies on the subarctic and temperate belts, had been completed before the war, and all this work was subsequently published in the series Problems of Physical Geography. Work on the subarctic, however, was seriously delayed by the war, but what subsequently emerged was much longer than its companion studies and was eventually recognized as a classic in its field. A second edition was published in 1956.[2] One reason for the additional length of both editions is emphasized by Grigor'ev when he states that, since most of the subarctic region lies within the territory of the USSR, an extended study is important for both scientific and practical reasons. Although Grigor'ev was never to specialize on the north only, it was to be a continuing part of his academic interests throughout his career.

This chapter is concerned to show not only how *The Subarctic* was a substantial contribution to both Soviet and international understanding of this important part of the globe but also that, together with associated research on natural zonation and the earth's heat and water balance, it advanced scientific understanding of the global environment as a whole. Thus despite, or perhaps to some degree because of, the difficulties associated with the Cold War,[3] our present-day conceptions of such processes as climate change are to some degree derived from Soviet scientific advances made during this period.

The Scientific Career of A. A. Grigor'ev

Andrei Aleksandrovich Grigor'ev (1883–1968), who directed the Academy of Sciences Institute of Geography from the 1930s to 1951, had a varied academic career.[4] From a middle-class background, he studied at Saint Petersburg University from 1901, graduating in 1907. Continuing his studies in Berlin and then Heidelberg, where he enrolled in the seminar of the eminent geographical philosopher Alfred Hettner, Grigor'ev returned to Russia in 1914, having been awarded a doctorate under Hettner's supervision. After working on the Brokgauz and Efron encyclopedia, he joined the Council for the Study of Productive Forces (KEPS), which had been established in 1915 under the chairmanship of V. I. Vernadskii and the auspices of the Academy of Sciences with a remit to survey the country's resources as a contribution to the war effort. He quickly rose to head of the organization's geographical section. Well into the 1920s, Grigor'ev was regarded as an economic (or socioeconomic) geographer and a strong proponent of Hettner's chorological[5] approach to geography. However, as the latter was coming under increasing political attack for violating Marxist ideology (for example, by allegedly subscribing to geographical determinism), he migrated into the physical side of the discipline. This move was encouraged by his participation in a number of geographical expeditions of a physical nature, including one to Iakutiia in 1925–26. His early studies on the north included one on the Bol'shezemel'skaia Tundra in northeast European Russia (1924) and another on the geology, relief, and soils of the northwestern part of the Lena-Aldan Plateau in the Soviet Far East (1925).[6] Meanwhile, on Grigor'ev's suggestion, KEPS sprouted a division to study the country's industrial geography, and the geographical activities of KEPS were reorganized in 1930 to become the Geomorphological Institute. Eventually, in 1936, this was transformed into the Institute of Geography in Moscow with A. A. Grigor'ev as director.

Grigor'ev's book, *The Subarctic*, was based upon a concept of physical geography that he termed "the single physical-geographical process." In Grigor'ev's view, this way of approaching geography was much more in keeping with the tenets of dialectical materialism than the then prevailing notion of landscape science.[7] The "single physical-geographical process" was conceptualized as a unity of the many physical processes operating in the earth's "geographical envelope," above the earth's core but below the upper atmosphere, under the influence of solar radiation and corresponding with the sphere of life or biosphere. Grigor'ev argued that this idea endowed geography with a distinctive subject matter in accordance with Friedrich Engels's teaching, which was that each science should study its own distinctive form of the "movement of matter."[8] Because, unlike landscape science, Grigor'ev's approach was focused on process rather than on a material entity (namely, landscape), it had a dynamic quality, which made it, in his view, commensurate with the principles of dialectical materialism. The idea of a "single physical-geographical process" was not a new one, being derived from nineteenth-century German concepts of the "geographical envelope." But it was Grigor'ev who endowed it with ideological and political significance in the conditions of the Stalinist USSR, declaring it to be the central focus of geography for the future. In an article published in 1946, for example, he described his idea as a "new approach" to geography, contrasting with all earlier approaches, and declared that "the study of the earth's surface precisely in this way most easily allows the discernment and study of the interconnections and interactions between the components of the environment, for which reason this must become the basic theoretical task of physical geography."[9] By this period, the process (*protsessual'nyi*) approach dominated the work of the institute's physical geographers, while Grigor'ev attempted by every means to achieve its dominance over the discipline as a whole.

Historical and Theoretical Background to *The Subarctic*

Ultimately both the process approach and landscape science derived from Russian studies of the environment, which dated back two centuries. In 1725, as part of his policy to modernize Russia, Peter the Great had founded the Imperial Academy of Sciences in Saint Petersburg with the express aim, among other things, of exploring the vast reaches of the Russian Empire, much of which was little known at the time, and of discovering and exploiting its enormous resources.

From 1725 the academy began to send out a series of scientific expeditions to explore, survey, and map Russia's territory. Although Russians had long been aware of the fact that the natural environment across Russia was far from uniform, only in the eighteenth century did the exact character of that variation begin to become clear. What was now being realized was that, at least in European Russia and West Siberia, the territory was spanned by a series of natural belts running from west to east and gradually merging from north to south: for example, the tundra in the north, the coniferous forest or taiga belt further south, and the steppe belt to the south of that. By the late nineteenth century, these latitudinal belts were becoming known as "natural" or "natural-historical" zones.[10]

By the middle to late nineteenth century, after more than a century of exploration and scientific study of Russia's territories, scientists had a fairly comprehensive understanding of the geographical character of their country's natural zones. What they lacked, however, was a well-founded understanding of the processes that produce them (to which Grigor'ev's later work was to make a significant contribution). Here, two nineteenth-century scholars were to make all the difference. The first was the soil scientist, Vasilii Vasil'evich Dokuchaev (1846–1903) who was to hold a chair in natural science at Saint Petersburg University. Dokuchaev's scientific trajectory took him by way of geology, quaternary studies, geomorphology, and hydrology into the study of soils, with particular reference to the black earths of the forest-steppe and steppe regions of European Russia. Since these territories were of vital importance to Russian agriculture at the time and were prone to drought, it was obviously important to develop a fully scientific understanding of their environment.

Dokuchaev developed two basic scientific ideas concerning soils that were to be of key significance for the future. Firstly, his understanding of soils was genetic, in the sense that he regarded them as being formed over long periods of time by the activity of a series of soil-forming factors, notably the underlying geology, relief, climate, hydrology, vegetation, fauna, and human society, with climate as the most significant factor. Soils were therefore to be seen as complex natural bodies in their own right, interlinking the inorganic and the organic in a unique way. Secondly, toward the end of his life, Dokuchaev came to see soil zones as arranged latitudinally to reflect the natural zones. Thus, tundra soils can only be found in the northern tundra, and similarly black earths only in the forest steppe and steppe to the south. And this was true not only of Russia but also globally. Thus, the climatologist M. I. Budyko later emphasized the importance of Dokuchaev's work: "It was Dokuchaev who first drew attention to the existence of geographical zones, noting that within wide territories (zones), natural conditions retain many common features that change perceptibly from zone to zone. ... Under the influence of the earth's spherical shape, climate, plants and animals are distributed from north to south over the earth's surface in a strictly determined order.[11]" This is also true of soils. What Budyko was pointing to here was the fact that, unlike earlier scholars, Dokuchaev was beginning to approach an understanding of the processes underlying the phenomenon of natural zones. However, he died before he could develop his ideas any further.

One other significant scholar who was to have a profound effect on views of the physical environment, including natural zonation and the processes that give rise to it, was the climatologist Alexander Ivanovich Voeikov (1842–1916). After university study in Saint Petersburg and Germany—specializing in meteorology, in which the Germans excelled at the time—Voeikov returned to Saint Petersburg to serve as secretary of the Russian Geographical Society's Meteorological Commission, and he also held a series of academic posts in the university. His major work, *The Climate of the Globe and of Russia in Particular*, published in 1884 and in German three years later, was a summary of meteorological understanding up to that point.[12] This particularly underlined the basic importance of solar radiation and its variations across the earth's surface to an understanding of meteorological and climatic processes and of climatic circulation. A key point, which was to have major significance for future meteorological studies, including of the north, was his insistence on the need to construct a credit and debit balance for the solar heat received and also lost by the globe with its atmospheric and hydrological envelopes and the ways in which this is distributed by atmospheric and oceanic circulation patterns. He also pointed to the need to gather more data on atmospheric moisture and on the balances between precipitation and evaporation in different places. He devoted considerable attention to snow cover as an important factor influencing the earth's heat balance.

In the early years of the twentieth century, the focus of physical geography, according to A. A. Grigor'ev,[13] swung toward empirical studies. Instead of seeking for the laws governing the variable character of the natural environment in theoretical studies, scholars tended to study empirical generalizations, such as variations in the ratio of annual precipitation to annual temperature, the ratio of precipitation to evaporability, and so on. However, it was found that such generalizations when mapped as isolines only very partially coincided with the boundaries of the natural zones and that this was because the basic relationships and processes in nature that govern such linkages were only partly understood. Gradually scientists came to the conclusion that the key to such understanding, as foreshadowed in the work of Dokuchaev and Voeikov, was the relationship in the environment between heat and moisture, or the heat and moisture balance, and a particular way of conceptualizing this, later known as the "radiation index of dryness."[14] Some of the most significant work in the study of the heat and water balance and its implications for the understanding of natural zones was to be undertaken by A. A. Grigor'ev of the Institute of Geography and M. I. Budyko, director of the Main Geophysical Observatory in Leningrad. This work began in the 1930s and extended into the 1960s.

Many problems stood in the way of the study of heat and moisture balances across the earth's surface. One was the acute lack of empirical data to support such studies. Not only were there few points where a reasonably comprehensive range of data was collected (and this was especially true for the northern regions), but even where this did occur the range was inadequate for measuring the wide variety of variables that needed to be calculated. Another was that it took many years to develop the theory required to explain the phenomena observed. Thus while it was argued that the successful development of such a theory would need to be based on the study of balances, quite how these balances worked was not well understood. Grigor'ev argued that his bid to reconstruct physical geography in the 1930s to move away from landscape science in order to focus on the geographical envelope and its spatial variations (a move that, as we have seen, had a political as well as a scientific motivation) would allow the science to develop a more sophisticated understanding of the material and energy exchanges and balances involved. Yet another problem was the sheer scale of the ambitions that propelled this program forward. Referring to his series of works between 1938 and 1946, which was designed to encapsulate his scheme, Grigor'ev wrote as follows:

> The basic aim of this work was a study of the structure, dynamics, and development of the geographic zones and subzones making up each geographic belt;[15] an investigation of the characteristics of the interrelationships and interdependencies, and of the interchange of matter and energy between components of the geographic environment; a determination ... of the biomass of the plant cover and animal life of the various zones ..., all ... done with the broadest possible utilization of the balance method. The aims of the study also included the determination of the characteristics of interaction and interchange between the zones making up the geographic belts and the determination, on the basis of all these data, of the basic laws of the structure, dynamics, and development of the geographic environment.[16]

Thus the scheme envisaged a truly comprehensive program, encompassing not only the nonliving parts of the environment but also its organic elements and exploring the relationships between them. Even now, many aspects of these relationships are only poorly understood, testifying to the enormity of the scientific ambitions that Grigor'ev embraced. Such ambitions can only be understood in the context of the grandiose schemes of nature transformation that were embraced by the Stalin regime from the 1930s onward.

The Subarctic

Grigor'ev claimed that the aim of the series to which *The Subarctic* belonged was "to develop the basis for formulating a theory of geographical zonality as one of the fundamental geographic laws."[17] He saw this as completing the work begun by Dokuchaev in the 1890s. Thus, Grigor'ev argued that his notion of the single physical-geographical process derived from two "general physical-geographical laws" discovered by Dokuchaev: namely the law of "the wholeness and indivisibility" of the natural environment, and that of geographical zonality.[18] But while Dokuchaev had arguably only begun to discern the heat and moisture balance as the key to understanding the exact character of these laws, Grigor'ev believed that herein lay the future of environmental understanding.

The heat and water balance idea focuses on the relationship between the heat available in the environment, derived largely from solar radiation, and available moisture to explain the basis for zonality, since both will vary by latitude. That relationship is far from straightforward, however, since it is affected by a variety of factors such as seasonality. Furthermore, the different geographical zones cannot be studied in isolation since they are all part of the earth's total environment and therefore have to be approached holistically. The need was to develop a series of indices to measure the effects of the different factors that influence zonality. Much of the basic work, as indicated already, was done by Grigor'ev and Budyko, at first separately and then in association. Particularly important for conceptions of zonality was the development of the idea of the "radiation index of dryness" (or of aridity), which calculates a thermal parameter in terms of radiation values or heat units (rather than the less reliable temperature values). The sum of heat units is then balanced against precipitation to form a moisture parameter. The balance between thermal and moisture parameters provides a basis for climate classification, which, when mapped, was found by Budyko and Grigor'ev to correspond well with the pattern of natural zones or belts, particularly in lowlands in temperate and tropical latitudes[19] (see table below).

The basic presentation of material in *The Subarctic* follows the lines already established in Grigor'ev's earlier publications of the late 1930s on the equatorial, tropical, and arctic belts.[20] The first chapter, just two pages long, considers the extent of the subarctic belt and its division into subzones. Like modern climatologists and ecologists, Grigor'ev avoids a strict definition of boundaries, preferring to consider the subarctic as a product of the prevalent heat and water balance in the region. He points to the following as the typical characteristics of this belt:

1. Low quantities of heat energy not only in the cold part of the year but also in the warm part, connected with the strongly evident negative annual balance of radiation energy and the clear predominance in summer atmospheric circulation of cold air masses, mainly of arctic origin.

2. Low levels of the average monthly indicators of the radiation balance in the lighter months of the year (May–July), both positive and negative.

3. Significant development of cyclonic activity and, connected with this, a clear predominance during the warm months of periods with a strongly marked positive moisture balance over periods with a negative balance.

4. Low average air temperatures in the warm months (no higher than ten to twelve degrees above zero at most) and very low temperatures in the thawing horizons of the soil.

A contemporaneous study by M. I. Budyko showed how these key characteristics related to the subarctic and the contrast with other natural zones.[21] The key relationships are illustrated in table 4.1.

Grigor'ev uses the key characteristics to identify the geographical extent of the subarctic. He notes that the climatic characteristics coincide with the tundra geobotanical zone, which is distributed along the northern and northeastern fringes of the continents of the northern hemisphere. In the eastern

Table 4.1. Geographic zonality.

Moisture Supply (radiation index of dryness)	Heat Energy Base (Radiation Balance)		
	Less than 0 (high latitude)	0–50 Cal/cm²/year (south Arctic, subarctic and middle Arctic latitudes)	50–75 Cal/cm²/year (subtropical latitudes)
Less than 0 (extremely excessive)	Perpetual snow		
0–1 (excessive)			
0–0.2		Arctic desert	
0.2–0.4		Tundra (tree patches in south)	Subtropical hemihylea with swamps
0.4–0.6		Northern and middle taiga	Subtropical rainforests
0.6–0.8		Southern taiga and mixed forests	Same
0.8–1.0		Deciduous forest and forest steppe	Same
1–2 (moderately inadequate)		Steppe	Hard-leaved subtropical forests and shrubs Subtropical steppe
2–3 (inadequate)		Semideserts of the temperate belt	Subtropical semidesert
More than 3 (extremely inadequate)		Deserts of the temperate belt	Subtropical desert

Source: A. A. Grigor'ev, "The Heat and Moisture Regime and Geographic Zonality," *Soviet Geography* 2, no. 7 (1961): 11–12.

part of the territory of the European USSR, where local radiation and climatic conditions (at least in the warmer months) are closest on average to those of the higher latitudes as a whole, the belt is found between 67 and 73 degrees north. Elsewhere it is displaced farther north or south according to local climatic circumstances. Thus, its exact position is affected by the harsh continental climate of eastern Asia, the warmer climatic effects of the North Atlantic Drift in the Barents Sea, or the cold climate of the northern Pacific. The focus of Grigor'ev's study, however, is the lowland part of northeastern European USSR, especially in the area of the Bol'shezemel'skaia Tundra (the focus of his earlier, 1920s study).

An earlier study of local environmental circumstances in the subarctic led him to subdivide the latter into two subzones: the near-arctic to the north (coinciding with the arctic tundra of the geobotanists) and the near-boreal to the south (coinciding with the subarctic tundra). A more precise definition of the relative location of these subzones is now given. Apart from their geobotanical differences, their locations depend on differences in the radiation balance and the effects of atmospheric circulation.

It is entirely in keeping with a study based on heat and moisture balances that chapter 2, consisting of twenty-two pages, should be devoted not to geomorphological processes, as would be traditional in Western physical geography, but to climate. As well as giving an overview of general climatic conditions, the chapter gives a detailed analysis of the radiation and thermal conditions of the summer period; atmospheric circulation in the warm months and associated phenomena such as wind, humidity, and precipitation; and an account of the climatic regime in the winter half of the year. In later studies of the subarctic belt, which compared this belt with other belts, the subarctic was defined as a region of excessive moisture supply in the environment and a low radiation balance (see table 4.1). In other words, there is insufficient heat to evaporate the moisture available. In Grigor'ev's view, this explained the entire character of the physical environment.

Chapters 3 and 4 are devoted to a discussion of hydro-geomorphological processes (notably, the effects of permafrost on hydro-geomorphological processes, the regimes of rivers and lakes, erosion and denudation, and microrelief) and soil-formation processes. Soils are, of course, essential to vegetation, but in cold, northern environments their evolution from ahumic soils (little more than fine rock debris in the simplest cases) to humic or organic soils may take hundreds or even thousands of years, inhibited by cold, permafrost, ground ice, and other factors. The character of these soils naturally restricts the kinds of vegetation that they can support.

Chapter 5, which runs to thirty pages, considers the vegetation of the subarctic or tundra. Tundra soils usually contain relatively little organic matter and are characterized by low levels of biological activity. Tundra vegetation develops during the limited period of the absence of snow cover and typically consists of mosses, lichens, and, in the south, bushes and stunted trees.

The principal feature of the landscapes of the subarctic is the fact that the region lies north of the tree line. Grigor'ev and Budyko believed that in these latitudes tree growth was inhibited not only by the low temperatures but also by moisture conditions unfavorable to tree growth.[22] Thus the considerable excess of available moisture over evaporability maintains a high humidity in the soil throughout the year. The development of the tree root system is impeded by the lack of gaseous oxygen in the soil.

Chapter 6 turns to a consideration of the fauna of the subarctic. As we might expect, the fauna is considered in its ecological context, including habitat, adaptation to climatic conditions, migrations, and so on.

The remaining chapters of *The Subarctic* summarize the basic energy and moisture balances of the region together with balances of minerals and organic materials; the variants of the subarctic environment to be found in East Siberia, the Far East, the Murmansk region, and North America; the character of vertical zonation within the subarctic; the region's long-term evolution (which was seen as a key to the understanding of the environment); and finally a summary of the book's main findings. The latter emphasizes the fact that, as expected, climatic conditions and other environmental circumstances are governed above all by the radiation balance and the relationship between heat and moisture. This confirmed Grigor'ev's earlier finding in respect of the earth's other belts. Also underlined is the subarctic's close relationship with the earth's other belts both in terms of atmospheric circulation and biological characteristics. Finally, in keeping with the Stalinist accent on the applied importance of science, the text makes a number of suggestions regarding better use of the belt's resources, such as improving the soils and making more use of the region's biological endowment.[23]

The Second Edition of *The Subarctic*

The first edition of *The Subarctic* had been published by the USSR Academy of Sciences in Moscow and Leningrad in 1946. By contrast, the second was published by the State Publishing House of Geographical Literature in Moscow in 1956.[24] In his introduction to the updated work, the author provides an explanation of why the new edition was considered necessary:

> In the ten years since the publication of the first edition of this book, geographical science has advanced rapidly. New very important data on solar radiation and its role in the geographical environment have emerged. The study of the structure and development of the earth's geographical environment has

led to the need to divide its components into those which operate everywhere and those which are restricted to defined zones, which in turn has led to more precise understanding of the roles that particular components play in the environment. Our understanding of geomorphological, climatic, and botanic processes operating within the environment, all of which play a leading role in the dynamics and development of that environment, have been deepened and become more precise. All these and other successes of geographical science have stimulated further work on the physical-geographical laws, and helped to throw new light on several important physical-geographical problems.[25]

Furthermore, he adds, the intervening period has added significantly to our knowledge of nature in the tundra belt in particular.

All this, according to Grigor'ev, has meant the need to rework the text significantly both from a theoretical perspective and in the light of the new data that have become available, but without increasing the book's overall length. Although Grigor'ev does not make the point, it seems possible that what also motivated the publication of a second edition was the growing Soviet interest in the north associated with prospective energy and mineral developments. Clearly a thoroughgoing scientific analysis of the subarctic's environment was likely to prove significant in the context of plans for the region's settlement and economic development.

The essential structure of the new edition follows that of the previous one. What is immediately noticeable, however, is that much more detail is provided about the spatial differences within the subarctic belt, both longitudinal and also latitudinal. In discussing the flora, use is also made of new theoretical concepts, such as the ecological concept of "phytotsenosis" (plant association).

Among the most important differences between the two editions was that much more was now known about northern climates, although there remained many gaps in the available data. Because of this, reliance still had to be placed on botanical maps, since plants were regarded as the best indicators of climate. More was now known about such matters as evaporation rates and moisture conditions, as well as biological processes, but much estimation was still involved, especially for the Siberian and Far Eastern regions. Nevertheless, overall there was greater possibility for precise measurement and thus for the development of quantitative rather than qualitative indices. With regard to theoretical matters, the previous edition had suffered from a lack of sufficient data on the distribution over the earth's surface of quantitative indices of components of the radiation and water balance equations due to the absence of methods for determining a number of the components. However, beginning in the mid-1940s, meteorologists, hydrologists, and oceanologists had begun to accumulate data on radiation and heat balances of the earth's surface and to work on the theory. Also, water-balance research expanded, including the composition of maps of a number of components of the water balance of the land. Much of this research was to be undertaken by Grigor'ev in association with M. I. Budyko. The latter was to develop several aspects of the research, especially those involving biological processes.

Grigor'ev's theoretical conclusion repeats many of the points made in the previous edition, including the fact that the same geographical laws operate in the subarctic as elsewhere and in respect of the complex interconnections between the subarctic and other belts.[26] He especially emphasizes the point that new data on radiational balances collected by the Main Geophysical Observatory in Leningrad have now permitted the explanation of some of the main latitudinal differences between parts of the subarctic.

With regard to his practical conclusions, Grigor'ev points to the significance of his work for possibilities of agricultural improvement in the subarctic, including making more use of the extended daylight hours in the summer period. The main hindrances to plant growth are noted as being the lack of heat resources, the lateness of the spring thaw, the excess moisture conditions, and the strong, cold winds, especially in early spring. Many of these, he believes, as well as problems associated with livestock farming and with making greater use of local faunal resources, can be resolved by taking appropriate measures, and he points to the work of the Ministry of Agriculture's Scientific Research Institute of Polar Agriculture in confirmation of this.[27] From a modern perspective, of course, what is missing is any apparent concern for the conservation of nature in this fragile region.

Conclusion

The international significance of the work of Grigor'ev and his associate M. I. Budyko was emphasized in the American editorial introduction to the 1974 English-language version of the latter's book *Climate and Life*:[28]

> This work warranted translation because 1. it is an authoritative statement of the new concepts of climatic analysis that are based on the laws of the conservation of mass and of energy that have developed in many parts of the world in the past twenty-five years, but nowhere as comprehensively as in the great Voeikov Geophysical Observatory in Leningrad and 2. It applies these energy-budget concepts to important questions in the biology of the planet. ... The first English-language summary of the research was first brought by Budyko to the World Meteorological Conference at Washington DC in 1956. The importance of the work was immediately recognized and it was then translated into English and later Japanese.[29]

The editor notes that the English translation of Budyko's 1950s work was undertaken by the Office of Climatology of the US Weather Bureau and other groups just getting involved in energy research and its applications. "Many areas of geophysics in North America, including climatology, hydrology and meteorology, were powerfully strengthened by the methods and global-scale data published in this translation as *The Heat Balance of the Earth's Surface* (1958)."[30] There were, he notes, two associated atlases, and the material subsequently provided the basis for many other studies at a variety of scales.

Grigor'ev's work on the subarctic, therefore, together with its associated work, was part of a pioneering venture by the Soviets casting new light on the character of the natural environment both at the global scale and at the regional. As we have seen, the venture had its origins in a long tradition of Russian environmental study, though it may well have been spurred on in the 1950s by Cold War considerations and undoubtedly contributed to our current understanding of global environmental change. Only now, with growing concern about the future of the planet, is the significance of some of this work beginning to be recognized.

Acknowledgments

The author wishes to thank the UK Economic and Social Research Council (ref. no. RES-062-23-1734) and the Arts and Humanities Research Council (ref. no. AH-G011028/1), who funded this research. Thanks are also due to Martin Parry (Imperial College, London), Richard Powell (SPRI, University of Cambridge), and John Thornes (University of Birmingham) for their incisive comments on an earlier draft of this chapter.

Denis J. B. Shaw is honorary senior research fellow in the School of Geography, Earth and Environmental Sciences, University of Birmingham. He is a specialist on the historical geography of Russia with particular reference to the history of geographical and related environmental sciences. Among other works, he is the author of *Russia in the Modern World: A New Geography* (1999), and, together with Jonathan D. Oldfield, of *The Development of Russian Environmental Thought: Scientific and Geographical Perspectives on the Natural Environment* (2016).

Notes

1. Andrei A. Grigor'ev, *Subarktika*, 1st ed. (Leningrad, Moscow, 1946).
2. Andrei A. Grigor'ev, *Subarktika*, 2nd ed. (Moscow, 1956).

3. It seems reasonable to suppose that Soviet interest in global environmental change at this point was partly motivated by military considerations.
4. Igor M. Zabelin, *Puteshestvie v glub' nauki (Akademik A. A. Grigor'ev)* (Moscow, 1976).
5. "Chorological" is derived from the Greek word *khoros*, meaning region or place. Thus a chorological geography would be a discipline focused on the study of regions or places.
6. Andrei A. Grigor'ev, *Geologiia i rel'ef Bol'shezemel'skoi tundry i sviazannye s nim problemy* (Moscow, 1924); Andrei A. Grigor'ev, *Geologiia, rel'ef i pochvy severo-zapadnoi chasti Lensko-Aldanskogo plato i Verkhoianskogo khrebta po dannym ekspeditsii 1925 g. Materialy Komissii po izucheniiu Iakutskoi Respubliki*, vol. 4 (Leningrad, 1926).
7. Denis J. B. Shaw and Jonathan D. Oldfield, "Landscape Science: A Russian Geographical Tradition," *Annals of the Association of American Geographers* 97 (2007).
8. Denis J. B. Shaw and Jonathan D. Oldfield, "Scientific, Institutional and Personal Rivalries among Soviet Geographers in the Late Stalin Era," *Europe-Asia Studies* 60, no. 8 (2008): 1397–1418.
9. Andrei A. Grigor'ev, "Nekotorye itogi razrabotki novykh idei v fizicheskoi geografii," *Izvestiia Akademiia Nauk SSSR Seriia geograficheskaia i geofizicheskaia* 10, no. 2 (1946): 139–68.
10. See note 20 below.
11. Mikhail I. Budyko, *Global Ecology* (Moscow, 1980), 136.
12. Alexander I. Voeikov, *Klimaty zemnogo shara: v osobennosti Rossii* (Saint Petersburg, 1884).
13. Andrei A. Grigor'ev, "The Heat and Moisture Regime and Geographic Zonality," *Soviet Geography* 2, no. 7 (1961): 3.
14. Ibid., 8. For more on this, see below.
15. See note 20 below regarding Grigor'ev's use of terminology here.
16. Grigor'ev, "Heat and Moisture Regime," 5–6.
17. Ibid., 5.
18. Andrei A. Grigor'ev, "O nekotorykh osnovnykh problemakh fizicheskoi geografii," *Izvestiia Akademii nauk SSSR: Seriia geograficheskaia*, no. 6 (1957): 3.
19. For further explanation of this idea regarding the balance of heat and moisture, see Grigor'ev, "Heat and Moisture Regime," 6–12, and Paul E. Lydolph, *Climates of the Soviet Union* (Amsterdam, New York, 1977), 357–59. The formula for the radiation index of dryness is R/Lr, where R is the yearly radiation balance at the earth's surface, L the latent heat of condensation, and r the mean annual precipitation.
20. One of the difficulties of this period is the inconsistent use by authors of terms like "zones" and "belts." Thus, Grigor'ev uses the term "belt" for what we have termed above "natural zone" (or in Dokuchaev's terminology, "natural-historical zone"), and uses the term "zone" as a subdivision of the belt. Henceforward we shall follow Grigor'ev's use of the term "belt," but use the term "subzone" for what he calls a "zone."
21. Mikhail I. Budyko, *Isparenie v estestvennykh usloviiakh* (Leningrad, 1948).
22. Andrei A. Grigor'ev and Mikhail I. Budyko, "Classification of Climates in the USSR," *Izvestiia Akademii nauk SSSR: Seriia geograficheskaia*, no. 3 (1959): 3–19.
23. This was of course the era of Lysenko, when exaggerated views regarding the prospects for environmental improvement were widely entertained.
24. Grigor'ev, *Subarktika*, 2nd ed. (1956).

25. Ibid., 3.
26. Ibid., 205.
27. Ibid., 206-9.
28. Mikhail I. Budyko, *Climate and Life* (New York, London, 1974).
29. Ibid., vii.
30. Ibid.

Bibliography

Budyko, Mikhail I. *Climate and Life*. New York, 1974.
———. *Global Ecology*. Moscow, 1980.
———. *Isparenie v estestvennykh usloviiakh*. Leningrad, 1948.
Grigor'ev, Andrei A. *Geologiia i rel'ef Bol'shezemel'skoi tundry I sviazannye s nim problem*. Moscow, 1924.
———. *Geologiia, rel'ef i pochvy severo-zapadnoi chasti Lensko-Aldanskogo plato i Verkhoianskogo khrebta po dannym ekspeditsii 1925 g. Materialy Komissii po izucheniiu Iakutskoi Respubliki*. Vol. 4. Leningrad, 1926.
———. "Nekotorye itogi razrabotki novykh idei v fizicheskoi geografii." *Izvestiia Akademiia Nauk SSSR Seriia geograficheskaia i geofizicheskaia* 10, no. 2 (1946): 139-68.
———. "O nekotorykh osnovnykh problemakh fizicheskoi geografii." *Izvestiia Akademii nauk SSSR: Seriia geograficheskaia*, no. 6 (1957): 3-17.
———. *Subarktika*. 1st ed. Leningrad, Moscow, 1946.
———. *Subarktika*. 2nd ed. Moscow, 1956.
———. "The Heat and Moisture Regime and Geographic Zonality." *Soviet Geography* 2, no. 7 (1961): 3-16.
Grigor'ev, Andrei A., and Mikhail I. Budyko. "Classification of Climates in the USSR." *Izvestiia Akademii nauk SSSR: Seriia geograficheskaia*, no. 3 (1959): 3-19.
Lydolph, Paul E. *Climates of the Soviet Union*. New York, 1977.
Shaw, Denis J. B., and Jonathan D. Oldfield. "Landscape Science: A Russian Geographical Tradition." *Annals of the Association of American Geographers* 97 (2007): 111-26.
———. "Scientific, Institutional and Personal Rivalries among Soviet Geographers in the Late Stalin Era." *Europe-Asia Studies* 60, no. 8 (2008): 1397-1418.
Voeikov, Alexander I. *Klimaty zemnogo shara: v osobennosti Rossii*. Saint Petersburg, 1884.
Zabelin, Igor M. *Puteshestvie v glub' nauki (Akademik A. A. Grigor'ev)*. Moscow, 1976.

 PART III

Images and Narratives

 CHAPTER 5

From a "Country of Cold and Gloom" to a "Welcoming Land"

Climate and the Image of Siberia in the Russian Periodical Press, 1860s to the Early 1900s

Nataliia Rodigina

The discourse on the "Siberian frosts" and their role in shaping the image of Siberia in nineteenth-century fiction has traditionally been the domain of literary scholars. For example, V. I. Tiupa foregrounded the role of metaphors of cold and ice in conceptualizing Siberia as a "godforsaken place," a liminal space in Russian culture, and a mythic place of death and subsequent resurrection.[1] K. V. Anisimov demonstrated the chronological mobility and metamorphoses of the content of the associative pair "Siberia/cold" in the literature of the seventeenth through nineteenth centuries, and showed that this content depended on the author's life experience and motives for creating the text.[2] His conclusion that the Siberian climate "warmed" as the region was integrated into the communicative space of Russian culture, which A. V. Remnev's work supports, is important for the analysis that follows.[3] Siberia was a recurrent topic in the Russian periodical press of the late nineteenth and early twentieth centuries, and its climate was part of the discussion about the region. However, the role of climate in representations of Siberia in the periodical press still has not attracted much scholarly attention.

This chapter examines the discourse about "Siberian frosts" in the late imperial Russian periodical press and analyzes its role in shaping ideas about Siberia. Texts about the region published between the second half of the nineteenth century and the beginning of the twentieth on the pages of leading social-political and literary journals—*Vestnik Evropy, Russkii vestnik, Russkoe bogatstvo,* and *Russkaia mysl'*—are the focus of my analysis. From the middle of the nineteenth century, "thick journals" were one of the fundamental institutions that formed, structured, and transmitted public opinion and occupied a central place in what educated Russians read. On the one hand, work published in these journals reflected collective and individual ideas about the regions of the

Russian Empire. On the other hand, however, the thick journals were crucial in shaping these ideas.

Understanding the journals as an instrument that shaped national, ideological, regional, and generational identity, I will show how, when, and why various "we-groups" actualized the theme of the Siberian cold in their struggles for symbolic power over the reading public. In what follows, I will discuss the historical context for the popularization of this topic. I will explore the ways in which discussions of the Siberian climate depended on the region's place in the geopolitical strategies of imperial power and the degree to which Siberia was integrated into the empire's socioeconomic and civilizational structures. I will also examine the relationship between the theme of Siberian cold and the ways in which readers of thick journals mentally assimilated the region—that is, how the region was included in the communicative space of "our own/inner Russia."

The Historical Context of the Image of Siberia in the Mid-Nineteenth-Century Russian Periodical Press

The number of periodical publications increased sharply at the beginning of Alexander II's reign, which opened a new era in the country's history, a period marked by liberal reforms and a newly energized public opinion. The press gained unprecedented opportunities to influence the social and political life of the empire. In the 1850s a new stage in Siberian administrative politics began, which was characterized by the local and central authorities' attempts to reexamine the administrative and territorial structure of the region, reorganize state institutions in the *krai*, and change the ways the local bureaucracy was structured.[4] Several factors sparked the public's interest in Siberia. Among these were the regime's search for different versions of the best administrative structure for the region and its efforts to define the region's status and place in imperial strategies as well as the notorious "Amur Affair."[5] All of these factors unfolded against a background in which Russian intellectuals searched for ways to define themselves, chose various civilizational orientations as part of their conceptual framework, and tried to identify the best models for state development.

Between the 1850s and 1870s, climate was hardly a burning topic in the Russian periodical press. N. A. Nekrasov's *Russian Women* (*Russkie zhenshchiny*) was one of the best known and most highly acclaimed texts in which climate plays an important role. In this poem, Siberian frost (the "murdering cold" or "*kholod-ubiitsa*") is one of the main heroes. It appears as one of the fundamental symbols of the theme of Siberia-as-prison—the "cursed country"—and creates an emotional background for the heroism of the Decembrists' wives.

In the first part of the poem, which is dedicated to Princess E. I. Trubetskaia and was first published in the April 1872 issue of *Otechestvennye zapiski*, we see some key elements of the theme of climate and the closely related theme of Siberia-as-prison:

> A harder frost, a more desolate path,
> The further to the east;
> Along three hundred versts
> Some kind of godforsaken settlement.[6]

As we know, Nekrasov's poem did a great deal to create an image of Siberia in the mass consciousness of his contemporaries. Travelers who went to the region of their own accord and those who made the journey under duress frequently quoted it in their journalistic writing and memoirs. The topic of climate periodically surfaced in the memoirs of the Decembrists and in a few travel essays and literary texts. As a rule, it could be reduced to clichés about the severity of Siberian frosts, the fertility of Siberian soil for its fortunate owners, and the abundance of the region's other natural resources.

Siberian Frost in the Conservative Press

The stereotype of Siberia as a land of abundance is seen vividly in publications in *Russkii vestnik*, a leading conservative journal, that describe Siberia as a territory that offered opportunities to rise above one's social status, gave people illusions about how easy it would be to improve one's material well-being, and encouraged adventure-seekers to undertake intrepid deeds.[7] The following fragment of autobiographical notes published by someone who signed himself "K. Zolotilov" shows how such ideas influenced the behavioral strategies and, at times, the biographies of contemporaries:

> There is a belief that Siberia, *although the country is certainly cold, on the other hand is rich, that this is our Russian El Dorado*, where both happiness and wealth await a bold seeker. Having succumbed to this seductive belief, I flew there to seek happiness and for my debut, I went to work for a gold-mining company, without the slightest idea about Siberian life or the people whom I had to deal with or gold mining, which is what I intended to do.[8]

Despite keen public interest in the "Amur question," there was very little discussion of the significance of and prospects for annexing the Amur or the influence of climate on the course of the region's economic development and the life of the new territory's population in conservative periodicals. Instead, writers spoke of various "natural" aspects of the region, like the fertility of the local soil and the new territory's abundant fish and game. However, the most important topics were the geopolitical and military-strategic role of the Far East and analysis of the successes and miscalculations of N. N. Murav"ev's administration.

At the beginning of the 1890s, German reviewers of George Kennan's *Siberia and the Exile System* addressed the topic of Siberia's climate. The structure of foreigners' narratives about Siberia and their reasons for examining topics connected with "Siberian life" are subjects that demand their own special coverage. Here I would like to note that in an overview of German reviews of Kennan's celebrated book that appeared in *Russkii vestnik*, one sees a striking, and surprising, similarity in foreign reviewers' opinions about political exile in the region and attitudes of the journal's editorial board. M. Berman, who wrote the overview, thought that in terms of the political exile system, for people who were morally ill, Siberia was a clinic that "needs to be ennobled to a somewhat greater degree," but, because contemporary "social life has an abundance of dark sides," such a "clinic" was simply necessary.[9] If one follows Berman's logic, Siberia was actually too good for exiles. Without going into detail about his analysis of foreign reviewers' attitudes toward exile, I would like to turn to this author's attempt to deconstruct myths about Siberia, which were widespread among compatriots. Berman wrote that

> people imagine Siberia as a polar country, with an eternal winter, white bears, and prison guards, and only a small circle of educated people knows that in some parts of Siberia the climate is almost tropical, that even in Kamchatka summer is such as we can find only in southern Europe, that in Europe it is hard to find anything like the diversity of Siberian flora or the warm, aromatic Siberian nights, that in Siberian cities there is a university, gymnasia, *Realschule*, and schools for women, theaters and museums, political and scholarly periodicals.[10]

Thus, the idea that the vast region of Siberia was notable for the diversity of its natural and climatic conditions, which was formulated in the first half of the nineteenth century, came into play again in the 1890s. Berman was the rare writer who articulated this idea, although it was not the focus of his version of Siberia. This idea was not widely represented in the periodical press as a whole. It was, however, broadly disseminated in the pages of *Russkii vestnik*.

The set phrases used to designate Siberia in articles and reviews in *Russkii vestnik* attest to the peripheral significance of the Siberian climate as a symbol of the region in one of the best-known conservative publications. Between the 1850s and 1870s, the provinces beyond the Urals were described as a "remote land" (*otdalennaia strana*), the "remote lands of Siberia" (*dalekie strany*

Sibiri), and a "land that is comparatively rich in nature" (*strana sravnitel'no bogataia ot prirody*). From the beginning of the 1880s, the semantic field of the toponym "Siberia" broadened in the lexicon of Russian conservatives, and new marker-words representing the region appeared: "our rich and still little-known Siberia" (*nasha bogataia i maloizvestnaia eshche Sibir'*); "the remote Siberian outskirts" (*dal'niaia sibirskaia okraina*) / "the remote eastern outskirts" (*dal'niaia vostochnaia okraina*) / "the remote and vast outskirts of our fatherland" (*dalekaia i obshirnaia okraina nashego otechestva*) / "our remote outskirts" (*dalekaia nasha okraina*) / "our remote parts" (*nashi dal'nie kraia*) / "the vast eastern outskirts" (*obshirnaia vostochnaia okraina*) / "our eastern outskirts" (*vostochnaia nasha okraina*); and "remote and cold Siberia" (*dalekaia i kholodnaia Sibir'*); "vast Siberia" (*obshirnaia Sibir'*) / "the vast Siberian *krai*" (*obshirnyi sibirskii krai*). Still more marker-words and common phrases included: "Siberia is the same kind of Russian land as all the other areas of the empire" (*Sibir' takaia zhe russkaia zemlia, kak i vse ostal'nye mestnosti imperii*); "a country of immense spaces, almost entirely populated by peasants" (*strana neob"iatnykh rasstoianii, pochti splosh' naselennaia krest'ianami*); "the remote Siberian steppes" (*dalekie sibirskie stepi*); and "a land where refuse of all kinds piles up" (*strana, gde skaplivaiutsia vsevozmozhnye otbrosy*).

From the 1850s through the 1870s the image of Siberia was interpreted mainly in the context of orientalist discourse as a little-known territory, an exotic colony celebrated for its natural riches, a place inhabited by "other" peoples, a region that attracted people dreaming about glory and making a career and a "Mecca" for geographers. At the same time, it was a frightening place, with its severe climatic conditions, enormous expanses, poor roads, and reputation as a place of exile and hard labor, which symbolized unlimited administrative *proizvol* (arbitrariness). Siberia was linked to the concept of a "country" (*strana*) and was seen as something separate, a place that was distinct from "our own" European Russia, even when it was described by people who had lived in the region for a long time. However, between 1850 and the beginning of the 1870s, the western outskirts of the empire gripped the attention of conservatives, and "sleeping," "cold" Siberia was designated as a repository of resources and an imperial reserve, not just in an economic but also in a sociopolitical sense.

From the 1880s through the early 1890s, Siberia became a priority in conservative journalistic discourse. It was no coincidence that in conservative journalism the metaphor of "awakening from sleep" was often used in this period to describe Siberia. Conservative journalists' reasons for paying attention to the region are well known. On the one hand, the social and economic problems of the European part of the country (the "impoverishment of the center") and the development of the ideological postulates of conservative doctrine (the idea of "the revenge of the nobility" and the fight against nihilism) drew the attention of conservatives. On the other hand, the government's changed policy about the region—a change that construction of the railroad, legalization of the resettlement movement, abolition of the exile system, and the extension to Siberia of certain provisions of judicial reform all confirmed—also made Siberia a focus for conservative journalists.

Several key meanings were attached to the toponym "Siberia" from the 1880s onward in the conservative press and in general. Firstly, Siberia was described as an outlying region. "Outlying" implies a relationship with something that is "inner," and Siberia's geographic position was described in terms of what writers and their readers understood as "inner" Russia—that is, the nucleus of the state. The idea that Siberia had a close relationship to Russia was reinforced by the possessive pronoun "ours" (*nasha, nashi*): for example, "our distant outskirts" (*dalekaia nasha okraina*), "our distant regions" (*nashi dal'nie kraia*), and "our eastern outskirts" (*vostochnaia nasha okraina*). As the use of the possessive pronoun suggests, Siberia was "growing into" Russian readers' mental map of Russia. The following quotations vividly illustrate the process whereby the idea of "our" Siberia was extended, and Siberia became "embedded" in this mental map: (1) "distant and at the same time nearby Siberia, which has been an integral possession of our fatherland since the time of Yermak";[11] (2) "Siberia is the same kind of Russian land as every other place in the empire."[12] The infrequent references to "distant, cold Siberia" are not accidental. In this context, the distinctive aspects of the Siberian climate were not particularly meaningful and were in fact peripheral to trends seen in the overarching depiction of the region. Secondly, the abundant references to Siberia's territorial extent, its vastness, and the "freedom" (*privol'nost'*) prevailing in the region are important to note. The adjectives "great" (*velikii*) and "vast" (*obshirnyi*) were used most often in descriptions of agrarian migration to the region; these words implicitly contrasted with the "crowding on the land" (*zemel'naia tesnota*) in the Russian "heartland" (*korennaia Rossiia*).

However, unlike liberal and populist journalists, conservatives had some reservations about the idea that peasant resettlement could be the answer to the agrarian question in European Russia. They thought that an outflow of workers would have a negative impact on the development of local landownership, and, in this context, they brought up the severe Siberian frosts, which would interfere with successful peasant farming "in the land of resettlement places." A review of a book presenting statistical and economic research on the peasant population of western Siberia is noteworthy in this respect:

> In the Tiumen *okrug* the climate is harsh, with frosts of below forty degrees Réaumur, there is an insignificant amount of black earth [and] harvests are usually average or bad. The springtime cold, which sometimes continues until June, harms young shoots, and the early autumn morning frosts, which

sometimes start at the end of July and the beginning of August, damage the buckwheat in bloom, and are harmful to the nascent wheat ear just as it is coming out ...[13]

Thus, mention of the "strength of Siberian frosts" and their influence on the region's development depended to some extent on the context in which the topic of the Siberian climate appeared.

The formulation of a nationalist doctrine, the oscillations of the autocracy's policy toward the periphery of the empire, and the ways individual authors interpreted the goals and meanings of Russification all influenced the ways in which Siberia was understood. Sometimes it was seen as an outlying region that the mercy of the monarchy had "awakened," a place that was connected with "inner Russia" by "iron paths" and conquered by Russian blood but also a place on the outskirts that had been forgotten until the present day. At other times it was seen as a "backward" and potentially dangerous territory, a "sewer [that collected] the entire Russian nation's most malignant scum."[14] In this image of the region, phobias connected with Siberia diverted attention from central Russia's problems, and the presence of enemies, from without (the countries bordering Russia, the European powers) and from within, was constantly emphasized. Political exiles often figured as the internal enemies. "Siberia—cold—gloom—exile" was a traditional formula from the seventeenth through the nineteenth centuries, but here "cold" and "gloom" have vanished, and Siberia has become another Russian province, but one with a certain distinctive character.

Content analysis of work published in another conservative monthly, *Russkoe obozrenie*, makes it possible to identify key recurring themes that created an "imagined Siberia" for the Russian reading public; content analysis also makes it possible to determine the role that discourse on climate played in constructing the region's image. In what follows, I will examine five recurring themes that shaped Russian readers' image of Siberia. One of these is a depiction of the region's landscape that includes some comparison with the empire's "heartland"—that is, European Russia. Another recurring theme is the description of distance, the modes of transportation across this distance, and road conditions. A third key theme is the collective characteristics of the region's population, with an emphasis on the "otherness" of Siberians. A fourth key theme is exaggerated attention to the aspects of Siberian life that corresponded to the sociocultural symbolism of Siberia prevailing in the mass consciousness (agrarian migration, penal servitude and exile, the lifestyles of officials, merchants, etc.). A fifth recurring theme is explication of the characteristics of personified symbols of the region, people whose activities were associated with Siberia.

Descriptions of the landscape—its natural and man-made features, including hamlets, villages, and other types of settlement—introduced readers to Siberian exoticness and, more broadly, were a mechanism that created a national identity and the cultural codes that not only supplied information about Siberia but also enabled readers to understand "internal" Russia. At the same time, distances rather than climate were most often the criterion that distinguished "self" from "other." "Here everything produces the impression of something immense, unbounded. The smallest rivers here are no narrower than the Volga; the peasant huts no smaller than the manor houses on Russian country estates, the larches (or, as they are incorrectly called there, the cedars) are taller than African palms. For some reason, even the grass there attains colossal dimensions," wrote the astonished traveler, Prince Konstantin Viazemskii.[15] At the same time, however, the journal's authors were more eager to record attributes that the surrounding landscape shared with internal Russia than its specifically Siberian features. In I. A. Goncharov's memoirs about Iakutsk we encounter the following notable dialogue with an imagined reader: "Yes all of this is in Petersburg too," says the reader, "a broad river, snow in abundance—pine trees—as many as you want, churches, we also have more than a few of those. And if you glance at the Petersburg or the Vyborg sides, then you will probably find something like yurts too."[16] As a rule, the rare references to the harshness of the Siberian climate were intended to emphasize Siberians' cordiality and warmth. As Goncharov put it, "However *cold and harsh nature* is, the people there are equally *soft and kind*. Tenderness and cordiality enveloped me, the desire of each inhabitant, vying with each other, to be pleasant and gracious in some way."[17]

The Discourse about "Cold and Gloom" in Representations of Siberia in the Liberal and Populist Press

In the 1860s and 1870s the liberal *Vestnik Evropy* actualized the image of Siberia as a territory that was little known to the intellectuals of European Russia, a distinctive "terra incognita" that should be studied and described. The journalists writing in *Vestnik Evropy* were among the first to see studying Asiatic Russia as part of the educated person's cultural mission and the first step toward colonizing the region. In the context of this journal's Western orientation, references to European travelers who published work about Siberia and the assertion that educated Russians did not feel similarly compelled to do this are noteworthy. For example, in a review of a collection of pieces by German travelers we see this comment:

> Given all the interest inherent in general in a very serious and scientific description of our lands, we unfortunately are poor in our own research and therefore will be satisfied with someone else's work, works written by foreign-

ers, where naturally one meets with a mixture of sensible observations and odd comments that expose their extreme lack of understanding of the milieu they are describing.[18]

An analysis of liberal periodicals confirms A. V. Remnev's observation that, like their Western counterparts, Russian liberals were not indifferent to colonialism and imperial expansion. The idea that the "scientific conquest" of new territories and peoples was a necessary condition for the success of Russian geopolitics in Asia was also widespread among the intellectual elite.[19] As a member of *Vestnik Evropy*'s staff argued, "Without doubt, acquiring land is important in the history of the state's development, not as an enlargement of its space on the map but as a new field for colonization. But colonization is due above all to knowledge of new places and, in most cases, the dissemination of this knowledge."[20]

The need to study the nature and climate, the natural history, and the geographic, socioeconomic, and cultural realities of Siberian life in order to debunk the myth of the cold and gloom of this "unknown land" is the red thread that runs through the majority of publications about Siberia in liberal journals. To ameliorate their contemporaries' lack of information about the composition of the population and the conditions in which it lived, as well as the cultural and economic development of the empire's eastern provinces, the editors of liberal journals strove to fill the information vacuum by publishing articles that popularized scientific knowledge about the region, sketches of life in Siberia, and travelers' notes. Most of their authors took note of the paucity and imprecision of Russian readers' ideas about the regions beyond the Urals. Sharing his impressions following a trip from Moscow to Tomsk, I. S. Levitov exclaimed that "the fear and trembling before Siberia, which is fed by many things, is devoid ... of sense. This [attitude] can only be explained by absolute ignorance of Siberia and those false facts that have taken root in us since childhood."[21] In travel sketches titled "To Distant Lands" ("V dalekie kraia"), which were first published in *Russkaia mysl'*, K. M. Staniukovich ironically noted the difference between the ease with which the Russian traveler could acquire information about many "exotic" locales and what it took to plan a trip to Siberia:

> [H]olding some sort of foreign railway timetable in your hands, it is incomparably easier to make an accurate estimate of a journey to Australia, China, California, or the Cape of Good Hope than, in the capital of the empire, to figure out the means of communication, how much time it will take, and what an excursion on the other side of the Urals will cost. Will you languish on the road for a month and a half, where can you get water, where is the postal road, at the stops along the way can you get hold of any kind of con-

veyance that does more to guarantee the integrity of your internal organs than the post-chaise does—for me all of this was shrouded in the deepest mystery. Siberian cities too, with their thirty-degree frosts and their classic "Siberian fires" were wrapped in the same sort of, romantic mystery, if not an even greater one.[22]

Exaggeration of the need to "discover" Siberia, despite longstanding scientific study of the region and the tradition of careful, precise descriptions of it in literary texts and memoirs, suggests that each new generation of intellectuals had to "discover their own Siberia" and endow it with those characteristics that, in terms of *Weltanschauung*, were significant for a particular "we-group." It was not an accident that various ideological communities mobilized the "Siberian theme" to draw attention to the burning issues of the day and to put forward their own interpretations and suggestions for resolving those problems.

In 1895 L. S. Lichkov, an official in the Ministry of State Domains who had taken part in statistical studies of Eastern Siberia, wrote in an article that appeared in *Russkaia mysl'* about the need for multifaceted study of the region in conjunction with building the railway and organizing settlement of the eastern provinces. He noted the pedestrian nature of the stereotypes about the region and the mythology that circulated among the public and insisted that it is wrong to ascribe features characteristic of some parts of Siberia to others:

> For many people Siberia is a gold mine and at the same time for many it is a kind of monotonous, impenetrable, wild, heavily forested wasteland where bears and yes, convicts live... But meanwhile, it is so large and extensive [*obshirna*] and, for this reason alone, it is already so diverse that the description given by a person who really knows one swathe of Siberia, although he knows it in some depth, in most cases it [his knowledge] turns out to be completely inappropriate when it comes to some other part of it ...[23]

Expressing a similar idea, an anonymous reviewer of a Russian translation of a book by the ethnographer and naturalist Otto Finsch and the zoologist Alfred Brehm wrote that "it seems no single corner of Russia has a reputation of such a variegated character as Siberia."[24]

It is notable that in numerous texts that call on readers to "get to know Siberia" and that intend to dispel numerous preconceptions about the region the topic of climate was virtually absent. I would argue that this silence was not by chance. Siberian frosts were indeed one of the stereotypical symbols of the region, and post-reform journalism called for this stereotype and others to be reexamined.

As Russian readers became acquainted with the literary and scientific work of the Siberian intelligentsia (many of whom were political exiles), as the "topic of Siberia" became increasingly popular in the periodical press, and as new expeditions for scientific research and for literary purposes began to be organized—that is, as the region became assimilated into the educated public's intellectual landscape—the image of Siberia as a separate, isolated country begins to fragment into images of its separate historical and cultural regions.[25] The publications in liberal journals clearly show the process whereby Iakutsk *Oblast'* and Altai, the island of Sakhalin, and the Priamur region, with all their inherent and specific climatic, environmental, geographic, social, economic, and cultural features, appeared on the mental map of educated Russians. Accordingly, the discourse about the Siberian climate is filled with new content: while readers continue to expect descriptions of the severe Siberian winter to feature in depictions of Iakutsk *Oblast'*, as a rule, descriptions of the Altai *Krai* and the Minusinskii district of Enisei Province include references to their gentle, warm climate, and the treacherous Priamur climate is not reduced to its severity but rather to its unpredictability. However, although they called for the destruction of stereotypical, mythic ideas about Siberia, authors writing for the "thick journals" created new images of Siberia, which did not always correspond in a precise way to reality. Although the discourse about the Siberian climate was not a vital element of efforts to justify the need for "intellectual colonization" of the region, it was a key topic in considering the prospects for peasant resettlement and political exile to the region.

Two images of the region that were directly connected with the topic of climate appeared consistently on the pages of liberal and populist journals in the early 1880s and continued to figure in characterizations of Siberia throughout the 1890s and the early years of the twentieth century. The first one is the image of Siberia as a peasant El Dorado, a promised land for settlers. With the increased land shortages in the European part of the empire and the growth of peasant settlements in Siberia, liberal and populist journalism began to treat Siberia as the main and most promising region for migration. Because they thought that voluntary colonization was a fundamental driving force of the Russian state's territorial and mental expansion, the liberal and populist intelligentsia came out in favor of legalizing resettlement and strong support for agrarian migrants. In accordance with this understanding of Siberia's destiny, its climate was called favorable for the development of agriculture, and there was an emphasis on the abundance of the region's natural gifts and the presence of the natural and climatic conditions that were necessary for the prosperity of the Russian tiller of the soil on the eastern outskirts of the empire. A. A. Isaev, an economist and active member of the Society for Aid to Needy Settlers, traveled to Siberia to become better acquainted with resettlement issues. His depiction of Siberian conditions is typical of this version of the region:

> Wherever you travel in Siberia, even as far as sixty degrees north, the extraordinary abundance of nature's gifts is striking. Along the Ob's middle course, where there are no wheel tracks and the distance between small settlements is measured in hundreds of versts, you see an enormous number of diverse and valuable fish and fur-bearing animals. You go a little south, to the region that is on the same latitude as the village of Narym, and you find such rich cattle raising, there is nothing like it in the Russian agricultural belt: the poorest peasant has five horses and five cows, it doesn't cost anything to take care of them, he mows so much hay that his large reserves often last for two winters.[26]

From the 1890s, the idea that resettlement was a "deeply conservative" measure began to predominate, first in populist and then in liberal publications. This opposition to resettlement incorporated a strange misunderstanding of what should be considered liberal. S. N. Iuzhakov, who wrote the "Chronicle of Domestic Affairs" ("Khronika vnutrennei zhizni") for *Russkoe bogatstvo*, set out the essential elements of this "new" view of agrarian migration:

> In principle it is unlikely that resettlement can find unconditional defenders since the state's task, when correctly understood, is to settle people where they are, in the *rodina*. Moreover, each person who is evicted is a loss for the country from whence he came, a loss that cannot be rectified in any way. For those who stay, it is also not easier since in most cases among us the land falls into the hands of kulaks.[27]

Publishing observations on resettlement agriculture, journalistic sketches, and articles presenting information about living conditions in Siberia promoted deconstruction of the myth of Siberia that prevailed in mass consciousness, which saw Siberia as a promised land for farmers, a free "Samara" [*razdol'naia* "Samara"], where there was "a lot of land and few authorities."[28] In fact, several factors that had little to do with Siberia per se doomed the effectiveness of resettlement in the eastern outskirts and ensured disappointment in its outcomes: intensive stratification of the peasantry under the influence of migrations; the fact that there were reverse migrations; and the excessive bureaucratization involved in resettlement.

A series of articles discussing the results of statistical studies of landownership and communal life appeared in populist journals, especially in the 1890s. These cast doubt on stereotypes of the territory as a storehouse of nature's riches with a favorable climate for agriculture.[29] Statistician N. O. Osipov's response to such articles and the stereotypes they challenged shows that there was a conscious effort to deconstruct myths about the region:

The vastness of the territory and the paucity of knowledge about Siberian life has always led and [still] leads to several fantastical ideas about both the nature of Siberia and, in particular, the life of its inhabitants. We are accustomed to think that Siberia is something like a land of miracles and inexhaustible riches of every kind. The research that has been carried out dispels this mistaken impression. ... Here there are neither miracles nor fairy-tale riches nor even an especially strikingly prosperous population, [and this article] sets the reader on the threshold of reality and lays out before us a rather well-known picture, one that in its general lines is reminiscent of the Ural steppes.[30]

In a similar vein, S. M. Ponomarev, another direct observer of peasant migration, noted that

poverty is progressively growing. Peasant communities who have lived [in Siberia] for a long time are groaning. The old-timers themselves are scattering. The conquerors of new lands are also fleeing. The country of rivers of milk and banks of jelly has ceased to be alluring and attractive. The time for settlement for no reason has passed. Time has put forth serious demands and they must be met by resolving the question seriously.[31]

The motives of such publications are clear—to show that Russia and Siberia have the same socioeconomic development problems and to make the once distant and little-known outskirts understandable and "our own" by including them in the world picture of the intelligentsia living in the capitals and the provinces of "internal" Russia. In other words, these journals were trying to make Siberia part of an area that the intelligentsia had mentally absorbed and integrated into their concept of what constituted Russian territory. Understanding the region as an organic and integral part of the empire gave birth to an image of the region as Siberia, the mirror of Russia. Informing the reading public about Siberia was seen not only as a way to draw society's attention to the needs of the *krai* but also as a way to struggle with the social ills of the entire country. The liberal and populist press used demonstrations of the abuses perpetrated by the Siberian administration—"every kind of outrage committed by the local kulaks and all kinds of robberies, which swept over and ravaged this unbelievably rich land, which is completely at the mercy of the local officialdom"[32]—as proof that in post-reform Russia, socioeconomic and cultural development were shared problems. In this context, S. Ia. Kapustin's image is noteworthy: "And thus, the Siberia of today, is she not Russia's daughter, like her mother in every way, with the only difference that the latter, as an adult, knows how to cover up many of her shortcomings but the former still does not know how to do this?"[33] Along the same lines, in a review in *Russ-*

kaia mysl' we read that "Siberia is neither a state nor in the intellectual sense is it a whole in and of itself. Indeed, it is nothing more than one of the many Russian provinces although it has many characteristic peculiarities."[34] When Siberia was understood in this way, discussing the Siberian climate was not particularly relevant. It was more important to demonstrate what Siberia and European Russia shared, rather than their differences, including nature and climatic ones.

The second persistent image of Siberia, which figured in the moderately oppositional press, is Siberia as a "cold and gloomy land of exile." This image conveyed the idea of Siberian exile as a stage in the career of a professional revolutionary, a place of exile for revolutionaries, where "their character is forged and tested." The heroization of Siberian exile is characteristic of both journalistic texts written by exiled Narodniki and Marxists and the personal writing of political exiles that appeared in the Russian periodical press at the turn of the nineteenth century.[35]

As happened at the beginning of the nineteenth century, the subject of Siberian frost and gloom plays a major role in post-reform discourse about political exile in Siberia. Cold in particular becomes one of the most vivid symbols of the country of "bondage" (*nevolia*) and lack of freedom. It is a punishment for the exile's beliefs that produces physical and emotional suffering. To create its own "poetics of a godforsaken place," a new generation of political exiles used the same elements on which their predecessors had relied during the first half of the century. The reflections of G. A. Machtet, who was exiled to Tobol'sk Province, are revealing here. "Of course, I don't think I could stay here," he wrote before leaving Siberia in 1885. "It would be simply horrible! ... To live out one's life in a pit, cold, godforsaken, alien to me in every way, only a dead man could spend five years in it and then keep living in it voluntarily."[36] K. M. Staniukovich, who was also a political exile, wrote:

> And again, over the course of a day not one building, not a single soul. Taiga and water, water and taiga, and masses of mosquitos—"midges" as the locals call them. And once again the weather was just right for this repellent/hateful nature. The sun showed its face stealthily and was stingy with its warmth at the beginning of June. Dull leaden clouds hung low over the leaden river. A sharp, cold wind from the near north stirred up the river, playing on it with white-crested waves, and sang a despondent song, shaking the tops of the trees on the banks. It was simply terrible. Melancholy involuntarily engulfed the newcomer. Is it really possible to live here?[37]

In terms of what representations of cold reveal about the mythology of "underground Russia," A. G. Tseitlin, well-known author who wrote under the pseudonym "Gedeonov," describes the conditions of exile in a fairly typical way:

> When you are trembling from the cold, which has not only made its way into every fiber of your clothing but has also insinuated itself into every pore of your body, battered by the cutting wind, hunger and sleeplessness—and you suddenly catch sight of a red flame, light flooding the yard of a Iakut's dwelling, when you hear the sound of a horse neighing and the anxious barking of dogs—then you become cheerful, you want to laugh and at that moment you feel a warm, friendly movement of your soul toward the Iakuts who are so kind to you.[38]

In Bolesław Onufrowich's memoirs, we meet with a widely accepted list of words used to describe the region: "I still vividly remember that bitterness and sense of injury that I experienced then from knowing that I had to spend five long years, some of the best years of my life, sitting in a godforsaken corner of unfamiliar, far-off, terrible Siberia for nothing."[39] Sometimes the concepts of "Siberia" and "prison" were used synonymously. For example, in his memoirs, Leo Deutsch noted that "until recently the characterization of Siberia as an enormous prison was justified, because, thanks to its natural conditions, it has a more reliable fence than what man-made walls and hired guards provide."[40]

Aestheticization of the suffering endured by the heroes of the struggle with the regime ensured that descriptions of the difficult conditions (including natural and climatic conditions) associated with a sojourn in the region would receive special attention, but at the same time this aestheticization accentuated the capacity of "heroes" to overcome difficulties and, in forced captivity, to find a way to use their skills honorably and gain the respect and admiration of the Siberians in their midst.

Unlike ideas about Siberia as a promised land, the metaphorical image of Siberia as a prison with its "cold and gloom" was fairly stable throughout the entire period studied here. It was actively circulated in texts of various genres written by political exiles despite the fact that many exiles experienced a change in their feelings about the region, moving from rejection to love for the land, its nature, and its people. In his memoirs, S. L. Chudnovskii called Siberia not a stepmother but a motherland.[41] One sees several different attitudes toward the *krai* in what Korolenko wrote in Siberia. Much of this was the result of being exiled, but, after a year in Siberia (1911) he wrote, "During my wanderings I managed to fall in love and now I often remember this harsh country with great future opportunities."[42]

***

Thus, the "thick journals" of the second half of the nineteenth century and the early twentieth century "reserved" the topic of the Siberian climate in order to discuss a broad spectrum of contemporary problems of Russian life (many of which were only connected indirectly with Siberia itself). These included the relationship of the regime and society (political exile as a punishment for dissidence); the economic position and prospects of the Russian peasantry (agrarian resettlement as a feature of "peasant life"); and the territorial expansion of the Russian empire and the "intellectual colonization" of its outlying territories. Depending on their goals, some ideological "we-groups" downplayed and some emphasized the severity of "Siberian frosts."

There was generational and ideational continuity in the way images of the region connected with its distinctive natural and climatic features worked. Both the Decembrists and the Narodniki used "Siberian gloom and frosts" to construct two images that, in essence, formed a binary: there was an image of an unfree country of exile and an image of a "Russian America" where, free and not knowing serfdom, the Russian *muzhik* flourished. Contradictory ideas about the impact of the Siberian climate on human beings peacefully coexisted in the minds of those "forced" to be Siberians, and they were used as a prism through which several different issues of value and significance were viewed—for example, the harshness and inhumanity of exile and the need to limit various types of bureaucratic constraints and extra-economic coercion to promote the effective development of agriculture.

Thus, the content of the discourse about the Siberian climate in the periodical press of the late nineteenth through the early twentieth centuries depended directly on the thematic context in which the "Siberian theme" functioned, the worldview and orientation of the periodicals and the degree to which the region was integrated into imperial space. My sources do not allow me to discuss the "warming" of the Siberian climate as a universal trend that was characteristic of representations of climate in the political press of the post-reform era. In discussions of the socioeconomic, social, political, and cultural problems of Siberia and Russia as a whole, differences in the climate of the European and Asian parts of the country were smoothed out as artistic and scientific knowledge of the empire's eastern outskirts increased and as the migration movement into the region developed and the Siberian railroad was constructed. The awakening of Siberians' regional self-consciousness and the vibrant journalistic activity of political exiles were other key developments that reduced the sense that there were disparities in climate in the two parts of the country. In the discourse about political exile, Siberian frosts were traditionally strong, and their severity did not really depend on the place where their victims served their sentences of exile. From the beginning of the nineteenth century and throughout the entire period under consideration, the severe Siberian cold remained a vivid symbol of the myth of "underground Russia."

Translation by Jacqueline Friedlander

Nataliia Rodigina, doctor of historical sciences, is a leading researcher at the Institute of History of the Siberian Branch of the Russian Academy of Sciences, and professor in the Department for Russian and Global History at the Novosibirsk State Pedagogical University. Her main research interests are: intellectual history, Siberia in the Russian Empire, and Russian literature. She is the author of *"Drugaia Rossiia": Obraz Sibiri v russkoi zhurnal'noi presse vtoroi poloviny XIX—nachala XX veka* (2006).

Notes

1. V. I. Tiupa, "Mifologema Sibiri: K voprosy o 'sibirskom tekste' russkoi literatury," *Sibirskii filologicheskii zhurnal* 1 (2002): 27–35.
2. K. V. Anisimov, "Klimat kak 'zakosnelyi separatist': Simvolicheskie i politicheskie metamorfozy sibirskogo moroza," *Novoe literaturnoe obozrenie* 99 (2009): 98–114.
3. A. V. Remnev, "Natsional'nost' 'sibiriak': Regional'naia identichnost' i istoricheskii konstruktivizm XIX v.," *Politiia* 3 (2011): 113–14.
4. See A. V. Remnev, *Samoderzhavie i Sibir': Administrativnaia politika vtoroi poloviny XIX–nachala XX v.* (Omsk, 1997), 14.
5. The Amur Affair refers here to public discussion about the prospects for the annexation of the Amur region to the Russian empire and the Far East's economic and geopolitical significance for Russia. The reasons why the "Amur question" arose, the ways it was treated in the periodical press, and the impact of public opinion on the evolution of government policy on the Far Eastern frontiers have already been widely covered in the Russian historiography. See N. N. Rodigina, *'Drugaia Rossiia': Obraz Sibiri v russkoi zhurnal'noi presse vtoroi poloviny XIX–nachala XX v.* (Novosibirsk, 2006), 98–103; Iu. D. Akashev, "Amurskii vopros i ego osveshchenie v periodicheskoi pechati (60–70-e gg. XIX v.)," in *Obshchestvenno-politicheskaia problematika periodicheskoi pechati Rossii XIX–nachala XX v.*, ed. A. V. Ushakov (Moscow, 1989), 130–43, etc. Here, the important point is that in discussions of the significance of the Amur during the 1850s and 1860s, the Far East was understood as part of Siberia, and its prospects were most often discussed alongside consideration of the role played by the entire eastern outskirts in imperial geopolitical strategies.
6. In Russian: "Moroz sil'nei, pustynnei put'/ Chem dale na vostok;/ Na trista verst kakoi-nibud'/Ubogii gorodok." N. A. Nekrasov, *Russkie zhenshchiny*, *Sobranie sochinenii*, ed. I. G. Iampolskii (Moscow, 1979), 2:254.
7. Although I understand the convention of describing *Russkii vestnik* as a conservative periodical, especially in reference to the period before 1863, I nonetheless follow the prevalent historiographic tradition of using the categories "conservatism," "liberalism," "populism" (*narodnichestvo*), etc. to characterize social thought; at the same time, I recognize the schematism, mobility, and Russian specificity of the content of this social thought.
8. K. Zolotilov, "Sibirskaia taiga," *Russkii vestnik* 1 (1863): 313. Emphasis mine.
9. "Nemtsy o knige Kennana," *Russkii vestnik* 1 (1894): 202.

10. Ibid., 203-4.
11. V. Belinskii, "Aktsionernoe uchreditel'stvo i neobkhodimaia ego reforma v Rossii," *Russkii vestnik* 12 (1898): 412.
12. "Vnutrennee obozrenie," *Russkii vestnik* 10 (1888): 332.
13. Review of A. A. Kaufman, *Materialy dlia izucheniia ekonomicheskogo byta gosudarstvennykh krest'ian i inorodtsev Zapadnoi Sibiri*, vols. 1-2 (Saint Petersburg, 1888-89), *Russkii vestnik* 3 (1890): 287.
14. "Vnutrennee obozrenie," *Russkii vestnik* 6 (1888): 345. See also A. Ia. Maksimov, "Ussuriiskii krai," *Russkii vestnik* 8 (1888): 19-46; A. S., "Ssylka i ostrov Sakhalin," *Russkii vestnik* 7 (1889): 59-90; "Vnutrennee obozrenie," *Russkii vestnik* 7 (1889): 333-39; N. N. Emel"ianov, "Tiur'ma i ssylka," *Russkii vestnik* 6 (1899): 713-20.
15. K. Viazemskii, "Puteshestvie vokrug Azii verkhom," *Russkoe obozrenie* 9 (1894): 343.
16. I. A. Goncharov, "Po Vostochnoi Sibiri: V Iakutske i Irkutske," *Russkoe obozrenie* 1 (1891): 6.
17. Ibid. Emphasis mine.
18. Review of A. Michi [Alexander Michie], *Puteshestvie po Amuru i Vostochnoi Sibiri* (Saint Petersburg, 1868), *Vestnik Evropy* 4 (1868): 982. *Puteshestvie po Amuru* is a translation from the German text, which was translated from Michie's original text of 1864, *The Siberian Overland Route from Peking to Petersburg, through the Deserts and Steppes of Mongolia, Tartary &c.* (London, 1864). The 1867 German translation was titled *Das Amur-Gebiet und seine Bedeutung: Reisen in Teilen der Mongolei, den angrenzenden Gegenden Ostsibiriens, am Amur und seinen Nebenflüssen, nach den neuesten Berichten, vornehmlich nach Aufzeichnungen von A. Michie, G. Radde, R. Maack u. A.* (Leipzig, 1867).
19. A. V. Remnev, *Rossiia Dal'nego Vostoka: Imperskaia geografiia vlasti XIX-nachala XX v.* (Omsk, 2004), 23-26.
20. Review of M. I. Veniukov, *Puteshestviia po okrainam russkoi Azii i zapiski o nikh* (Saint Petersburg, 1868), *Vestnik Evropy* 2 (1868): 900.
21. I. Levitov, "Ot Moskvy do Tomska," *Russkaia mysl'* 7 (1883): 3.
22. K. M. Staniukovich, *V dalekie kraia*, in *Sobranie sochinenii v 10 tomakh*, vol. 1, ed. M. P. Eremin (Moscow, 1977), 238. Staniukovich's travel sketches first appeared in *Russkaia mysl'*, nos. 1, 2, 4, 12 (1886) under the pseudonym L. Nel'min.
23. L. S. Lichkov, "Gde pravda? (K voprosu o 'poezdakh' dlia issledovaniia Sibiri)," *Russkaia mysl'* 3 (1895): 107.
24. Review of O. Finsh [Otto Finsch] and A. Brem [Alfred Brehm], *Puteshestvie v Zapadnuiu Sibir'* (Moscow, 1882), *Russkaia mysl'* 5 (1882): 37.
25. The use of the word "country" (*strana*) to identify the region was far from accidental. *Strana* was commonly and widely used in conjunction with Siberia.
26. A. A. Isaev, "Kak otnosit'sia v Sibiri k pereselentsam? (Po lichnym nabliudeniiam)," *Russkaia mysl'* 12 (1890): 83-84.
27. [S. N. Iuzhakov], "Khronika vnutrennei zhizni," *Russkoe bogatstvo* 12 (1893): 153.
28. See, for example, V. Vladislavlev, "Khozaistvennoe polozhenie tobol'skikh novoselov," *Russkoe bogatstvo* 6 (1899): 102-27.
29. S. N. Iuzhakov, "Khronika vnutrennei zhizni," *Russkoe bogatstvo* 7 (1894): 148-52; review of S. I. Zalesskii, *Issledovanie prigodnosti nekotorykh malovodnykh mestnostei Barnaul'skogo i Kainskogo okrugov k zaseleniiu pereselentsami iz Evropeiskoi Rossii* (Tomsk,

1893), *Russkoe bogatstvo* 3 (1894): 53–54; review of A. A. Kaufman, *Krest"ianskaia obshchina v Sibiri: Po mestnym issledovaniiam, 1886-1892* (Saint Petersburg, 1897), *Russkoe bogatstvo* 5 (1897): 54–58.

30. N. O. Osipov, "K voprosu o pozemel'nom ustroistve krest"ian Zapadnoi Sibiri," *Russkoe bogatstvo* 5 (1894): 53.
31. S. M. Ponomarev, "Sibirskaia obshchina i pereselenie," *Severnyi vestnik* 5 (1887): 89.
32. Review of N. I. Naumov, *Sobranie sochinenii*, *Russkaia mysl'* 2 (1898): 51.
33. K-tin [S. Kapustin], "Zerkalo Rossii? (Po povodu knigi Iadrintseva *Sibir' kak koloniia*)," *Russkaia mysl'* 1 (1883): 29.
34. Review of M. G. Vasil'ev, *Pesni sibiriachki* (Saint Petersburg, 1901), *Russkoe bogatstvo* 10 (1901): 37.
35. N. N. Rodigina, "Mat' ili machekha? Obraz Sibiri u politicheskikh ssyl'nykh vtoroi poloviny XIX v.," in *Sotsial'nye konflikty v istorii Rossii*, ed. V. N. Khudiakov, T. A. Saburova, and I. I. Krott (Omsk, 2006), 235–45; A. Iu. Ledovskikh, "Konstruirovanie obrazov geroev i antigeroev sibirskoi ssylki v rossiiskoi zhurnal'noi presse vtoroi polovine XIX–nachala XX veka," in *Obrazovanie v istorii, istoriia v obrazovanii*, ed. V. A. Zverev (Novosibirsk, 2011), 270–78.
36. Quoted in V. M Fizikov, "G. A. Machtet v sibirskoi ssylke," *Uchenye zapiski Omskogo gosudarstvennogo pedagogicheskogo instituta* 36 (1968): 60.
37. Staniukovich, *V dalekie kraia*, 324–25.
38. A. Gedeonov, "Za severnym poliarnym krugom," *Russkoe bogatstvo* 6 (1896): 133.
39. B. O-ch, "V mesta otdalennye (Vospominaniia administrativnogo ssyl'nogo)," *Minuvshie gody* 8 (1908): 285.
40. L. G. Deich [Deutsch], *16 let v Sibiri* (Saint Petersburg, n.d.), 143.
41. S. L. Chudnovskii, *Iz davnikh let: Vospominaniia* (Moscow, 1934), 266.
42. Quoted in A. Khrabrovitskii, "Neopublikovannye vospominaniia V. G. Korolenko o Sibiri," *Sibirskie ogni* 10 (1962): 173.

Bibliography

Akashev, Iu. D. "Amurskii vopros i ego osveshchenie v periodicheskoi pechati (60–70-e gg. XIX v.)." In *Obshchestvenno-politicheskaia problematika periodicheskoi pechati Rossii XIX–nachala XX v.*, edited by A. V. Ushakov, 130–43. Moscow, 1989.

Andree, Richard. *Das Amur-Gebiet und seine Bedeutung: Reisen in Teilen der Mongolei, den angrenzenden Gegenden Ostsibiriens, am Amur und seinen Nebenflüssen, nach den neuesten Berichten, vornehmlich nach Aufzeichnungen von A. Michie, G. Radde, R. Maack u. A.* Leipzig, 1867.

Anisimov, K. V. "Klimat kak 'zakosnelyi separatist': Simvolicheskie i politicheskie metamorfozy sibirskogo moroza." *Novoe literaturnoe obozrenie* 99 (2009): 98–114.

A. S. "Ssylka i ostrov Sakhalin." *Russkii vestnik* 7 (1889): 59–90.

Belinskii, V. "Aktsionernoe uchreditel'stvo i neobkhodimaia ego reforma v Rossii." *Russkii vestnik* 12 (1898): 408–29.

Chudnovskii, S. L. *Iz davnikh let: Vospominaniia*. Moscow, 1934.

Deich [Deutsch], L. G. *16 let v Sibiri*. Saint Petersburg, n.d.

Emel"ianov, N. N. "Tiur'ma i ssylka." *Russkii vestnik* 6 (1899): 713-20.

Fizikov, V. M. "G. A. Machtet v sibirskoi ssylke." *Uchenye zapiski Omskogo gosudarstvennogo pedagogicheskogo instituta* 36 (1968): 54-62.

Gedeonov, A. "Za severnym poliarnym krugom." *Russkoe bogatstvo* 6 (1896): 116-52.

Goncharov, I. A. "Po Vostochnoi Sibiri: V Iakutske i Irkutske." *Russkoe obozrenie* 1 (1891): 5-29.

Isaev, A. A. "Kak otnosit'sia v Sibiri k pereselentsam? (Po lichnym nabliudeniiam)." *Russkaia mysl'* 12 (1890): 80-90.

[Iuzhakov, S. N.] "Khronika vnutrennei zhizni." *Russkoe bogatstvo* 12 (1893): 145-59.

———. "Khronika vnutrennei zhizni," *Russkoe bogatstvo* 7 (1894): 127-53.

K-tin [Kapustin, S.] "Zerkalo Rossii? (Po povodu knigi Iadrintseva Sibir' kak koloniia)." *Russkaia mysl'* 1 (1883): 27-39.

Khrabrovitskii, A. "Neopublikovannye vospominaniia V. G. Korolenko o Sibiri." *Sibirskie ogni* 10 (1962): 173.

Ledovskikh, A. Iu. "Konstruirovanie obrazov geroev i antigeroev sibirskoi ssylki v rossiiskoi zhurnal'noi presse vtoroi polovine XIX-nachala XX veka." In *Obrazovanie v istorii, istoriia v obrazovanii*, edited by V. A. Zverev, 269-78. Novosibirsk, 2011.

Levitov, I. "Ot Moskvy do Tomska." *Russkaia mysl'* 7 (1883): 1-30.

Lichkov, L. S. "Gde pravda? (K voprosu o 'poezdakh' dlia issledovaniia Sibiri)." *Russkaia mysl'* 3 (1895): 105-33.

Maksimov, A. Ia. "Ussuriiskii krai." *Russkii vestnik* 8 (1888): 244-75.

Michie, Alexander. *The Siberian Overland Route from Peking to Petersburg, through the Deserts and Steppes of Mongolia, Tartary &c.* London, 1864.

Nekrasov, N. A. *Russkie zhenshchiny, Sobranie sochinenii*. Vol. 2. Edited by I. G. Iampolskii. Moscow, 1979.

"Nemtsy o knige Kennana." *Russkii vestnik* 1 (1894): 193-224.

O-ch, B. "V mesta otdalennye (Vospominaniia administrativnogo ssyl'nogo)." *Minuvshie gody* 8 (1908): 285-311.

Osipov, N. O. "K voprosu o pozemel'nom ustroistve krest'ian Zapadnoi Sibiri." *Russkoe bogatstvo* 5 (1894): 52-79.

Ponomarev, S. M. "Sibirskaia obshchina i pereselenie." *Severnyi vestnik* 5 (1887): 60-89.

Remnev, A. V. "Natsional'nost' 'sibiriak': Regional'naia identichnost' i istoricheskii konstruktivizm XIX v." *Politiia* 3 (2011): 109-28.

———. *Rossiia Dal'nego Vostoka: Imperskaia geografiia vlasti XIX-nachala XX v.* Omsk, 2004.

———. *Samoderzhavie i Sibir': Administrativnaia politika vtoroi poloviny XIX-nachala XX v.* Omsk, 1997.

Review of O. Finsh [Otto Finsch] and A. Brem [Alfred Brehm], *Puteshestvie v Zapadnuiu Sibir'* (Moscow, 1882). *Russkaia mysl'* 5 (1882): 37-41.

Review of A. A. Kaufman, *Krest'ianskaia obshchina v Sibiri: Po mestnym issledovaniiam, 1886-1892* (Saint Petersburg, 1897). *Russkoe bogatstvo* 5 (1897): 54-58.

Review of A. A. Kaufman, *Materialy dlia izucheniia ekonomicheskogo byta gosudarstvennykh krest'ian i inorodtsev Zapadnoi Sibiri*. Vols. 1-2 (Saint Petersburg, 1888-89). *Russkii vestnik* 3 (1890): 287-92.

Review of A. Michi [Alexander Michie], *Puteshestvie po Amuru i Vostochnoi Sibiri* (Saint Petersburg, 1868). *Vestnik Evropy* 4 (1868): 981-82.

Review of N. I. Naumov, Sobranie sochinenii. *Russkaia mysl'* 2 (1898): 51.
Review of M. G. Vasil'ev, Pesni sibiriachki (Saint Petersburg, 1901). *Russkoe bogatstvo* 10 (1901): 36-39.
Review of M. I. Veniukov, *Puteshestviia po okrainam russkoi Azii i zapiski o nikh* (Saint Petersburg, 1868). *Vestnik Evropy* 2 (1868): 900.
Review of S. I. Zalesskii, *Issledovanie prigodnosti nekotorykh malovodnykh mestnostei Barnaul'skogo i Kainskogo okrugov k zaseleniiu pereselentsami iz Evropeiskoi Rossii* (Tomsk, 1893). *Russkoe bogatstvo* 3 (1894): 53-54.
Rodigina, N. N. *"Drugaia Rossiia": Obraz Sibiri v russkoi zhurnal'noi presse vtoroi poloviny XIX-nachala XX v.* Novosibirsk, 2006.
———. "Mat' ili machekha? Obraz Sibiri u politicheskikh ssyl'nykh vtoroi poloviny XIX v." In *Sotsial'nye konflikty v istorii Rossii,* edited by V. N. Khudiakov, T. A. Saburova, and I. I. Krott, 235-45. Omsk, 2006.
Staniukovich, K. M. "V dalekie kraia." In *Sobranie sochinenii v 10 tomakh.* Vol. 1. Edited by M. P. Eremin. Moscow, 1977.
Tiupa, V. I. "Mifologema Sibiri: K voprosy o 'sibirskom tekste' russkoi literatury." *Sibirskii filologicheskii zhurnal* 1 (2002): 27-35.
Viazemskii, K. "Puteshestvie vokrug Azii verkhom." *Russkoe obozrenie* 9 (1894): 317-53.
Vladislavlev, V. "Khozaistvennoe polozhenie tobol'skikh novoselov." *Russkoe bogatstvo* 6 (1899): 102-27.
"Vnutrennee obozrenie." *Russkii vestnik* 6 (1888): 338-57.
"Vnutrennee obozrenie." *Russkii vestnik* 10 (1888): 324-42.
"Vnutrennee obozrenie." *Russkii vestnik* 7 (1889): 322-41.
Zolotilov, K. "Sibirskaia taiga." *Russkii vestnik* 1 (1863): 313-46.

 CHAPTER 6

Local Warming
Cold, Ice, and Snow in Russian and Soviet Cinema

Oksana Bulgakowa

> *Rus', you are a kiss in the frost.*
> —Mikhail Kul'chitskii

Cold and snow—popular topics in a period of global warming—have frequently accompanied storylines associated with Russian identity, creeping into the historical and contemporary narratives of national and foreign "storytellers" alike. The Russia created by Hollywood was a country of "imperial ballet dancers, terrorists, polar bears, snowy steppes, and Grand Dukes."[1] Icicles and snow-covered fields visualized the cliché of "Russian." Both Russian and Soviet artists put the naked bodies of Russian Venuses in an icy landscape, depicting kisses in the snow and bathing in snowdrifts. Boris Kustodiev painted Russian Shrovetide (*Maslenitsa*, 1903) and the Russian Revolution (*Bol'shevik*, 1919–20) in one and the same festive snowy landscape. Arkadii Plastov gave his painting of a naked beauty in falling snow the title *Spring* (*Vesna*, 1954).

With the appearance of films, this situation changed somewhat. Shooting on location in snowy landscapes was problematic: the automatic and mechanical features of movie cameras did not work, film lost its elasticity, becoming brittle, and its photosensitivity decreased. The dazzling surface of snow, which reflects and intensifies direct sunlight, did not allow enough light to be transmitted, and film crews had to use filters. Cameraman Vladimir Shneiderov, who shot a polar expedition on the icebreaker *Sibiriak*, noted that the artists on board did not have problems like these.[2] In this sense, older technologies of representation were more reliable.

In spite of this, throughout the totalitarian and post-totalitarian periods, the national winter coloring figured in Russian and Soviet films of all formats and genres: adventure (*Two Captains/Dva kapitana*, 1955 and 1976); ethnographic (*One Sixth of the World/Shestaia chast' mira*, 1926), fantasy (*Sannikov Land/Zemlia Sannikova*, 1973); fairy-tale (*Jack Frost/Morozko*, 1964);

comic (*Neptune's Holiday/Prazdnik Neptuna*, 1987); and biographical (films about the fates of Ermak, Dezhnev, Bering, Sedov, Nansen, Shmidt, Papanin, and the doomed crew of the steamship *Cheliuskin*). An icy landscape was the setting for parables (*Spotted Dog Running at the Edge of the Sea/Pegii pes, begushchii kraem moria*, 1990), films for children (*Chuk and Gek/Chuk i Gek*, 1955), films about animals (*Little Napoleon the Third/Nedopesok Napoleon Tretii*, 1978), and the beauties of nature (*Under the Northern Lights/ Pod Severnym siianem*, 1990). Expensive joint productions like Mikhail Kalatozov's *The Red Tent* (*Krasnaia palatka*, 1971), with its "all-star cast," about the mission to rescue Umberto Nobile; Sergei Bondarchuk's film version of Tolstoi's *War and Peace* (1966–68); or Andrei Mikhalkov-Konchalovskii's epic *Siberiade* (*Sibiriada*, 1978) coexisted with low-budget films. They recounted the conquest of the North Pole and Siberia, and the existential problems of life at polar stations (*72 Degrees Below Zero/72 gradusa nizhe nulia*, 1976; *How I Spent This Summer/Kak ia provel etim letom*, 2009); narrated the heroic feats of geologists, radio operators, surveyors, and pilots in peace and war (*Victory/Pobeda*, 1938; *Valerii Chkalov*, 1942; *A Story About a Real Man/Povest' o nastoiashchem cheloveke*, 1946); depicted the machinations of saboteurs and spies (*Traces in the Snow/Sledy na snegu*, 1955; *There Are No Strangers Here/ Chuzhie zdes' ne khodiat*, 1985); and presented dramas about the heroes of the Arctic in valiantly painted stories of the conquest of nature (*Hero of the Arctic/Geroi Arktiki*, 1934; *Seven Brave Men/Semero smelykh*, 1937; *The Ordinary Arctic/Obyknovennaia Arktika*, 1976), a theme that was treated with equal success in post-Soviet films profaning the pathos of their predecessors (*Comrade Chkalov Crosses the North Pole/Perekhod tovarishcha Chkalova cherez Severnyi polius*, 1993). However, the words "winter," "snow," "cold," and "ice" were rarely used in their titles.[3]

It is striking that Soviet films whose action is connected with the cold, snow, and ice are studied mainly by fans, who put together long lists and upload pirated copies of films to the internet. Film historians, however, have paid almost no attention to this theme, which might not be accidental. Only in the last two years have several articles about documentaries and video installations involving Arctic landscapes appeared.[4] Here the cold is not a physical or a meteorological phenomenon that can change the way the temperature does. In the visual arts and film this is, above all, an *image* that refers to symbolic connotations, metaphors, and myths. However, film not only creates pictures but also stimulates the imagination associated with those pictures. It creates a cliché that links snow with certain narratives, most often those involving an extreme crisis, an ordeal, or a threatening situation, thereby intensifying the dramatic tension. In films, cold as a *sensation* can be created suggestively, forcing not only the hero on the screen but also the audience to freeze. At the same time, the feeling of coldness does not have be transmitted by using pictures of snow. For example, Alain Resnais was able to create an icy atmosphere in a film whose action takes place in the summer (*Last Year at Marienbad*, 1961).

Representation, imagination, sensation, and narratives associated with snow and ice do not concur. Images of cold and snow refer to aesthetics and aesthesia; the former is concerned with the visual imagination and the metaphorical connotations of snow and ice, but aesthesia is the bodily perception of cold mediated by the senses and the means by which this perception is created in art. Analysis of this displacement from aesthetics to aesthesia and the move from symbolic to metaphoric and atmospheric conceptualization of the nation's climate and landscape in Soviet cinema defines the dynamics of my chapter. I begin by looking at the "iconography of ice and snow as Russian clichés and global metaphors," Russian references *to* and specific divergences *from* them. Then I trace the ways that Soviet cinema wrote a conflict situation connected with prevailing over the cold into the topic of modernization and used it to create Soviet identity during the crucial decade of Stalinist industrialization, from the end of the 1920s to the late 1930s.

The "narrativization" of cold remained the traditional realm of the masculine ordeal and adventure. But since Russia was associated with woman in the popular imagination, the image of the Rodina or motherland had to be inscribed in the new historical subject, which is the focus of the section titled "Nature and Human Nature: Climate, Bodies, and Modernization."

The third part of my chapter, "Nature and History, or a Philosophy of the Seasons of the Year," is therefore devoted to Soviet cinematography's attempt in the mid- to late 1930s to present a radical Soviet history as a natural cycle. Using metaphors from nature to designate historical cycles in Russia is not an isolated phenomenon. The metaphorical label of the "thaw" (*ottepel'*) described the process of de-Stalinization as a natural phenomenon. During this period, a movement in the opposite direction begins on the Soviet screen. In film narratives of this period, the way cold is assessed changes. It begins to be treated not as an integral part of the national identity but as a climatic condition that threatens the manifestation of what is human. There are changes in the expressive means that help to create cold as sensation and *atmosphere*, which act suggestively on the viewer. The final section, "The Temperature of the Screen," examines how testing these means begins in wartime films and continues into the stagnation era.

The Iconography of Ice and Snow: Russian Clichés and Global Metaphors

Like the desert, a snowy plain creates an abstract background against which a different visuality is possible: there are no details to distract the eyes there.

It is no coincidence that in *The Seven Pillars of Wisdom*, T. E. Lawrence connects the origins of religion with the special—bare—desert landscape, which he characterizes as a spiritual icehouse.[5] This abstractness might be one of the reasons why a snowy landscape, cold, and ice so frequently attracted the attention not only of meteorologists, geographers, and physicists but also of artists, poets, linguists, philosophers, and psychoanalysts interested in the metaphors associated with these phenomena.[6] The rich metaphoric capacity of snow and ice migrated into the popular imagination long ago, and film made use of it.

The metaphors associated with images of snow and ice are striking in their simultaneous references to oppositions—fragility and hardiness; death and eternal life; the ephemeral, the transient, and the everlasting—which is associated with the capacity of materials to undergo transformations (the easy transition from solid to liquid and vice versa), the disappearance and dissolution of their own materiality. Snow and ice are therefore often associated with the mystical idea of overcoming physicality. Like glass, ice was understood by mystics and alchemists as a filter for spirituality. For the Romantics it became the source of illusion and was associated with images of melancholia and death in the Symbolists' imagination. Artists and philosophers often saw in snowflake crystals an archetype standing between nature and culture, the embodiment of a sublime form and absolute beauty. To the extent that both materials were associated with disappearance, they were often brought together with another time-limited phenomenon: female beauty. Theodor Adorno connected the nature of snow and ice with the idea of the beautiful and the aesthetic in general, which finds its expression and its essence in the moment of its own passing.[7]

This paradox is also preserved in the way a vision engendered by the snowy landscape is understood. In antiquity, Apollo, the god of light, was the personification of perfect sight and the rational mind; the sons of Boreus—that is, the North Wind—and the Hyperboreans, who lived on the other side of the northern mountains, were subjugated to him. The snowy landscape was identified with the clear, sober, form-and-order-encompassing Apollonian glance. At the same time, this landscape lacked reference points (far and near): the dramatic situation of a snowstorm was blinding—and called for another way to understand sight. The human gaze, which is usually distracted by inessential details, falls into a state of perfect contemplation when internal insight and imagination take the place of incomplete perception. Made complete by blindness, the hero was ready to see the essence. This motif was often used in literature. In the impenetrable darkness created by a snowstorm, writers forced their protagonists to confront a fate that they could not control, which is how Pushkin brought the predestined pair together in his *Blizzard* (*Metel'*).

Invoking the concept of rational sight, which is distinct from individual perception, the Enlightenment connected this with the metaphor of the cold mind while the Symbolists preferred blind Providence to clarity of sight. At the same time, the capacity of the cold to protect organic nature from decomposition connected the form of ice with the appearance—the preservation—of memory. However, the ephemeral nature of materials that can melt and evaporate was associated with the absence of traces and referred to the vanishing of memory.[8]

These paradoxical metaphors, which are connected with images of snow and ice, can be found in Andrei Tarkovsky's films. In *Solaris* (*Soliaris*, 1972) the director created a winter landscape with an iconographic motif, not just of Russia but also of earthly civilization. In *Mirror* (*Zerkalo*, 1974), the image of historical memory was associated with this landscape.

Thus, in *Solaris* Tarkovsky uses the image of snow to explain to Hari—the clone of neutrinos, the creation of a formless ocean of thinking matter that is capable of imitation but does not have a memory—something that she cannot know: earth. Astronaut Kris shows Hari an amateur film depicting a bonfire in snow. But she sees only an image, without knowing what the sensation of cold is like. Hari also scrutinizes a similar winter landscape, which is depicted in a painting by Pieter Bruegel, a copy of which is hanging in the space station's library. Here the picture is brought to life by the movement of the camera, which enters the painted landscape as if it is the gaze of an unearthly civilization, trying to understand this sign. At this moment the animation of nature, with the help of cinematic technology, passes to the clone, who takes on human emotions along with the cultural memory of humankind. What Tarkovsky does here can be understood as a reference to the popular hypothesis that human civilization began in the Ice Age, which was central to psychoanalyst Sándor Ferenczi's theory of evolution. However, in the moment that this artificial being is animated, it kills itself with the help of cold oxygen. This directorial decision could be interpreted as a reference to the universal connotations of cold and ice as metaphors of death. However, a distinctive feature of ice and snow is the fact that they are capable of transformation and therefore occupy a place between the opposition of life and death. In a few seconds, Hari thaws and is resurrected from the dead, like a northern Christ. In *Andrei Rublev* (1966/1972), Tarkovsky, staging a crucifixion in the snow, worked with the motif of a northern Golgotha, which was popular in Netherlandish painting. At the same time, Hari can be interpreted as the transformed incarnation of the sleeping—ice—beauty.

Here, snow, cold, and ice are associated with death and melancholy but at the same time with the idea of eternal life, the imperishable body. This paradoxical metaphorics also extends to the way memory is understood. Tarkovsky finds the same wintry landscape inspired by Bruegel's painting in the natural world of central Russia, and he uses it in his autobiographical film *Mirror* to represent an episode from 1943. This motif appears at the moment when the boundaries between individual perception, memory, and historical memory are blurred. In a single second, the child, who does not yet have a historical memory, sees a panorama of events that take place later—the capture of the Reichstag, the atomic bomb exploding, the cadres of the Chinese Cultural Revolution. At that moment he becomes the keeper of historical memory about the future and the mediator of film's fragile memory. However, in the film this hero without memory, who lost his parents during the blockade winter, is resurrected only by the imagination of Tarkovsky remembering *his own* childhood. Here, cold and ice are connected with both the vanishing of memory and its eternal existence.

These three metaphorically saturated scenes refer to the accepted connotations of ice, cold, and snow in the global imagination, with "local" adjustments. These connotations are personified by the director, who declared that his art's goal was the salvation of individual memory and vanishing intimate time.

The cold associated with pictures of snow and ice was used much more frequently, however, in the genre of adventure films involving extreme situations, all the way up to apocalyptic stories about a global catastrophe that turns the earth into an uninhabitable, snowy desert (Steven Spielberg's *Artificial Intelligence*, 2001; Roland Emmerich's *The Day after Tomorrow*, 2004). The Soviet school of cinema created its own variant of the dramatic ordeal in cold landscapes.

Nature and Human Nature: Climate, Bodies, and Modernization

The conflict between harsh nature and the weak human body was used dramatically and expressively in Swedish cinema (Mauritz Stiller's 1923 *Gunnar Hedes Saga*, which is known in English as *The Blizzard*) and in German cinema, where the very popular genre of the mountain film was created. Arnold Fanck, who directed *The Holy Mountain (Der heilige Berg*, 1926) and *The White Ecstasy (Der weiße Rausch*, 1931), and his leading lady, Leni Riefenstahl, who made her own mountain film, *The Blue Light (Das blaue Licht*, 1929), had a decisive influence on the development of this genre. Siegfried Kracauer saw in these pieces not a heroic myth but the political implications of national socialism. Luis Trenker was the leading figure in films of this type. In his hands—for example, *The Doomed Battalion (Berge in Flammen*, 1931)—the mountain film and its hero "conform to a political regime which relies on intuition, worships nature and cultivates myths."[9] It extols the mountaineers' military victories and "ennobles their fight," which includes fighting against natural catastrophes and inhuman nature, "transforming it into a 'tragic duty.'"[10] The mountaineer "is the type of man on whom regimes ... can rely,"[11] and it is in precisely this heroic glorification of the duel with nature, in which men must prove that they are genuine heroes, that Kracauer, the sociologist of culture, discovered a "German pattern," the fantasies about "perpetual adolescents" that fascism exploited.[12] In these plots, ice has a magical power, which attracts the protagonists and makes death ready for them.

Russian directors transformed this plot. On the Soviet screen it moved from ethnographic and exotic films about the life of the Russian Nenets people and expeditions to Pamir and Tian-Shan to a story about the conquest of nature. The formation of a national hero was inscribed in a plot about the protagonist confronting the climate and his own body, which asserted the metaphysical values of the spirit.

Mikhail Kalatozov's film *Salt for Svanetiia* (*Sol' Svanetii*, 1929) was the turning point. It began as a feature film and was shot as an ethnographic film, using the method of observation and dramatization. It was influenced by Robert J. Flaherty, who made the first internationally successful ethnographic documentary film about the life of the Inuit (*Nanook of the North*, 1922). However, Kalatozov developed a completely different view of the relationship of nature and man. He did not tell a story about a person adapting to natural conditions, but instead made the conquest, the subordination of nature, the subject of the film, which later became a meta-narrative of the Stalinist cinema of the 1930s and 1940s.

Sergei Tret'iakov, a leading theoretician of the Left Front of the Arts (LEF), wrote the screenplay for Kalatozov's film. Based on the "bio-interview" genre introduced by Tret'iakov, it is the true story of a blind woman from a village inhabited by the Svans, who lived in a mountain region virtually cut off from the civilized world. The blind woman regains her sight after a successful operation in the city. In film technology, Tret'iakov sought ways to convey the changes in the blind woman's subjective vision: the transition from an out-of-focus image of blurry circles and distorted outlines to the usual sharpness, from darkness to bright white light, sharp contrasts, distinct geometric forms. The literal and figurative meanings of the recovery of sight coalesced in the storyline of his visual cinematic prose. The blind woman does not just become sighted; she sees the light, is emancipated, and has an epiphany of the film camera's liberated, futuristic vision, the perfect sight of Dziga Vertov's kino-eye, which replaced the imperfect human eye.

Kalatozov, who shot and directed the film himself, used filters specially prepared for the film to create expressive pictures of ice, stone, and snow. He showed the film in Moscow for people in the Left Front circle, and it was a flop. With Viktor Shklovsky, a specialist in re-editing, Kalatozov used the material he had already shot to put together an ethnographic documentary about the life of the Svans, their customs and rituals, called *Salt for Svanetiia*. He got rid of the blind heroine and replaced the drama of individual enlightenment with a semidocumentary account of the collision of the old (a preindustrial society that survived by hauling salt through the mountain pass) and the new, which comes into the far-off settlement with machinery that blasts through the ice to make a road.

Kalatozov used film—an art that deploys fragmentation, speed, simultaneity, and technology—to depict an archaic lifestyle. He dismembered bodies by turning them into shots of mouths, hands, and backs and opted for low camera shots and the diagonal compositions of Alexander Rodchenko's photographs and Dziga Vertov's city films. Rodchenko and Vertov used these techniques to emphasize geometric, Constructivist buildings and to convey the sense of speed in a changed perceptual situation. In the world of the Svans there were neither modernistic buildings nor quick means of transport. Instead of skyscrapers, bridges, and radio towers, Kalatozov shot triangular mountain peaks, the Svans' towers, waterfalls, and mountain landscapes. He suggested the feeling of speed with accelerated footage of drifting clouds, an avalanche, and a galloping horse. He reduced the Svans' life to a few activities—tilling the soil and breeding cattle, childbirth, and burying the dead. From rituals seen with an ethnographer's eye he made a parable about the fragility of a life determined by hunger, cold, and privations, a life dictated by ice, snow, sun, avalanches, and drought. Nothing in the beginning of the film corresponds to the idea of subduing nature to the human will, which was the foundation of Stalinist modernization. Here, humans are part of nature, a weak part. Women weave, people till the soil in the snow, and their archaic tools seem like surrealistic artifacts. Human figures in black appear in the snowy landscape like ornamental, rhythmic segments that structure the whiteness. The film observes the changing seasons, but the color white is dominant—white clouds and snow, white smoke, radiant ice, white stones, the Svans' white towers, snow-covered mountains, white mules carrying white salt to women dressed in black. The expressive face of a screaming woman juxtaposes the white face of a corpse and the legs of a man who died in an avalanche whose open mouth was filled up with snow. The montage sequence does not follow a narrative logic but creates a rhythmic composition.

The funeral of the man who died in an avalanche while bringing salt through the mountain pass alternates with scenes of a woman giving birth. She has been banished from society, and her child dies. The ritual of the funeral, the sacrifice of a lamb, and the physical suffering of childbirth are compared. The animal's blood, the woman's blood, the blood covering the newborn that a dog licks, drops of milk from the mother's breast irrigate the desiccated soil. The baby dies, the lamb is sacrificed. Male choruses during the burial, female choruses during the mourning for the dead, the ritual of burial, the physiology of childbirth, human blood, the blood of the sacrificed animal. The montage brings Christian and pagan rituals together, preserving the mythical and mystical character of the fatal subordination to nature and fate by virtue of the film's ethnographic orientation.

Kalatozov trusted neither the mystic ornamentality of archaic rituals nor the tragedy of poverty found in Andrei Platonov's early stories about famine, drought, a disembodied utopia, and the existential abyss (*Dzhan* and *Kotlovan* or *The Foundation Pit*). At the end of the film, however, the drama of hardships is resolved, and a new story begins. Modernization must overcome hardships and subdue nature to technology, which is more powerful than an avalanche. Women vanish from the frames—along with ice and snow. Modernization is connected with male bodies, the half-naked bodies of the roadbuilders, which present physical work as an athletic exercise. Powerful explosions that blast through the mountain rock complete the masculine work, the word "Bolsheviks" appears on an intertitle, and a Stalinist tractor brings not only salt but also a new myth to Svanetiia. A road is put through the mountain pass, joining the old and the new, and the timeless icy landscape gives way to futuristic speed.

The films of the 1930s replicated this theme. Nature is "raw," feminine, a merciless force associated with hardships, threats, crises, death; it was subdued by civilization, which is presented as a mechanized force that frees people from biological afflictions. Technology—icebreakers, airplanes, sleighs with propellers—appears in snowy landscapes as man's helper. Sergei Gerasimov's *Seven Brave Men* (1937), the first film about a polar station, followed this narrative arc. The transformation of nature was also associated with the validation of a special protagonist who could conquer it. During the war this hero was capable of similar feats, even without the help of mechanized mediators, as Aleksandr Stolper showed in *The Story of a Real Man* (*Povest' o nastoiashchem cheloveke*, 1948). The story of the flyer Meres'ev (the fictional hero's name) was based on what actually happened to the pilot Aleksei Mares'ev, who was shot down on 4 April 1941 near Kursk and, eighteen days later, made his way back to the Soviet front lines, at first walking on his badly injured legs and then crawling. The film put the hero in a winter landscape and showed how the pilot prevailed over snow and cold with the help of his strength of spirit, although he was wounded and his physical strength was gradually diminishing.

The philosophy of this mystical strength was close to the mythical idea of a higher, northern race whose bodies were tempered by frost and whose imagination was stimulated by darkness. These heroes had inner vision. They set out for snowy, icy spaces to conquer the forbidden zone as also happened in other cultures in relation to the Arctic and the Antarctic.[13] Cold, snow, and ice were presented in the framework of a plot turning on struggle and subordination, but forays into nature meant the triumph of the spirit over nature's dangerous, frightening power. The idea that the human body was vulnerable and fragile is suppressed, and taking risks in confronting a natural disaster helps the heroes to become acquainted with their own manliness and strength. They are not created by the fire that melts steel but by ice. In the framework of these ideas, the cold is deprived of negative connotations and does not become a realm of suffering but the arena of an ordeal. It gave birth to a special national character, which became the myth of a higher civilization. The cold of Russia, the northern empire, was warm for Russians but deadly for others; the victory over Napoleon, and later Hitler, was blended into this climatic myth.[14]

The gendered aspect of the narrativization of cold was unambiguous: climatic ordeals in snowy landscapes remained a male domain. Female narratives associated with cold were situated in the realm of fairy tales about Russian Snegurochka, the Snow Queen, Sleeping Beauty, and the lazy sister and the hardworking one, who find themselves in the kingdom of the mistress of snow, Old Mother Frost (Gospozha Metelitsa, from the German Frau Holle; in the Russian version this is a man, Morozko), characters who are no different from the Western European ones. Most of them are said to have the magic power of perfect beauty, which is frightening, cold, soulless, and evil, like a power-seeking woman. The Snow Queen was also interpreted either as menacing nature personified in a body made of ice or as the embodiment of ominous, rational knowledge, a kind of a female version of the Faustian quest. In the romantic variant, she was a girl who was incapable of feeling love: Snegurochka, or a sleeping virgin, whose sexuality is waiting to be awakened and who can come back to life only when Prince Charming appears. These beauties were laid to rest in a crystal—ice—coffin. In popular cinema they were transformed into frigid career women, which is how Camille Paglia interprets the female ice myths.[15] Kazimir Malevich connected this female ice myth with the image of the ruler of the new Russian history and suggested putting Lenin's embalmed body into a crystal coffin like a sleeping beauty, bringing together the idea of the eternal state that has done away with history and an imperishable body that does not know death. This is not as paradoxical as it seems at first glance. Russia—the Snow Queen—must be inscribed in a historical narrative and Lenin, or more accurately his death on a very cold winter day during the Epiphany frosts, helped to establish the new myth—with the aid of Soviet cinema.

Nature and History, or a Philosophy of the Seasons of the Year

In the 1920s, Soviet cinema was already using natural phenomena—drifting ice in Vsevolod Pudovkin's *Mother* (*Mat'*, 1926), a storm in his *The Heir of*

Genghis Khan (*Potomok Chingiz-Khan*, 1927)—as signs of historical cataclysms: the parallel montage of ice breaking up compared the awakening of nature with an eruption of revolutionary energy. The director wrote historical time into the natural cycle, and this metaphor of the correlation of history, understood as inevitable progress, with the eternal return of the natural cycle, became the characteristic trait of Soviet mythological cinematic thought. However, the decisions made by Pudovkin, Vertov, and Eisenstein were rooted in the dual nature of film editing. The montage of the 1920s—the juxtaposition of fragmented spaces and bodies—was the ideal way to convey an idea about materialized, "precisely measurable" time, "which became physical space," as Georg Lukács formulated it. In his analysis of reification, he described time as a montage of abstract particles. By rationalizing the work process and breaking it down into separate operations, man was made into the incarnation of time and was transformed into a mechanized part of a mechanical system: "Thus time sheds its qualitative, variable, flowing nature; it freezes into an exactly delimited, quantifiable continuum filled with quantifiable 'things' (the reified, mechanically objectified 'performance' of the worker, wholly separated from his total human personality): in short, it becomes space."[16] In *History and Class Consciousness* Lukács contrasts the understanding of time as the expression of a mechanical process established by a spatial continuum with a different feeling: the proletariat understands history as the present and the present as a product of history, thereby restoring processuality to time. Thus, in his view, the idea of the end of history could be dropped in philosophy, and all unresolved problems of the "accidental" and the transition from nature to logic could be rethought.

In the 1930s, Soviet directors resolved this transition in the framework of the genuine possibilities of film, which made it feasible to manipulate time and present the transition from nature to history as a product of modern cinematic magic. Films about the October uprising were made each decade for the forthcoming anniversary of the revolution with a ready-made set of approved components. The October Revolution was consolidated as an initiation event, and it returned every decade in a new filmic incarnation as a kind of seasonal rebirth: in 1927 in Eisenstein's *October* (*Oktiabr'*); in 1937–38 in a whole group of films, including Mikhail Romm's *Lenin in October* (*Lenin v Oktiabre*) and *Lenin in 1918* (*Lenin v 1918 godu*), Mikheil Chiaureli's *The Great Dawn* (*Velikoe zarevo*), Grigorii Kozintsev and Leonid Trauberg's *The Vyborg Side* (*Vyborgskaia storona*), and Sergei Iutkevich's *The Man with a Gun* (*Chelovek s ruzh'em*); in 1958 in Fridrikh Ermler's *The First Day* (*Den' pervyi*) and Sergei Vasil'ev's *October Days* (*V dni oktiabria*); and in 1982 in Sergei Bondarchuk's *I Saw the Birth of a New World* (*Ia videl rozhdenie novogo mira*). This ritual commemorative film production interrupted linear historical time. At the same time, whenever the history of the revolution was adjusted, characters were cleared out and heroes and details were replaced with new ones. In this way, history was affirmed in the figure of the eternal return as an infinitely variable present, and the cinema became a truly collective effort and creation that went beyond the framework of a single film.

In 1934, when Lenin's death had to be staged as a shared experience like the revolution, Vertov presented in *Three Songs about Lenin* (*Tri pesni o Lenine*, 1934) not the biography of a real Soviet politician but a metaphorical parable about a dead prophet whose rebirth as light of all kinds—from a beam of light to an Ilych light bulb—led to magical transformations. The movement of the film is subordinated to the transition of "emancipation → death → rebirth," which helped to create a semantic and a figurative halo around the concept of "Lenin." By using film techniques, Vertov connected the Soviet rhetorical figure of "Lenin dead is more alive than all living beings" with the metaphor of the cold as death embodied in frozen nature, which experiences a rebirth in the spring. In this way the life of a human being was presented as a cycle of eternal renewal. In order to convey this strange condition, Vertov experimented with inverting "movement-immovability" (the basic phenomena of film, on which the illusion of making unmoving images mobile is built) as synonyms of "life-death." Lenin's death was represented through a series of freeze frames forcing moving objects—locomotives, machines, engineering tools, and finally the camera itself—to stand still. His death was perceived as a rupture of the film— and of history. But since a film can be both put in motion and stopped, Vertov juxtaposes frames of the corpse with shots of Lenin gesticulating and talking, shots of the immobile body, and a stream of people walking by his coffin. The moving mass—grieving soldiers, children, women, old people—compensates for the immobility of one body. The oppositions that were formulated in the intertitles (Lenin moving—then motionless, Lenin motionless—the masses moving) preceded the fundamental transformation—of a dead man into "the one who was the most alive."

In the film, "Lenin" and "Stalin" were not presented as real figures but as symbolic incarnations of "light," "water," "spring." In the first version of the screenplay, a reference to the word "Stalin" was replaced by a metaphorical description: Lenin is spring, "the spring of a desert, which is turned into a garden. The spring of the land to which a tractor comes, a Stalinist, socialist spring."[17]

The film's first and second songs begin and end with a sequence of three shots: the estate in Gorki (frontal, a long shot, neutral), the view from Lenin's window to the bench (a medium shot, diagonal composition, implying a subjective view, possibly the last thing the dying Lenin saw), and then a medium close-up, showing the empty bench. These three shots are shown over and over again. A photograph of Lenin sitting on the bench is shown once in this montage sequence. In the collective memory of the generation of the film's first audiences, the bench was associated with the figures of Lenin *and* Stalin, the image of whom, sitting on this bench, was frequently reproduced. But in the film, the empty bench is repeated, shot in summer, winter, and spring and edited by using dissolves. This repetition is not just a compositional bridge. The montage series creates a system of juxtapositions in which the bench—an everyday object without mythological projections—refers to the film's fundamental semantic figure of "presence in absence," which recalls the figure of "eternal life in death." This garden bench in the park of an estate outside Moscow in summer, winter, and spring becomes a Mecca and the film's refrain. Vertov's montage sequence, with its rhythmic repetitions, refers to music and poetry on the formal level but simultaneously supports the mythological idea of cyclic time, which replaces historical time.[18]

Organizing the shots into montage sequences connects not only sound and image but two types of thought. Here, montage, the analytic method of dismembering and assembling, which is always associated with the typographic culture of linear thought, is subordinated to the logic of the accumulative, nonanalytical, superfluous structures of oral poetry. The repetition of certain frames, the same titles, entire montage phrases would have helped the viewer of the film (as repetition used to help the narrator in oral composition) not to lose the thread connecting these scattered pictures and sounds. This assisted in highlighting the qualities that gave the technical art of film the "organic," natural attributes of complex thought. Therefore, development in Vertov's montage phrases moves forward slowly, returning several times to what has already been shown and heard, making it easier to keep track of what is going on and simplifying perception. The refrain of the film relies on the oral techniques of mnemonics but simultaneously refers to the mental figures defined by this type of thought: classifications based on an analogy of forms, united not by temporal causality but through spatial contiguity, ignoring the differences between the past and the future, conceptions of cyclical time. Vertov therefore treated historical time like natural time and transformed Lenin into a god who dies and rises from the dead, a god of eternal return like Osiris, Atis, Adonis, Bacchus.

In 1937 Eisenstein used this figure to describe montage. That method was not understood as the mechanical process of assembling and constructing a poultry farm or a water supply system as it was in the 1920s[19] but was now understood by analogy with the body of a dismembered, reassembled, and resurrected god, a Dionysus or an Osiris.[20] The metaphor of eternal return was taken up by Russian writers and poets at the beginning of the 1930s: Boris Pasternak called his cycle of poems *Second Birth* (*Vtoroe rozhdenie*, 1932) and Mikhail Zoshchenko titled his book *Youth Restored* (*Vozvrashchennaia molodost'*, 1933). At the end of the 1930s Eisenstein interprets narrative as an expression of mythological thought and ritual as its foundation, for example a god's death and resurrection. In ritual the narrative is embodied in rhythmic movement leading to an ecstatic experience, a sacral state accessible through physical imitation. In literature and film the narrative unites kinetics with mimetic and symbolist meanings. It is just this multilayered union that Eisenstein tries to embody in his late films. In his sketch *Moscow*, historical time is transformed into a spiral with repetitive, isomorphic events.[21]

It was not an accident that Vertov could not set down in writing the composition he came upon as a screenplay or convey the content of the film in words; he tried to do this in prose and in poetry but did not succeed.[22] For most of his screenplays, it was simpler to resort to diagrams that looked like circles and ellipses. The diagrams were not simply a schema of the screenplay, they also graphically conveyed nonlinearly organized, associative thinking and cyclical time. In this sense, Vertov's spiraling, circular screenplays were not just stopgap solutions for expressing the impossibility of putting montage structure into writing. The narrative forms are inseparable from representations of time. With his return to pre-Christian, folkloric ideas, the director had to arrive at pre-linear ideas about time as a circle, to the narrative as a figure of the eternal return with repeating structures. The pseudoreligiosity of the culture of Stalin's time was never better expressed than in this figure, although Stalin was not pleased with Vertov's film.[23] But a similar cyclic perception of time is not peculiar to myths alone. Prison inmates come to lose a sense of time, and only the alteration of day and night or the changing seasons are preserved as the sensation of the current time.

The Temperature of the Screen

In Soviet films, winter nature was part of the exoticism of the Russian landscape. At the same time, conveying the sensation of cold as temperature and atmosphere was ignored. The short day (and the lack of light) made nature in winter expensive in terms of producing a film. Therefore, winter in films was shot most often in the studio or in summer, with the help of things that were already used in the theater—salt, naphthalene, and sawdust. In *Alexander Nevsky* (1938) the central episode of the Ice Battle was shot at the height of summer, in July. The film immediately became unusually popular, but audiences commented scornfully on its props. In fact, *Alexander Nevsky* did not pretend to be an authentic reconstruction of either atmospheric or historical events. It was not about ancient Rus and the fight against the Teutonic Order but about a possible war with Germany, and the film turned out to be prophetic: the cold climate prepared death for the enemy on Lake Peipus and helped the Russians, who were in harmony with their nation's natural features and climate. However, beginning with wartime films, frost began to lose its decorative features and gradually was transformed into a savage cold, which was dangerous, not only for foreign intruders but also for Russian bodies, especially the bodies of Russian women.

In Russian war films, whose style changed radically in both documentary and feature films after the war began—moving to a harsh naturalism with shocking close-ups of people put to the sword and killed, their mutilated faces and dismembered bodies marked with unaesthetic traces of violence—the cold appeared as a torment and a form of torture used by the enemy. Documentary footage from besieged Leningrad, mass graves, photographs of the executed Zoia Kosmodemianskaia, and frozen corpses of soldiers hit Soviet screens. This oppressive atmosphere of icy horror was expressively conveyed in Mark Donskoi's *The Rainbow* (*Raduga*), the 1944 film adaptation of a story by Polish-Ukrainian writer Wanda Wasilewska. Donskoi transmitted the feeling of cold from the screen to the audience. The film's plot and mise-en-scène referred to biblical symbols and followed Christian iconography.

Olena, a pregnant partisan, returns to her village, which is occupied by the Germans, and is betrayed and arrested. On Christmas Eve, she gives birth to a son in a freezing cow shed blanketed with snow. To force her to confess, as the mother watches, the German officer tortures her naked, newly born child in the cold and kills him. As she walks to the gallows barefoot, clad only in a thin shirt, Olena's path is staged like the road to Golgotha, a northern Golgotha in the snow. The tortured and executed Ukrainian Madonna is surrounded by two figures who repeat her fate—a mother and her murdered son. The biblical narrative—the sacrificial death of children and the martyrdom of their mothers—is enhanced by the composition of the frames: a young adolescent who tries to help Olena is shot and falls onto barbed wire, which leaves traces of Jesus's torment on his forehead. The shots of his dead body in the coffin repeat the composition of Mantegna's well-known painting of the dead body of Christ.

Donskoi and his cameraman, Boris Monastyrskii, created a suggestive, icy atmosphere of oppressive physical terror, which they shot in artificial snow in the unbearable summer heat of Tashkent, where the studio had been evacuated. This atmosphere was created not only by the contrast of the defenseless, warm body and the putatively cold snow but also, above all, by the rhythmic, sloweddown, "frozen" development of the film and its special affective strategy, which heightened the state of being powerless in confronting terror. This impotence was lifted in the film's last scene—a scene in which, skiing lightly and very fast, the partisans attack. Only here could the accumulated constraint of movements be discharged in a sensorimotor manner and bring liberation to the viewer. The fact that flying, liberating movement was associated with snow gave the icy landscape an unexpectedly different connotation. On 18 November 1944 the American critic James Agee published a review of this film in *The Nation*, in which he asserted that *The Rainbow* had no artistic value: he described the impact of the film as aesthetic blackmail that paralyzes viewers' ability to make moral and aesthetic judgments. Therefore, ethics and aesthetics destroy each other, and the film does not attempt to understand the cruelty of war.[24]

This film cast doubt on a narrative about heroes of the ice who are able to overcome the cold and suggested another way to present it on the screen. The heroes' lack of the opportunity to move, their isolation from the world, and the impossibility of communication were attributed to the snowy landscape, the freezing of the film's rhythm, and its special affective strategy (the long infusion of terror without resolution). The image and the sensation of cold coalesced and, in conveying cold, not the plot but the atmosphere and the way it was created also became important.

This change in the "temperature" of the screen intensified even more during the "Thaw." The Russian film historian Vitalii Troianovskii called that period the "cinema of a 'cold snap'" and he considered *Ivan's Childhood* (*Ivanovo detstvo*, 1961) the first Soviet "genuinely cold film" (whose action, by the way, does not take place in winter). He associated this cooling with a change in the "dominant generation of filmmakers" and the appearance of "aesthetic, philosophical, and moral alternatives."[25] A series of new war films in the 1970s and 1980s (Aleksei German's 1971 *Trial on the Road/Proverka na dorogakh*; Larisa Shepit'ko's 1977 *The Ascent/Voskhozhdenie*; Semen Aranovich's 1983 *Tornado Bombers/Tornedonostsy*, among others) and Nikolai Dostal's later Gulag series (*Lenin's Testament/Zaveshchanie Lenina*, 2007) created the image of a "ferocious winter." Beautiful snowy landscapes were preserved only in fairy tales, adventure films, or historical epics.

Winter and frost had previously been presented as majestic nature, purifying civilization and yielding to it, creating and transforming the Soviet person's character. In Thaw and post-Thaw films, the symbolic temperature of the culture dropped. In this culture, cold began to be assessed not as a healthy, inalienable part of the national identity but as a life-threatening climatic condition. Mystical illumination no longer helped. This shift attested to a change in self-assessments of the national character and signified a local warming: while Russian heroes did not freeze on the screen in the 1920s and 1930s, and in its cinematic representation cold was warm, now Russian films presented the cold as cold.

There were also changes in the film techniques that made it possible to transmit the sensation of cold from the screen to the audience. The intent was not to dramatize a situation but to ensure a perceptual shift from heightened beauty to the corporeal sensation of something that is unbearable, which had to be conveyed suggestively. This meant a change in how films were shot. Previously the aesthetic perception of the decorativeness of a snowy landscape had been supported not only by narratives but, above all, by ways to light the snow and the actors' bodily movements. For shooting in the studio, powerful lighting and orange filters were used, supporting a "warm" radiance of the white surface. This same effect could be achieved when shooting in nature in bright sunlight.

German, Shepit'ko, and Aranovich shot their films without sun and without additional lighting. In the composition of the shot it is not the earth's white covering but the gray, gloomy background of the sky that dominates. The snow does not sparkle, the light is dim and almost like twilight, the landscape reflects the dark sky, and the sun, even if it appears in the clouds, does not change its grayish color. This white-gray surface of a broad expanse without structuring elements (trees, houses, poles, bridges) creates the sense of a complete loss of orientation. The sparkling whiteness is not important; instead it is the inability to figure out what is close and what is far away. The contrasts are insignificant, reduced by a thin layer of pyrotechnic smoke, which is perceived as icy fog. This fog is supported by the effect of steam from the actors' mouths. The steam not only is authentic, pointing to the effect of the actual temperature (although this effect in the cinema is an illusion that can easily be achieved or overcome by using certain techniques), but it also has an atmospheric impact, supporting the contrast between a warm body and the cold environment, which vanishes at the moment in the film when the external temperature surrounding that body is established and the corpse loses its warm breath.

Neither Aleksandr Rou in *Jack Frost* (*Morozko*) nor Sergei Gerasimov in most of the scenes in *Seven Brave Men* intended to achieve this effect in close-ups of their heroes freezing to death in a fairy-tale winter forest in the former or in a snowy cave in the latter, after the protagonists get lost on the way to the polar station. Steam coming out of the actor's mouth could be artificially created in these films, but the directors did not need it. Therefore, in *Jack Frost*, an actress can easily wear a light dress and play a scene of freezing in the snow, which the viewer perceives as a striking visual sleight of hand but does not experience as something frightening. The artificiality of this comfortable movie-winter was emphasized pointedly. In *Seven Brave Men* the director combined close-ups and extended dialogues in medium shots against a background of artificial snowy landscapes, which were filmed in a warm studio, and very long shots with a skier in real snow. The long shots in nature were captured in bright sunlight, enhancing the snow's decorative beauty and glittering whiteness. Warm orange filters removed the feeling of cold light. On the screen, even the polar explorer, dressed in a fur jumpsuit but dying, whose face Gerasimov covered with hoarfrost, does not convey the sense of becoming stiff from the cold. His body remains warm and he is dying from general exhaustion.

The ways to represent bodies in the snow also changed. Stolper's and Gerasimov's films accentuated their polar explorers' and flyers' warm clothing, which protected their bodies—fur jumpsuits and hats, thick gloves. Donskoi, Shepit'ko, and German sent their partisans into the snow in ragged overcoats, thin boots, and underwear, emphasizing their defenselessness. Unlike the films of the 1930s, fur, *valenki* (felt snow boots), and equipment were absent from the screen. Indeed, the films ignored the fact that cars will not start in the cold, but after the Soviet screen taught the viewer to always see snow in combination with either motorized sleds or an icebreaker, this change was felt visually as a shift. Equipment enabled the heroes of the films of the 1930s to overcome insurmountable space. Even Gerasimov's and Stolper's heroes, who did not have equipment, were not stopped for a minute. This unstoppable movement surmounted cold with kinetics.

New films were based on the impossibility of forward movement in snow and on obstacles that the protagonists, falling into a state of complete immobility, could not overcome. Kalatozov used just this gradual congealing of movement in *The Unsent Letter* (*Neotpravlennoe pis'mo*). The face of a geologist lost in the taiga was covered with snow or hoarfrost and was gradually transformed into an immobile—dead—mask. German and Shepit'ko chose eccentric details to emphasize the contrast of warm and cold as living and dead. A cow lost in the snow, a house without a roof, the impossibility of drawing water from a frozen well. Cold in films received an extremely unpleasant acoustic equivalent. The crackle of frost was created by a high-pitched, grating noise, intensifying the feeling of "inhumanity."

The cold's radical inhumanity was carried into Gulag films. In *Kolyma Tales* (*Kolymskie rasskazy*) Varlam Shalamov presented the feeling of cold that he and his hero experienced, impressively suggestively and rhythmically, like the falling of breath: "My body trembled from every blast of the wind, I writhed, I could not stop all of my skin from trembling—from my toes to the back of my head."[26]

Cold—along with hunger, exhaustion, and terror—destroys the prisoners' humanity. It is striking, however, that Shalamov, the son of a priest, ignores the ambivalent nature of the situation. Monks voluntarily subjected their bodies to these deprivations, and cold, hunger, silence, and pain entered the arsenal of their ways to achieve the transcendental state of a special spirituality while suppressing corporeality. The heating system in the Solovki monastery hardly changed when the monastery was turned into a camp. Although the monks did not complain about the cold, the Gulag prisoners perceived the temperature differently. The absence of free choice—the inability to choose to attain or block the sensation of the cold—was decisive in the perception of the sensation of cold.

This is exactly what one notices in comparing how the winter landscape is represented in two of Nikolai Dostal's films, the 2007 TV series *Lenin's Testament* and the film *Petia on the Road to the Kingdom of Heaven* (*Petia po doroge v tsarstvie nebesnoe*, 2009), which describes life in the zone where people who had been freed from the camps lived. *Lenin's Testament* is about the fate of Varlam Shalamov. Iurii Arabov, who wrote the screenplay, wove stories from several of the *Kolyma Tales* into this partly fictional biography of Shalamov. (The seventh and eighth episodes of the series are devoted to his time in Kolyma.)

Petia on the Road to the Kingdom of Heaven depicts an episode from the life of a young *iurodivyi* (holy fool), whose sojourn on earth represents only a brief stop on the road to another kingdom. The action takes place in March 1953, on the eve of the amnesty for Gulag prisoners, when several convicts try to flee and accidentally murder Petia while the authorities are pursuing them. Both the film and the TV series were shot in the same place, the settlement of Kandaksha in Murmansk *Oblast'*. The contrast between frost as warmth and cold, beauty and death, is achieved by using different kinds of lighting, color grading, and framing. Outside the camp, frost appears as the beauty of the snowy landscape, which can be apprehended aesthetically. Inside the camp all aesthetic categories are destroyed, and the film tries to connect the same landscape with unpleasant sensations on the level of visuality as well as the level of dramaturgy. The film about Petia could have been called "The Warm Winter of '53." The visual range of the film is defined by the fairy-tale splendor of the decorative landscape. The snow cover turns into a surface radiating light. All the heroes are dressed in light-colored fur jackets, and the whiteness is not soiled by human bodies but is only clearly, rhythmically structured by dark fir trees, wooden structures, rails, and sleepers. Petia builds a mausoleum out of snow that is like a castle for a sleeping beauty from which he inspects a parade of prisoners every morning. However, the snowy whiteness and the shining light are not associated with the dark, undifferentiated mass that the prisoners represent. When they appear in the frame, the whiteness is replaced by a dirty, gray-brown color. In one episode they have to trample this untouched whiteness in order lay the road. Visually, this leads to the destruction of the decorative, sparkling whiteness.

The television series follows other settings. Its dominant color is the dark, indistinguishable brown mass of earth and barracks and the prisoners' gray bodies. Their dark colors—dark clothing, dark buildings—force the festive whiteness completely out of the frame. The gray-brown mass dominates, and the snow itself looks like dirt. Not only are the bodies concealed in quilted jackets but the faces also are almost invisible from under their bulky *ushankas*.

Shalamov describes cold as an unstoppable, dynamic, and all-annihilating force of nature, which breaks the human body and many other materials: "The Kolyma frost tests any building material, asphalt board, plywood—it crumbles, breaks it."[27]

Each episode begins with a panorama of a snowy landscape structured by the crosses in the cemetery and tightly links the picture of the snow with an image of death. This is supported by many of the episodes' storylines, in which the cold is the reason several heroes die: the unheated barrack becomes a mass grave; Shalamov's sister dies from hypothermia. Snow does not appear as an aesthetic sublime but as an ugly and dangerous phenomenon. In the television series, the light is suppressed. While the film about Petia was shot at midday and in sunlight, all the footage of the TV series was shot in the afternoon, when the sun was hidden by clouds, and at twilight. The sun does not shine; the temperature of the light is cold, and this feeling is transmitted to the screen. Freedom decides whether the snow is cold or warm, whether it can strike the imagination as a visual impression or shock as a deadly force. The temperature of the light and the color grading determine whether we perceive this element aesthetically or aesthesically.

The abstractness of the snow removes the visual dirt and distracting details. But instead of a sublime picture and spirituality, the TV series shows the viewers ugliness linked with death. The Gulag does not contribute to the development of aesthetic perception. Whiteness does not lead the prisoners to the suppression of corporeality necessary to enhance the internal sight needed by the seer whose body was wasting away in the wilderness. The cultural significance of the cold, which would often be seen as part of the sacral, mystical spirit of the North, is destroyed, and the cold is associated with a catastrophe, a threat, a border zone that is far from civilization and slows down all processes, above all, speed, which is associated with the coordinates of modernism.

In various epochs, Soviet films delineated quite different pictures of cold, ice, and snow, which changed the perception of Russian natural and climatic conditions. If a way of living—be it clothing (*valenki*, furs), food (Siberian pelmeni), or the *bania*—creates adaptational mechanisms, then images and films have always been a powerful way to condition sensations and emotions. They make winter feel warm and beautiful or harsh and dangerous. The change in screen temperature, and, at the same time, Russian identity and the culture's symbolic temperature, can be interpreted in this context as a crisis of the community, the singling out of individual, differentiated perception that does not coincide with the national cliché. However, even in the very coldest period, when pictures of cold already appeared as the end of civilization in Hollywood films, Tarkovsky's films returned to the snowy landscape as its beginning.

Translation by Jacqueline Friedlander

Oksana Bulgakowa is professor emeritus of film studies at Johannes Gutenberg University Mainz. She has published several books on Russian and German cinema (*Eisenstein: Three Utopias; Architectural Drafts for a Film Theory*, 1996; *The Adventures of Doctor Mabuse in the Country of Bolsheviks*, 1995; *Eisenstein: A Biography*, German edition 1998, English 2003, Russian 2017; *Factory of Gestures*, 2005; *Soviet Hearing Eye: Film and Its Senses*, 2010), directed films (*Stalin—A Mosfilmproduction*, 1993; *The Different Faces of Sergei Eisenstein*, 1998), curated exhibits (film section of the exhibit *Moscow–Berlin, Berlin–Moscow 1900–1950*), and developed multimedia projects (The Visual Universe of Sergei Eisenstein, website, Daniel Langlois Foundation, 2005; *Factory of Gestures: On Body Language in Film*, DVD, 2008; *Eisenstein: My Art in Life*, Google Arts & Culture, 2017). She has taught at FU Berlin, Stanford, and UC Berkeley.

Appendix: Filmography

72 Degrees Below Zero (*72 gradusa nizhe nulia*, 1976), directed by Sergei Danilin and Evgenii Tatarskii. Adventure film about how a unique research station at the South Geomagnetic Pole is saved.

Above Us the Southern Cross (*Nad nami iuzhnyi krest*, 1965), directed by Vadim Il'enko and Igor Bolgarin. Period drama about the Arctic.

Alder Island (*Ostrov ol'khovyi*, 1962), directed by Tatiana Berezantseva. About looking for iron ore near Sakhalin.

Alitet Leaves for the Mountains (*Alitet ukhodit v gory*, 1949), directed by Mark Donskoi. Ethnographic film about how the Soviet regime was established in Chukotka.

Alesha's Love (*Aleshkina liubov'*, 1960), directed by Georgii Shchukin and Semen Tumanov. Melodrama about Alesha, a geologist at a drilling site on the Kazakh steppe who falls in love with Zinka.

Animal Hunters (*Zverolovy*, 1959), directed by Gleb Nifontov. Film about hunting a tiger.

An Antarctic Tale (*Antarkticheskaia povest'*, 1979), directed by Sergei Tarasov. Musical period drama about brave polar explorers as they began to explore Antarctica.

The Ascent (*Voskhozhdenie*, 1976), directed by Larisa Shepit'ko. About the fate of partisans in occupied Belorussia during the winter of 1942.

At the North Pole (*Na Severnom poliuse*, 1937), directed by Iakov M. Posel'skii. Documentary about the heroes of the Arctic.

Attention, Tsunami Coming! (*Vnimanie, tsunami!*, 1969), directed by Georgii Iungval'd-Khil'kevich. Adventure film about sailors sending out alerts about a tsunami.

Avalanche (*Lavina*, 1975), directed by Nikolai Koshelev and Valentin Morozov. A story about the enthusiasts of the 1930s who were the first to explore the Khibinskii Mountains and conquer the ice tundra.

The Ballad of Bering and His Friends (*Ballada o Beringe i ego druz"iakh*, 1970), directed by Iurii Shvyrev. About the discoveries made on an expedition led by Vitus Bering, a Danish cartographer and explorer who served in the Russian navy during the reign of Peter I.

The Battle of Stalingrad (*Stalingradskaia bitva*, 1949), directed by Vladimir Petrov. About the heroic defense of Stalingrad in 1942.

The Bay of Happiness (*Zaliv schast"ia*, 1987), directed by Vladimir Laptev. Biopic and adventure film about the life and work of Admiral G. I. Nevel'skoi.

Bearskin for Sale (Prodaetsia medvezh"ia shkura, 1980), directed by Aleksandr Itygilov. Drama about a bear who pursues a hunter who has killed his she-bear.

Blow the Whistle Twice in the Fog (*Dva dolgikh gudka v tumane*, 1980), directed by Valerii Rodchenko. Crime film whose action takes place at the beginning of the 1980s in a northern region of the USSR. An AN-2 hydroplane carrying bags of money is forced to make an unplanned landing in a sparsely settled area near a lake. The crew leaves the plane, but a strong wind comes up and carries the plane to the opposite shore of the lake. An unknown person who comes upon the AN-2 takes some of the money, burns the plane, and kills an inadvertent witness to the theft. The captain of the plane takes it upon himself to investigate.

Bonfire on a White Night (*Koster v beloi nochi*, 1984), directed by Boris Buneev. Disaster film about a group of geologists who are doing exploratory work in Siberia and accidently set fire to forests.

Born Twice (Dvazhdy rozdennyi, 1983), directed by Arkadii Sirenko. War drama about a young soldier who is the sole survivor of a Soviet ship that was sunk by the Germans. As he makes his way through an unforgiving, snowy landscape, he is relentlessly pursued by a German plane whose pilot is determined to kill him.

The Boss (*Nachal'nik*, 1989), directed by Dmitrii Gendenshtein. Adventure film about geologists.

The Boss of Chukotka (*Nachal'nik chukotki*, 1966), directed by Vitalii Mel'nikov. Film about Alesha, a young clerk who by chance becomes the head of Chukotka.

Caravan (*Karavan*, 1974), directed by Uchkun Nazarov. A film about geologists. A brigade of oil drillers comes to an Uzbek mountain village. A driller named Afzal falls in love with a young widow with a child named Kholinsu.

Chuk and Gek (*Chuk i Gek*, 1953), directed by Ivan Lukinskii. The story of how seven-year-old Chuk and six-year-old Gek went with their mother to join their father, who was on a geological expedition to a remote location in Siberia.

Cheliuskin (1934), directed by Iakov M. Posel'skii. Documentary about the heroes of the Arctic.

Cheliuskintsy (1984), directed by Mikhail Ershov. Period drama about the Cheliuskintsy, the members of an expedition made by the steamship *Cheliuskin*.

The Commandant of Bird Island (*Komendant Ptich'ego ostrova*, 1939), directed by Vasilii Pronin. Adventure film about a border guard who finds himself on an uninhabited island and stands guard over Japanese smugglers.

The Commander of the Lucky "Pike" (*Komandir schastlivoi "Shchuki,"* 1972), directed by Boris Volchek. Film about the heroism of the submariners of the Northern Fleet who defended the sea lanes providing access to Murmansk in 1942.

Convoy PQ-17 (*Konvoi PQ-17*, 2004), directed by Aleksandr Kott. About the heroism and courage of sailors on an Allied Arctic convoy during World War II.

The Defence of Volochaevka (*Volochaevskie dni*, 1937), directed by Georgii Vasil'ev and Sergei Vasil'ev. War film about Japanese commandos supporting the Whites during the Russian Civil War.

Dersu Uzala (1961), directed by Agasi Babaian. Film based on Russian traveler Vladimir Arsen'ev's 1923 book of the same title about his journeys through the Ussuriisk region.

Dersu Uzala (1975), directed by Akira Kurosawa. Soviet-Japanese coproduction about the travels of Russian scientist and writer Vladimir Arsen'ev. Dersu Uzala, a hunter in the taiga, was Arsen'ev's friend and is at the center of the story.

Diamonds (*Almazy*, 1947), directed by Aleksandr Olenin and Ivan Pravov. Young geologist Sergei Nesterov has returned from the army and is continuing the work that the war interrupted, a search for deposits of diamonds for industrial use in the Urals. He finally succeeds.

Diamond Trail (*Almaznaia tropa*, 1978), directed by Vladimir Khmelnitskii. Historical, five-episode TV adventure film about geologists.

Dima Gorin's Career (*Kar'era Dimy Gorina*, 1961), directed by Frunze Dovlatian and Lev Mirskii. Comedy about how Dima Gorin goes, as a result of a series of coincidences, to a construction site in Siberia where he meets his true love.

A Dream in Polar Fog (*Son v nachale tumana*, 1994), directed by Baras Khalzanov. Period drama about a European's integration into the culture and traditions of Chukotka.

Eagle Island (*Orlinyi ostrov*, 1961), directed by Mikhail Izrailev and Marianna Roshal'. About the work done by Moldavian archaeologists on the mysterious Eagle Island.

Ermak (1996), directed by Vladimir Krasnopol'skii and Valerii Uskov. Action-packed historical film about Ermak Timofeevich, one of the most brilliant, controversial, and tragic figures of the era of Ivan the Terrible.

The Evil Spirit of Iambui (*Zloi dukh iambuia*, 1978), directed by Boris Buneev. A story based on Grigorii Fedoseev's story, which is itself based on real events and people, is the film's starting point. About topographers, prospectors, and surveyors.

Far from Moscow (*Daleko ot Moskvy*, 1950), directed by Aleksandr Stolper. Film version of Vasilii Azhaev's novel of the same title about the construction of an oil pipeline in the Far East at the beginning of World War II.

From Snow to Snow (*Ot snega do snega*, 1968), directed by Iurii Petrov. Melodrama about how a young woman who has just graduated from an institute travels to a remote meteorological station in the north. Circumstances force her to go through the winter alone.

Georgii Sedov (1975), directed by Boris Grigor'ev. About the preparations for an expedition to the North Pole and the expedition itself, which was led by the well-known Arctic researcher, sailor, and hydrographer Georgii Iakovlevich Sedov (1877–1914), who funded the expedition with private donations.

Glass Beads (*Stekliannye busy*, 1978), directed by Igor Nikolaev. Children's film about a father's relationship with his young daughter and their trip to Kamchatka.

Golden Lake (*Zolotoe ozero*, 1935), directed by Vladimir Shneiderov. About a fight between members of a gold-prospecting expedition and a predatory band on the run from justice in the Altai taiga.

The Golden Woman (*Zolotaia baba*, 1986), directed by Viktor Kobzev. Adventure film about the search for a golden statue in the Urals.

The Great Sami (*Velikii samoed*, 1981), directed by Arkadii Kordon. The story of Tyko Vylka, the first Nenets artist, cartographer, and polar researcher. He fought in World War II and was the chair of the Island Council of Novaia Zemlia.

How I Spent This Summer (*Kak ia provel etim letom*, 2008), directed by Aleksei Popogrebskii. Film about polar explorers. Petty conflicts and human morals are at the center of the story.

An Icy Fate (*Ledianaia sud'ba*, 1930), directed by Vladimir Petrov. Adventure film about the staff of a meteorological station beyond the Arctic Circle. The film has not been preserved.

If I Fall in Love (*Esli ia poliubliu*, 1976), directed by Lev Tsutsul'kovskii. Melodrama about Shura's first expedition. She is a young woman who has recently graduated from a geological institute.

I'm Going to You Arctica (*Idu k tebe Arktika*, 1985), directed by Iosif Pasternak. Documentary about polar explorers.

Incident in the Taiga (*Sluchai v taiga*, 1953), directed by Iurii Egorov and Iurii Pobedonostsev. Adventure film that takes place in a Siberian enterprise, involving a local hunter and a young scientist from Moscow who wants to introduce a new method for breeding sables.

Island (*Ostrov*, 2006), directed by Pavel Lungin. Mystical story about a modern saint in a northern monastery.

It Happened at Mine Number Eight (*Sluchai v shakhte vosem'*, 1957), directed by Vladimir Basov. About the development of Siberia and the discovery of coal deposits.

It's Quiet Here (*Mesta tyt tikhie*, 1967), directed by Georgii Shchukin. War film about polar flyers.

Jack Frost (*Morozko*, 1964), directed by Aleksandr Rou. Children's fairy-tale film about the fate of modest Nasten'ka and her stepmother's unappeasable greed.

Just One Life (*Vsego odna zhizn'*, 1968), directed by Sergei Mikaelian. A joint Soviet-Norwegian film about Fridtjof Nansen, the famous polar researcher and traveler.

Komsomol'sk (1938), directed by Sergei Gerasimov. About the construction of Komsomol'sk-on-Amur and sabotage in factories.

The Last Hunt (*Posledniaia okhota*, 1979), directed by Igor Sheshukov. Ethno-drama that takes place during the 1920s. Foreign pirates moor their schooner on the shore of the Arctic Ocean near Russian East Siberian settlements. They buy valuable furs and gold from the locals on the cheap. The pirates decide to steal the treasure. Ivan Shatokhin, the manager of the trading post, and the local Eskimos band together to fight them.

The Last Year of the Golden Eagle (*Poslednii god Berkuta*, 1987), directed by Vadim Lysenko. Period drama about the fight against the White Guards.

The Law of the Antarctic (*Zakon Antarktidy*, 1965), directed by Timofei Levchuk. About the rescue of a group of Belgian polar explorers whose airplane crashed on New Year's Eve. Soviet flyers were the only ones to come to the aid of the passengers.

Lieutenant Klimov's Truth (*Pravda leitenanta Klimova*, 1981), directed by Oleg Dashkevich. War drama.

Little Napoleon III (*Nedopesok Napoleon III*, 1979), directed by Eduard Bocharov. Film about an Arctic fox who has escaped from a fur farm. The fox saves a six-year-old boy.

Love Me the Way I Love You (*Liubi menia, kak ia tebia*, 1986), directed by Vera Tokareva. Polar explorer Fedor meets and falls in love with Ksenia. Ksenia responds to Fedor's kindness and sensitivity.

The Man from Nowhere (*Chelovek niotkuda*, 1957), directed by El'dar Riazanov. Fantasy comedy about finding Big Foot, the attempts to socialize him, and the adventures that are part of these efforts.

The Man Who Was Lucky (*Chelovek, kotoromu vezlo*, 1978), directed by Konstantin Ershov. A story about a father, the talented geologist Vladimir Ishutin, as he is seen through his sons' eyes. The film recreates the 1920s–30s.

Master of the Taiga (*Khozain taigi*, 1968), directed by Vladimir Nazarov. A crime story about a young, inexperienced police detective.

Mishka in the North (*Mishka na severe*, 1979), directed by Sergei Shpakovskii. About the surprising twists and turns in the fate of Mikhail Ruchkin, the driver of an all-terrain vehicle who decides to take a vacation from his job in the Arctic and go to Moscow.

Moonstone (*Lunnyi kamen'*, 1935), directed by Adol'f Minkin and Igor Sorokhtin. In 1912 Russian geologist Ivan Popov discovers deposits of a rare mineral, the so-called moonstone, in the Pamir region, and the Academy of Sciences of the USSR sends an expedition there.

A Mysterious Discovery (*Tainstvennaia nakhodka*, 1954), directed by Boris Buneev. What three schoolboys from a polar settlement learn about the history of the region when they find an old gun in a cave.

The Mystery of the Golden Mountain (*Taina zolotoi gory*, 1985), directed by Nikolai Gusarov. About how the serf Mikhailo Volkov, German geologist Friedrich Nagel, and Siberians Khariton and Kornei discovered coal deposits on Gora Gorelaia, near the future city of Kemerovo.

Nameless Island (*Ostrov bezymiannyi*, 1946), directed by Adol'f Bergunker. War film that takes place on a northern island.

New Horizon (*Novyi gorizont*, 1940), directed by Grigorii Braginskii and Aga-Rza Kuliev. A story about a young geologist's struggle against time-servers and careerists who are only interested in what helps them and who get in the way of the work of developing new oil reservoirs.

Nisso: Youth's First Morning (*Nisso: Iunosti pervoe utro*, 1979), directed by Davlat Khudonazarov. In 1919 an echo of the October Revolution rolls along the Pamir Mountains. However, in hard-to-reach villages, life continues as it did before.

The Northern Option (*Severnyi variant*, 1975), directed by Ol'gerd Vorontsov. A story about geologists and drilling for oil in the north.

On Active Duty (*Pri ispolnenii sluzhebnykh obiazannostei*, 1963), directed by Ilia Gurin. About polar flyers, friendship, and mutual help.

On the Ruler's Tracks (*Po sledu vlastelina*, 1979), directed by Vadim Derbenev. Adventure film about rescuing animals and the fight against poachers.

On the Winds of the Taiga (*Na taezhnykh vetrakh*, 1979), directed by Anatolii Nitochkin. About geologists prospecting for oil who are developing the USSR's northern regions.

Once There Lived a Capitan Brave (*Zhil otvazhnyi kapitan*, 1985), directed by Rudol'f Fruntov. War film about the heroic deeds of Tosia, the captain of a fishing trawler who becomes a naval officer.
Operation Wunderland (*Operatsiia Vunderland*, 1989), directed by Otar Koberidze. War film about how a small detachment of Soviet sailors helped to thwart the German military's Operation Wunderland, a large-scale effort to destroy Soviet ships. The setting is the far north in 1942.
An Order (*Prikaz*, 1987), directed by Iurii Oksanchenko. In the Arctic Circle, men doing their military training are ordered to set up a temporary lighthouse on the shoreline. The task must be completed within three days.
The Ordinary Arctic (*Obyknovennaia Arktika*, 1976), directed by Aleksei Simonov. A two-episode TV film based on Boris Gorbatov's socialist-realist stories about the everyday life of the Soviet conquerors of the Arctic.
Pamir (1929), directed by Vladimir Erofeev. Documentary about the heroes of the Arctic.
People in the Ocean (*Liudi v okeane*, 1980), directed by Pavel Chukhrai. Story about the daily life of border guards and danger lurking in the ocean.
The Polynin Case (*Sluchai s Polyninym*, 1970), directed by Aleksei Sakharov. War film. The film's action takes place in the late autumn of 1941 on the Karelian front. Polynin, the commander of an aviation regiment, falls in love with a young actress.
The Possessed (*Oderzhimye*, 1962), directed by Takhir Sabirov. A film about oil-prospecting geologists who are developing the northern regions of the country.
Princess Liuska's Shore (*Bereg printsessy Lius'ki*, 1967), directed by Viacheslav Nikiforov. About the work of a small group of geologists.
The Rainbow (*Raduga*, 1943), directed by Mark Donskoi. About the heroic struggle that Soviet partisans and the people who lived in the Ukrainian village of Nova Lebedivka waged against the Nazi occupiers.
The Red Tent (*Krasnaia palatka*, 1969), directed by Mikhail Kalatozov. Historical drama about a 1928 air expedition to the Arctic led by General Umberto Nobile.
Reserve Aerodrome (*Zapasnoi aerodrom*, 1978), directed by Ilia Gurin. Children's film about polar flyers.
The Return (*Vozvrashchenie*, 1968), directed by Viktor Ryzhkov. A soldier returns home after the end of the war. A story about how he has to start once again to get used to life in peacetime, his wife, and the children who grew up without him.
Riches (*Bogatstvo*, 2004), directed by El'dor Urazbaev. A TV adventure series based on Valentin Pikul's historical novel about defending Kamchatka and the Far East from the Japanese during the Russo-Japanese War.
The Rider with a Lightning Bolt in His Hand (*Vsadnik s molniei v ruke*, 1975), directed by Khasan Khazhkasimov. On the heroic deeds of Komsomol member Vera Flerova, who was the first to discover the largest deposit of tungsten and molybdenum in Kabardino-Balkariia in the early 1930s.
A Risk-Taking Strategy (*Strategiia riska*, 1978), directed by Aleksandr Proshkin. A story about the career path of a petroleum expert who goes from being in charge of exploratory geologic expeditions to the head geologist of the trust.
The River (*Reka*, 2002), directed by Aleksei Balabanov. Period film about a leper colony in the Iakutiian taiga.
The Roof of the World (*Krysha mira*, 1928), directed by V. Erofeev.

The Route (*Trassa*, 1978), directed by Anatolii Vekhotko and Nataliia Troshchenko. About a Czech investigator who finds himself in a complicated situation while laying an oil pipeline to the north of Tiumen'.

Sannikov Land (*Zemlia Sannikova*, 1973), directed by Albert Mkrtchian and Leonid Popov. Fantasy film based on science-fiction writer Vladimir Obruchev's novel of the same title about a dramatic expedition to a legendary warm land beyond the Arctic Circle.

The Scarlet Stone (*Alyi kamen'*, 1986), directed by Valerii Isakov. Romance about a young geologist and his bride, a tragic event, a rescue, and complications many years later.

Sea Cadet of the Northern Fleet (*Iunga severnogo flota*, 1973), directed by Vladimir Rogovoi. Four teenagers do not want to wait for the victory over the Germans, so they set out—each taking his own route—to a school for apprentice seamen on the Solovetsky Islands that was created at the beginning of the war.

The Secret of the Ancestors (*Taina predkov*, 1972), directed by Marat Aripov. Based on Nikolai Iakutskii's novel *The Golden Stream* (*Zolotoi Ruchei*). In Iakutiia merchants have bent the local inhabitants to their will. The merchant Oparin tries in vain to discover the secret of the golden stream.

The Secret of the Cave of Kaniut (*Taina peshchery Kaniiuta*, 1967), directed by Habib Faiziev. Adventure film about contemporary heroes—geologists—and people who lived long ago.

Semen Dezhnev (1983), directed by Nikolai Gusarov. Biopic about the seventeenth-century traveler Semen Dezhnev who was the first to discover the new Siberian lands.

Seven Brave Men (*Semero smelykh*, 1936), directed by Sergei Gerasimov. About the first team to spend the winter at a polar station in the Arctic.

Seven Hours until Death (*Sem' chasov do gibeli*, 1983), directed by Anatolii Vekhotko. About a surgeon on a steamship in the far north who saves a sailor's life.

The Seventeenth Transatlantic (*Semnadtsatyi transatlanticheskii*, 1972), directed by Vladimir Dovgan'. About how valuable shipments of military supplies for the USSR being carried by transport ships and protected by a British command were lost during World War II.

Short Summer in the Mountains (*Korotkoe leto v gorakh*, 1964), directed by Aida Manasarova. Feature film about Galia Ustinovich, a young woman who has come to a remote area for a geological training course.

Siberiade (*Sibiriada*, 1979), directed by Andrei Mikhalkov-Konchalovskii. Film about the subduing of Siberia told as a saga of two feuding families.

Skirmish in a Blizzard (*Skhvatka v purge*, 1978), directed by Aleksandr Gordon. Crime drama about a hijacked bus and the rescue of the passengers.

The Snow Queen (*Snezhnaia koroleva*, 1966), directed by Gennadii Kazanskii. Children's film based on the story by Hans Christian Andersen.

SOS from the Taiga (*SOS nad taigoi*, 1976), directed by Arkadii Kol'tsatyi and Valentin Perov. About a former prisoner named Zhamin who is on a work assignment with a colleague. They decide to travel separately through the taiga to a village, but the colleague does not arrive at the village. Zhamin is suspected of murdering this colleague, who is his enemy, during this journey.

Spotted Dog Running at the Edge of the Sea (*Pegii pes, begushchii kraem moria*, 1990), directed by Karen Gevorkian. The heroes of the film are Nivkhs, members of a small northern ethnic group, who give their lives to save a young boy.

Stalingrad (1943), directed by Leonid Varlamov. Soviet documentary about the battle of Stalingrad during World War II.

Stalingrad (1989), directed by Iurii Ozerov. War film.

The Stewardess (*Stiuardessa*, 1967), directed by Vladimir Krasnopol'skii and Valerii Uskov. About a woman who becomes a stewardess on the northern route of a domestic airline to have a chance to meet with her beloved, who is a geologist.

Story of the "Furious" (*Povest' o "Neistovom,"* 1947), directed by Boris Babochkin. About the destruction of a German submarine by the Soviet destroyer *Furious*.

Story of a Real Man (*Povest' o nastoiashchem cheloveke*, 1948), directed by Aleksandr Stolper. The dramatic story told in the film is based on actual events in the life of celebrated fighter pilot Aleksei Meres'ev.

The Sullen Vangur (*Khmuryi Vangur*, 1959), directed by Anatolii Dudorov. Feature film about geologists.

Summer Holiday Time (*Vremia letnikh otpuskov*, 1960), directed by Konstantin Voinov. As soon as summer comes to the northern regions, Svetlana, a geotechnical engineer who has been dreaming all winter about the southern sea, plans to go on vacation. But the day she is due to leave, she is given an unexpected assignment—to temporarily take charge of an oil field.

Taiga Landing (*Taezhnyi desant*, 1965), directed by Vladimir Krasnopol'skii and Valerii Uskov. About a youth brigade of builders in the taiga laying track for the Abakan-Taishet railway.

A Taiga Story (*Taezhnaia povest'*, 1979), directed by Vladimir Fetin. About hunters. A parable based on Viktor Astaf'ev's "A Dream about White Mountains," a short story in his *Tsar-Fish* (*Tsar'-ryba*) collection.

Territory (*Territoriia*, 1979), directed by Aleksandr Surin. The heroes of this film, which takes place in the mid-1950s, are geologists prospecting for gold at the Arctic Circle.

There Are No Strangers Here (*Chuzhie zdes' ne khodiat*, 1975), directed by Anatolii Vekhotko. A crime film about geologists in Siberia.

Those Who Go beyond the Horizon (*Idushchie za gorizont*, 1972), directed by Nikolai Kalinin. Ethno-drama about geologists and their travels to the far north.

The Time of the Taiga Snowdrop (*Pora taezhnogo podshnezhnika*, 1958), directed by Iaropolk Lapshin. Period film about events after the October Revolution.

Torpedo Bombers (*Torpedonostsy*, 1983), directed by Semen Arnovich. Film based on Iurii German's war novels that incorporates actual wartime footage. About a Soviet marine air force unit stationed in Murmansk.

Traces in the Snow (*Sledy na snegu*, 1955), directed by Adol'f Bergunker. An investigation of a murder and the capture of the criminals in the postwar years.

Transit (*Peregon*, 1984), directed by Oleg Riabokon'. Film about daily life in the navy, the honor of officers, and true male friendship, which shows itself in times of danger.

Trial on the Road (also known as *Checkpoint*) (*Proverka na dorogakh*, 1971), directed by Aleksei German. About partisan warfare during the winter of 1942.

Turn On the Northern Lights (*Vkliuchite Severnoe Siianie*, 1972), directed by Radomir Vasilevskii. Children's film about youngsters who disappear and are rescued.

The Turning Point (*Tochka vozvrata*, 1986), directed by Viacheslav Kolegaev. A film based on a novella by Vladimir Sanin about polar flyers, the development of Siberia, and the discovery of mineral deposits.

The Twelve Months (1956), directed by Ivan Ivanov-Vano and Mikhail Botov. Children's fairy-tale cartoon film.

Twilight (*Polumgla*, 2005), directed by Artem Antonov. It is the winter of 1945, and the war is drawing to a close. In a remote northern village, a brigade of German prisoners of war are building a tower for a radio beacon. The people living in the village—women and old people whose husbands and sons are fighting or have died at the front—meet the POWs with obvious animosity.

Two + Dog B. (*Dva + Sobaka B.*, 2002), directed by Dmitrii Vasil'ev. Adventure film about the conquest of the North Pole.

The Two Captains (*Dva kapitana*, 1955), directed by Vladimir Vengerov. Adventure film based on Veniamin Kaverin's novel of the same title about flyer Sania Grigor'ev, who found the traces of a missing expedition in the Arctic.

The Two Captains (*Dva kapitana*, 1976), directed by Evgenii Karelov. Television series based on Kaverin's novel about flyer Sania Grigor'ev.

Tymancha's Friend (*Drug Tymanchi*, 1960), directed by Anatolii Nitochkin. Adventure film telling the story of a wolf's friendship with humans.

Under the North Star (*Pod poliarnoi zvezdoi*, 2001), directed by Maksim Voronkov. A film about life in the far north.

Under the Northern Lights (*Pod Severnym Siianiem*, 1990), directed by Toshio Goto, Piatras Abukiavichus, and Sergei Vronskii. The story of a friendship between a Japanese hunter abandoned by fate in Siberia and a wolf he tamed and nicknamed Buran (Snowstorm).

Under a Stone Sky (*Pod kamennym nebom*, 1974), directed by Knut Andersen and Igor Maslennikov. War film about Norwegians rescued by the Red Army.

The Unsent Letter (*Neotpravlennoe pis'mo*, 1959), directed by Mikhail Kalatozov. Film about the search for diamonds and about geologists who get lost, are gradually freezing in the snowy taiga, and are trying to find ways to send information about the deposits of diamonds that they have found.

Valery Chkalov (1941), directed by Mikhail Kalatozov. A film about polar flyers.

Valley of the Blue Rocks (*Dolina sinikh skal*, 1956), directed by Nikolai Krasii. About young geologists scouting for oil reserves.

Vertical (*Vertikal'*, 1966), directed by Boris Durov and Stanislav Govorukhin. About the courage and experiences of mountaineers who were caught in a storm in the mountains.

Victory (*Pobeda*, 1938), directed by Vsevolod Pudovkin. A film about polar flyers.

Wait for Letters (*Zhdite pisem*, 1960), directed by Iulii Karasik. Story about eager young people who leave the city to work in Siberia.

The Wanderer (*Strannik*, 1987), directed by Mikhail Vedyshev. Adventure film based on Evgenii Feodorovskii's short story "A Fresh Ocean Breeze," which is part of his collection of short stories titled *Tsar-Fish* (*Tsar-ryba*).

When the Whales Leave (*Kogda ukhodiat kity*, 1981), directed by Anatolii Nitochkin. About the love of the beautiful Tintin and the hunter Gilgil for each other.

Where Winter Is Long (*Tam, gde dlinnaia zima*, 1967), directed by Aleksandr Davidson. About oil exploration and the construction of a camp to house drillers if oil is discovered.
While the Mountains Stand (*Poka stoiat gory*, 1976), directed by Vadim Mikhailov. Psychological drama about mountaineers.
White Curse (*Beloe prokliat'e*, 1987), directed by Nikolai Koval'skii. About the descent of an avalanche on a resort area and the courageous, last-minute rescue of the vacationers.
White Explosion (*Belyi vzriv*, 1971), directed by Stanislav Govorukhin. About the feats of Soviet soldiers in mountaineering divisions during World War II.
White Shaman (*Belyi shaman*, 1982), directed by Anatolii Nitochkin. The action takes place in 1930–40. The hero of the film is a hunter who becomes the chair of the first collective farm in Chukotka.
Wild Dog Dingo (*Dikaia sobaka Dingo*, 1962), directed by Iulii Karasik. A story about first love.
Wild Honey (*Dikii med*, 1966), directed by Vladimir Chebotarev. War drama about the fate of frontline photojournalist Varvara Kniazhich.
Wish Upon a Pike (*Po shchuch'emu velen'iu*, 1938), directed by Aleksandr Rou. Children's fairy-tale film about Emelia the lazybones who catches a magic pike that fulfils his wishes.
The Witness Disappeared (*Propazha svidetelia*, 1971), directed by Vladimir Nazarov. Thriller about an investigation of the murder of a zoologist.
Wolf Island (*Ostrov volchii*, 1969), directed by Nikolai Il'inskii. Film about polar flyers.
The Wolverine's Track (*Sled rosomakhi*, 1978), directed by Georgii Kropachev. Contemporary interpretation of an ancient Chukchi legend about love.
Zoia (1944), directed by Lev Arnshtam. About the life and heroism of Zoia Kosmodemianskaia, a young partisan who became a Hero of the Soviet Union after she was murdered by the Germans.

Acknowledgments

I would like to thank Viktoria Gökhan-Rotermel for her help in compiling this list.

Notes

1. A. Morskoi, "Moda na russkoe," *Illiustrirovannaia Rossiia*, no. 5 (1929): 15.
2. V. Shneiderov, *Pokhod Sibiriakov* (Moscow, 1933), 87. Vladimir Erofeev described the same difficulties experienced in shooting the Pamir ascension in *The Roof of the World* (*Krysha mira*, 1928). V. Erofeev, *Po kryshe mira s kino-apparatom: Puteshestvie na Pamir* (Moscow, 1929), 70, 16.
3. "Winter" appears in film titles 13 times and occupies the last place in the statistical hierarchy in comparison with "love" (225 times), "happiness" (61 times), "man" or "person" (*chelovek*) (59 times), and "death" (46 times). I am using Miroslav Segida's statistical analysis of the titles of 6,500 Soviet films and 1,060 pre-revolutionary Russian films that appeared between 1907 and 1991. See M. Segida and S. Zemlianukhin, *Domashniaia sinemateka: Otechestvennoe kino 1918–1996* (Moscow, 1996), 8.

4. Here I have in mind two essays: Oksana Sarkisova, "Arctic Travelogues: Conquering the Soviet North," in *Films on Ice: Cinemas of the Arctic*, edited by Scott MacKenzie and Anna Westerståhl Stenport (Edinburgh, 2015), 222–31; and Lilya Kaganovsky, "The Negative Space in the National Imagination: Russia and the Arctic," in *Arctic Environmental Modernities: From the Age of Polar Exploration to the Era of the Anthropocene*, edited by Lill Ann Körber, Scott MacKenzie, and Anna Westerståhl Stenport (Basingstoke, 2017), 169–82. Both essays are devoted to documentary films from the 1920s and 1930s. They concentrate on the production history, historical context, and artistic expression of three films: *One Sixth of the World* (1926); Dziga Vertov's *Beyond the Arctic Circle* (*Za poliarnym krugom*, 1927); and Vladimir Erofeev's film about the Vasil'ev brothers, *Feat on the Ice* (*Podvig vo l'dakh*, 1928). Kaganovsky also discusses *Solovki Power* (*Solovetskaia vlast'*, 1988), Marina Goldovskaya's late film about the first Gulag camp. In addition, she mentions two recent films without analyzing them: Aleksei Popogrebskii's *How I Spent This Summer* (2009) and Ivan Tverdovskii's *Island of Communism* (*Ostrov kommunizma*, 2014). Sarkisova's and Kaganovsky's pieces are contributions to essay collections that examine the relationship between modernization (countermodernities and multiple modernities) and the specific geographic, political, and climatic space of the Arctic. The essays in both volumes analyze narratives associated with this space in various cultures and the visual representation of this space in film (moving images), narratives that, as the editors put it, "play a central role in the global representation of Arctic modernities" (Körber, MacKenzie, and Westerståhl Stenport, "Introduction: Arctic Modernities, Environmental Politics, and the Era of the Anthropocene," in Körber, MacKenzie, and Westerståhl Stenport, *Arctic Environmental Modernities*, 15). In Kaganovsky's and Sarkisova's factually rich essays, however, the emphasis is not on representation of the "cold" and the metaphorical contexts associated with it but rather on the influence of the political paradigms of Russian imperialism of the beginning of the century, which were supplanted by the expansionist policy of the Stalin era. In other words, the heroic conquest of the Arctic and its transformation into a habitable, "warm" space. The Gulag camp system was supposed to carry out this project, but there is no documentary material about this. Film fell under the influence of various ideologemes and, in accordance with these, changed the image of the Arctic. New works resist these ideologemes: for example, work done by Ursula Biemann, the Swiss experimental video artist and political activist, whose installations are not presented in movie theaters but in art galleries, museums, and various contemporary art biennales. They are meant to mobilize viewers to fight against environmental pollution, the destruction of the Arctic landscape, and climate change in the Anthropocene epoch. For example, in her 2013 installation *Deep Weather*, Biemann uses aerial photography, which initially shows enchanting natural beauty, but then the camera reveals the dimensions of what industrial terrorism has done to the landscape. Lisa E. Bloom's essay, "Invisible Landscapes: Extreme Oil and the Arctic in Experimental Film and Activist Art Practices" (in Körber, MacKenzie, and Westerståhl Stenport, *Arctic Environmental Modernities*, 183–95), is devoted to this installation and similar works.
5. Thomas Edward Lawrence, *Seven Pillars of Wisdom: A Triumph* (London, 1935), 39–41. Emphasis mine.

6. These metaphors have been analyzed in recent scholarship. See for example, Helmut Lethen, "Lob der Kälte: Ein Motiv der historischen Avantgarden," in *Die unvollendete Vernunft: Moderne versus Postmoderne*, edited by Dietmar Kamper and Willem van Reijen (Frankfurt/Main, 1987), 282–324; Helmut Lethen, *Verhaltenslehren der Kälte: Lebensversuche zwischen den Kriegen* (Frankfurt/Main, 1994); Andrea Dortmann, *Winter Facets: Traces and Tropes of the Cold* (Bern, 2007); and Heidi Hansson and Cathrin Norberg, eds., *Cold Matters: Cultural Perceptions of Snow, Ice and Cold* (Umeå, 2009), among many others.
7. Theodor W. Adorno, *Ästhetische Theorie* (Frankfurt/Main, 1970), 13. Alexander Kluge recently presented some aspects of this symbolic connotation in his four-hour film *Landscapes with Ice and Snow* (*Landschaften mit Eis und Schnee*, 2010), which draws on Adorno's ideas.
8. Bettine Menke, "Die Polargebiete der Bibliothek: Über eine metapoetische Metapher," *Deutsche Vierteljahresschrift für Literaturwissenschaft und Geistesgeschichte* 4 (December 2000): 545–97.
9. Siegfried Kracauer, *From Caligari to Hitler: A Psychological History of the German Film* (Princeton, NJ, 1974), 259.
10. Ibid., 261.
11. Ibid.
12. Ibid., 258.
13. Robert G. David, *The Arctic in the British Imagination, 1818–1914* (Manchester, 2000).
14. In the political mythology of the 1930s–50s there is, however, a strange paradox, which Vladimir Papernyi revealed, using the architecture of Moscow as an example. The plan for the general reconstruction of the city used models from Italian architecture, which, like Peter I, Stalin preferred. With its warm Mediterranean architecture, the wide balconies and sunny terraces that compelled one to forget about the short summer and the severe winter, the northern, landlocked capital looked like Venice. Vladimir Papernyi, *Kul'tura dva* (Moscow, 1996), 174–78.
15. Camille Paglia, "Ice Queen, Drag Queen," *New Republic*, 4 March 1996, 24–26.
16. Georg Lukács, "Reification and the Consciousness of the Proletariat," in *History and Class Consciousness: Studies in Marxist Dialectics*, trans. Rodney Livingstone (Cambridge, MA, 1971), 90. In the original: "Die Zeit verliert damit ihren qualitativen, veränderlichen, flussartigen Charakter: sie erstarrt zu einem genau umgrenzten, quantitativ messbaren, von quantitativ messbaren 'Dingen' (den verdinglichten, mechanisch objektivierten, von der menschlichen Gesamtpersönlichkeit genau abgetrennten 'Leistungen' des Arbeiters) erfüllten Kontinuum: zu einem Raum." Georg Lukács, "Die Verdinglichung und das Bewußtsein des Proletariats," in *Werke*, vol. 2: *Frühschriften: Geschichte und Klassenbewußtsein* [1923] (Berlin, 1963), 264.
17. Dziga Vertov, *Dramaturgicheskie opyty*, vol. 1 of *Iz naslediia*, ed. Aleksandr Deriabin (Moscow, 2004), 168.
18. Ten years later, in *The Vow* (*Kliatva*) Mikheil Chiaureli took over this bench as a ready-made sign: "There, near a bench where Lenin's shadow appears to be imprinted in the snow, the voice of the dead man speaks to the conscience of Stalin. But lest the allusion to the mystical coronation of Moses and to the mystical transmission of Mosaic law be missed, the director has Stalin look up *to heaven*. A beam of sunlight pierces through

the branches of the fir trees and strikes the forehead of the new Moses." André Bazin, "The Myth of Stalin in the Soviet Cinema," *Bazin at Work: Major Essays & Reviews from the Forties & Fifties*, ed. Bert Cardullo, trans. Alain Piette and Bert Cardullo (New York, 1997), 34.
19. Sergej Eisenstein, "Massenkino," *Die Weltbühne*, no. 49 (1927). The quotation is from the reprint of Eisenstein's article in *Filmwissenschaftliche Mitteilungen*, no. 3 (1967): 1015.
20. Sergei Eisenstein, *Montazh*, ed. Naum I. Kleiman (Moscow, 2000), 221-27.
21. On this project, see Oksana Bulgakowa, "Symbolische Topographie des neuen Moskau," in *Mastering Russian Spaces: Raum und Raumbewältigung als Probleme der russischen Geschichte*, ed. Karl Schlögel and Elisabeth Müller-Luckner (Munich, 2011), 253-78.
22. E. I. Vertova-Svilova and V. I. Frutichev, comps., *Tri pesni o Lenine: Sbornik* (Moscow, 1972), 113.
23. L. Maksimenkov, K. M. Anderson et al., comps., *Kremlevskii kinoteatr, 1928-1953: Dokumenty* (Moscow, 2005), 961-62.
24. James Agee, *Agee on Film* (New York, 1958), 1:123-26.
25. V. A. Troianovskii, "Novye liudi shestidesiatykh godov," in *Kinematograf ottepeli* (Moscow, 2002), 2:57, 59.
26. Vladimir Shalamov, "Perchatka," *Perchatka, ili KR-2*, in *Sobranie sochinenii v chetyrekh tomakh* (Moscow, 1998), 2:291.
27. Shalamov, "Iakov Ovseevich Zavodnik," *Sobranie sochinenii*, 2:384.

Bibliography

Adorno, Theodor W. *Ästhetische Theorie*. Frankfurt/Main, 1970.
Bazin, André. "The Myth of Stalin in the Soviet Cinema." In *Bazin at Work: Major Essays & Reviews from the Forties & Fifties*, edited by Bert Cardullo, translated by Alain Piette and Bert Cardullo, 23-40. New York, 1997.
Bloom, Lisa E. "Invisible Landscapes: Extreme Oil and the Arctic in Experimental Film and Activist Art Practices." In *Arctic Environmental Modernities: From the Age of Polar Exploration to the Era of the Anthropocene*, edited by Lill Ann Körber, Scott MacKenzie, and Anna Westerståhl Stenport, 183-95. Basingstoke, 2017.
Bulgakowa, Oksana. "Symbolische Topographie des neuen Moskau." In *Mastering Russian Spaces: Raum und Raumbewältigung als Probleme der russischen Geschichte*, edited by Karl Schlögel and Elisabeth Müller-Luckner, 253-78. Munich, 2011.
David, Robert G. *The Arctic in the British Imagination, 1818-1914*. Manchester, 2000.
Dortmann, Andrea. *Winter Facets: Traces and Tropes of the Cold*. Bern, 2007.
Eisenstein, Sergej. *Montazh*, ed. Naum I. Kleiman. Moscow, 2000.
Eisenstein, Sergej. "Massenkino." *Die Weltbühne*, no. 49 (1927): 858-60.
———. "Massenkino." *Filmwissenschaftliche Mitteilungen*, no. 3 (1967): 1015.
Erofeev, V. *Po kryshe mira s kino-apparatom: Puteshestvie na Pamir*. Moscow, 1929.

Hansson, Heidi, and Cathrin Norberg, eds. *Cold Matters: Cultural Perceptions of Snow, Ice and Cold*. Umeå, 2009.
James Agee, *Agee on Film*. Vol. 1. New York, 1958.
Kaganovsky, Lilya. "The Negative Space in the National Imagination: Russia and the Arctic." In *Arctic Environmental Modernities: From the Age of Polar Exploration to the Era of the Anthropocene*, edited by Lill Ann Körber, Scott MacKenzie, and Anna Westerståhl Stenport, 169–82. Basingstoke, 2017.
Körber, Lill Ann, Scott MacKenzie, and Anna Westerståhl Stenport. "Introduction: Arctic Modernities, Environmental Politics, and the Era of the Anthropocene." In *Arctic Environmental Modernities: From the Age of Polar Exploration to the Era of the Anthropocene*, edited by Lill Ann Körber, Scott MacKenzie, and Anna Westerståhl Stenport, 1–20. Basingstoke, 2017.
Kracauer, Siegfried. *From Caligari to Hitler: A Psychological History of the German Film*. Princeton, NJ, 1974.
Lawrence, Thomas Edward. *Seven Pillars of Wisdom: A Triumph*. London, 1935.
Lethen, Helmut. "Lob der Kälte: Ein Motiv der historischen Avantgarden." In *Die unvollendete Vernunft: Moderne versus Postmoderne*, eds. Dietmar Kamper and Willem van Reijen, 282–324. Frankfurt/Main, 1987.
———. *Verhaltenslehren der Kälte: Lebensversuche zwischen den Kriegen*. Frankfurt/Main, 1994.
Lukács, Georg. "Die Verdinglichung und das Bewußtsein des Proletariats." In *Werke*. Vol. 2: *Frühschriften: Geschichte und Klassenbewußtsein* [1923]. Berlin, 1963.
———. "Reification and the Consciousness of the Proletariat." In *History and Class Consciousness: Studies in Marxist Dialectics*. Translated by Rodney Livingstone. Cambridge, MA, 1971.
Maksimenkov, L., K. M. Anderson, et al., comps. *Kremlevskii kinoteatr, 1928–1953: Dokumenty*. Moscow, 2005.
Menke, Bettine. "Die Polargebiete der Bibliothek: Über eine metapoetische Metapher." *Deutsche Vierteljahresschrift für Literaturwissenschaft und Geistesgeschichte* 4 (December 2000): 545–99.
Morskoi, A. "Moda na russkoe." *Illiustrirovannaia Rossiia*, no. 5 (1929): 15.
Paglia, Camille. "Ice Queen, Drag Queen." *New Republic*, 4 March 1996, 24–26.
Papernyi, Vladimir. *Kul'tura dva*. Moscow, 1996.
Sarkisova, Oksana. "Arctic Travelogues: Conquering the Soviet North." In *Films on Ice: Cinemas of the Arctic*, edited by Scott MacKenzie and Anna Westerståhl Stenport, 222–34. Edinburgh, 2015.
Segida, M., and S. Zemlianukhin. *Domashniaia sinemateka: Otechestvennoe kino 1918–1996*. Moscow, 1996.
Shalamov, Vladimir. "Iakov Ovseevich Zavodnik." In *Sobranie sochinenii*, 2:377–88. Moscow, 1998.
———. "Perchatka." *Perchatka, ili KR-2*. In *Sobranie sochinenii v chetyrekh tomakh*, 2:291. Moscow, 1998.
Shneiderov, V. *Pokhod Sibiriakov*. Moscow, 1933.
Troianovskii, V. A. "Novye liudi shestidesiatykh godov." In *Kinematograf ottepeli*, 2:6–60. Moscow, 2002.

Vertov, Dziga. *Dramaturgicheskie opyty*. Vol. 1 of *Iz naslediia*, edited by Aleksandr Deriabin. Moscow, 2004.

Vertova-Svilova, E. I., and V. I. Frutichev, comps. *Tri pesni o Lenine: Sbornik*. Moscow, 1972.

CHAPTER 7

The Aesthetics of Cold
Narrating National Trauma in Film

Roman Mauer

The TV miniseries *As Far as My Feet Will Carry Me* (1959, directed by Fritz Umgelter) achieved such high viewing figures that it went down in German TV history as one of the first "street sweepers"—shows that emptied the streets when it aired. The miniseries is about Clemens Forell (Heinz Weiss), a German soldier in Hitler's army, who escapes from a Soviet prisoner-of-war (POW) camp in Cape Deschnev and embarks on a dangerous trek through icy Siberia. Released four years after the last German POW returned home from Soviet captivity, the miniseries is generally thought to have met with such an overwhelming response from the public because, on the one hand, it thematized a collective experience; on the other hand, however, it did not present the Germans as perpetrators but as victims of Soviet repression. This also sheds some light on the issue: the same year saw the release of director Frank Wisbar's movie on the Battle of Stalingrad, *Dogs, Do You Want to Live Forever?* (1959). The image of German soldiers suffering from the Russian cold or perishing can be understood as an iconic intensification of national socialism's failed megalomaniac fantasies; this angst-ridden image of a dead-end trap has engraved itself as "Geschichtszeichen Stalingrad" ("Stalingrad as Historical Sign")[1] into Germany's cultural memory—the embodiment of a collective trauma—and also put in place the image of a hostile Soviet Russia. But in *As Far as My Feet Will Carry Me*, when Clemens Forell overcomes Siberia's coldness to escape the icy grip of the Soviet Union, he seems to create a counterimage of the German soldiers' defeat in Stalingrad. Stalin, who in 1929 had developed Soviet POW camps into a comprehensive system of state oppression, used the camps after the surrender of Germany to intern about 3.15 million German soldiers and exploit their labor force. Especially the prisons in Siberia became symbols of inhuman experience, in part because of the extreme subzero temperatures and the hostile environment. Besides the hunger, the cold was an important functional component of the prison, which made it easier to control people; it took away any hope of flight. The indifference of nature and its absolutist power became the epitome both of the repressive practices of the regime and of the impotence of the captives. The situation of the prisoners of war, both Soviets in Nazi Germany and Germans in the Soviet Union, remained an emotionally charged topic and a marked taboo within historical treatment, which resulted in falsified representations (and false statistics in particular). The following chapter focuses on the symbolic mechanisms to compensate for these traumatic experiences within German popular culture, specifically film and television. Therefore, three successive images of masculinity are interrelated: from the superhuman perseverance of the male body in the ice, glorified as an act of self-control in the Weimar Cinema, to the decline of the heroic soldiers in the icy trap of Stalingrad in German postwar movies, which was paralleled with the image of an individual who, by his liberation from cold Siberia, representatively overcomes the national trauma of powerlessness. There is a correlation between body image, coldness, and social and historical experience that manifests itself within cinematic atmospheres.

At first glance, this chapter may appear strikingly different from the thematic framework of this volume as it attains the German perspective on the Russian cold as represented in films about Stalingrad and the returning home from Siberian internment camp. This, however, is to show that the phenomenon of coldness regarding historical context must not be limited to the country (Soviet Union) itself; instead, it offers an external perspective, which helps to develop a transnational and international discourse in multi-perspectivity. After all, phenomena such as these with the inherent clashing of cultures on grounds of, for example, world wars or related types of conflict are not limited solely to one country. On the one hand, the cold does not arrange and limit itself to national borders; on the other hand, individuals who take it upon themselves to cross these scenic zones are inevitably confronted with the cold and will most certainly carry their experiences back into their own country.

Atmospheric Positions in the Cinematic Dispositive

The aesthetics of cold is a phenomena of atmosphere. Analyzing film history with the focus on atmosphere is a new research approach that is just about to be explored in film studies.[2] In the following, I suggest to conceptualize the issue of atmosphere within the cinematic experience as consisting of four basic components: first, there is the atmosphere of the spatial dispositive (movie theater auditorium or TV room); second, the atmosphere of the film, which makes an impact on viewers through light and sound; third, the individual mood of a singular spectator; and fourth, the social atmosphere that is created through the collective viewing experience of the audience (anonymously in a movie theater auditorium or more intimately in a TV room).

Atmospheres can be understood as emotional forces that have an affective influence on the body. Their position is an intermediate one: they are part of the objects that produce them and at the same time of the subjects that perceive them.[3] Although topographies and objects can be described precisely (in terms of temperature, color, haptics, texture, and consistency), it is difficult to determine the atmospheric effect they will have. The "ecstasy of things" is what German philosopher Gernot Böhme calls an object or a body's expressive force, which fills the space with "tensions and suggestions of movement."[4] It is hard to determine, because this expressive effect is first realized in the subject and its perceptions. And since experienced moods (unlike emotions) are diffuse and cannot be attributed to a clear-cut cause, a person—in the attempt to ascribe a mood to an external stimulus (for example, an atmosphere)—can make misattributions. Atmospheres are therefore "'just' constructions…, which are formed based on moods."[5] At the latest, since Marcel Proust's epoch-making novel *In Search of Lost Time* (1913–27) and the madeleine experience, we have been aware of the extent to which a person's sensory perception is subjectively determined by past experiences. As a result of personal disposition and history, as well as social climates and socialization, each individual acts as a highly individualized filter for effects from the outside.

Similarly, social atmospheres are not firmly defined or clearly demarcated phenomena. They change over time and are determined by major sociopolitical shifts and their echo in the media and culture. So the German reaction to depictions of national socialism and its crimes was clearly different immediately after World War II compared to what it is today and to how other cultures react to it. German film theorist and sociologist Siegfried Kracauer speaks in his famous but controversial film sociology book *From Caligari to Hitler* (1947) of a "collective mentality" and tries to research its deep layers, especially in films. In the book's introduction, even if he states that he is not using the term to fabricate a "fixed national character," a collective mentality still implies exactly this, that a people have a psychological disposition. Moreover, this approach misguides Kracauer into drawing a direct connection between the films of the Weimar Republic and the rise of national socialism.[6] Indeed, these films are expressions of a collective experience—however, not to be understood as a pre-fascist kind that anticipated national socialism but as a post-traumatic reaction in succession to World War I.[7]

By combining the spatial, medial, individual, and social dimensions, we produce a square of the atmospheric positions in the cinematic or TV dispositive. These four components can interact in ways that are either harmonious or dissonant. The interaction would be dissonant if, for example, within a collective atmosphere of joy during a screening of a comedy there were an individual mood of mourning (a viewer mourns the loss of a loved one). This may cause a sensual conflict; but within the viewing process, the mood of the viewer may possibly adapt to the surrounding. The interaction would also be dissonant if a film on coldness were shown in an overheated movie theater. For example, Arnold Fanck's film *The Holy Mountain*, which takes place in snow and ice and which I will also discuss later, was first presented at the turn of 1925/1926 in the UFA-Filmpalast am Zoo, a movie theater in Berlin, which had a sophisticated and comfortable interior: "all in red and gold; heavy rich purple on the floors and walls," while an "electric zeppelin" sprayed Eau de Cologne and kept the air fresh.[8] The contrast between depictions of nature and coldness in the film and the coziness and artificiality of the movie theater auditorium leads to an atmospheric dissonance. In the 1920s, when the movie theater still had to establish itself as part of the middle-class art scene, cinema auditoriums were furnished very opulently. In the United States, architect John Eberson had designed some of the most beautiful "atmospheric theaters" with curved cloud-and-star ceilings, which, according to British architect Dennis Sharp, were supposed to serve a calming, therapeutic function: "We credit the deep azure blue of the Mediterranean sky with a therapeutic value, soothing the nerves and calming perturbing thoughts."[9]

In view of the atmospheric dissonances that can arise between the film and the movie theater auditorium or between collective and individual atmospheres, does a director's attempt to generate the same feelings among all viewers, and to do this through cinematic atmospheres, not come across as absurd and impossible? The viewer can still understand a film's intended atmosphere, since medial atmospheres are based on conventions the viewer is familiar with. Even if viewers do not perceive the atmospheres emotionally, they can understand them. Moreover, through a homogenous interplay between the various artistic elements (the acting, music, camera, montage sequences), the filmmaker tries to attain a clarity and a power that overrides any feelings the audience may otherwise be having. The cognitive model (convention) and the emotional impact (the synergy of the creative means) made by a medial atmosphere can, in other words, keep the viewer in check, so that individual, spatial, or collective deviations do not occur. However, if the four atmospheres interact harmoniously, they have the potential to create an intense, uniform quality of feeling. Where, then, can film history studies commence in its analysis? It cannot take the viewer's individual sensual mood as its starting point. The movie theater auditoriums and TV rooms are also too numerous to be able to draw any conclusions about their particular, spatial atmospheres. But the medial atmosphere (the cinema or TV film) and the social atmosphere (for a specific time) can indeed be discussed and set into relation to one another.

Coldness and Heroic Masculinity in Weimar Republic Mountain Films

Heroic masculinity as a physical statement against coldness is very vividly presented in Weimar Republic mountain films, which became classics of film history. The pioneer of this uniquely German genre was director Arnold Fanck, who was willing to take risks and who shot his successful films at original locations: among the Alps' icy ranges in *The Holy Mountain* (1926) and *The White Hell of Pitz Palu* (1928, codirected by G. W. Pabst), or even between Greenland's glaciers in *S.O.S. Iceberg* (1932). At the time, moviegoers were captivated by the breathtaking nature shots. One viewer even comments on the atmospheric transference he experienced between the medial body and his own body: "The dangerous ascents and descents, jumping over crevasses between glaciers, overcoming snow holes and things like that, that all has something unusual and exciting to it. You feel the dangerous thrill of this sport in your own body …"[10] In the final scene of *The Holy Mountain*, Fanck depicts two mountain climbers' struggle to survive when they are forced to persevere on an icy overhang during a snowstorm. Vigo (Ernst Petersen) falls off and dangles from the safety rope, secured by his "friend" Karl (Luis Trenker), who is partially responsible for the fall and out of loyalty does not let go of the rope even after Vigo has long since frozen to death. Frozen stiff and covered in ice, Karl holds onto the rope all night until morning when, in a state of delirious exhaustion, he plunges into the depths.

The main aesthetic technique the black-and-white film employs in this sequence to create a medial atmosphere of coldness is contrasting that coldness with warm scenes. In a parallel montage, the people in the village are shown engaged in festive activities. The contrast provided by their warm, cozy living room in the valley intensifies the effect of the cold, inhospitable mountain heights. Fanck heightens the effect by tinting the black-and-white film. He immerses the hut's atmosphere in a warm sepia tone and the nighttime mountain shots in cold blue. But the atmospheric counterpoint is, above all, intensified through the correlations that take place between body and movement. While the dance-like dynamics in the interior room trigger associations of warmth (and life), the rigid bodies on the mountain trigger associations of coldness (and death). This sequence shows that, in film, movement serves as an indicator of a heated organism with good blood flow and, through synesthetic transfer, is perceived as an atmosphere of warmth. The high points in the scenes depicting coldness are the close-ups of the friend's frozen face, his radiant bluish skin covered in ice. Ice on bare skin, snow crystals in a beard, a face contorted with pain, all surrounded by swirling snowdrifts—those are the most direct and most impressive aesthetic calls to the viewer's own memories of bodily experiences. They show that the screen's cold temperature, above all, functions via the body: the skin as a resonance field is what first makes the effects of coldness visible.

The final scene in *S.O.S. Iceberg* is similar: lost in Greenland's white frozen wastelands, a man (Gustav Diessl) and his dog swim through glacier water, fight their way from ice floe to ice floe, trying to attract a pilot's (Leni Riefenstahl) attention. In both films' final scenes, Arnold Fanck shows the male body in its fight against the pain of coldness, thereby celebrating images of toughness and willpower. The completely frozen-looking man in *The Holy Mountain* soon resembles a statue or the petrification of an idea. The camera repeatedly zeroes in on the figure, elevating him to a symbol of heroic masculinity—the image of a man who is willing to set aside his own needs and make sacrifices until death.

The discussions in film studies on Arnold Fanck's mountain films were strongly influenced by Siegfried Kracauer's book *From Caligari to Hitler*. Kracauer puts the glorification of the male hero in a national socialist context: "Although this kind of heroism was perhaps too demanding and too eccentric to serve as a pattern for the people in the valleys, it was already rooted in a mentality that was kindred to national socialism."[11] When Germany started to work through its film history, this position gradually began to change.[12] In his 1999 dissertation, Thomas Bogner stated that the connection between mountain films and the Hitler cult could, above all, be found at the personnel level, since both German director Leni Riefenstahl and her cameramen, Sepp Allgeier and Hans Schneeberger, were trained by Arnold Fanck: "Nevertheless, A. Fanck is not to blame that his talented student, Leni Riefenstahl, connected images of sublime nature and the heroic man in a way that was typical for Arnold Fanck and that she did so in a national socialist context. Fanck's film *The Holy Mountain* ... often played a role in discourses that national socialism could exploit for itself, without it being the case that a direct connection could be made between the two."[13]

Fanck was not a national socialist when he shot this film. As a child he had a serious lung disease and had found his ideal lifestyle while attending a Davos boarding school where the focus was on self-discipline and rigor ("The motto was: tough it out! ... During the five winter months, we had to go out on the ice daily regardless of how cold it was. And it was often 20°C and 25°C below zero in Davos"[14]). At this time, he discovered his passion for skiing, the mountains, and filmmaking.[15] Inspired by Friedrich Nietzsche's Zarathustra, he dedicated himself to a "heroic concept of life" until his death.[16] Bogner looks at this ideal image of heroic masculinity and anchors it in ideas from the 1920s, which had been shaped by nineteenth-century militarism, the ethics of the *Männerbünde* (men's associations), and the idealization of comradeship and front experiences in World War I. Bogner presents how at the time it was popular to equate mountain climbers and soldiers: the extreme situation of conquering a mountain was equated with heroism during the war. Both were understood as "existence-heightening experiences": "The more people a man kills and the more four-thousand-meter peaks he climbs, the more war injuries and medals he reaps, and the more serious falls and avalanche disasters he survives, the more recognition he earns."[17] Like death in war, death on a mountain was referred to as a death on the "battlefield of honor." With regard to the final scene in *The Holy Mountain*, Bogner emphasizes: "While climbing up Santo's north face, Vigo and 'his friend' are not in a trench's storm of steel, but in the ice and snow avalanches of an 'unleashed nature.'"[18] Moreover, by showing them climbing up together, secured together, and with the physical proximity of mountain climbing, a type of comradeship is articulated that is similar to fighting on a front, where your own personal interests take a backseat to group loyalty. As is the case in trenches, it is only in the life-threatening fight with nature that "true" friendship between men manifests itself. Bogner situates the elevated role of male friendship in Fanck's *The Holy Mountain* in the German tradition of the *Männerbünde*, which defines masculinity through strength, order, and courage; masculinity becomes possible when one is isolated from wife and family and when it is differentiated from the softness and indecision attributed to femininity.[19] This means that from the point of view of this elevated friendship, masculinity and comradeship can only be constituted through extreme situations on the mountains and in war. And in mountain films, this vibrantly comes to the foreground through the image of the tough, rugged body withstanding the cold.

What this all amounts to is that, in the mentioned examples of the aesthetics of coldness, an atmospheric transmission upon the spectator is aspired. This transmission operates less on a spatial level than by means of the representation of the body, which is exposed to the climatic conditions of a certain space. In this regard, it appears as reasonable to further differentiate the aspect of medial atmosphere into its components: space and body of characters. The empathy of the viewer may first be conceived as a sheer sensual process that comes clear of any ascription of meaning and, in an synesthetic act, is meant to provide a quality of sensation. On the cognitive level of the cinematic experience, the body becomes a figure and the corporal experience is filled with meanings, which result from the system of significance and values of the film, like masculine toughness, willpower, readiness to make sacrifices, which through narration are condensed into a heroic myth. The sensual experience and the denotative cognitive meaning have to be regarded within a historical context, because society fills them with current discourses (like here the liminal experience of the mountaineer is equated with the heroism of the soldier). In this manner a connection between the body and the society arises, and the individual body may become a collective body image.

In the following, the objective is to address the aforementioned connection between media atmospheres and historical experiences. Thereby, theoretical assumptions will be related to a particular historical context. Focus is placed on the period of time in the immediate aftermath of World War II.

The Icy Grave in Stalingrad: *Dogs, Do You Want to Live Forever?* (FRG 1959)

After 1945, the war movie genre reflected the political and ideological reorientation of the Federal Republic of Germany (FRG), which in the early stages of the Cold War had put itself under the patronage of the United States. Starting in 1949, American war movies were imported to the FRG in large numbers and ushered in a wave of war films. The wave peaked between 1957 and 1960 and significantly decreased between 1961 and 1964. West German war movies began to be produced in 1953 and comprised a quarter of these movies.[20] American war movies served a pilot function: they laid the groundwork for the reception of this new genre and prepared the market for it. With ruthless images of the physical horrors, these films also influenced West German productions. There is a definite trend to separate the successes and qualifications of the German military in World War II from national socialism to thereby make concessions to the FRG, which was its new political and military ally.[21] *The Desert Fox* (USA 1951) was highly successful in the FRG and started a trend; it idealized General Field Marshal Erwin Rommel as the symbol of a brave, fair soldier who is betrayed by his political leaders. West German war movies, such as *Canaris* (FRG 1954), *It Happened on July 20th* (FRG 1955), and *The Plot to Assassinate Hitler* (FRG 1955), initially followed this model of politically rehabilitating war heroes and reducing antifascist resistance to military figures.[22] At the same time, American war movies reflected the anti-communism prevalent at the time and increased the fear that existed, which saw Communist countries as a huge military threat.

If we look at these two trends—rehabilitating the German military and anti-communism—and do so with regard to the Battle of Stalingrad, then things get tricky for a director in the 1950s: the total defeat of the German army and the Russian victory contradict these attempts of idealization and relief. *Dogs, Do You Want to Live Forever?* (FRG 1959), the second installment in Frank Wisbar's war film trilogy,[23] is one of the few movies in the 1950s that depicts the war on the Eastern Front. Right at the start, there is a montage where images of the German army marching in a parade are juxtaposed with images of fallen German soldiers in Stalingrad, whose naked feet jut out in the snow; the film thereby confronts the image the Nazi regime had of itself, the regime's megalomaniac fantasies, and contrasts them with an iconic consolidation of the Nazis' catastrophic failure. The images of fallen soldiers are iconic because of their icy grave: the dead cannot be buried properly because they are frozen in the ice. Since their naked injuries are not covered up and they are exposed to the aggressions of nature, these people's injuries are prolonged in a symbolic way. The image of their frozen suffering is preserved by the cold. The permanence of trauma (indeed, the failure within the Russian coldness) is therefore inscribed in these images: one is forced to work through this trauma, and it is not possible to forget the unthinkable.

Although the beginning of *Dogs, Do You Want to Live Forever?* immediately positions the movie as an antiwar film, it follows the trend of films that seek to rehabilitate the German army. The causes, objectives, and methods behind this war of extermination against Russia are not taken into consideration, and the German officers are presented as men of integrity who know what they are doing but who are betrayed by Hitler. The film argues that these brave heroes only fail because they are not adequately supplied with military equipment, food, and winter clothing and are led into catastrophe by Hitler's irrational commands. The tragedy of their situation is illustrated by the depictions of coldness. In the frozen steppes, we see the soldiers hacking into the ground so they can build dugouts, as if they are digging their own grave in the ice. When their defeat becomes obvious, the film shows images of a white inferno. Various soldiers carry the wounded through wind and snow, past frozen corpses. The white nothingness that surrounds them symbolizes their extraterritorial situation: defenseless, they are far removed from the concrete world. A surreal road sign listing the distance to Berlin (2,431 km) makes them aware of how far away from home they are: "What are we doing in this part of the world? ... We haven't lost anything here." The film sets up a visual contrast between their powerlessness in the snow flurries and the superiority of the Russian tanks racing toward them: "What the Russians don't accomplish, the cold will take care of" is the main statement. The film ends with freezing, silent German prisoners of war, who are being escorted through the snowy landscape in a long line, accompanied by funeral music. Left behind on the wayside are the sick, the weak, and the dead.

The German soldiers are not only reenvisioned in their presentation as victims of their leadership, of the cold, and of their deportation: in the few scenes showing personal contact with the Russians, the Germans are depicted as people who are helpful and human. They give a single farm mother a meal, save a student from being deported, let prisoners walk free, and delight Russian soldiers with piano music during a ceasefire. Cynically, these scenes where the two cultures meet end with the Russians looking at their invaders with a sense of thankfulness. While, on the German side, the film mainly shows cultivated officers, the Russians it presents are reduced to naïve representatives of the common people. The only exception among the Russians is the student Katja (played by Sonja Ziemann, star of the escapist "heimatfilm" genre in postwar cinema), who speaks German and quickly succumbs to the charms of Lieutenant Colonel Gerd Wisse (Joachim Hansen). The only exception among the Germans is Major Linkmann (Wolfgang Preiss), a national socialist and coward, who becomes a deserter and is executed by his own soldiers. In summary, it is a stereotypical characterization and moral connotation of national representatives.

If we compare Frank Wisbar's film to director Aleksandr Stolper's *Vozmezdiye* (*Man wird nicht als Soldat geboren*, USSR 1970), the film made ten years later that deals with the Battle of Stalingrad from the Soviet point of view, some striking differences are apparent. Stolper does not look for the army's opponents in the cold or among the Russians' own leadership but addresses the Russian losses and hardships. The film pays tribute to the way the people collectively stick together: the mothers who work in the steelworks where they cast war materials, the young ladies who care for the wounded in military hospitals, the experienced officers who are deeply concerned about their soldiers. Compared to those of *Dogs, Do You Want to Live Forever?* the Russian officers' conversations take on a much more personal and less formal tone. Under the banner of socialism, the film thus stages the solidarity and brotherliness of the collective, where all the individuals selflessly fulfill their role, so that the jointly fought battle finally ends in victory. While the German movie works off a national guilt, but finally chooses a strategy of repression, Aleksandr Stolper's *Vozmezdiye* does seem to integrate an immense national loss into a self-perception of social and moral superiority. Furthermore, here coldness is not depicted as an existential problem but as a matter of course, which is faced with adequate equipment.

Atmospheric Relief: *As Far as My Feet Will Carry Me* (FRG 1959)

By the end of 1949, two million German soldiers, who after 1947 had remained in POW camps, returned to civilian life. The Soviet Union continued to detain about thirty thousand prisoners. It was only in 1956 that the last of them were released to Germany. The experiences of the former soldiers returning home and of the families waiting for them were still fresh in people's minds in 1959, which was not only when Frank Wisbar's film on Stalingrad was released in cinemas but also when the TV series *As Far as My Feet Will Carry Me* aired. It was the first major German TV production and the first enormous success. Directed by Fritz Umgelter, it was shot over five months and based on the eponymous bestseller by Josef Martin Bauer. The series is about German soldier Clemens Forell (Heinz Weiss) and his escape from a Soviet POW camp in

Siberia, where he had been sentenced to twenty-five years of forced labor in a lead mine in the Arctic Circle.

The film opens with succinct images that capture the topography and coldness. The German prisoners are deported to Siberia by freight train. The trip takes weeks, and during this time they try to get an idea of the size of the Soviet empire. One man draws Russian rivers and cities on a layer of snow coating the wall of the freight train. He has two problems: Firstly, the wooden wall is definitely not big enough to draw the entire Soviet Union. Secondly, his fingers soon hurt from drawing a map in the snow. In this way, the film profoundly illustrates how foreign the context is for the German prisoners: they see the Soviet Union as an empire of inconceivable dimensions and as a country that is permanently cold. Since the film does not waste any words describing the reason for their captivity—their involvement in national socialism and the war of extermination against Russia—the German prisoners from the start are presented as victims with whom German viewers have to sympathize. This empathy for the prisoners is intensified by the way the Russian guards are portrayed, as cruel and cynical. Wearing thick fur coats, the Russians stand next to shivering Germans, indifferent to their suffering and the countless typhus casualties whose bodies are thrown from the train.

For viewers, Clemens Forell's escape from the lead mine's inhuman conditions serves to articulate a collective dream of liberation from Russian captivity. However, what is also crucial is that he escapes through an icy Siberian landscape. Unlike the thousands of German soldiers who died from hunger and the cold Russian winter during the Battle of Stalingrad, the German here is able to survive the inhospitable cold. What is decisive is that Forell is much better equipped than the soldiers in Stalingrad. The camp physician, Dr. Heinz Stauffer (Wolfgang Büttner), who plans Forell's escape, can be read as the positive counterimage to the political leadership of the German army: in the country where Hitler refused to let the encircled German troops escape, Stauffer encourages Forell to dare the impossible. During Forell's escape through the Siberian ice, Stauffer's off-screen voice accompanies him like the voice of a father, giving him rational pieces of advice. He also equips Forell with everything he will need to survive in the cold landscape: clothes, a compass, and food. In *As Far as My Feet Will Carry Me*, Clemens Forell appears to present a counterimage of the German soldiers' defeat in Stalingrad. The film brings a sense of atmospheric relief to a traumatized postwar Germany in two different ways: it falsely presents the German war prisoners as innocent victims of Hitler's horrible deportation and exploitation, and it suggests that German war prisoners have the competence to triumph over the Soviet Union as a country of coldness—because this time the strategic planning and the equipment are right. "I must go home!" is the sentence that draws Forell to Germany like a magnet and at the end of an adventurous plot also lets him reach his destination.

With regard to the interaction between film and social atmosphere, an interesting continuity can be found in the cold aesthetics and the body images, which connect Weimar Republic mountain films with West German war movies about the Eastern Front in World War II. These films are determined by an atmosphere of extreme coldness, which a male body is struggling against, a struggle that is compacted into an iconic image, which represents the societal atmosphere of a certain time.

With Arnold Fanck, in the Weimar Republic, it is yet the heroic body willing to make sacrifices, which is purposefully looking for the challenge of ice and snow so as to withstand it by hardship, and which, in its superhuman mode, solidifies into a statue. Within this glorification, the film can be situated in the German tradition of *Männerbünde*, in which comradery and masculinity only prove themselves within maintenance in extreme situations. In societal perception, there was a tendency to equate the reliability of a comrade on the mountain with the reliability on the battlefield. The fact that this heroism was shattered by the Russian cold in the failure of Stalingrad becomes evident in Frank Wisbar's antiwar movie. Here we see the damaged, fallen body, vulnerably frozen in the ice, as a memorial of the national trauma of megalomania—however, the collective guilt is suppressed in this film. With Fritz Umgelter, the body gains the struggle against coldness and disorientation in the Siberian ice through its will to survive, its logistic competence, and its optimism, and it frees itself, in place of the German people, from the pitfall of history. In *As Far as My Feet Will Carry Me*, the experience of Stalingrad and the POW camps has led to the aim of protecting and of rescuing the body.

In further exploration, the task is to extend the scope to encompass remakes from the recent past—*Stalingrad* (Germany 1993) by director Joseph Vilsmaier and *As Far as My Feet Will Carry Me* (Germany 2001) by director Hardy Martins—because the value structures shift again in these films.

The major success of 1959's *As Far as My Feet Will Carry Me* has a lot to do with the assumption that it is based on a true story. In 2010, the radio author Arthur Dittlmann and the historian Jürgen Zarusky expressed serious doubts about this: many of the events that Cornelius Rost—that is Clemens Forell's real name—describes in the original interview are historically inaccurate. According to Zarusky, there never was a lead mine in Cap Deshnew. If this thesis is true, then the escape story described in *As Far as My Feet Will Carry Me* is a myth, and as a construction, it offered the perfect form of atmospheric relief for the traumatized psyche of postwar Germany.

Roman Mauer is a research assistant in the field of film studies at Johannes Gutenberg University Mainz. He studied film studies, literature, and social anthropology in Mainz and received his doctorate in 2004 with a study on Jim Jarmusch. He has taught at the University of Film and Television Munich (HFF), the German Film and Television Academy Berlin (DFFB), the Film University Babelsberg "Konrad Wolf," and the Mainz University of Applied Sciences. Since 2008 he has organized international lecture series and media cooperation projects with ZDF/arte, the Friedrich Wilhelm Murnau Foundation, and Deutsche Kinemathek Berlin. His main research topics are the aesthetics of simultaneity, the narratology of film and comics, film style, audiovisual film didactics, methods of visualization, and inter- and transculturalism in film.

Notes

1. Helmut Lethen, "Stalingrad als Geschichtszeichen," in *Unheimliche Nachbarschaften: Essays zum Kälte-Kult und der Schlaflosigkeit der Philosophischen Anthropologie im 20. Jahrhundert* (Freiburg i.Br., 2009), 187–214.
2. Also see, Philipp Brunner, Jörg Schweinitz, and Margrit Tröhler, eds., *Filmische Atmosphären* (Marburg, 2012).
3. Gernot Böhme, *Atmosphäre: Essays zur neuen Ästhetik* (Frankfurt/Main, 1997), 21.
4. Ibid., 33.
5. Fritz Strack and Atilla Höfling, "Von Atmosphären, Stimmungen & Gefühlen," in *Atmosphäre(n): Interdisziplinäre Annäherungen an einen unscharfen Begriff*, ed. Rainer Goetz and Stefan Graupner (Munich, 2007), 106.
6. Siegfried Kracauer, *Von Caligari bis Hitler: Ein Beitrag zur Geschichte des deutschen Films* (Hamburg, 1958), 8.
7. Also see, Anton Kaes, *Shell Shock Cinema: Weimar Culture and the Wounds of War* (Princeton, NJ, 2009).
8. Thomas Bogner, "Zur Rekonstruktion filmischer Naturdarstellung am Beispiel einer Fallstudie: Natur im Film 'Der heilige Berg' von Doktor Arnold Fanck" (PhD diss., Hamburg University, 1999), 1.
9. Dennis Sharp, *The Picture Palace and Other Buildings for the Movies* (New York, 1969), 74. Also see Paolo Caneppele and Anna Lisa Balboni, "Film als Heilmittel? Die Kino-Debatte in der medizinischen Welt während der Stummfilmzeit," in *Psyche im Kino: Sigmund Freud und der Film*, ed. Thomas Ballhausen, Günther Krenn, and Lydia Marinelli (Vienna, 2006), 76.
10. Anonymous, 1921, quoted by Bogner, "Zur Rekonstruktion filmischer Naturdarstellung am Beispiel einer Fallstudie," 20.
11. Kracauer, *Von Caligari bis Hitler*, 72.
12. Also see Thomas Brandlmeier, "Arnold Fanck," in *CineGraph*, ed. Hans-Michael Bock (Munich, 1984), E2; and Eric Rentschler, "Hochgebirge und Moderne: Eine Standortbestimmung des Bergfilms," *Film und Kritik 1* (1992): 9–12.
13. Bogner, "Zur Rekonstruktion filmischer Naturdarstellung am Beispiel einer Fallstudie," 3.
14. Arnold Fanck, *Er führte Regie mit Gletschern, Stürmen und Lawinen: Ein Filmpionier erzählt* (Munich, 1973), 10.

15. Bogner, "Zur Rekonstruktion filmischer Naturdarstellung am Beispiel einer Fallstudie," 67–68.
16. Fanck, *Er führte Regie mit Gletschern, Stürmen und Lawinen*, 52.
17. Bogner, "Zur Rekonstruktion filmischer Naturdarstellung am Beispiel einer Fallstudie," 64.
18. Ibid., 60.
19. Also see, Klaus Theweleit, *Männerphantasien*, vol. 1: *Frauen, Fluten, Körper, Geschichte* (Frankfurt/Main, 1977); Klaus Theweleit, *Männerphantasien*, vol. 2: *Männerkörper— zur Psychoanalyse des weißen Terrors* (Reinbek, 1980).
20. See Wolfgang Wegmann, "Der westdeutsche Kriegsfilm der fünfziger Jahre" (PhD diss., Cologne University, 1980), 110–13.
21. Also see Wolfgang Wegmann, "Der westdeutsche Kriegsfilm der fünfziger Jahre," 107–8.
22. Also see ibid., 126.
23. The war movie trilogy also includes *Sharks and Little Fish* (dir. Frank Wisbar, Germany, 1957) and *Darkness Fell on Gotenhafen* (dir. Frank Wisbar, Germany, 1960).

Bibliography

Bogner, Thomas. "Zur Rekonstruktion filmischer Naturdarstellung am Beispiel einer Fallstudie: Natur im Film 'Der heilige Berg' von Doktor Arnold Fanck." PhD diss., Hamburg University, 1999.

Böhme, Gernot. *Atmosphäre: Essays zur neuen Ästhetik*. Frankfurt/Main, 1997.

Brandlmeier, Thomas. "Arnold Fanck." In *CineGraph*, edited by Hans-Michael Bock, E2. Munich, 1984.

Brunner, Philipp, Jörg Schweinitz, and Margrit Tröhler, eds. *Filmische Atmosphären*. Marburg, 2012.

Caneppele, Paolo, and Anna Lisa Balboni. "Film als Heilmittel? Die Kino-Debatte in der medizinischen Welt während der Stummfilmzeit." In *Psyche im Kino: Sigmund Freud und der Film*, edited by Thomas Ballhausen, Günther Krenn, and Lydia Marinelli, 55–76. Vienna, 2006.

Fanck, Arnold. *Er führte Regie mit Gletschern, Stürmen und Lawinen: Ein Filmpionier erzählt*. Munich, 1973.

Kaes, Anton. *Shell Shock Cinema: Weimar Culture and the Wounds of War*. Princeton, NJ, 2009.

Kracauer, Siegfried. *Von Caligari bis Hitler: Ein Beitrag zur Geschichte des deutschen Films*. Hamburg, 1958.

Lethen, Helmut. "Stalingrad als Geschichtszeichen." In *Unheimliche Nachbarschaften: Essays zum Kälte-Kult und der Schlaflosigkeit der Philosophischen Anthropologie im 20. Jahrhundert*, 187–214. Freiburg i.Br., 2009.

Rentschler, Eric. "Hochgebirge und Moderne: Eine Standortbestimmung des Bergfilms." *Film und Kritik* 1 (1992): 8–27.

Sharp, Dennis. *The Picture Palace and Other Buildings for the Movies*. New York, 1969.

Strack, Fritz, and Atilla Höfling. "Von Atmosphären, Stimmungen & Gefühlen." In *Atmosphäre(n): Interdisziplinäre Annäherungen an einen unscharfen Begriff*, edited by Rainer Goetz and Stefan Graupner, 103–10. Munich, 2007.

Theweleit, Klaus. *Männerphantasien.* Vol. 1: *Frauen, Fluten, Körper, Geschichte.* Frankfurt/Main, 1977.

———. *Männerphantasien.* Vol. 2: *Männerkörper—zur Psychoanalyse des weißen Terrors.* Reinbek, 1980.

Wegmann, Wolfgang. "Der westdeutsche Kriegsfilm der fünfziger Jahre." PhD diss., Cologne University, 1980.

 PART IV

Pain and Pleasure

 CHAPTER 8

The Wehrmacht and the Russian Winter
The Impact of Climate at the Front and in Soviet Captivity

Aleksandr Kuzminykh

Traditionally, Soviet historians have ignored the impact of climate on the events of World War II. They have ascribed their foreign colleagues' reflections on the way the Soviet military command used certain distinctive features of Russia's climate to their desire to diminish the Red Army's successes and their eagerness to explain the German troops' defeat by emphasizing the impact of secondary factors. A. N. Mertsalov, a highly regarded Soviet historian of World War II, wrote that as a factor in warfare, climatic conditions "in and of themselves were never of decisive significance," and instead concluded that "purposeful human agency determines the outcome of a war."[1]

Outside the Soviet Union, things were different, especially in the postwar West German historiography, where the concept of geographic determinism featured widely in analyzing the reasons for Germany's defeat in the war with the USSR. To varying degrees, German historians and memoirists attributed the Wehrmacht's crushing defeat to the impact of the "Russian summer with its dust, intense heat, and thirst," "autumn with its rain, which forcibly choked off every movement in the mud," and the "incredibly early and cold winter."[2] The titles of these works speak for themselves: *Tigers in the Mud*, *War in a White Hell*, and *Frozen Victory*.[3]

In the post-Soviet historiography, the role climate played during World War II—in planning military operations, carrying them out, and their results—has received considerable attention. For example, among the reasons for the Red Army's failures and significant losses during the Soviet-Finnish war (the Winter War) of 1939–40, researchers cite Soviet troops' lack of preparation for military action in winter conditions and severe frosts.[4] Although most Russian historians are critical of the proposition that "General Frost" and "General Winter" were the determining factor in the Red Army's victories in World War II, the view that the harsh winter was the Soviet troops' most reliable "ally" in the Battle of Moscow and at Stalingrad is becoming more common. Mikhail Zefirov and Dmitrii Degtev proposed a "winter success" syndrome: the Russians advanced successfully in the winter, the Germans in the summer.[5] However, this concept certainly does not explain the reasons for the Soviet troops' victories on the Kursk salient and during Operation Bagration in the summer campaigns of 1943 and 1944 respectively.

This chapter examines the impact of climate on the fighting capacity of Wehrmacht troops during World War II and in Soviet captivity. It is based on new sources, including both official documents (NKVD-MVD records) and those of personal provenance (diaries and memoirs), which reflect the process whereby German soldiers and prisoners of war adapted to what they perceived as extreme cold. I argue that experiencing the cold became a part of the collective German experience that connected war and captivity and that German soldiers' experience of the cold had a tangible influence on the image of Russia that took shape in wartime and postwar Germany.

Cold as a Factor in the Conditions at the Front

As is well known, Russia is considered the world's coldest country. While the average annual temperature in Finland is 1.5°C and 7.8°C in Germany, in Russia it is -5.5°C. In Russia's northern regions, winter and low temperatures persist for most of the year. Historians S. M. Solovev, V. O. Kliuchevskii, L. N. Gumilev, and L. V. Milov all noted the influence of the natural environment on Russian history.[6] The works of Stephen Wheatcroft, R. W. Davies, N. M. Dronin, and A. P. Kirilenko show that there was a direct relationship between climate and economics and politics in twentieth-century Russian history.[7]

According to meteorological data, the winter of 1941–42 was one of the coldest winters on Russian territory in the twentieth century. During the three winter months of 1941–42, the air temperature remained 5.7 degrees lower than the norm (figure 8.1) In 1942 the temperature in Leningrad was 10 degrees below the normal temperature and frosts reached -32°C. This blockade winter ranks third in severity among the January temperatures in the twentieth century. During the same period in Kalinin and Iakhroma, towns in Moscow *Oblast'*, the temperature fell to -50°C, which is characteristic of Siberian cities like Chita and Irkutsk.[8]

Analogous data can be found in the specialized military literature. For example, *The Rout of German Forces near Moscow*, a secret 1943 publication of the General Staff of the Red Army compiled under the direction of Marshal B. M. Shaposhnikov, indicates that during the winter of 1941–42 the temperature of the Moscow region was lower than normal. More specifically, in November the average temperature was 5 degrees below zero, in December it was 12 degrees below zero, and in January it was 19 degrees below zero. In comparison, the average long-term winter temperature values for the same region are -3°C

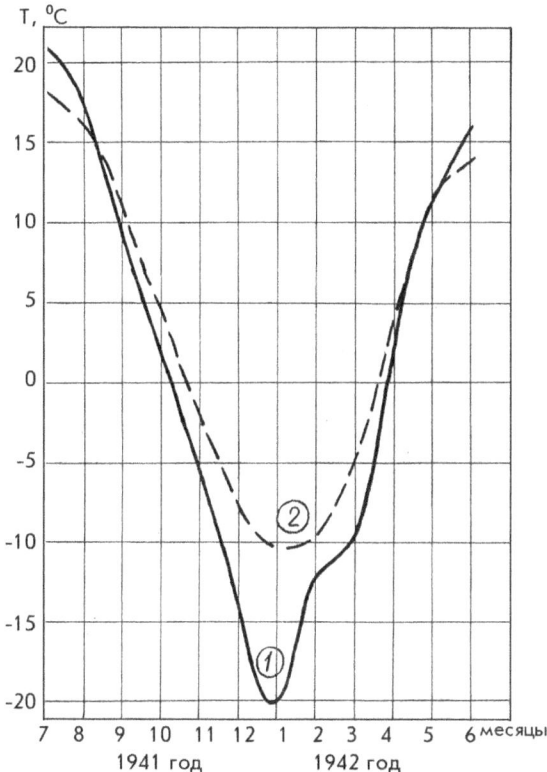

Figure 8.1. Average monthly air temperature in Moscow in 1941–42 and "normal" (mean annual) temperature values (second curve). Reproduced from V. N. Razuvaev, "Pogoda i klimat v Rossii v XX veke," in *Rossiia v okruzhaiushchem mire: Analiticheskii ezhegodnik* (2001), retrieved 12 December 2011 from http://www.rus-stat.ru/stat/3932001-6.pdf.

in November, -8°C in December, and -11°C in January. In some periods in January, frosts were as low as -35 to -40°C. The amount of snow reached 50–65 centimeters during the winter of 1941–42.[9]

In planning and implementing the concept of the blitzkrieg, the German leadership made a serious miscalculation—it did not prepare its troops for a winter campaign. When the Wehrmacht approached Moscow in October 1941, Hitler announced that the "Soviets" would soon be destroyed completely. This meant that the fighting would be over before the cold set in. On the basis of this propagandistic premise, the Wehrmacht's rear services stockpiled warm clothing for only 20 percent of the personnel, they did not provide antifreeze for the motorized units, and they did not give the military's technical personnel a lubricant for winter weapons. On top of this, a timely campaign to collect warm clothing for the troops was not organized in Germany during the autumn of 1941.[10]

As is well known, reality disrupted the plans made by Hitler's command. The first month of war under winter conditions showed that the German army was poorly equipped for the cold period of the year; from the onset of the frosts, they experienced enormous difficulties. Fierce storms and prolonged periods of freezing temperatures demoralized the German troops, seriously undermining their ability to fight. As someone who took part in the Eastern campaign of 1941–42 wrote, "We were advancing through frozen bogs, the ice kept cracking, and icy water poured into my boots. My gloves were soaked through, I had to take them off and wrap a towel around my numb hands. I wanted to howl from the pain."[11]

A unique document attests to how complicated it was for Wehrmacht soldiers to adapt to the Russian winter. This is the diary of Gerhardt Linke, a lieutenant of the 185th Infantry Regiment of the 87th Infantry Division who fought in the battles outside Moscow. Here are some of the more typical entries:

> 16 November 1941 ... Several freezing days were enough for illnesses and cases of frostbite to start. Our fighting strength is visibly diminishing. ... We Germans are generally not used to waging war in winter and our equipment doesn't match the [demands of] the latter. ... 5 December 1941 At night, the temperature dropped to minus 26 degrees. ... The radio doesn't work in strong frosts. Our position is oppressive, uncertain. ... An icy wind blows prickly needles of snow into your face. A hard crust from your breath settles on your balaclava. The rest of your face quickly becomes white and after just a few minutes in the frost you come back frostbitten. Many people on guard duty try to warm themselves up at miserable campfires because the feet are the most sensitive to the cold. Our kit doesn't bear comparison with the Russians'. The enemy has insulated pants and jackets. He wears *valenki* [felt boots] and fur hats. Recently a few sheepskin coats arrived, they gave them out to the soldiers who have to spend the most time in the frost. Our footwear isn't enough, especially with the condition our boots and socks are in. ... 15 December 1941 The cold is penetrating everywhere. I am trying to protect myself with a blanket and two overcoats, but my feet are getting numb from the frost. A snowstorm is raging, the snow is covering us and our carts. ... 26 December 1941 In the morning on a truck to the place where they are issuing ammunition. The motors are refusing to work because of the severe cold. ... 2 January 1942 From minus 33 to minus 37 degrees. ... There is a numbing frost. I got hold of a pair of local *valenki*. They are amazingly warm on my feet. Little by little our division is getting them. Unfortunately, what we can get is far less than what we need.[12]

Lieutenant Linke did not live to see the warm weather. He died in the battles around the village of Oshchepkovo (in Smolensk *Oblast'*) in February 1942.

Of course, both sides experienced the same weather conditions. But unlike the Soviet army, the German troops did not have appropriate winter attire and warm boots. To combat the cold, German soldiers had only summer field caps, knitted woolen balaclavas, cloth overcoats and ersatz *valenki* made from straw with wooden soles, which created additional problems rather than offering much protection from the cold. There were not enough fur-lined coats, fur caps, sheepskin jackets, and fur-lined gloves, but the footwear was the worst of it—the nails reinforcing the soles of the mid-calf-length leather boots were ideal conductors of cold.[13] As a result, during the winter of 1941, cases of frostbitten feet reached 40 percent in many Wehrmacht divisions at the front.[14]

The frost not only put soldiers out of action, it also incapacitated machinery: the oil in automobile engines froze, tank motors did not start, and rifles and machine guns would not shoot. Under these conditions, the German army's offensive was doomed to fail. As Herbert Kraft noted in his memoirs: "The Soviets took care of their soldiers in good time. Valenki, insulated pants and padded jackets, fur-lined gloves and caps, skis and sledges were standard equipment for them. Their weapons also worked well in the severe cold. But we lay in our ice-cold caves without winter outfits. We threw blankets on top of summer overcoats as if they were the capes of Napoleon's army. The icy wind blew through our ridiculously thin woolen gloves."[15] Boris Slutskii says something similar in his memoirs: "During the winter of 1941–1942, warmed by our own breath, our snowy lair outside Moscow vanquished the German inability to adapt to snowy lairs."[16]

It should be noted that the German leadership did try to learn from the unsuccessful experience of fighting during the winter in the USSR. In August 1942, Franz Halder, the chief of the General Staff of the Ground Forces, approved and signed off on a handbook on how to wage war in the winter, which generalized from the experience of the 1941–42 campaign. This handbook was used as a textbook on developing practical skills for successful military campaigns during the Russian winter. It contained recommendations, accompanied by illustrations, on insulation for clothing and footwear, how to manufacture and wear gear for the face ("snow glasses") that would provide protection from the wind and the cold, how to build huts, how to use sleds for transporting various things, how to lay roads in virgin snow, and the like. Because the handbook was a weighty tome (around 400 pages), an abridged version, the *Pocket Handbook for Winter War* (*Taschenbuch für den Winterkrieg*), was published in September 1942. This 270-page edition contained only the mandatory provisions for rank-and-file soldiers. The fact that it was almost immediately reprinted with revisions and additions in 1943 shows how much demand there was for this practical handbook.[17]

In the winter of 1942–43, insulated winter clothing was introduced in the German army. This measure was the result of the experience of the previous winter, when thousands of German soldiers fighting on the Eastern Front suffered from the cold. This kind of uniform turned out to be very convenient since it gave soldiers freedom of movement and permitted them to use equipment while simultaneously protecting them from severe cold and from overheating during intensive movement. The uniform included a thick, double-breasted parka and matching pants.

It was much more complicated to overcome the Wehrmacht soldiers' fear of the Russian winter, which the Soviet political organs actively exploited in their special propaganda for the enemy troops. One leaflet addressed to the Germans reads as follows: "Remember what the winter of 1941 was like in Russia. … In the German trenches, the advancing Russian units found curled up, frozen corpses of soldiers, entire platoons and companies of them. The white death. … This year you will have to spend the winter in treeless regions. There is no cover from terrible frosts and snowstorms. There is no firewood for huts and dugouts. Under the conditions of the Russian frosts, the most insignificant wound is fatal. … Whoever doesn't die from the Russian bullets will die in the arms of the white death!"[18] The success of this leaflet was guaranteed since it was based on rumors circulating among German soldiers.

It is not surprising that in wartime Germany the "Russian winter" was a metaphor for terrible suffering and death in extreme cold.[19] For the German population and the generals alike, the Russian winter was associated, consciously or unwittingly, with the destruction of Napoleon's army in Russia. The well-known director Leni Riefenstahl wrote in her memoirs that for her, the German soldiers who died in the snow and ice in Russia and the Russian winter were very strongly connected, and the Russian winter gave her a feeling of enduring horror that resided in the depths of her soul.[20] M. V. Datsishina concludes that "[the fact that] frost is an intrinsic feature of Russia and an inevitable death from frost in Russia were inextricably interlinked in the consciousness of the German nation."[21]

Soviet fighters also noted how strongly climate affected the troops. Vladimir Krylov, who took part in the battles for Leningrad, wrote that "in its terrible consequences, intense oppressiveness, and destructive impact on the human psyche, cold is the only thing that can be compared with hunger." He went on to say that "cold has a bulldog's grip. It doesn't care about our feelings. It only needs them for support, in order to drive out and freeze out consciousness, to hammer it out and turn it off."[22] Former frontline soldiers remember how, after hours of lying in the snow, they would pull off their ammunition, which had iced over, rip open their valenki and tear off their footcloths, and the skin that came with them. Those who fought in winter battles were often stricken with what was called "frozen consciousness syndrome," which was characterized by an acute decline in physical and mental activity.

The Soviet military leaders' use of climate during World War II was an outstanding, indeed crucial, contribution to the Red Army's victories. The ways the military leadership used the climatic factor, along with the heroism and courage of Soviet soldiers, enabled them to defeat the German troops in the battles of Moscow and Stalingrad. The Red Army command repeatedly issued orders to destroy all residential buildings that could serve as housing in the enemy's rear in order to force the Germans to quarter their units in the open air. In particular, Order Number 0428, issued by the Headquarters of the Supreme High Command on 17 November 1941, instructed all army units "to deprive the German army of the possibility of settling in villages and cities, to drive the German aggressors out of all population points into the cold, into the fields, to smoke them out of every lodging and warm refuge and force them to freeze under the open sky."[23] The Soviet commanders' calculation turned out to be correct: blizzards and snowstorms did no worse than bullets and missiles to mow down enemy soldiers. Judging by General Gotthard Heinrici's frontline letters, there were more Wehrmacht losses from frostbite near Moscow in some parts of the front than there were dead and wounded men.[24] It was not a coincidence that, with bitter irony, German soldiers called the medal for the 1941–42 winter campaign the "Order of Frozen Meat."

A similar tactic was used successfully during the battle for Stalingrad. General P. I. Batov, who took part in those battles, wrote: "Toward the middle of January we drove the fascist troops out into the open steppe, to the frost, without water. Whichever way you look—boundless steppe. Nowhere to hide and warm up."[25] In the absence of winter clothing, the German soldiers in their trenches were helpless against the icy steppe winds. Many of them froze to death or suffered from frostbite.[26] This is how Joachim Wieder, a German officer who survived Stalingrad, describes the situation in his memoirs:

> There were sharp frosts and the mercury column in the thermometer went down below 30 degrees. Our unit—the pitiful remnants of a regiment that long ago had been divided into battle groups—fell back in a disorderly fashion along the uninhabited, snowy steppe. Behind them stretched long columns of stragglers, lightly wounded and frostbitten. Unable to withstand the inhuman stress, hunger, and the extreme cold, during those days many of those whom the Russian missiles spared perished. Our path was strewn with corpses that the snowstorm covered with snow, as if out of compassion.[27]

At the end of January 1943, there were more than fifty thousand wounded, sick, and frostbitten soldiers in the "Stalingrad cauldron."[28] Eyewitnesses remember that many refuse pits at field hospitals were filled to the brim with frozen limbs that had been amputated. Berlin physician Hans Diebold, who had been sent to Stalingrad at the end of December 1942, confirmed the mass mortality of German soldiers in the "cauldron" from hypothermia. Explaining the reasons for the contingent's mass mortality rate to his commanding officer, Zhuravelev, the senior military *feldsher* (medical assistant) of Camp No. 50 for German prisoners of war, came to a similar conclusion.[29] Around 60 percent of the German soldiers taken prisoner at Stalingrad had frostbite complicated by gangrene and blood poisoning.[30]

At the beginning of February 1943, the German troops in the "Stalingrad cauldron" began to capitulate. Joachim Wieder describes this in his memoirs:

> The Russians gathered and took away crowds of exhausted soldiers who were worn out by endless suffering and apathetically resigned to their fate, the way people brush off sluggish, half-dead flies with their hands in late autumn. ... The first thing that struck my eye was how the victors looked. These were healthy, good-looking people. They were wearing winter outfits and were well armed. It was impossible not to envy them. The soldiers ... were dressed in sheepskin coats or padded jackets, felt boots, and fur caps with earflaps. The warmly dressed, well fed, brilliantly equipped Red Army men with their broad, mostly red-cheeked faces were a striking contrast to our pitiable, deadly pale, unwashed, unshaven figures, trembling from the cold. Weakened and exhausted, we were dressed in motley, multicolored uniforms: overcoats and fur coats of every possible type, blankets, scarves, grey-green balaclavas, woolen rags and our footwear was completely unsuited to the Russian winter. This sudden meeting and the sharp contrast showed me at once how terribly low we had fallen and how little we were prepared for a death struggle.[31]

Cold in Captivity

The impact of climate on German military personnel in Soviet captivity was equally important. A significant number of the camps for prisoners of war were in remote regions of the European north of the USSR, the Urals, and Siberia. This contravened Article Nine of the Geneva Convention (the Convention Relative to the Treatment of Prisoners of War, signed on 27 July 1929), which forbade holding prisoners of war in places with adverse climatic conditions.[32] The NKVD leadership initially tried to take climate into consideration when deciding where to put prisoners of war (POWs). For example, Italian POWs, who found it difficult to endure the conditions in the northern regions of the USSR, were sent to Pakhta-Aral'skii (in Iuzhno-Kazakhstanskaia *Oblast'*), the Andizhan camps (Uzbekistan SSSR), and the Temink camps (Mordovian ASSR).[33] The French, the Belgians, and the Luxembourgers were shipped to Radinskii Camp No. 188, which was near Tambov.[34] Nonetheless the policy of separating prisoners of war by nationality was applied inconsistently and was never fully implemented. Eventually prisoners of war of more than thirty nationalities were placed in camps in the northern regions of the USSR. These included French, Italian, Spanish, Yugoslavian, Greek, Bosnian, Albanian, and even Brazilian prisoners.[35]

According to Article Nine of the Geneva Convention, in harsh climatic conditions special measures should be taken in terms of providing food and material goods for prisoners of war and using their labor. However, the "Regulations on Prisoners of War" adopted by the Council of Peoples' Commissars of the USSR in July 1941 did not follow the guidelines laid down in Article Nine. The "Regulations on Prisoners of War" did not say anything about any kind of differentiation, including the need to take the particulars of the climate into account in placing unarmed enemy soldiers in camps, providing food and clothing for them, and using their labor.[36]

It was hard for prisoners of war to get used to the freezing Russian winter. It was not by chance that Soviet camps were described in terms of the severe climatic conditions in the questionnaires filled out by repatriated POWs after they returned to their home countries; swamp-like moisture and dampness were often mentioned alongside the cold winters.[37] In their memoirs, former prisoners of war speak of how hard it was for them become acclimated to the cold. These memoirs describe terrible frosts of negative 50 degrees, birds falling from the sky because of the hellish cold, saliva freezing as it was spit out, and similar horrors. Rumors that things of this type often happened in Russia—the "country of eternal cold, bears, and darkness"—were widespread in the West.[38]

This evidence should certainly be taken with some skepticism. Deaths of prisoners of war from cold are, however, mentioned in archival documents. Thus, on 8 February 1947 Helmut Brandt died suddenly in the Dedovo Pole camp department in Vologda *Oblast'*. According to the medical examination, the cause of death was heart failure due to hypothermia. According to the camp doctor's notes, on that day the temperature fell to -35°C.[39]

The reports from camps and special hospitals show that the first and fourth quarters of the year saw an increase in indicators of mortality and morbidity. For example, in Camp No. 447 (in the Karelian-Finnish SSR) in November 1945, 153 people (4.1 percent of the entire contingent of POWs) died. In December 1945, there were 259 deaths (7.2 percent of all prisoners). In January 1946, there were 203 deaths (6.1 percent), 132 in February (4.2 percent), and 49 in March (1.6 percent).[40] Similar dynamics are observed for the USSR as a whole. Thus, out of 126,834 German POWs who died in 1945 in the first quarter, there were 62,714 deaths (49.4 percent). In the second quarter there were

22,319 deaths (17.6 percent of the total) and 16,613 deaths in the third quarter (13.1 percent). In the fourth quarter, there were 25,188 deaths (19.9 percent).[41] This data shows that there was an overall decrease in morbidity over the course of the year, but the number of deaths increased with the onset of winter.

There was a very high incidence of frostbite during the winter. Thus, in March 1945, of 540 people admitted to Special Hospital No. 2715 (in the settlement of Chagoda), 39 (7 percent) were suffering from frostbite.[42] The situation at Special Hospitals No. 1825 and No. 5091 (in Cherepovets) and Special Hospital No. 337 (in Babaevo) was similar.[43] During the winter of 1944–45, more than thirty amputations of frostbitten upper and lower extremities were performed at Special Hospital No. 1825, and two POWs died of hypothermia.[44] It is noteworthy that the first autumn frosts led to the mass incidence of frostbite. Thus, in October 1945, twenty-nine cases of third-degree frostbite were recorded by the sanitary department of Griazovetskii Camp No. 150.[45] Tissue damage as a result of activity in low temperatures cannot be considered unique to prisoner-of-war camps in the northern regions of the USSR. In December 1946, more than five hundred cases of frostbite were recorded at Camp No. 229 (Krimskaia *Oblast'*) and Camp No. 288 (Uzbekistan SSR).[46]

Labor productivity fell sharply during the winter months. Thus, although the POWs in Camp No. 158 (Cherepovets), who were rebuilding the railway bed of the Suda-Sheksna section of the Northern Railway, fulfilled the plan by 101 percent in the second and third quarters of 1946, in the fourth quarter they only fulfilled it by 83.6 percent. Something similar happened in 1947: during the first quarter 63 percent of the plan was fulfilled, 87.5 percent was fulfilled in the second quarter, and 107 percent in the third.[47] In Griazovetskii Camp No. 150 the contingents of POWs sent out for external work during the winter decreased from 54.5 percent to 23 percent.[48]

Aggregate productivity indicators for prisoner-of-war camps in the Soviet Union also had a pronounced seasonal character. Thus, the average labor productivity for POWs' work in 1944 was 93.7 percent in January, 107 percent in April, 101.4 percent in July, 91.5 percent in October, and 87.5 percent in December.[49] Something similar happened in 1947. In the first quarter of 1947, the gross output of German POWs amounted to 831 million rubles, 927 million in the second quarter, 970 million in the third quarter, and 743 million in the fourth.[50] As is evident from this data, the lowest percentages in the yearly production cycle occurred during the coldest winter months.

The memoirs of Robert Prinzing, who worked on a logging squad in Vologda *Oblast'* during the winter of 1945–46, show how difficult and complicated it was to fulfill the production plan in winter:

> The weather during the last few days was very cold but on New Year's Eve the frost became even more severe. After getting up in the morning, we no-

ticed that the curtain that we had hung in front of the flimsy entry door, was covered with hoar frost. The day was going to be an ordeal. Before going out on the road, I tied a piece of fabric to my cap that covered my nose, cheeks, and the entire lower part of my face, leaving only a small slit for my eyes. Eight of us set out for the forest. A cold northeast wind was blowing. Filled with light clouds, the sky was a gray-blue color that heralded a severe frost. My neighbor hadn't wrapped himself as well as I had, and he was constantly rubbing his nose, which had turned white. I noticed that the slit for my eyes was becoming narrower and narrower. My fur hat and my eyelashes were encrusted with frost. The first thing we did after we got to the place where we were going to log was to make a big fire to warm ourselves. But in this kind of frost it was a senseless business. The fire gave out practically no heat. Our salvation was that after working for a few minutes, all the axe handles broke into matchstick-sized fragments, which gave us a valid reason to return to the camp ...[51]

Prisoners of war often saw bad weather as a reason to cut their work short. Thus, in February 1947, POWs Prikkert, Moltrecht, and Wolff appealed to their compatriots to refuse to go out to work "because of the cold weather." They suggested staging a hunger strike if the camp administration opposed this.[52] On 17 December 1944 in the dining hall of Solombalsk Camp No. 211 (Arkhangel'sk), the medic Russo, a prisoner of war who was Polish by nationality, spoke persuasively to his fellow POWs: "The Hungarian commanders want to curry favor with the Russian commanders and send everyone to work in the cold weather so people are going to die. Your clothes aren't good [so] don't go out to work and if the commanders send [us] out, let's give them a beating."[53]

The camp authorities had a difficult task: under the circumstances they were responsible for not only the lives but also the work of the prisoners of war in a climate that was disastrous for them. Directive No. 28/K/21676 from the NKVD came out on 31 December 1943. This obligated the heads of front-line reception and transfer camps to maintain a temperature that did not fall below 16°C in living quarters; in invalid brigades the temperature could not be lower than 18°C and in infirmaries a temperature of at least 20°C had to be maintained. It was obligatory to install thermometers in the POWs' living quarters.[54] When there were frosts below 15°C, POWs were forbidden to leave their quarters, and in the absence of warm clothing and shoes, they were required to remain inside at temperatures below 8°C. The workday was not to exceed six hours on days when there were frosts.[55]

In industrial camps several restrictions limited the use of POWs' labor during the winter. A specially created commission consisting of representatives from the *khozorgan* (economic organs) and camps supplying the labor force drew up a document about terminating work in extreme weather conditions. Directive No. 28/126727 of 19 November 1942, "On Measures for the Prevention of Frostbite in Prisoners of War," issued by the administration of the NKVD and Decree No. 848 of 29 December 1947 from the Ministry of Internal Affairs (MVD) ordered the heads of POW camps to establish temperature boundaries for each camp by taking into account the local and climatic factors specific to each camp (air temperature, humidity, etc.) that would keep POWs from going outside the camp to work. In fact, this meant that the determination of the minimum temperature was made at the discretion of the camp authorities. Thus, in Camp No. 158 (Cherepovets), prisoners of war were not allowed to leave for external work in temperatures lower than -25°C but in Camp No. 437 (Cherepovets) the low-temperature threshold was considered -30°C.[56]

As a rule, work stopped when wind speeds were higher than twenty meters per second, independent of the air temperature. In weather conditions like that it was recommended that POWs be used for work in enclosed facilities. In work outside, in temperatures lower than -15°C, making fires in safe places to warm POWs or providing heat for fifteen to twenty minutes for every two hours of work in special buildings (warming points) was envisioned. Those who did not have winter clothes were not allowed to be sent out to work. Work points were equipped with stoves, and it was strictly prohibited to send weak POWs out to work. In addition, camp personnel were supposed to talk with the prisoners of war about how to prevent frostbite, and in freezing weather convoys and foremen were supposed to be given a special ointment for frostbite.[57]

According to Directive No. 375 of 24 July 1943, "On the Timely Provision of Prisoners of War with Warm Clothing," issued by S. N. Kruglov, the deputy commissar for internal affairs, former soldiers of enemy armies who were being held in the northern camps were to be given half-length fur coats (*polushubki*), cotton-wool padded jackets (*telogreiki*), and trousers, sweaters, or warm shirts.[58] The economic apparatus and the sanitary services of the camps were entrusted with establishing "daily monitoring of the condition of clothes and footwear" to ensure the "quick and careful repair and drying out of uniforms which provide warmth."[59] An NKVD telegram of 16 November 1945 demanded that every camp and all camp departments that were not prepared to maintain POWs under winter conditions be closed.[60] For gross violations of these NKVD decrees and directives, officials had administrative or criminal liability. Thus, the head of Camp No. 211 (Arkhangel'sk), who failed to ensure the maintenance of prisoners of war in winter conditions, was dismissed from his post, and the deputy head of Camp No. 220 (in Molotovsk) was placed under strict arrest for the same reason.[61]

To summarize, studying the influence of climate on the events of World War II does not mean denying or diminishing the contribution of Soviet troops to the Wehrmacht's crushing defeat. Climate in and of itself certainly could not stop the German army's offensives at Moscow and Stalingrad, but to discount its role in these battles distorts historical reality—that is, what actually happened. Russia's severe climatic conditions negatively affected the morale as well as the psychological and physical condition of Wehrmacht soldiers at the front and in Soviet prisoner-of-war camps. At the same time, the camp personnel took the necessary measures to improve living conditions and the use of prisoner-of-war labor, which helped former enemy combatants to adapt to the conditions of life in a natural and climatic environment to which they were unaccustomed.

Acknowledgments

This chapter was completed with support from the Russian Foundation for the Humanities (Rossiiskii gumanitarnyi nauchnyi fond, RGNF), grant no 12-01-00344a.

Translation by Jacqueline Friedlander

Aleksandr Kuzminykh is professor in the Department of Philosophy and History at the Vologda Institute of Law and Economics of the Federal Penitentiary Service. His research interests are the history of military captivity and internment in World War II, the history of internal affairs agencies, and the Russian penal system. He is the author of several books, including *Voennyi plen i internirovanie v SSSR (1939–1956 gody)* (2016) and *Archipelag GUPVI na Evropeiskom severe (1939–1949 gg.)* (2017).

Notes

1. A. N. Mertsalov, *Zapadnogermanskaia burzhuaznaia istoriografiia Vtoroi mirovoi voiny* (Moscow, 1978), 244.
2. Ibid., 243.
3. Otto Karius, *'Tigry' v griazi: Vospominaniia nemetskogo tankista*, trans. S. V. Lisogorskii (Moscow, 2006); Zhan Mabir, *Voina v belom adu: Nemetskie parashiutisty na Vostochnom fronte, 1941–1945 gg.*, trans. N. A. Egorova (Moscow, 2005); Wolfgang Paul, *Erfrorener Sieg: Die Schlacht um Moskau 1941–1942* (Esslingen, 1976).
4. See, for example, A. E. Taras, ed. and comp., *Sovetsko-finskaia voina 1939–1940 gg.* (Minsk, 1999), 154–77.
5. Mikhail V. Zefirov and Dmitrii M. Degtev, *'Laptezhnik' protiv 'chernoi smerti': Obzor razvitiia i deistvii nemetskoi i sovetskoi shtrumovoi aviatsii v khode Vtoroi mirovoi voiny* (Moscow, 2008), 108.
6. See "Vliianie na russkuiu istoriiu prirodno-klimaticheskogo faktora," in *Rossiia i mir*, ed. A. A. Danilov, part 1 (Moscow, 1994), 10–12.

7. Nikolai M. Dronin and Edward G. Bellinger, *Climate Dependence and Food Problems in Russia (1900–1990)* (Budapest, 2005); Stephen G. Wheatcroft and Robert W. Davies, "Agriculture," in *The Economic Transformation of the Soviet Union, 1913–1945*, ed. Robert W. Davies, Mark Harrison, and Stephen G. Wheatcroft (Cambridge, 1994), 106–15; Nikolai M. Dronin and A. P. Kirilenko, "Rol' klimaticheskogo i politekonomicheskogo faktorov v dinamike urozhainosti zernovykh v otechestvennoi istorii XX vek," *Vestnik Moskovskogo universiteta*, Seriia 5, Geografiia 5 (2012): 13–18.
8. V. N. Razuvaev, "Pogoda i klimat v Rossii v XX veke," in *Rossiia v okruzhaiushchem mire: Analiticheskii ezhegodnik* (2001), retrieved 12 December 2011 from http://www.rus-stat.ru/stat/3932001-6.pdf.
9. Boris Mikhailovich Shaposhnikov, ed., *Razgrom nemetskikh voisk pod Moskvoi: Kniga pervaia (Moskovskaia operatsiia Zapadnogo fronta 18 noiabria 1941 g.–31 ianvaria 1942 g.* (Moscow, 1943), retrieved 16 December 2011 from http://www.1942.ru/book/msk/index1.htm.
10. M. V. Datsishina, "Tema Napoleona i voiny 1812 goda v sovetskoi i natsistskoi propagande v khode Velikoi Otechestvennoi voiny," *Voprosy istorii*, no. 6 (2011): 151.
11. Quoted in S. Voropaev, comp., *Entsiklopediia Tret'ego Reikha* (Moscow, 1996), 54.
12. See T. V. Domracheva and S. D. Miakushev, eds., "'Nam ne udalos' slomit' soprotivlenie protivnika': Dnevnik nemetskogo ofitsera G. Linke, ubitogo pod Moskvoi, 1941–1942 gg.," *Otechestvennye arkhivy*, no. 1 (2011): 75–113.
13. Guido Knopp, *Istoriia vermakhta: Itogi* (Saint Petersburg, 2009), 91.
14. P. Carel' [Paul Carrell], *Gitler idet na Vostok, 1941–1943*, trans. A. Kolin, *Vostochnyi front*, vol. 1 (Moscow, 2003), 154.
15. G. Kraft [Herbert Kraft], *Frontovyi dnevnik esesovtsa: 'Mertvaia golova' v boiu*, trans. S. Lipatova (Moscow, 2010), 206.
16. Quoted in Ia. Dukhan, "Eshche odno pravdivoe slovo o voine," review of Boris Slutskii, *Zapiski o voine*, *Neva*, no. 6 (2001): 197.
17. *Taschenbuch für den Winterkrieg*, abridged ed. of 1 September 1942, with additional material from November 1942 (Berlin, 1943).
18. Quoted in N. N. Iakovlev, *Izbrannye proizvedeniia* (Moscow, 1990), 438.
19. Datsishina, "Tema Napoleona," 152.
20. L. Rifenshtal' [Leni Riefenstahl], *Memuary* (Moscow, 2006), 266–67.
21. Datsishina, "Tema Napoleona," 152.
22. Vladimir Krylov, "Gody dalekie, gody ushedshie," *Sever*, no. 4 (2000): 71.
23. *Russkii arkhiv: Velikaia Otechestvennaia: Stavka Verkhovnogo Glavnokomandovaniia: Dokumenty i materialy: 1941 god*, vol. 16 (5–1) (Moscow, 1996), 299.
24. I. Khiurter [Johannes Hürter], ed., *Zametki o voine na unichtozhenie: Vostochnyi front 1941–1942 gg. v zapisiakh generala Kheinritsi*, trans. O. I. Beida and I. P. Petrov (Saint Petersburg, 2018), 151. The original German edition is Johannes Hürter, ed., *Notizen aus dem Vernichtungskrieg: Die Ostfront 1941/42 in den Aufzeichnungen des Generals Heinrici* (Darmstadt, 2016). In contrast Iurii Veremeev estimates that during the fall and winter of 1941–42 approximately three thousand Wehrmacht soldiers died from frostbite. See Iurii G. Veremeev. *Krasnaia Armia v nachale Vtoroi mirovoi: Kak gotovilis' v voine soldaty i marshaly* (Moscow, 2010), 44–45.
25. Pavel Ivanovich Batov, *V boiakh i pokhodakh*, 4th ed. (Moscow, 1984), 246.

26. V. Adam [Wilhelm Adam], *Katastrofa na Volge: Memuary ad"iutanta F. Paulius* (Smolensk, 2001), 221.
27. I. Wider [Joachim Wieder], *Stalingradskaia tragediia: Za kulisami katastrofy* (Moscow, 2006), 92–93.
28. Ibid., 100, 131.
29. Aleksandr E. Epifanov, *Stalingradskii plen 1942–1956 gody: Nemetskie voennopleny v SSSR* (Moscow, 1999), 230.
30. Ibid., 28, 40–41, 59.
31. Vider, *Stalingradskaia tragediia*, 161, 162.
32. Maksim Matveevich Zagorul'ko, ed., *Voennoplennye v SSSR, 1939–1956: Dokumenty i materialy* (Moscow, 2000), 1013.
33. Ibid., 32.
34. Evgenii N. Pisarev, *Rada, Pot'ma, t'ma GULAGa: Ocherk* (Tambov, 1999), 11.
35. Ibid., 218–19, 255–56.
36. Zagorul'ko, *Voennoplennye v SSSR*, 65–68.
37. A. S. Shil'nikov and V. A. Gorobchenko, "Lager'-peresylka voennoplennykh i uznikov vtoroi mirovoi voiny pod Rybinskom," in *Problemy voennogo plena: Istoriia i sovremennost'; Materialy Mezhdunarodnoi nauchno-prakticheskoi konferentsii*, part 1 (Vologda, 1997), 157.
38. Surprisingly similar descriptions of the Russian winter can be found in the memoirs of Swedish soldiers taken prisoner at Poltava in 1709. See Evgenii V. Anisimov, *Vremia petrovskikh reform* (Leningrad, 1989), 185.
39. Arkhiv Upravleniia ministerstva vnutrennikh del Rossiiskoi Federatsii po Vologodskoi oblasti (hereafter Arkhiv UMVD Rossii po VO), f. 10, op. 1, d. 231, l. 24.
40. Calculated from data in Zagorul'ko, *Voennoplennye v SSSR*, 491.
41. Calculated from data in ibid., 504.
42. Gosudarstvennyi arkhiv Vologodskoi oblasti (hereafter GAVO), f. 1876, op. 1, d. 238, l. 3.
43. Ibid., f. 1876, op. 1, d. 142, l. 3, 48; f. 1876, op. 1, d. 236, l. 11–11 ob.
44. Ibid., f. 1876, op. 1, d. 233, l. 4.
45. Arkhiv UMVD Rossii po VO, f. 10, op. 1, d. 17, l. 44.
46. Ibid., f. 6, op. 1, d. 487, l. 13; f. 6, op. 1, d. 488, l. 1.
47. Rossiiskii gosudarstvennyi voennyi arkhiv (hereafter RGVA), f. 1/p., op. 35a, d. 26, l. 20.
48. Arkhiv UMVD Rossii po VO, f. 10, op. 1, d. 13, l. 3 ob.
49. Maksim Matveevich Zagorul'ko, ed., *Glavnoe upravlenie po delam voennoplennykh i internirovannykh NKVD-MVD SSSR: Otchetno-informatsionnye materialy, Voennoplennye v SSSR*, vol. 4 (Volgograd, 2004), 569.
50. Ibid., 587.
51. Quoted in Aleksandr L. Kuzminykh, S. I. Starostin, and A. B. Sychev, *"'Teper' ia pribyl na krai sveta ...'": Iz istorii uchrezhdenii dlia soderzhaniia inostrannykh voennoplennykh i internirovannykh v Vologodskoi oblasti (1939–1949 gg.): Ocherki i dokumenty* (Vologda, 2009), 1:146.
52. Arkhiv UMVD Rossii po VO, f. 10, op. 1, d. 44, l. 87 ob.
53. RGVA, f. 1/p, op. 9v, d. 78, l. 36.

54. Arkhiv UMVD Rossii po VO, f. 10, op. 1, d. 105, l. 103 ob.
55. *Russkii arkhiv: Velikaia Otechestvennaia*, vol. 16 (5-1), 125-27.
56. Arkhiv UMVD Rossii po VO, f. 10, op. 1, d. 194, l. 86; f. 10, d. 325, l. 232.
57. Ibid., f. 10, op. 1, d. 194, l. 86.
58. Ibid., f. 6, op. 1, d. 451, l. 287-287 ob.
59. Ibid., f. 6, op. 1, d. 463, l. 54 ob.; f. 6, op. 1, d. 471, l. 15; f. 6, op. 1, d. 483a, l. 533-533 ob.
60. *Russkii arkhiv: Velikaia Otechestvennaia: Inostrannye voennoplennye Vtoroi mirovoi voiny*, vol. 24 (13-1), 265-66.
61. Arkhiv UMVD Rossii po Arkhangel'skoi oblasti, f. 3, d. 61, l. 32; f. 3, d. 62, l. 287.

Bibliography

Adam, V. [Wilhelm Adam]. *Katastrofa na Volge: Memuary ad"iutanta F. Paulius*. Smolensk, 2001.
Anisimov, Evgenii V. *Vremia petrovskikh reform*. Leningrad, 1989.
Batov, Pavel Ivanovich. *V boiakh i pokhodakh*. 4th ed. Moscow, 1984.
Carel', P. [Paul Carrel]. *Gitler idet na Vostok, 1941-1943*. Translated by A. Kolin. *Vostochnyi front*. Vol. 1. Moscow, 2003.
Datsishina, M. V. "Tema Napoleona i voiny 1812 goda v sovetskoi i natsistskoi propagande v khode Velikoi Otechestvennoi voiny." *Voprosy istorii*, no. 6 (2011): 149-56.
Domracheva, T. V., and S. D. Miakushev, eds. "'Nam ne udalos' slomit' soprotivlenie protivnika': Dnevnik nemetskogo ofitsera G. Linke, ubitogo pod Moskvoi, 1941-1942 gg." *Otechestvennye arkhivy*, no. 1 (2011): 75-113.
Dronin, Nikolai M., and Edward G. Bellinger. *Climate Dependence and Food Problems in Russia (1900-1990)*. Budapest, 2005.
Dronin, Nikolai M., and A. P. Kirilenko. "Rol' klimaticheskogo i politekonomicheskogo faktorov v dinamike urozhainosti zernovykh v otechestvennoi istorii XX vek." *Vestnik Moskovskogo universiteta*, Seriia 5, Geografiia 5 (2012): 13-18.
Dukhan, Ia. "Eshche odno pravdivoe slovo o voine." Review of Boris Slutskii, *Zapiski o voine*. *Neva*, no. 6 (2001): 195-97.
Epifanov, Aleksandr E. *Stalingradskii plen 1942-1956 gody: Nemetskie voennopleny v SSSR*. Moscow, 1999.
Johannes Hürter, ed. *Notizen aus dem Vernichtungskrieg: Die Ostfront 1941/42 in den Aufzeichnungen des Generals Heinrici*. Darmstadt, 2016.
Iakovlev, N. N. *Izbrannye proizvedeniia*. Moscow, 1990.
Karius, Otto. *'Tigry' v griazi: Vospominaniia nemetskogo tankista*. Translated by S. V. Lisogorskii. Moscow, 2006.
Khiurter, I. [Johannes Hürter], ed. *Zametki o voine na unichtozhenie: Vostochnyi front 1941-1942 gg. v zapisiakh generala Kheinritsi*. Translated by O. I. Beida and I. P. Petrov. Saint Petersburg, 2018.
Knopp, Guido. *Istoriia vermakhta: Itogi*. Saint Petersburg, 2009.
Kraft, G. [Herbert Kraft]. *Frontovyi dnevnik esesovtsa: 'Mertvaia golova'v boiu*. Translated by S. Lipatova. Moscow, 2010.

Krylov, Vladimir. "Gody dalekie, gody ushedshie." *Sever*, no. 4 (2000): 58–80.

Kuzminykh, Aleksandr L., S. I. Starostin, and A. B. Sychev. "'Teper' ia pribyl na krai sveta ...'": *Iz istorii uchrezhdenii dlia soderzhaniia inostrannykh voennoplennykh i internirovannykh v Vologodskoi oblasti (1939–1949 gg.); Ocherki i dokumenty*. Vol. 1. Vologda, 2009.

Mabir, Zhan. *Voina v belom adu: Nemetskie parashiutisty na Vostochnom fronte, 1941–1945 gg*. Trans. N. A. Egorova. Moscow, 2005.

Mertsalov, A. N. *Zapadnogermanskaia burzhuaznaia istoriografiia Vtoroi mirovoi voiny*. Moscow, 1978.

Paul, Wolfgang. *Erfrorener Sieg: Die Schlacht um Moskau 1941–1942*. Esslingen, 1976.

Pisarev, Evgenii N. *Rada, Pot'ma, t'ma GULAGa: Ocherk*. Tambov, 1999.

Razuvaev, V. N. "Pogoda i klimat v Rossii v XX veke." In *Rossiia v okruzhaiushchem mire: Analiticheskii ezhegodnik*. 2001. Retrieved 12 December 2011 from http://www.russtat.ru/stat/3932001-6.pdf.

Rifenshtal', L. [Leni Riefenstahl]. *Memuary*. Moscow, 2006.

Russkii arkhiv: Velikaia Otechestvennaia: Inostrannye voennoplennye Vtoroi mirovoi voiny. Vol. 24 (13-1). Moscow, 1996.

Russkii arkhiv: Velikaia Otechestvennaia: Stavka Verkhovnogo Glavnokomandovaniia: Dokumenty i materialy: 1941 god. Vol. 16 (5-1). Moscow, 1996.

Shaposhnikov, Boris Mikhailovich, ed. *Razgrom nemetskikh voisk pod Moskvoi: Kniga pervaia (Moskovskaia operatsiia Zapadnogo fronta 18 noiabria 1941 g.–31 ianvaria 1942 g*. Moscow, 1943. Retrieved 16 December 2011 from http://www.1942.ru/book/msk/index1.htm.

Shil'nikov, A. S., and V.A. Gorobchenko. "Lager'-peresylka voennoplennykh i uznikov vtoroi mirovoi voiny pod Rybinskom." In *Problemy voennogo plena: Istoriia i sovremennost'; Materialy Mezhdunarodnoi nauchno-prakticheskoi konferentsii*, part 1, 156–60. Vologda, 1997.

Taras, A. E., ed. and comp. *Sovetsko-finskaia voina 1939–1940 gg*. Minsk, 1999.

Taschenbuch für den Winterkrieg. Abridged edition of 1 September 1942, with additional material from November 1942. Berlin, 1943.

Veremeev, Iurii G. *Krasnaia Armia v nachale Vtoroi mirovoi: Kak gotovilis' v voine soldaty i marshaly*. Moscow 2010.

"Vliianie na russkuiu istoriiu prirodno-klimaticheskogo faktora." In *Rossiia i mir*, ed. A. A. Danilov, part 1, 10–12. Moscow, 1994.

Voropaev, S., comp. *Entsiklopediia Tret'ego Reikha*. Moscow, 1996.

Wheatcroft, Stephen G., and Robert W. Davies. "Agriculture." In *The Economic Transformation of the Soviet Union, 1913–1945*, edited by Robert W. Davies, Mark Harrison, and Stephen G. Wheatcroft, 106–30. Cambridge, 1994.

Wider, I. [Joachim Wieder]. *Stalingradskaia tragediia: Za kulisami katastrofy*. Moscow, 2006.

Zagorul'ko, Maksim Matveevich, ed. *Glavnoe upravlenie po delam voennoplennykh i internirovannykh NKVD-MVD SSSR: Otchetno-informatsionnye materialy, Voennoplennye v SSSR*. Vol. 4. Volgograd, 2004.

———. *Voennoplennye v SSSR, 1939–1956: Dokumenty i materialy*. Moscow, 2000.

Zefirov, Mikhail V., and Dmitrii M. Degtev. *'Laptezhnik' protiv 'chernoi smerti': Obzor razvitiia i deistvii nemetskoi i sovetskoi shtrumovoi aviatsii v khode Vtoroi mirovoi voiny*. Moscow, 2008.

 CHAPTER 9

Winter Tourism and Skiing in the Soviet Union
School of Courage, Source of Health, National Pastime

Aleksei Popov

> *Our future fighters can, must, and will be excellent skiers.*
> —A. Tarasov-Kaslinskii, 1932

> *Physical conditions and frosty air are your best physician, and winter tourism is an excellent vitamin for health.*
> —V. Sergeev, 1982

Several significant works on tourism and recreation in the Soviet Union have recently appeared, including works by Western scholars.[1] Scholarship on Soviet tourism and recreation is usually structured chronologically, geographically, or in terms of institutional frameworks. In this chapter, however, for the first time the focus is on one particular type of tourism whose development is directly connected with a specific season and its attendant features: winter ski tourism, the quintessential activity of Soviet citizens during the cold, snowy period of the year. Between the second half of the 1920s and the end of the 1980s, the nature of winter ski tourism changed in some significant ways that reflect changes in Soviet society as a whole.

During winter, Soviet daily life was inextricably connected with skiing. In 1923, soon after the Soviet regime was established, seven thousand pairs of skis were manufactured in artisan workshops throughout the USSR.[2] However, ski production expanded steadily in the decades that followed: in the second half of the 1930s, the yearly output of skis in the country was already more than 1.8 million pairs, and in the 1970s–80s this number reached five million pairs each year.[3] Before the war, the Petrozavodsk ski factory, which opened in 1931 and whose employees included several foreign craftsmen from the Scandinavian countries, was considered the best Soviet ski manufacturer.[4] During the postwar period, ski-manufacturing combines in Kirov, Mukachevo, and Tallinn became the country's largest producers of skis.[5]

Throughout the Soviet period, skis remained the fundamental attribute of winter tourism. They were much more popular than time-honored modes of winter transportation like horse-drawn sleighs and sledges drawn by reindeer or dogs, but skis also enjoyed greater popularity than the newest fruits of scientific and technological progress, such as sleighs with propellers, snowmobiles, and other motorized snow vehicles. Usually made from wood, skis were both traditional and modern. They were used for work and leisure by people of all ages, from all social strata, and of different nationalities. The mass distribution of skis in the USSR was in many ways a result of the country's natural and climatic conditions—that is, a long period of subzero temperatures and a stable snow cover over a large part of the country's territory. But social, political, economic, and cultural factors also played significant roles in their popularity. At the same time, the nature and functions of skiing practices evolved, which indicates their dependence on the historical transformations of Soviet society.

Proletarian Tourists—To Skis!

The proletarian tourist movement began to develop in the Soviet Union in 1927. It was centered around public organizations, the first of which was the Russian Society for Tourists (Rossiiskoe obshchestvo turistov), which was followed by the Society for Proletarian Tourism of the RSFSR (Obshchestvo proletarskogo turizma RSFSR) and, in 1930–36, the All-Union Voluntary Society for Proletarian Tourism and Excursions (Vsesoiuznoe dobrovol'noe obshchestvo proletarskogo turizma i ekskursii, or OPTE). This mass public organization had virtually complete control over domestic tourism in the USSR. Its chief mission was to use tourist hikes, trips, and excursions in the state's interest—that is, to build socialism.[6] As Russian historian Evgeniia Oborina notes, the goal of Stalin-era Soviet tourism was not rest, relaxation, or enjoyment. Instead, it demanded of tourists significant effort (labor, endurance, concentration), which was supposed to transform both external reality and the internal world of the tourists themselves.[7] The long-lasting concept of "tourism as a school of courage," which, to varying extents, was intrinsic to the tourist movement throughout the entire period of the USSR's existence, took shape in the 1930s.[8] The main slogans of proletarian tourism proclaimed that "whoever does not get lost in snowy mountains does not panic in battle," "proletarian tourism is the way to bring up courageous fighters," and "proletarian tourism develops an iron will, bravery, quick-wittedness, and a keen eye."[9]

Envisioning tourism as a "school of courage" included deliberately renouncing comfort while hiking or traveling. Adverse or even extreme natural and climatic conditions were considered advantageous to the physical development of future fighters and helpful for perfecting their moral and psychological qualities. This led to propaganda of such types of active tourism as winter ski trips and mountain climbing.[10] At the same time, ski tourism had a much greater potential for mass development than mountaineering. From the geographic point of view, ski tourism could take place in practically every territory of the USSR except the southernmost regions, and even before the proletarian tourism movement began, a significant proportion of the population knew how to ski. Moreover, teaching someone to ski took less time and effort than training a mountaineer. Ski equipment was also less expensive to purchase than mountain-climbing equipment, and it was easier to come by for both city and country dwellers. As a result of all of these factors, from the first years of proletarian tourism onward, the slogan "All tourists, put on your skis!" resounded.[11]

During the proletarian tourism era, winter tourism on skis took two basic forms—day trips (which were called *vylazki* or "sorties") and multiday campaigns. Both of these were militarized as much as possible. Ski sorties were relatively short trips to nearby areas, which took place mainly on weekends. They were very important for training beginners who did not have much experience with ski trips or with checking their skis and other equipment. This kind of work had the potential to involve the largest number of proletarian tourists. Therefore, at the beginning of the 1930s the slogan "Not a single winter day off without skiing expeditions!" appeared.[12] In the winter of 1932–33, in the context of the mass campaign "For a Model Ski Winter," the OPTE's Central Council called for teaching skiing skills to at least three million proletarian tourists. To popularize this initiative throughout the country, numerous winter holidays, relay races on skis, and "skiing days" were organized at industrial enterprises.[13]

Experienced skiers went on multiday skiing trips when taking a vacation during the cold period of the year. During the prewar period, the most popular regions for multiday trips were Soviet Karelia and Murmansk *Krai*, the Urals, and the North Caucasus.[14] Participants of this type of excursion could work out their itinerary independently, but they then had to coordinate it with the enterprise's proletarian tourist cell and confirm it with the city or regional OPTE council at the point of departure. This way of organizing tourist trips was usually called "independent tourism." The tourists themselves paid their travel expenses, but they had to coordinate with the OPTE cell to get what was called a "route sheet." This document allowed them to purchase train tickets (or tickets for any other type of transport) at a reduced price, buy products with ration cards (at the time there was a ration-card system in the USSR) in the places on their itineraries, and receive a certificate attesting to successful completion of their trip. Traveling without coordinating with an OPTE cell was called "vagrancy" and not socially acceptable.

The methodological literature on proletarian tourism was addressed to activists who wanted to create an OPTE cell and popularize its activities. It emphasized that making ski "sorties" and trips was an excellent way to wake an OPTE cell from its winter "hibernation" and inspire it to organize winter activities that were as vigourous and socially important as its summer activities.[15]

Trips made by ski tourists during the late 1920s and in the first five years of the 1930s were usually intended to improve the participants' skiing technique (sporting and training trips) and to work on other applied military skills (war-readiness trips), but they were also undertaken to do socially useful work in the course of the journey (agitational trips, trips to exchange industrial experience). However, the ski trip most frequently included all of these elements. Participants of ski trips benefited personally: they became stronger and improved their overall physical health, expanded their knowledge, and raised their cultural level. However, in the prewar period, these gains were seen as byproducts; the main goal was social utility.[16]

The period when OPTE was active coincided with the height of the militarization of tourism and what was called "war preparation" tourism. During a time when Soviet propaganda was constantly talking about the threat that the capitalist countries might attack the Soviet Union, increasing the country's defenses became one of the proletarian tourism movement's most important tasks.[17] Ski tourism was strongly influenced by mass militarization. Participants of war-readiness ski trips led by regular officers set up military-style camps, practiced shooting, and studied the basics of camouflage and orientation under winter conditions. To develop these kinds of skills, tourists on militarized ski trips were even given rifles and gas masks.[18] In 1931, the OPTE Central Council announced a competition for carrying out a war-readiness ski trip of a distance of at least twenty-five kilometers. Its program had to include such elements as having the participants transport a machine gun installation through the snow, orient themselves to the terrain at night by using field communications, throw training grenades, and use winter camouflage.[19] The goal of educating the potential soldier-patriot, someone with the New Person's strong body and resolute mind, linked the OPTE's activities with the war-readiness practices of another Stalinist-era mass organization, the Society for Assistance to Defense, Aviation, and Chemical Construction (Obshchestvo sodeistviia oborone, aviatsionnomu i khimicheskomu stroitel'stvu or OSOAVIAKhIM).[20]

From the late 1920s through the 1930s, another important task of ski tourism was to strengthen communication (a linkage or *smichka*) between the city and the countryside. As A. Tarasov-Kaslinskii put it in his book *Skiing in the*

USSR (*Lyzhi v SSSR*), which came out in 1932, "How much the link [*smichka*] between town and country gains, how the younger rural generation's, especially the women's, horizons expand if excursions from remote places make their way to the city on skis! And how many city dwellers know the country, its way of life and work only from stories and books. ... Organized excursions, strolls on skis, will aid cultural and political growth."[21] In short, as a guide to productive action, Tarasov-Kaslinskii called on his compatriots to take to their skis: "On skis we will bring culture to the *kolkhozy* and the *sovkhozy*! With skis we will link our 'bear-like' back of the beyond with the city! On skis—into battle for cultural revolution!"[22]

Although the process of making a ski "connection" between the city and the countryside was envisaged as a two-sided undertaking, politically well-prepared urban ski tourists were supposed to be especially active in this activity. *On Skis around the Outskirts of Leningrad* (*Na lyzhakh po okrestnostiam Leningrada*), which was published in 1932, offered readers a fairly detailed list of things urban skiers could do to help Soviet villages as they went through collectivization. They were encouraged to give lectures, read reports, and hold conversations with villagers in reading rooms, red corners, and village councils. During such events they needed to explain the correctness of the policy of Stalinist modernization of the USSR, show the superiority of collective forms of agriculture, and popularize participation in electing deputies and in various social-political campaigns. City tourists were also supposed to give peasants practical help during the winter by repairing agricultural equipment.[23]

Anti-religious propaganda was an important part of OPTE members' winter activities. Instructions for proletarian tourist cells on organizing ski tourism stated that "ski tourists can help put on an anti-religious event in a village (for example, at a 'christening,' which is one of the most important and one of the most drunken religious holidays). Tourists can organize cultural entertainments for peasant youth, aiding the fight against drunkenness and hooliganism (for example, during 'Shrovetide')."[24] After returning from a trip, tourists were obligated to report on the socially useful work that they had done during the excursion in order to avoid being accused of bourgeois idleness and "tramping about aimlessly."[25]

OPTE was liquidated in 1936, but throughout the Stalinist period the basic ideas about the significance of winter trips did not change.[26] For example, a 1940 editorial in *Pravda* argued that "winter tourism—[to places] far and near, short-term and multiday trips on skis—is also absorbing and useful as are summer trips. The tourist who completes even a small winter trip strengthens his health, trains his muscles, acquires many skills which will be useful *in peace and in war*. It is necessary to strive in all possible ways so that tourism not only does not decrease during winter but also acquires an even broader scope."[27]

The Skiing of Courage and Memory

The second half of the 1950s through the late 1980s was a period when various kinds of tourism developed that preserved certain archetypes of the Stalinist period. As well-known Russian geographer Boris Rodoman justly observes, during the period of "stagnation" the Soviet tourist movement retained its genetic link with the militarized tourism of the first five-year plans. This connection can be traced in characteristic features of tourism in this period (marches, reports, formations), specific objects of material culture (tents, rucksacks, cooking pots that were much like military mess tins), and touristic terminology (the "tourist *lager*," the "tourist campaign," "coming to a halt").[28] Researcher Irina Sandomirskaia goes even further and sees the cultural connotations of proletarian tourism not only in the Soviet hiking tourism of the 1960s but even in the post-Soviet tourist practices of the 1990s.[29]

Independent tourism was still an organizational form for multiday ski trips except that instead of OPTE cells, now there were tourist clubs. Participants in independent tourist trips compiled an itinerary on their own, but then they had to get an authorized "itinerary list," give the leadership of the tourist club the names of the group members, and inform the rescue service about their movements.[30] Independent ski trips were as popular with Soviet citizens as bicycle and boat trips. Walking trips were the only tourist activity that drew more participants. The optimal size of a group ski hike was eight to twelve participants. For a trained group of ski tourists, the standard distance for a day hike was twenty-five to thirty kilometers, and for schoolchildren, twelve to twenty kilometers. As was the case in the prewar period, a winter sleepover in field conditions for groups of school-age and secondary-school children and adult tourists without enough hiking experience was considered undesirable.[31] Sleeping outside in tents during the winter was usually something done only by experienced ski tourists when they were visiting sparsely settled parts of the country. Temperatures below -20 to -25°C were considered hazardous to the health of people on ski hikes.[32]

The leaders of the Communist Party and All-Union Leninist Young Communist League (Komsomol) encouraged events that maintained the continuity of late Soviet winter tourism with the heroics of the first decades of the USSR. For example, in the 1970s and 1980s, Komsomol members in Arkhangel'sk made a yearly two-day ski trip of sixty kilometers, starting from the town on Mud'iug Island where there was a memorial to soldiers who died while establishing Soviet rule in northern Russia.[33] The word "courage"—for example, as in "routes of courage," "roads of courage," and "the skiing of courage"—was still used to describe these events, which were intended to foster the military and patriotic education of the rising generation. Popular books about winter sport or winter tourism described how Soviet soldiers and partisans on skis inspired fear in the Nazi occupiers during World War II.[34] On the metaphorical level the skis themselves sometimes continued to be perceived as a weapon of sorts in the struggle with dangerous snowstorms. "Don't think of facing snow *without weapons*, of refusing to use skis," warned the author of a tourist publication of the 1970s.[35] Such publications also emphasized winter tourism's positive influence on the physical development and the moral and psychological qualities of the Soviet person. Responding to the question of "What is winter experience?" the author of an article that appeared in the magazine *Tourist* (*Turist*) said, "This is the experience of dealing with snow, that cheerful mood not only on the first day on the road but also [the act of] gathering your will on the tenth day of frosts, snowstorms, and blizzards. Winter experience includes both physical and moral preparation."[36]

Some citizens of the USSR still understood winter tourism in these terms. These were romantically minded individuals with a certain nostalgia for the "heroic epoch," as they saw the first decades of Soviet power. They satisfied their craving for the romanticism of struggle and victories by organizing complicated independent trips in winter, returning on their own initiative to the Stalinist model of the "tourism of courage and surmounting obstacles." Even those who could not participate directly in demanding ski trips were intensely interested in such feats. Thus, the public responded with great enthusiasm to the first ever ski hike to the North Pole, which was completed in 1979 by participants of an expedition led by Dmitrii Shparo and organized by the newspaper *Komsomol'skaia pravda*.[37] Extreme winter trips gave their participants, who were largely members of the postwar generation, the feeling of risk, the sense of playing a game of sorts with fate in which the stakes were one's own life. At the same time, the risk of death was not far-fetched in this context. For example, a group of nine university student ski tourists led by Igor Diatlov mysteriously died in the Northern Urals in February 1959, their bodies found at varying distances from a snow-covered tent.[38] Equally tragic cases of ski hikes took place later as well. Thus, during a ski hike in the Eastern Saian mountains in 1971, nine members of a tourist group perished. Seven tourists died suddenly in the winter of 1982 in the Polar Urals; five more tourists did not return from a hike in 1983 on the Kola Peninsula. During 1988, a "snowstorm took the lives" of eighteen ski tourists.[39]

Various government bodies and members of the public made some efforts to reduce fatal winter tourism accidents. For independent tourists, compliance with the official procedures for independent tourism was called their security pledge—that is, their guarantee of a safe trip. Before leaving, they were required to inform the local commission that evaluated and classified itineraries (*marshrutno-kvalifikatsionnaia komissiia*) about their route and provide the names of the group members; they also had to let the control and safety service know in a timely manner when the trip would start. According to statistics from the early 1980s, 90 percent of accidents involving participants in winter tourist hikes took place in groups that neglected the formal rules for organizing a trip.[40] Special publications for tourists constantly published information about how to survive in extreme winter situations, for example, by erecting a temporary shelter made from so-called "snow bricks," handmade blocks of hard-packed snow.[41]

Another aspect of late Soviet winter tourism that was reminiscent of the Stalinist model of proletarian tourism was the socially useful work done by people on ski hikes. During visits to remote villages, they sometimes gave lectures and amateur concerts for the local population, did career guidance work with rural schoolchildren, and took down historical testimony from veterans of war and labor.[42]

The Soviet Winter Tourism Industry

After the OPTE was eliminated in 1936, the tourist and excursion departments of Soviet trade unions were put in charge of Soviet domestic tourism. The social and economic aspects of developing tourism and recreation were especially important for these trade-union bodies. A "tourist boom" began in the Soviet Union in the 1960s. There was a rapid increase in the scale of organized excursions, tours, and trips that the participants paid for with vouchers (*putevki*). The vouchers were a cost-sharing arrangement whereby the trade-union organizations at enterprises paid part of the value of the vouchers and the tourist who purchased the voucher paid the rest. In 1970, 9.8 million people purchased vouchers for tourist trips, but in 1975, 25.4 million people took trips using vouchers. In 1982, 34.1 million people took trips using vouchers, and in 1990, the number of people using vouchers for tourism increased to 40.2 million.[43] As part of this overall increase, the number of people taking winter trips on vouchers from trade-union organizations rose. Between December 1985 and February 1986 alone, approximately 13.4 million tourists used vouchers.[44]

From mid-October to mid-April there was a stable snow cover in many regions of the Soviet Union, and in some mountainous regions (for example, on Mount Elbrus) it was even possible to ski during the summer, so the ski season could be extended beyond the three winter months. But December, January, and February remained the traditional time for the ski trips people took on days off and holidays, during the winter vacations, and in the school vacation. For Soviet tourist organizations, winter tourism was especially important inasmuch as it ensured that tourist bases and hotels were filled throughout the year, making it more financially effective to operate them.[45]

In 1931, of the OPTE's winter itineraries for which one could buy vouchers, only one was a ski trip. This was an eleven-day route through Karelia and Murmansk *Krai*, which cost between forty-four and seventy-five rubles, depending on the level of amenities chosen.[46] By contrast, during the Brezhnev period, each year the trade-union tourist organizations offered ten different skiing itineraries for which people could purchase vouchers. As *Tourist* (*Turist*) magazine pointed out, a broad array of possibilities was opening up for Soviet fans of winter tourism. They could choose to "go skiing in the bewitching forests of Karelia, the Urals, or Central Russia or the slalom slopes of the Caucasus, the Tian-Shan Range, the Carpathians, the Khibiny Mountains, [or] Sakhalin; take a romantic trip in a horse-drawn sleigh or fly through virgin snow in a Buran snowmobile"[47] (see table 9.1). A wide range of local ski itineraries for trips of two to sixteen days was also on offer. The most popular of these were trips in the northwestern part of the RSFSR, the Northern Caucasus, the Altai Mountains, and the Estonian SSR (through the Nelijärve nature reserve).[48]

In the proletarian tourism period, people taking part in winter campaigns (*zimnye pokhody*) could stay in the OPTE's so-called "ski stations" (*lyzhnye stantsii*). In areas where there were no ski stations, ski tourists had to spend the night in the homes of members of the local population, in the village club's building, or in buildings housing other public institutions. In the 1960s–80s there were hundreds of tourist bases operating during the winter. As early as the early 1960s, the idea that "winter recreation needs impeccable organization in a harmonious combination with snowy expanses and welcoming comfort" began to be voiced.[49] In practice, however, the level of comfort available during winter trips was often quite low. To increase the number of guests that tourist bases could take in and to reduce the costs of serving tourists, multiday ski trips were included in the programs of planned tourist itineraries. For example, the fourteen-day local itinerary "Across the Northern Taiga" offered by the Arkhangel'sk regional council for tourism and excursions included an eight-day ski hike of 160 kilometers.[50] On these hikes ski tourists would spend the night in fairly primitive wooden huts (which were called "shelters" or *priiuty*), which they had to heat with logs, and they would cook over a campfire.[51]

Trips on "winter weekend trains," which departed from many of the country's major cities, were a distinctive form of voucher tourism. Each tourist train carried four to six hundred aficionados of active winter recreation. The trains were both a means of transportation and a place to spend the night. For example, during the winter the *Mountain* (*Gornyi*) was a train that left from Novosibirsk every weekend while the *Snowflake* (*Snezhinka*) departed from Barnaul and Tiumen' on the weekends.[52]

The infrastructure for downhill-skiing resorts developed particularly slowly in the Soviet Union. A significant financial outlay was needed to create com-

Table 9.1. Winter tourist routes across the Soviet Union involving active means of travel (1980).

Route name	Brief description of the route	Number of days	Period when voucher was valid	Cost of voucher (in rubles)
Polar (ski trip)	3 days in Murmansk —15 days in Tulom (including an 8-day hike on skis)	18	Feb.–April	125
Monchegorsk (ski trip)	Murmansk Regional Council for Tourism and Excursions	15	Jan.–May	98
Dombai (ski trip)	Tourist hotel Dombai or tourist hotel Krokus	15	Jan.–April	113–118
Elbrus (ski trip)	Tourist base Azau, tourist base Cheget, or tourist hotel Itkol	15	Jan.–April, Oct.–Dec.	103–113
Transcarpathian (downhill skiing)	Rakhiv (Ukrainian SSR), tourist base Tisa (including ski hikes)	16	Jan.–April, Dec.	71
Through the high Carpathians (downhill skiing)	Iasinia (Ukrainian SSR), Edelweiss tourist base, including trips to Kozmeshchik ski shelter and Dragobrat ski shelter	14	Jan.–April, Dec.	64

Source: *Turistskie marshruty*, ed. Tsentral'nyi sovet po turizmu i ekskursiiam VTSSPS (Moscow, 1980), 42–43, 40, 52, 59, 66, 78–79.

fortable facilities for tourists in the Caucasus and the Ukrainian Carpathians. The cost increased because ski slopes had to be constructed and lifts and cable cars equipped to carry skiers. Despite the rapidly increasing popularity of downhill-skiing tourism, the corresponding material and technical bases were not developed intensively enough, and the number of vouchers available for downhill ski trips did not match the demand. According to sociological research carried out in the first half of the 1980s, the demand for winter vouchers for the regions of the country that were the most popular among Soviet downhill skiers (Bakuriani, Dombai, Mount Elbrus, and the Carpathians) was about twenty times higher than their supply.[53]

The history of downhill-skiing sport and tourism in the USSR should be examined in its own right, but here we will discuss it only briefly. Like cross-country skiing, downhill skiing had its roots in the period of proletarian tourism when the ski section of OPTE's Central Council organized the first winter ski campaign through the mountain passes of the Caucasus in February 1931.[54] However, downhill skiing in the Soviet Union did not become a mass activity but instead remained an elite pastime until the end of the Soviet period. In the 1960s–80s the Caucasus was still Soviet downhill skiers' favorite place to ski; however, their equipment was different from what the masses of cross-country skiing enthusiasts used. Soviet Alpine skiers looked down on Soviet-made skis, and even skis made in the Eastern Bloc countries were considered insufficiently prestigious. People joked about a Bulgarian-made brand of downhill skis: "If you want to be the nastiest—give your friend Mladost." At the same time, those who owned Western brands of downhill skis like Fischer, Leki, Kästle, K2Race, and Salomon commanded respect and envy as these typical examples of Soviet downhill-skiing folklore from the 1980s indicate: "Any slope will be won, / because you bought Salomon!"; "Like a bird, on Fischers I fly down the mountain / With a cry of 'Hurrah,' conquering the bumps!"; "The holy host cries out to me / To go to heaven, drop your skis, / I say heaven's not for me, / Please give me back my K2 skis!"[55]

People brought home popular Western brands of skis, often bought secondhand, from their relatively rare trips abroad. In several cities in the USSR, there were improvised "ski flea markets." For example, in Moscow there was a ski flea market on Saikina Street (at the Avtozavodskaia metro station).[56] Ski flea markets had a much better assortment of skis than what sporting goods stores offered. Among Soviet skiers of the 1960s–80s, eye-catching foreign sports gear became fashionable: bright ski outfits, high-quality sunglasses, and plastic downhill ski boots with clips.

During the Brezhnev period the traditional geography of winter tourism in the USSR expanded to include the Soviet Central Asian republics. The Chimbulak (Kazakhstan), Chimgan (Uzbekistan), and Takov (Tazhikistan) downhill ski resorts gradually became more popular. Kamchatka and Sakhalin in the Soviet Far East were also considered promising places to develop this type of recreation.[57]

The Ski Slopes of Health and Fun

Irina Sandomirskaia emphasizes the fact that improving health, especially overcoming "Soviet fatigue" and the chronic neuroticism that bedeviled the first generation of the builders of the "bright future," was an important aspect of proletarian tourism. She takes note of the medical and public health discourse of proletarian tourism, especially the focus on how it could redirect neurotic energy into a socially useful track. A source she cites from the late 1920s demonstrates this: "Our epoch demands clear thought, muscles of steel, cheerfulness, and perseverance in meeting goals. ... These qualities ... are necessary for our young people, who are standing on the threshold of historic class battles."[58] This quotation highlights the fact that proletarian tourist practices, including ski campaigns, treated recreation as something that should actively improve the tourist's health. However, Stalin-era conceptualizations of recreation saw improving the health of tourists as individuals only as an intermediate objective on the way to the final goal, which was to use their physical and psychological faculties to the greatest possible extent in the interests of society and the state.

However, the image of an enemy as a foreign invader or a "traitor to the Motherland" gradually lost its relevance during the post-Stalinist period, and the mobilizational logic of Soviet tourism underwent an interesting transformation. The orientation of the late Soviet person's values changed a great deal: personal (private) interests supplanted social usefulness to a significant degree. Therefore, winter tourism became a way to carry on an abstract struggle with new "enemies" of humankind—diseases, stressors, laziness, and boredom. This change was rooted in ongoing urbanization, which meant that an increasing number of Soviet people were experiencing negative consequences associated with city life such as low energy, stressful situations, and chronic fatigue.

In the 1960s–80s ski tourist itineraries increasingly began to be called both "roads of courage" and "routes of health." Popular articles from those years devoted a great deal of attention to the health benefits of winter sports and winter tourism. On the one hand, they emphasized the general health-improving effect of active winter recreation: "Ski campaigns are the elixir of high spirits for everyone!" and "Winter tourism is a wonderful vitamin for good health."[59]

On the other hand, winter tourism's ability to treat specific illnesses and other problematic physical conditions was also accentuated. For example, "Ski tourism is one of the most effective and reliable ways to develop the stamina of the heart muscle and the entire organism."[60] Or, "Frosty air is a miracle drink for the lungs. A ski trip is the best medicine for an exhausted nervous system."[61] And, "Frosty air and ... pictures of a winter landscape take away tiredness / fatigue and stress, they charge [people] with cheerfulness and a good mood for the entire work week."[62]

The mass ski trips, relay races, and other races on skis that took place in many parts of the Soviet Union in the 1960s–80s became a kind of a compromise between the ideological education and recreational aspects of winter tourism. The ski races near the Moscow suburb of Odintsovo, which took place from 1969 onward on the initiative of the well-known skier Nikolai Manzhosov, are one example of this compromise. The mass Sarma ski trips organized every year by the tourist club of the Latvian Republic are another example. Events combining tourism and sports were included in the programs of events to celebrate the traditional winter holidays of the cities of the Russian far north: the Belomorsk games (Arkhangel'sk), the Festival of the North games (Murmansk), and the Northern Lights competitions (Nar'ian-Mar).[63]

On 28 February 1982, on the initiative of the newspaper *Soviet Sport* (*Sovetskii sport*) the first All-Union Day of the Skier took place; throughout the country approximately 10 million people simultaneously took part in winter sports competitions.[64] Calling on the citizens of the USSR to participate in this mass event, *Soviet Sport* wrote: "On this day, may millions of ski tracks laid down by each [skier] merge into a single, large snowy road of health stretching from the Pacific Ocean to the western edges of our Motherland."[65]

The mass nature of Soviet winter tourism during the era of "stagnation" was one reason why winter tourism lost its identification with masculinity.[66] Many women and children were participating in independent ski trips, which "softened" the psychological climate and the emotional mood of tourist groups. No one was surprised when a group of winter tourists with twice as many women as men set off to storm the mountain passes.[67] Toddlers took their first steps on skis when they were two and three years old, and parents were advised to get five- and six-year-olds used to going on eight- to ten-kilometer weekend ski trips.

The following quotation from *Tourist* (*Turist*) magazine does a good job of conveying the point that the family was at the heart of the new paradigm of winter tourism: "It is better when both parents go skiing with their child. Then Papa plays the role of the draft horse and Mama makes sure that the little one doesn't freeze, and simultaneously brushes off excess snow, changes his soaked mittens for dry ones, feeds him, amuses him."[68]

The very relationship to snow noticeably softened. Tourists perceived it much more frequently not as an enemy but as a friend. In the tourist texts of the 1970s and 1980s, lyrical epithets for snow like "gentle," "fluffy," "soft," "beautiful," "lovely," and "golden" predominate.[69]

The new winter tourism of the Thaw, and especially during the "stagnation" period, needed steadily decreasing oversight from the state and the structures under its control (tourist organizations, societies, and clubs). From the early 1960s there was a boom in unorganized ("wild") tourism, which was gravitating toward complete self-organization. Soviet "wild" tourists were usually associated with seaside summer holidaying in Crimea or the Black Sea coast of the Caucasus; however, this social phenomenon also had a winter variant.[70] On the outskirts of practically any Soviet city during the cold season, one could see crowds of skiers spontaneously taking over "small mountains" (*malye gory*)—snow-covered slopes of mountains, hills, and ravines that were suitable for skiing and sledding. On weekends, holidays, and school vacations such places attracted numerous ski tourists from the nearby city.

For example, in parts of Moscow and its outlying areas, skiing enthusiasts actively made use of the "small mountains." On weekends and holidays the Lenin Hills, Krylatskoe, Skhodnia, Podreznikovo, Iakhroma, the area near the Tourist (Turist) train station on the Savelovskoe line, and other places like these became destinations for mass family recreation—skiing, sledding, and using various homemade devices for going down snowy, icy slopes.[71] Using the "small mountains" was spontaneous initially; however, volunteer athletic societies and clubs and the trade-union organizations of enterprises soon got involved in organizing the use of such places. As a result of their efforts, the simplest possible drag lifts were built, and rental points for ski equipment and other sporting goods opened.[72]

Conclusion: The "Looping" Ski Track of Soviet Winter Tourism

Changes in the essential attributes of winter tourism during the Soviet period are reflected in the ways it was visually represented from the 1930s to the 1980s. Stalin-era images feature columns and rows of male skiers wearing military-style clothing, often carrying weapons, which reinforces the masculine nature of their activity, even if these skiers were not actually soldiers. The discourse of manly physicality determined the external manifestations of proletarian tourism, and readiness—both for a war with any enemy and engaging in socially useful work—was its animating idea.[73] The local OPTE organization—not the family—brought together people, predominantly men, who worked at the same enterprise, for a ski sortie or campaign. Various data sources put female membership in the OPTE at no more than 5 percent of the total membership.[74] The gender division in OSOAVIAKhIM, another Soviet mass organization of the prewar period, was similar: 10–20 percent of the members were women, but a significantly lower percentage of the female members actually took part in military preparedness activities.[75] Under such conditions, the tourist group's solidarity was not based on kinship or friendship ties but instead on a shared social mission and the idea of mutual assistance when faced with an imagined enemy.

In the post-Stalinist period, the state's eagerness to use winter tourism for its own purposes inevitably had to take new forms. As technological progress, urbanization, and the social and economic development of the country's vast territory accelerated, the significance of skiing as a seasonal mode of transportation and as a channel for "cultural communication" between cities and the countryside decreased. Advances in weapons technology and changes in combat strategies reduced the military applications of skiing. In a "cold war" between political blocs with nuclear weapons, mobilizing soldier-skiers was hardly of decisive importance. In official discourse, the glorification of skiing practices was redirected from future wars to past victories.[76] However, in terms of individual perceptions, Soviet citizens continued to acclaim those who took part in skiing campaigns, even in the present, but only when skiers took the most extreme routes or when they faced emergency situations with fatal outcomes. Otherwise, heroic winter trips were seen as a thing of the past and part of the memory of the feats accomplished by the heroes of the first Soviet decades.

From the 1950s on, there was a notable increase in the importance of the social and economic, recreational, and enjoyment-oriented aspects of winter tourism. Ski tourists contributed directly to the USSR's domestic economy by spending money on vouchers and/or ski equipment made in the Soviet Union. In addition, people who participated in active winter recreation were more productive and missed fewer days of work due to illness. However, against expectations, Soviet skiing enthusiasts' mass exodus to the "winter slopes of health" escaped the state's control. Skis, sleds, and skates became features of family recreation, which could be independent, autonomous, and apolitical.

The new visual image of Soviet winter tourism included not only skis but also fashionable, often foreign-made, equipment. Little by little, the figure of the courageous male skier was supplanted by the sparkling, elegant image of the female skier. An example of this image, which reflects the new, underlying realities of winter tourism, can be seen in the 1984 Soviet animated film *Winter in Prostokvashino* (*Zima v Prostokvashino*). Dressed in a skiing outfit, with a New Year's tree in the background, the hero's mother sings this song:

> If winter never was
> In towns and villages
> We would never know
> These *days are fun*

A little one would never circle
Around a snow-woman
The *ski track would not loop in and out*[77]
If not, if not, if not ...[78]

These lines, which are filled with optimism, could be considered the anthem of the new winter tourism of the last Soviet decades—which had already ceased to be a "school of courage." It was still the "elixir of health," but at the same time it seemed more and more like "national fun." Enjoyment was a recurring motif in Soviet public discourse about winter sports in the 1970s and 1980s. For example, phrases like "snowy tracks of health and *a good mood*" and "slopes of strength and *fun*" were used in a description of ski trips.[79] Health, happiness, and spending time with family members and friends became the values defining winter tourism in the USSR. Although the regime wanted to frame it as a socially useful activity, this was increasingly a mere formality.

Climate—the unchanging cold, snowy winter—was the only constant, the one thing that did not depend on the will of particular individuals or the state in general. It was the background against which the significant changes in the external form and internal content of the skiing practices discussed here took place. This natural constant was unchanging throughout the years of the Stalinist mobilization, the liberal romanticism of the thaw, and the late Soviet period. The annual call to "tame" snow as a force of nature through skiing practices enabled the Soviet regime to prompt its citizens to engage in social, physical, and emotional activity during the yearly period of prolonged cold. However, in terms of historical dynamics, the development of Soviet winter tourism took a "looping" trajectory and included too many individual and collective strategies for the state to easily or effectively control it.

Translation by Jacqueline Friedlander

Aleksei Popov is an associate professor of Russian history at the V. I. Vernadskii Crimean Federal University. His research interests include the history of tourism, international relations, and cultural diplomacy in the Cold War era; Soviet everyday life; social history; and historical memory of World War II. He has published several books, including *Skvoz' "Zheleznyi zanaves": Russo Turisto; Sovetskii vyezdnoi turizm, 1955-1991* (together with Igor Orlov, 2016), *Skvoz' "Zheleznyi zanaves": See USSR! Inostrannye turisty i prizrak potemkinskikh dereven'* (together with Igor Orlov 2018), and *Vsesoiuznaiia zdravnitsa: Istoriia turizma i kurortnogo dela Kryma v 1920-1980-e gody* (2019).

Notes

1. Anne E. Gorsuch, *All This Is Your World: Soviet Tourism at Home and Abroad after Stalin* (New York, 2011); Diane P. Koenker, "Whose Right to Rest? Contesting the Family Vacation in the Postwar Soviet Union," *Comparative Studies in Society and History* 51, no. 2 (2009): 401–25; Diane P. Koenker, *Club Red: Vacation Travel and the Soviet Dream* (New York, 2013); Alan D. Roe, "Into Soviet Nature: Tourism, Environmental Protection, and the Formation of Soviet National Parks, 1950s–1990s" (PhD diss., Georgetown University, 2015).
2. "Razvitie lyzhnogo sporta v SSSR," fizsport.ru, retrieved 1 December 2019 from http://www.fizsport.ru/story-lyzhnogo-sport/razvitie-lyzhnogo-sporta-v-sssr.
3. Ibid.
4. In the 1920s and 1930s, Scandinavian influence was even present in the language used by Soviet skiers. For example, ski boots were called *peksi* (from the Finnish *pieksu*) and the broad Finnish-style skis known as *Murtomaa* skis (from the Finnish *murtomaa*) were widely used.
5. "Ot 'maliutki' do 'Rossii'," *Ogonek*, no. 9 (1973): 32–33.
6. For a more detailed discussion of proletarian tourism, see Diane P. Koenker, "The Proletarian Tourist in the 1930s: Between Mass Excursion and Mass Escape," in *Turizm: The Russian and East European Tourist under Capitalism and Socialism*, ed. Anne E. Gorsuch and Diane P. Koenker (New York, 2006), 119–40; I. I. Sandomirskaia, "Novaia zhizn' na marshe: Stalinskii turizm kak 'praktika puti'," *Obshchestvennye nauki i sovremennost'*, no. 4 (1996): 163–72; E. A. Oborina, "'Proletarskii' turizm 1920-kh–serediny 1950-kh gg. kak sotsial'no-kul'turnoe iavlenie," *Vestnik Permskogo universiteta, Seriia Istoriia* 1, no. 9 (2010): 110–13; I. B. Orlov and E. V Iurchikova, *Massovyi turizm v stalinskoi povsednevnosti* (Moscow, 2010), 224.
7. Oborina, "'Proletarskii' turizm," 110.
8. See for example, A. P. Gashchuk and V. S. Vukolov, *Turizm—shkola muzhestva* (Moscow, 1987).
9. V. Antonov-Saratovskii, *Besedy o turizme: Azbuka sovetskogo (proletarskogo) turizma* (Moscow/Leningrad, 1930), 137.
10. For more detail on the history of Soviet mountaineering, including the period when the OPTE was active, see Eva Maurer, "An Academic Escape to the Periphery? The Social and Cultural Milieu of Soviet Mountaineering from the 1920s to the 1960s," in *Euphoria and Exhaustion: Modern Sport in Soviet Culture and Society*, ed. Nikolaus Katzer (Frankfurt, 2010), 159–78.
11. I. Cherepov, "Na lyzhi!" *Na sushe i na more*, no. 28–30 (1932): 16.
12. Iu. Blinov, "Ni odnogo vykhodnogo dnia bez lyzhnykh vylazok," *Na sushe i na more*, no. 18 (1933): 9.
13. "Kazhdyi turist dolzhen umet' khodit na lyzhakh," *Turist-aktivist*, nos. 11–12 (1932): 14.
14. "Zimnie marshruty," *Na sushe i na more*, nos. 33–34 (1931): 18.
15. "Rabota iacheek O.P.T. po lyzhnomu turizmu," *Vestnik Permskogo universiteta, Seriia Istoriia* 1, no. 12 (2010): 114.
16. A. A. Tarasov-Kaslinskii, *Lyzhi v SSSR* (Moscow/Leningrad, 1932), 5–9, 16–18; Cherepov, "Na lyzhi!" 16.
17. V. Perlin, "Prevratim turizm v moshchnoe sredstvo ukrepleniia oborony SSSR," *Turist-aktivist*, no. 3 (1931): 7.

18. I. Cherepov, "Lyzhnye voenno-ispytatel'nye pokhody," *Na sushe i na more*, no. 4 (1933): 14.
19. "Konkurs na luchshee provedenie lyzhnogo voenizirovannogo pokhoda," *Turist-aktivist*, no. 3 (1931): 11.
20. For more detail, see O. Iu. Nikonova, *Vospitanie patriotov: Osoaviakhim i voennaia podgotovka naseleniia v ural'skoi provintsii (1927–1941 gg.)* (Moscow, 2010).
21. Tarasov-Kaslinskii, *Lyzhi v SSSR*, 7.
22. Ibid., 16.
23. N. Kh. Vilenskaia and V. N. Klychin, *Na lyzhakh po okrestnostiam Leningrada* (Moscow/Leningrad, 1930), retrieved 3 December 2018 from https://skitalets.ru/infomation/books/4623.
24. "Rabota iacheek," 115.
25. A. D. Popov, "Deiatel'nost' v Krymu Vsesoiuznogo dobrovol'nogo obshchestva proletarskogo turzima i ekskursii (1930–1936 gg.)," *Uchenie zapiski Tavricheskogo natsional'nogo universiteta im. V.I. Vernadskogo, Seriia Istoriia* 16, no. 6 (2003): 57.
26. For more information about domestic tourism during late Stalinism, see Anne E. Gorsuch, "There's No Place Like Home: Soviet Tourism in Late Stalinism," in *All This Is Your World*, Anne E. Gorsuch (New York, 2011), 26–48.
27. "Na lyzhakh—v turistskii pokhod," *Pravda*, 11 December 1940. Emphasis added.
28. Boris Rodoman, "Dosug vne gosudarstva: samoorganizatsiia pokhodnykh turistov," *Otechestvennye zapiski*, no. 6 (2005), retrieved 3 December 2018 from http://www.strana-oz.ru/?numid=27&article=1183.
29. Sandomirskaia, "Novaia zhizn'," 163.
30. The following figures indicate the scale of independent tourism in the USSR: While 15.2 million people took part in independent tourist trips in 1973, in 1975 there were 18.3 million participants. This number increased to 19.5 million in 1982. See A. Kh. Abukov, *Turizm na novom etape: Sotsial'nye aspekty razvitiia turizma v SSSR* (Moscow, 1983), 170.
31. B. P. Morgunov, "Organizatsiia i provedenie lyzhnykh pokhodov," in *Turizm: Uchebnoe posobie* (Moscow, 1978), 100–101.
32. Dmitriev, "Tekhnika lyzhnoi vylazki," *Turist-aktivist*, no. 1 (1931): 30.
33. B. I. Ogorodnikov, *Turizm i sportivnoe orientirovanie v komplekse GTO* (Moscow, 1983), 73.
34. B. V. Minenkov, *Zimnii sport dlia vsekh* (Moscow, 1983), 11.
35. B. Miasoedov, "Sneg—drug i vrag," *Turist*, no. 2 (1970): 17. Emphasis added.
36. Ibid.
37. For more detail about this seventy-six-day trip, see V. Snegirev, *Nash polius* (Moscow, 1982).
38. "2 fevralia 1959 g. gibel' turisticheskoi gruppy Diatlova," Novyi Gerodot: Obshche-istoricheskii forum, retrieved 15 November 2018 from http://gerodot.ru/viewtopic.php?f=7&t=14466.
39. "Nesluchainye sluchainosti," *Turist*, no. 12 (1989): 48–49. These accidents were usually connected with an unexpected avalanche. Many reasons for the deaths of the Diatlov group have been put forward, but what actually caused this tragedy is still unclear.
40. A. Akselevich, "Esli nachnetsia purga," *Turist*, no. 1 (1982): 29.
41. For example, see L. Lukoianov, "Sam sebe spasatel'," *Turist*, no. 1 (1980): 10–11.
42. A. Ryzhkov, "Lyzhno prokladyvaiut omichi," *Turist*, no. 1 (1983): 5.

43. Abukov, *Turizm na novom etape*, 27; V. A. Kvartal'nov, *Turizm, ekskursii, obmeny: Sovremennaia praktika* (Moscow, 1993), 10.
44. "Zima—pora otpusknaia," *Pravda*, 8 January 1986.
45. Ibid.; R. Iurasov, "Zimoi, slovno letom," *Turist*, no. 2 (1978): 21.
46. "Zimnie marshruty OPTE," *Turist-aktivist*, no. 1 (1931): 47.
47. "Zima vstupaet v prava," *Turist*, no. 11 (1982): 4.
48. *Turistskie marshruty*, ed. Tsentral'nyi sovet po turizmu i ekskursiiam VTSSPS (Moscow, 1980), 7–8, 11–12, 24, 26.
49. V. Viktorov, "'Marshrutniki' i 'radikulisty'," *Ogonek*, no. 7 (1962): 28–29.
50. M. Strel'nikova, "Liubiteliam severnoi ekzotiki," *Turist*, no. 1 (1988): 20.
51. For example, see A. Shcherbak, "Zapoliarnyi lyzhnyi," *Turist*, no. 1 (1973): 10; A. Ryzhkov, "Il'menskaia panorama," *Turist*, no. 2 (1979): 6; Strel'nikova, "Liubiteliam," 20.
52. "Poezd idet v Gornyiu Shoriiu," *Turist*, no. 2 (1975): 24. On the *Snowflake* from Barnaul, see T. Tarasova, "I sneg, i smekh, i zdorov'e," *Turist*, no. 3 (1988): 12–13, and from Tiumen', see "Zimnii den' Tiumeni," *Turist*, no. 1 (1982): 3–4.
53. "V poiskakh Snezhnogor'ia: Kruglyi stol Turista," *Turist*, no. 2 (1985): 17.
54. A. Zhemchuzhnikov, "Turisty—na gornye lyzhi," *Na sushe i na more*, no. 2 (1933): 7.
55. "Ski folk," Krichalki, retrieved 25 November 2018 from http://tomba.rasc.ru/s0010.html.
56. "Kak eto bylo: Gornye lyzhi v SSSR," Ski Master, retrieved 25 November 2018 from http://www.skimaster.ru/info/page_277_20.html.
57. "Zima—pora otpusknaia," 34.
58. Sandomirskaia, "Novaia zhizn'," 165.
59. "Zima vstupaet v prava."
60. P. I. Lukoianov, *Zimnie sportivnye pokhody* (Moscow, 1988), 3–4.
61. V. Sergeev, "Pliusy moroznykh dnei," *Turist*, no. 1 (1982): 21.
62. Lukoianov, *Zimnie sportivnye pokhody*, 4.
63. Minenkov, *Zimnii sport*, 13–14.
64. Ibid., 13. The All-Union Day of the Skier was subsequently held annually, on the last Sunday in February.
65. "Vykhodi, tovarishch, na start!" *Sovetskii sport*, 26 February 1982.
66. On the social causes of the "crisis of masculinity" in the late Soviet period, see Elena Zdravomyslova and Anna Temkina, "The Crisis of Masculinity in Late Soviet Discourse," *Russian Studies in History* 51, no. 2 (2012): 13–34.
67. Akselevich, "Esli nachnetsia purga," 29.
68. O. Kalashnikov, "Semeinyi eksperiment," *Turist*, no. 2 (1975): 20.
69. For example, see "Zolotye snega Zakarpat'ia," *Turist*, no. 1 (1970): 29.
70. More detail can be found in Christian Noack, "Coping with the Tourist: Planned and 'Wild' Mass Tourism on the Soviet Black Sea Coast," in *Turizm: The Russian and East European Tourist under Capitalism and Socialism*, ed. Anne E. Gorsuch and Diane P. Koenker (New York, 2006), 281–304; A. Popov, "'My ishchem to, chego ne teriali': Sovetskie dikari 'v poiskakh mesta pod solntsem'," *Ab Imperio*, no. 2 (2012): 261–98.
71. "V poiskakh Snezhnogor'ia," 17–19.
72. Ibid.
73. Sandomirskaia, "Novaia zhizn'," 166.
74. V. Vorob'ev, "Zhenshchina i turizm," *Na sushe i na more*, nos. 5–6 (1931): 2.

75. O. Iu. Nikonova, "Kak iz krest'ianki Gaidinoi sdelat' Marinu Raskovu, ili o teorii i praktike vospitaniia sovetskikh patriotok," *Novoe literaturnoe obozrenie*, no. 112 (2011), retrieved 25 November 2018 from http://magazines.russ.ru/nlo/2011/112/ni 14-pr.html.
76. Nina Tumarkin was the first to write about this "memorial turn." See Nina Tumarkin, *The Living and the Dead: The Rise and Fall of the Cult of World War II in Russia* (New York, 1994).
77. The Russian verb *petliat'* ("to loop," that is, to move in a nonlinear looping or winding manner) is used in this line of the song. See S. Ozhegov, *Tolkovyi slovar' russkogo iazyka* (Moscow, 2011). "Looping" is a good metaphor to describe the twists and turns in the way winter tourism developed in the Soviet Union.
78. Evgenii Krylatov wrote the music and Iurii Entin wrote the lyrics. In the animated film, Soviet singer Valentina Tolkunova sang the song. Emphasis added.
79. *Sovetskii sport*, 1 January and 13 February 1982.

Bibliography

"2 fevralia 1959 g. gibel' turisticheskoi gruppy Diatlova." Novyi Gerodot: Obshcheistoricheskii forum. Retrieved 15 November 2018 from http://gerodot.ru/viewtopic.php?f=7&t=14466.
Abukov, A. Kh. *Turizm na novom etape: Sotsial'nye aspekty razvitiia turizma v SSSR*. Moscow, 1983.
Akselevich, A. "Esli nachnetsia purga." *Turist*, no. 1 (1982): 29.
Antonov-Saratovskii, V. *Besedy o turizme: Azbuka sovetskogo (proletarskogo) turizma*. Moscow/Leningrad, 1930.
Blinov, Iu. "Ni odnogo vykhodnogo dnia bez lyzhnykh vylazok." *Na sushe i na more*, no. 18 (1933): 9.
Cherepov, I. "Lyzhnye voenno-ispytatel'nye pokhody." *Na sushe i na more*, no. 4 (1933): 14.
———. "Na lyzhi!" *Na sushe i na more*, no. 28–30 (1932): 16.
Dmitriev. "Tekhnika lyzhnoi vylazki." *Turist-aktivist*, no. 1 (1931): 30.
Gashchuk, A. P., and V. S. Vukolov. *Turizm—shkola muzhestva*. Moscow, 1987.
Gorsuch, Anne E. *All This Is Your World: Soviet Tourism at Home and Abroad after Stalin*. New York, 2011.
Iurasov, R. "Zimoi, slovno letom." *Turist*, no. 2 (1978): 21.
"Kak eto bylo: Gornye lyzhi v SSSR." Ski Master. Retrieved 25 November 2018 from http://www.skimaster.ru/info/page_277_20.html.
Kalashnikov, O. "Semeinyi eksperiment." *Turist*, no. 2 (1975): 20.
"Kazhdyi turist dolzhen umet' khodit na lyzhakh." *Turist-aktivist*, nos. 11–12 (1932): 14.
Koenker, Diane P. *Club Red: Vacation Travel and the Soviet Dream*. New York, 2013.
———. "The Proletarian Tourist in the 1930s: Between Mass Excursion and Mass Escape." In *Turizm: The Russian and East European Tourist under Capitalism and Socialism*, edited by Anne E. Gorsuch and Diane P. Koenker, 119–40. New York, 2006.
———. "Whose Right to Rest? Contesting the Family Vacation in the Postwar Soviet Union." *Comparative Studies in Society and History* 51, no. 2 (2009): 401–25.
"Konkurs na luchshee provedenie lyzhnogo venizirovannogo pokhoda." *Turist-aktivist*, no. 3 (1931): 11.

Kvartal'nov, Valerii A. *Turizm, ekskursii, obmeny: Sovremennaia praktika.* Moscow, 1993.
Lukoianov, L. "Sam sebe spasatel'." *Turist*, no. 1 (1980): 10–11.
Lukoianov, P. I. *Zimnie sportivnye pokhody.* Moscow, 1988.
Maurer, Eva. "An Academic Escape to the Periphery? The Social and Cultural Milieu of Soviet Mountaineering from the 1920s to the 1960s." In *Euphoria and Exhaustion: Modern Sport in Soviet Culture and Society*, edited by Nikolaus Katzer, 159–78. Frankfurt, 2010.
Miasoedov, B. "Sneg—drug i vrag." *Turist*, no. 2 (1970): 17.
Minenkov, B. V. *Zimnii sport dlia vsekh.* Moscow, 1983.
Morgunov, B. P. "Organizatsiia i provedenie lyzhnykh pokhodov." In *Turizm: Uchebnoe posobie*, 100–116. Moscow, 1978.
"Na lyzhakh—v turistskii pokhod." *Pravda*, 11 December 1940.
"Nesluchainye sluchainosti." *Turist*, no. 12 (1989): 48–49.
Nikonova, O. Iu. "Kak iz krest'ianki Gaidinoi sdelat' Marinu Raskovu, ili o teorii i praktike vospitaniia sovetskikh patriotok." *Novoe literaturnoe obozrenie*, no. 112 (2011). Retrieved 25 November 2018 from http://magazines.russ.ru/nlo/2011/112/ni14-pr.html.
———. *Vospitanie patriotov: Osoaviakhim i voennaia podgotovka naseleniia v ural'skoi provintsii (1927–1941 gg.).* Moscow, 2010.
Noack, Christian. "Coping with the Tourist: Planned and 'Wild' Mass Tourism on the Soviet Black Sea Coast." In *Turizm: The Russian and East European Tourist under Capitalism and Socialism*, edited by Anne E. Gorsuch and Diane P. Koenker, 281–304. New York, 2006.
Oborina, E. A. "'Proletarskii' turizm 1920-kh–serediny 1950-kh gg. kak sotsial'no-kul'turnoe iavlenie." *Vestnik Permskogo universiteta, Seriia Istoriia* 1, no. 9 (2010): 110–13.
Ogorodnikov, B. I. *Turizm i sportivnoe orientirovanie v komplekse GTO.* Moscow, 1983.
Orlov, I., and E. V. Iurchikova. *Massovyi turizm v stalinskoi povsednevnosti.* Moscow, 2010.
"Ot 'maliutki' do 'Rossii.'" *Ogonek*, no. 9 (1973): 32–33.
Ozhegov, S. *Tolkovyi slovar' russkogo iazyka.* Moscow, 2011.
Perlin, V. "Prevratim turizm v moshchnoe sredstvo ukrepleniia oborony SSSR." *Turist-aktivist*, no. 3 (1931): 7–8.
"Poezd idet v Gornyiu Shoriiu." *Turist*, no. 2 (1975): 24.
Popov, A. D. "Deiatel'nost' v Krymu Vsesoiuznogo dobrovol'nogo obshchestva proletarskogo turzima i ekskursii (1930–1936 gg.)." *Uchenie zapiski Tavricheskogo natsional'nogo universiteta im. V.I. Vernadskogo, Seriia Istoriia* 16, no. 6 (2003): 54–63.
———. "'My ishchem to, chego ne teriali': Sovetskie dikari 'v poiskakh mesta pod solntsem." *Ab Imperio*, no. 2 (2012): 261–98.
"Rabota iacheek O.P.T. po lyzhnomu turizmu." *Vestnik Permskogo universiteta, Seriia Istoriia* 1, no. 12 (2010): 114–16.
"Razvitie lyzhnogo sporta v SSSR." Fizsport.ru, retrieved 1 December 2019 from http://www.fizsport.ru/story-lyzhnogo-sport/razvitie-lyzhnogo-sporta-v-sssr.
Rodoman, Boris. "Dosug vne gosudarstva: Samoorganizatsiia pokhodnykh turistov." *Otechestvennye zapiski*, no. 6 (2005). Retrieved 3 December 2018 from http://www.strana-oz.ru/?numid=27&article=1183.
Roe, Alan D. "Into Soviet Nature: Tourism, Environmental Protection, and the Formation of Soviet National Parks, 1950s–1990s." PhD diss., Georgetown University, 2015.
Ryzhkov, A. "Il'menskaia panorama." *Turist*, no. 2 (1979): 6.

———. "Lyzhno prokladyvaiut omichi." *Turist*, no. 1 (1983): 5.
Sandomirskaia, I. I. "Novaia zhizn' na marshe: Stalinskii turizm kak 'praktika puti.'" *Obshchestvennye nauki i sovremennost'*, no. 4 (1996): 163–72.
Sergeev, V. "Pliusy moroznykh dnei." *Turist*, no. 1 (1982): 21.
Shcherbak, A. "Zapoliarnyi lyzhnyi." *Turist*, no. 1 (1973): 10.
"Ski folk." Krichalki. Retrieved 25 November 2018 from http://tomba.rasc.ru/s0010.html.
Snegirev, V. *Nash polius*. Moscow, 1982.
Sovetskii sport. 1 January and 13 February 1982.
Strel'nikova, M. "Liubiteliam severnoi ekzotiki." *Turist*, no. 1 (1988): 20.
Tarasov-Kaslinskii, A. A. *Lyzhi v SSSR*. Moscow/Leningrad, 1932.
Tarasova, T. "I sneg, i smekh, i zdorov'e." *Turist*, no. 3 (1988): 12–13.
Tumarkin, Nina. *The Living and the Dead: The Rise and Fall of the Cult of World War II in Russia*. New York, 1994.
Turistskie marshruty, edited by Tsentral'nyi sovet po turizmu i ekskursiiam VTSSPS. Moscow, 1980.
"V poiskakh Snezhnogor'ia: Kruglyi stol Turista." *Turist*, no. 2 (1985): 17–19.
Viktorov, V. "'Marshrutniki' i 'radikulisty.'" *Ogonek*, no. 7 (1962): 28–29.
Vilenskaia, N. Kh., and V. N. Klychin. *Na lyzhakh po okrestnostiam Leningrada*. Moscow/Leningrad, 1930. Retrieved 3 December 2018 from https://skitalets.ru/infomation/books/4623.
Vorob'ev, V. "Zhenshchina i turizm." *Na sushe i na more*, nos. 5–6 (1931): 1–3.
"Vykhodi, tovarishch, na start!" *Sovetskii sport*, 26 February 1982.
Zdravomyslova, Elena, and Anna Temkina, "The Crisis of Masculinity in Late Soviet Discourse." *Russian Studies in History* 51, no. 2 (2012): 13–34.
Zhemchuzhnikov, A. "Turisty—na gornye lyzhi." *Na sushe i na more*, no. 2 (1933): 7.
"Zima—pora otpusknaia." *Pravda*, 8 January 1986.
"Zima vstupaet v prava." *Turist*, no. 11 (1982): 4.
"Zimnie marshruty." *Na sushe i na more*, nos. 33–34 (1931): 18.
"Zimnie marshruty OPTE." *Turist-aktivist*, no. 1 (1931): 47.
"Zimnii den' Tiumeni." *Turist*, no. 1 (1982): 3–4.
"Zolotye snega Zakarpat'ia." *Turist*, no. 1 (1970): 29.

 CHAPTER 10

Heroes of the Ice
The Polar Explorer and the Ice Hockey Player as Two Masculine Identity Scripts of the Soviet Era

Alexander Ananyev

Ice has often had a key place in Russian and Soviet history. As a result of climate and geography, important military and political events took place on the ice. In the thirteenth century, the Battle on the Ice (Ledovoe poboishche, 5 April 1242) on Lake Peipus (Chudskoe ozero) brought the forces led by Aleksandr Nevskii, Prince of Novgorod, victory over the Livonian Order. In the twentieth century, the Ice Road of Life built across Lake Ladoga made it possible to get supplies to besieged Leningrad during World War II. Heroic scenarios directly connected with ice also had a place in peacetime. Thus, acting in severe climatic conditions, individuals and groups of professionals were at various times encircled by a special "warmth of the Motherland," which, under certain historical circumstances, gave them specific obligations. Therefore, activity on an icy field of endeavor attracted attention from society, and success was rewarded with respect and honor, which created new images of heroes of the ice and disseminated them across broad social strata.[1]

This chapter focuses on two such images. Taking the polar explorer and the ice hockey player as examples, I would like to present several key components of these two scenarios of Soviet masculine identity that arose during the twentieth century. These two groups have been chosen because, as media exemplars of positive masculinity, they have some key features in common (indicating some continuities in Soviet masculine identity) yet the differences between these two groups are also tied to important changes in the society in which their images as ice heroes arose and were popularized.

The image of the polar hero developed and was spread in the mass media in conjunction with the polar expeditions of the "Papanin Four" in the 1930s and the ice hockey players of "Larionov's line" in the 1980s. Based primarily on memoirs and journalism (print media, radio, and television), this chapter addresses four questions: Given that the ice was the main place where their activities took place, under what kinds of conditions did polar explorers and ice hockey players live and work? Within each professional group, what were the characteristics of particular intergroup relationships that were connected with living and working conditions, and what were each group's interactions with the outside world like? How do official incentives and rewards and public adulation reflect the importance of the work done by prominent representatives of the two professional groups? What kind of a place in state policy and propaganda do the images of "heroes of the ice" examined here have?

The Image of the Heroic Polar Explorer: The "Papanin Four"

"Fighters on the Polar Front," an article that appeared in December 1935 in a special Arctic issue of the magazine *Technology for Young People* (*Tekhnika-molodezhi*), vividly demonstrates the increased interest in the profession of polar explorer during the first half of the twentieth century[2]:

> Thousands of them are young, strong, determined Soviet people who want to make their way to the Arctic—to a ship, a winter camp, a fur factory, a reindeer herding collective farm [*sovkhoz*]. Thousands fall asleep [while writing] letters to the leading figure in polar work in the Soviet Union, Otto Iul'evich Shmidt, with ardent requests to set off on another polar expedition. … But brilliant leader O. Iu. Shmidt chooses people carefully. The Arctic does not need jacks of all trades. … Therefore, comrades, don't write to O. Iu. Shmidt telling him that you are ready for "any" work, it's better to let him know that you are a meteorologist or a veterinarian, a machinist, or a cook. Those are the people Otto Iul'evich needs.[3]

The need to create a single state structure that would be responsible for all aspects of developing the North Pole was already an urgent problem for the Soviet regime in the late 1920s. As a result, the Council of People's Commissars (Sovet narodnykh komissarov or SNK) published a decree on 17 December 1932 that established the Main Directorate of the Northern Sea Route (Glavnoe upravlenie Severnogo morskogo puti or GUSMP). O. Iu. Shmidt, who helped to create the new structure, was appointed as its head. The new head of the directorate enjoyed the rights of the People's Commissariat (Narodnyi komissariiat or Narkomat). Shmidt, whom the author of the article called a "brilliant leader," headed this organization in 1932–39.

GUSMP's main task was to equip expeditions and ensure safe passage through the Northern Sea Route from the White Sea to the Bering Strait and the Pacific coast, that is, along the seaways of the northern territories above the sixty-second parallel. In conjunction with this, the development and maintenance of polar stations in the Arctic was an equally important government project. To accomplish this, all of the USSR's purpose-built icebreakers, several hunting and river vessels, and a few airplanes were transferred to GUMSP.

As soon as the new directorate was created, a new battle began in the Soviet Union: a fight against the country of eternal ice. The opposition of cold and warmth was heightened, which gave rise to a new heroic epoch with its own myths, legends, and heroes. Among these the so-called "Papanin Four" had a central place. This was the team of scientists who carried out experiments at the first Soviet drifting station, which was established on Arctic ice floes on 21 May 1937.

The North Pole-1 (Severnyi polius-1or SP-1) drifting station was staffed by four people and operated for nine months, covering more than two thousand kilometers. As it moved southward from the North Pole, the ice floe on which the research station was situated gradually became smaller and smaller. The situation became critical in the winter of 1938. An airplane and three steamers were sent to the Greenland Sea to evacuate the researchers. After their successful removal from the ice on 19 February 1938, work at the drifting station was officially terminated. The coverage by Soviet media such as the daily newspaper *Pravda* and the popular magazine *Ogonek* celebrated their mission as a triumph. On 20 February the front page of *Pravda* was devoted to the Papanin Four: "The head of the station is Hero of the Soviet Union Ivan Papanin, who fought in the Civil War; Petr Shirshov is a hydrologist, an indefatigable scientist; Ernst Krenkel' is the fearless, cheerful radio operator who gained worldwide renown during the epic voyage of the *Cheliuskin*; Evgenii Fedorov is an astronomer and magnetologist. The entire country knows their names, their life stories, their portraits."[4] Soon afterward, *Ogonek* published a separate brochure about them, declaring in the preface that "we have no doubt that the feat of Papanin's team [*papanintsy*] will nourish more than one generation with remarkable books in poetry and prose, and adults, young people, and children alike will read them. These works will be stories, novels, plays, diaries, epic poems, lyric poetry, and songs."[5] These were prophetic words. Lines written by the poet Vasilii Lebedev-Kumach were long retained in collective memory: "The fragments float away and melt / The famous Papanin ice floes, / But their descendants will remember for centuries / This tale of heroic labors."[6]

Shortly after the end of the drift, several publications about the first drifting station at the North Pole followed. Diaries and memoir accounts of the expedition, especially Papanin's *Life on the Ice Floe* (*Zhizn' na l'dine*) and Krenkel''s *Four Comrades* (*Chetyre tovarishcha*) became extremely popular.[7] These books were produced by an editorial group led by Iurii Lukin, who also edited Mikhail Sholokhov's literary work. Papanin's and Krenkel''s books about life and work on North Pole-1 came out at the same time in 1940. Both were soon reprinted and were very similar to each other in terms of the size of their respective print runs and price.[8] Both literary diaries give detailed descriptions of the life and work of the Papanin Four while they were drifting on the ice floe. These artistic works, which both have "diary" in the title and a first-person narrator, draw the reader in with their apparently documentary character. As will be shown below, they persuasively and colorfully created the narrative for a masculine epic about heroes of the ice.

Working and Living Conditions on the Ice

Let us look at how the winterers' living quarters and the main shelter, which they built and lived in during ferocious blizzards, hard frosts, and the endless polar night, are described. The diary written by Papanin, who was the expedition's "manager," gives the technical specifics of the tent:

> With the beds, our tent weighed fifty-three kilograms; it was two and a half meters wide, three and seven-tenths meters long, two meters high. We made the tent very warm, [it consisted of] four layers: two layers of eiderdown were placed between two layers of heavy tarpaulins. A vestibule was attached to the tent … There was an inflatable "air" floor; the air cushion that separated the floor [of the tent] from the ice was fifteen centimeters thick.[9]

In addition to the tent, which they called the "Central House of the North Pole" and which was the winterers' main living quarters,[10] several other buildings were erected on the ice, including the "Cooking Facility [*Kukhnestroi*]," which the winterers called the "grandiose edifice for catering at the North Pole station."[11] The kitchen was built from "snow bricks or snow mixed with water."[12] Krenkel' added a bit of a military tone, with a touch of fancifulness, to the description of the kitchen: "The kitchen's ice walls were so strong they were more like the walls of a dugout. We will rename our encampment in the American style: 'Fort Four' or 'Fort Winds.'"[13]

If one leaves out the climatic component and the absence of communal amenities, at times the descriptions of the Papanin Four's daily life on the ice could sound like the men were living at a resort. While the country was experiencing food shortages, in the assortment of comestibles the winterers had there were forty-six different foods to choose from, including caviar, smoked pork loin, lard, chocolate, coffee, and cognac. The Institute of Food Supply Engineers helped to make the preparations for the expedition. As a result, Papanin recalled that "we not only had the possibility of really eating every day but on holidays we were also able to organize 'banquets' when the table was laden with ham, cheese, caviar, butter, condensed milk, sweets, and cake."[14] The winterers also had an ample supply of spiritual nourishment: "We brought with us a small library whose holdings included books by Lenin, Stalin, Chernyshevskii, Gor'kii, Tolstoi, Balzac, and Stendhal."[15] However, as Krenkel' emphasized, during the first period of drift, because they had almost no free time, the winterers' "only daily reading [was] the inscription on the tent, which was 'The Glavsevmorput Drifting Expedition.'"[16]

In addition, the winterers had an impressive collection of garments: "Our clothing consisted of silk and woolen underwear, wool [suits], socks, stockings made from dog's hair, high fur boots, *valenki* with galoshes, pants and shirts of fur pelts, fur deerstalker caps, woolen mittens and fur mittens, fur and eiderdown overalls, leather boots, a leather coat, canvas raincoats, and *malitsy.*"[17]

However, after three months on the ice floe their calculations showed that a change of underwear actually took place only "once in two months," after which the leader of the station drew the following conclusion: "Now we will have to change clothes on a monthly basis."[18] A note from a month earlier shows the researchers' attitude toward hygiene: "I went to the cupboard, got underwear for myself and Teodorych [a diminutive of "Teodorovich," Krenkel"s patronymic], went back to the tent and changed my clothes, taking the old ones off—socks I had been wearing for two months. Incidentally, we really didn't want to take the old underwear off. We had gotten used to it. Never mind: we are getting used to the new ones."[19]

It was even more amusing (and dramatic) when someone reading Papanin's or Krenkel"s diary learns that of the expedition's four participants, in general only one of them (Shirshov) washed his hands, with snow, and only in good weather. The others treated hygiene somewhat differently: "On major national holidays and the twenty-first of each month (on our anniversary day) we become unrecognizable: we shave, wash, sometimes even clean our teeth."[20] In this rather gloomy situation, the men did a lot of joking around: "On those days we usually joke with each other that 'It's for sure, you are women's favorite! Aren't you?' Followed by the answer: 'Oh, no! Nothing like that!'"[21]

It is striking that the winterers' reactions to the "hostile" weather conditions surrounding them very often took on a lyric tone: "Frosty but clear weather is always pleasant to me. When the sky is clear, the frost is especially sharp, and the gleaming stars delight me."[22] However, the "semantic reading on the thermometer" used to assess the ice that surrounded them varies quite a bit. Sometimes the landscape of the drifting ice floes is depicted in romantic terms: "On a moonlit night, our camp looks something like a fairy-tale kingdom. The ice surrounding us is very beautiful."[23] On another occasion, the reality of the North Pole reminds Papanin of a situation that is the diametric opposite of the kingdom of eternal ice: "The ice is beginning to break up again. All the time we are hearing a distant rumble that sounds like guns firing. When this happens, it always reminds me of the front."[24]

On the whole, if one excludes the narratives about various crises that flared up while the researchers were wintering on the ice floe, an expressive picture emerges, one that combines both delight in the surrounding nature and a sense of its inherent dangerousness: "As far as the eye can see—everywhere there are fields, fields, fields strewn with ice hummocks of the most varied outlines. The ice hummocks are already covered with snow. A resounding, almost oppressive quiet. Both beautiful and fear-inducing."[25]

Relationships within the Group and with the Outside World

It is important to look at the relationships the members of the expedition had with each other. In the case of the Papanin Four, these are observations about a group of four adult men who had firsthand experience of the daily life of winterers and had shared the sorrows and joys of polar expeditions more than once. Although the diaries do not explicitly mention serious interpersonal conflicts, emotions do have a place in both books. Beneath the surface of the narrative about daily life on the ice floe as it drifted, the emotional life of the individual participants and emotions connected with relationships among them are part of the story.[26] There were certainly quarrels and times when they tried to clarify their relationships with each other.[27] In the published documents about wintering, however, there are no vivid examples of explicit disagreements within the collective. Other published sources also do not recount any stories of serious clashes or protracted disputes among the winterers. Evidently such things were not supposed to appear in Soviet propaganda. In fact, the diaries' main goal was clear and precisely targeted: to reinforce the image of the new Soviet hero as someone who could overcome the most severe conditions of both the natural and the human environment. It is logical that the idea of heroes of the ice was constructed on the basis of positive motifs, thereby creating a narrative about how new territories were being subdued for the country by the group of brave men on the ice floe. This was a narrative that aimed to refute bourgeois theories, demonstrate scientific discoveries, and show the entire world the heroism of the Soviet people as well as the USSR's titanic might.

The motif of a cohesive group of polar explorers heroically confronting and successfully battling the North Pole's "hostile" external conditions grew out of the broader context of Soviet social politics at a time when society was waging a war on internal enemies. In fact, while the winterers were drifting on the ice floe, there was a noticeable "thinning out" of the Glavsevmorput leadership. At the end of 1937 and the beginning of 1938, dismissals and arrests began at GUSMP. These repressions were the result of the failure of the navigation system, which was necessary for safe passage along the Northern Sea Route. Many leaders at GUSMP were charged with disrupting the navigation project, which, in the language of the Chekists, meant that they were nothing other than "wreckers." High-circulation publications about the expedition disseminated the idea that the winterers' reaction to these events was immediate and unambiguous, as Papanin states in his diary: "In the afternoon they told us over the radio about the enemies of the people, wreckers, and saboteurs who had made their way into the Main Directory of the Northern Sea Route. These rascals, despicable traitors to the Motherland, did a great deal of harm. Our indignation has no bounds!"[28]

While they were drifting, the radio connection was the winterers' sole means of communication with the outside world. Overcoming vast distances with the help of the radio station, the "amazing product of Soviet technology,"[29] the Papanin Four were in continuous contact with Moscow and the cities across the Soviet Union and, as popular publications emphasized, with the whole world. In a telegram sent to the highest Soviet leadership at the very beginning of the expedition, the members of the expedition assured them that morally, they felt they were in unity with their fellow Soviet citizens: "Dear Iosif Vissarionovich, here in a desert of ice, many thousands of kilometers from our native Moscow, we do not feel that we have been torn away from our country."[30] Actually, throughout the entire drift, musical concerts were transmitted "By special request," as were many radio broadcasts "For the North Pole" in which the winterers' wives, children, and relatives made appearances. And private contacts with Soviet and foreign amateur radio hobbyists kept the participants of the expedition from feeling that they were alone on the ice floe amid the snow and the cold.

The smaller the melting ice floe became, the more intense the public's interest in the men at the ice station. While some parts of their memoirs indicate that the winterers tried to express their displeasure with the adulation and praise that was lavished on them ("They are styling us as knights and *bogatryi* and heroes. ... We smile at this: Which of us are *bogatryri*?"),[31] what they say about the increased public interest in the expedition compels us to reevaluate their relationship with the outside world: "Stroimilov reports that today the Moscow papers published telegrams about our landing at the pole. People are queuing to buy newspapers."[32] From Bol'shaia Zemlia (the Great Land) the winterers received reports via the radio that new expressions based on their experiences on the drifting station were making the rounds: "Ivan Ivanovich, where are you calling from, give us your coordinates ..."; "Mama, where are you? Give me your call sign ..."; "(On the tram) Citizen, don't push! I'm drifting ..."[33] The growing interest in the expedition took on a mass character and raised the winterers to new, almost unreachable heights, which of course came to their attention through daily radio communication:

> Judging by reports from Moscow, our life has become a frequent topic of conversation on the tram and at home. In spite of the weather reports published every day, on the tram they are sure that on the ice floe it is one hundred

times colder. Cold is identical with our expedition. It was almost as if the word for ice cream was no longer "popsicle" but "papanino." Our names are on advertisements. It would not be surprising if after we return perfumeries ask us to be photographed specially, for some kind of perfume called Krenkel or Dmitrich.[34]

Rewards and Glorification

During the dramatic evacuation of the Papanintsy, mass interest in the "heroes of the ice" gradually intensified. Even during the first stage of the evacuation, the crews on the icebreakers that went to rescue the expedition argued about which ship would take which members of the expedition. In the end they drew lots. The *Murmansk* took Papanin and Krenkel', and the *Taimyr* took Fedorov and Shirshov. A while later the "heroic quartet" went on board the legendary icebreaker *Yermak* led by O. Iu. Shmidt. When they came back from the ice floe, a triumphal greeting awaited them on their native soil. After reaching Leningrad, where a "sea of people" met them and a rally at the port took place, the "quartet" took the Moscow train to the capital. That is where the main celebrations began. A crowd numbering in the thousands filled Komsomol'skaia Square. All of them wanted to see the new heroes and hear their voices. After another meeting, at which Papanin spoke, the heroes went to the Kremlin.[35]

The participants of the drifting station received the highest state honors. Krenkel', Fedorov, and Shirshov were given the title Hero of the Soviet Union, and Papanin received the Order of Lenin.[36] The heroes were also awarded doctorates of geographical sciences without having to defend dissertations. Millions of the people across the "immense country" wanted to see the new Stalinist heroes and hear fascinating stories about their heroic work. An itinerary for a new propaganda and educational mission was assigned to each of the four Papanisty. The mass circulation publications, such as books devoted to the winterers' daily lives on the Soviet Union's first drifting station, played a key part in this mission. At this point, we will leave the complicated 1930s and turn to the 1980s in the next part of the chapter to look at how the image of new heroes of the ice—hockey players—took shape against the backdrop of the development of this sport.

The Image of the Ice Hockey Player: "Larionov's Line"

An observation about the world of sport made by literary theorist Hans Ulrich Gumbrecht describes quite precisely the conditions under which the polar explorers of the 1930s became objects of fervent admiration:

> It need not always be the objectively greatest of all times and best of the world for sports to transfigure its heroes in the eyes of passionate spectators. All that it takes to become addicted to sports is a distance between the athlete and the beholder—a distance large enough for the beholder to believe that his heroes inhabit a different world. For it is under this condition that athletes turn into objects of admiration and desire.[37]

While the Papanin Four's ice floe at the North Pole was just this kind of a "different world" in the 1930s, in the second half of the twentieth century, "heroes of the ice" who carried out their work on ice-skating rinks gradually became the objects of mass adoration.

As is well known, Soviet ice hockey entered the international arena in the 1950s. From that time on, Moscow became a center of ice battles. Young, talented players from provincial ice hockey teams usually ended up in one of the capital's teams, TsSKA (Tsentralnyi Sportivnyi Klub Armii or Central Army Sports Club), Spartak, Dinamo, or Kryl'ia Sovetov. Ice hockey gradually became more of a mass spectator sport and more professional.[38] The number of fans also increased; at the end of the 1960s, the games during the intra-union ice hockey tournament attracted more than a million spectators annually.[39] Leonid Brezhnev was a fan, and he often went to ice hockey matches. In addition to the Party leadership's personal interest in ice hockey, this sport turned out to be an attractive spectator sport that met the needs of the state.[40] As emphasized by historian of sport Robert Edelman, who devoted one of his books to the "big three" sports in the USSR (football, ice hockey, and basketball), the entertainment ice hockey provided worked well with the "predictability and stability" of both the official sports structures for ice hockey and the conditions of the game:

> Tensions between the needs of the national team and those of the clubs were minimal, and the internal league season was organized around the demands of the international schedule. Beyond this, the Soviet style of play contrasted sharply with the brawling physicality of the Canadian game. As a result, there was much less violence by players. Fans were more easily controlled within the confines of indoor arenas than could be accomplished in larger stadiums. The result was a spectacle far better suited than football to official needs and concerns. Finally, the fact that the entire enterprise enjoyed considerable international success made ice hockey especially attractive to Party members.[41]

Given the very successful way this sport developed in the 1960s and 1970s, it is not surprising that a whole galaxy of Russian ice hockey stars appeared. These athletes were examples for the ice hockey players of the following decades to emulate. The so-called "Larionov Five" had a special place among them.

Living and Working Conditions on the Ice

By highlighting and providing commentary on the successes of the USSR's first national ice hockey team in the 1980s, contemporary journalism had a significant influence on the way the image of the ice hockey player took shape. As a group, the Larionov line, a group of players who were known as the Green Unit and the KLM line outside the USSR, defined the fashion in ice hockey for an entire decade. In fact, this group's playing style set new standards of excellence in the world of international sports.

The five men performed an athletic spectacle on the ice: Igor Larionov was the "dispatcher" (in the Soviet ice hockey tradition, a "line" is given the center forward's surname), Vladimir Krutov and Sergei Makarov played offense (their initials and Larionov's made up the team's international name, the KLM line), and Viacheslav Fetisov and Aleksei Kasatonov acted as the legendary defensemen. Each of the athletes played a specific position in the line, showing much of their individuality, yet they were perfectly convincing as a group. This is how sports journalist Leonid Reizer describes the Larionov line in his book *Multiplying by Five* (*Umnozhenie na piat'*), which came out at the height of the players' popularity:

> Fetisov: He is … particularly attractive. … He might have been asked to star in a film where the hero has to be tall … and well-built … and elegant. … He is amazingly well proportioned.
>
> Kasatonov: A glowing flush on his cheeks. The picture of health. Inner calm. … Broad-shouldered. Takes his time, the kind of slow and steady pace you see in everyday life.
>
> Makarov: The eyes of a person who knows what he wants from life and how to get it. … The smallest one. Tight and springy.
>
> Larionov: A friendly look, conducive to conversation. No sign of hockey machismo. … He gives the impression that he is always on a starvation diet.
>
> Krutov: His face is round, even a bit childish. Sort of a somewhat ordinary face, he looks nothing like a star. … Strongly and well built. Somewhat stocky, he always has a Bickford fuse at hand, which ignites him and, turning on a crazy speed, he becomes a battering ram, powerful and maneuverable in equal parts.[42]

Although in the preceding decades Soviet ice hockey players preferred not to rely on brute strength, in the 1980s ice hockey changed. The nature of the game became noticeably tougher: "Techniques that depend on strength are applied everywhere, they don't yield an inch of ice without violent resistance and they run faster than they used to."[43] In pointing this out, Reizer, a regular contributor to the weekly *Football. Hockey* (*Futbol. Khokkei*) in the 1980s and the head of the hockey section of the newspaper *Soviet Sport* in the 1990s, paid special attention to the physical aspects of the team members' behavior on the ice. Thanks to his colorful reporting, the reader learns about how the hockey "supermen" move on artificial ice, each in his own way. For example:

> Makarov: He glides, oh how he glides on the ice! He does not knock out a hurried shot with his skates but remains, as if magnetized to the light blue ice. And out of loyalty to this, Makarov's steel blades skate sharply and at the same time smoothly. ... He goes toward his opponent swinging like a pendulum—here, inclining his trunk a bit to the left, there, making a deceptive move to the right. And he cuts through the defense. It's rare to see him sprawled on the ice.[44]

Of the way center forward Larionov skates, he says, "His skating is low key. And deceptive, like a deceptive exterior that hides true possibilities! ... He flits like a butterfly and is always in the right place at the right time."[45] Reizer's attentiveness to the physical qualities of the players' movements during the game, the individualized characteristics of the techniques, and the beauty of the players' exceptional actions on the ice field persuasively show that the category of "heroes of the ice" has by no means become an empty metaphor. In the context of professional sports in the 1980s, this category certainly acquired a new essence.

The high level of professionalism characteristic of the ice hockey of this time was the result of a harsh schedule of constant training and competition. This motif appears in the memoirs of players, in particular Fetisov's, who writes in his 1998 book *Overtime* (*Overtaim*):

> From the time I was sixteen, I lived under the order of the competition cycle's system. Eleven months of the year, practice on the ice, sometimes twice a day, on a strictly defined schedule. ... I lived by a precise schedule: you practice for three months, there's a break, preparing for the Izvestiia Cup, a break, getting ready for the world championships, a big break. ... I was trained to carry certain loads, the way a champion hunting dog is trained—to go after game.[46]

This was the same kind exhausting regime of "daily work on the ice" that organized the life and work of the members of Larionov's line. On the whole, it did not allow the athletes to have a normal private life. In the press of the 1980s we see numerous metaphors that develop this theme. Thus, for the players, their family life, their home was "this fortress where you could catch your breath and stock up on cordial warmth and have the feeling that in this life you are not only necessary to millions like a knight on the ice without fear and reproach but are also necessary for two specific people, your wife and child."[47]

The harsh conditions of training and competition and their husbands' lack of free time greatly distressed the players' wives, who witnessed the results of hockey battles. Their voices fill out the picture of the work done by the "heroes of the ice," who were in the popular mass media's spotlight almost every day.[48] Thus, usually well hidden behind a chunk of an "iceberg" who embodies the strength and courage of the ice hockey player, certain intimate and emotional details appear, coming from lips of his beloved wife, supplementing the image that the fans saw during a match: "Behind his strength and apparent reserve, that is, his manly qualities, somehow it is not immediately obvious that he is gentle, even vulnerable. He is as sensitive as, well, I don't really know, as sensitive as a child!"[49]

In interviews with sports journalists, the wives of the knights of the ice expressed their unhappiness about their husbands' frequent absences: "at home he's an infrequent guest," someone they only saw now and then.[50] It is telling that in this context Kasatonov's wife Janna compared her husband's working conditions with those of the polar explorers, the "heroes of the ice" of previous eras: "My father was a polar flyer. Papa took part in one of the first expeditions to the Antarctic. ... From childhood in fact, I got used to the way I am living now. Mama was also eternally waiting for Papa. He stayed on the drifting stations for a month and longer. This, by the way, is worse than hockey. Here, on the hockey rink, you don't have ice floes breaking under you."[51] The absence of risk from the forces of nature is obvious, inasmuch as hockey players move on artificial ice in covered stadiums. However, other problems and complications make up for this. Therefore, the diet of professional athletes comes up over and over again. It is connected with the motif of hockey players' strict self-discipline and voluntary self-restraint. Instead of confronting the external conditions of "work on the ice" like frosts and blizzards, the hockey player has a daily struggle with the internal demands of his own organism. Here, there is another striking difference in the way the conditions of work on the ice done by the two types of "heroes of the ice" were evaluated. Although what the winterers said about their provisions emphasized the relative abundance of food at their disposal, despite prevailing widespread food shortages and, in some places, famine, the deliberate rejection of any excesses against a backdrop of relative prosperity is a fundamental motif of the male ice hockey players' relationship to food. And that motif is often expressed through the lens of their wives' lack of understanding: "We are always arguing about food. 'Look, can't you understand that I don't eat very much,' he complains. And I want him to eat properly. He eats very little: a child's serving of soup and a very small second course."[52]

In general, the wives of the ice hockey players of the 1980s received a lot of attention from the press and television, much more than athletes' wives usually had in the preceding decades and even more attention than polar explorers' wives had enjoyed in the 1930s. Obviously, the increased interest in female partners of public persons came as the result of the broader social and cultural changes that took place in the second half of the twentieth century. Yet the images of the women who stood at the side of the new heroes of the ice were to a significant degree different from representations of the wives of polar explorers, who were present in the narrative but remained on the periphery of the main story. For example, polar explorers' wives appeared as participants in radio communications. They were depicted in newspapers or their voices transmitted while talking with their husbands over the radio, but their appearance, attire, or hairstyles were not described in the press explicitly. The wives of ice hockey players, however, became vivid phenomena in their own right, reinforcing the aureoles of the heroes of the ice. In the 1980s journalists emphasized the striking, fashionable clothes that Lada Fetisova, Vera Makarova, Lena Larionova, Nina Krutova, and Janna Kasatonova wore. In addition to their distinctive external appearance, they could also be recognized in other ways: "They arrive, not without some swagger, in their own cars or in taxis, turning up their noses at the subway. And there is no question about their destination. Anyone can see when they get out of the car that yes, these are the wives of hockey players!"[53]

Rewards and Glorification

The wives of the ice hockey players became the public mouthpieces for dissatisfaction with their husbands' earnings. Judging by the statements recorded in an interview with the wives of the players of Larionov's line at a time when most Soviet citizens were experiencing difficulty with their salaries and access to cash, the wives of the ice hockey players, in particular, Janna Kasatonova, seemed to be living in a "different reality":

> Of course, Lyosha and the guys from his quintet earned more than average players. All this is mainly because of trips abroad. They earned more than highly qualified engineers. ... My Lyosha has the rank of major and his rate of pay, for a hockey player of the first category, is five hundred rubles. ... I remember that when they went to FRG [the Federal Republic of Germany or West Germany] they got around four hundred marks for winning, half for a tie, and nothing if they lost. Is that a lot? A nice women's sweater costs as much as [they get for] winning two matches, jeans, ninety marks and children's jeans, sixty ...[54]

However, one also gets a sense of the players' income by taking note of their wives' clothes, which fascinated the press and the public. Reizer's descriptions of the wives of the Larionov Five are very colorful and quite revealing:

> They were noticeable from afar. In winter passersby even turned their heads: mink, Arctic fox, fox fur coats on their slender figures; on their heads were hats also made from the fur of strange little animals or [just] their hair, daringly exposed to the icy wind, coiffed in the latest fashion; and the heels of their modern ankle boots click in the same haughty way. And their faces, faces that are so striking, either on their own or from skillfully applied, name-brand cosmetics. Well, these were downright free appearances [made by] fashion models right out of *Burda Moden*!⁵⁵

The Papanin Four were also dressed in silk and furs, which, to a significant degree, ensured physical survival under the conditions of life on the ice floe. In the context of the new image of heroes of the ice in the 1980s, fur clothing, which the Papanintsy wore for its functionality, acquired a new meaning. It became an ornament and a sign of luxury.

Material rewards for ice hockey players became a constant motif. In many interviews the players (or their wives) denied that ice hockey players enjoyed "super-profits" while they attempted to show that being a ice hockey player at the international level entailed objective mental and physical difficulties: "Look, they say hockey players are 'shoveling in the dough.' Well, fine, take someone who is a doctor of the sciences [*kandidat nauk*, i.e., someone who has earned a doctorate], he does intellectual work and at the most he runs the risk of a pen going into his eye. But the guys are taking risks all the time."⁵⁶

The Soviet regime loved to reward the heroes of the ice for their victories, because they brought the country Olympic gold and numerous medals from international championships and the prestige that went along with these. Here is how Fetisov remembers the regime's rewards in his memoirs:

> In the middle of June [1988] at the height of the holidays, a telegram from the government came to our hotel in Yalta. All of us, the whole company, Kasatonov, Makarov … and our wives were on holiday. We read the text: "Urgent: Come to the Kremlin to receive an award." With the help of this telegram we bought plane tickets (at the height of the summer season to just buy tickets was impossible but with a telegram like this they sold them to us). … In the morning we went to the Kremlin for the ceremony. We were all in a good mood: They are giving me the Order of Lenin, everything is great, life is wonderful. At home I dressed in my Olympic uniform. … I received the order and after it was awarded, there is a buffet, everyone is walking around

the Kremlin hall, a lot of people come up to me, they congratulate me. And Grammov comes up to me and Gorbachev is with him and says: Mikhail Sergeevich! This is our famous hockey player Firsov [sic]! ... I was beside myself. Everything was happening at the same time! The order. The Kremlin, Gorbachev, permission from Iazov [to go to the NHL] just like a fairy tale.[57]

Not all of them received the USSR's highest state decoration, the one that Fetisov writes about. However, all of Larionov's linemen received numerous high state honors, including Honored Master of Sport of the USSR, for Distinguished Labor, the Order of the Red Banner of Labor, and the Order of the Badge of Honor. The patronage of the leader of the country helped the Five—who were able to keep playing in US National Hockey League clubs in the 1990s—develop their professional careers.

Relationships within the Group and with the Outside World

The line's cohesion, which had become the hallmark of the style of ice hockey during the Soviet period, was also characteristic of the relationships among the players. The memoir literature and journalism confirm this cohesion. This did not prevent the press of that time from emphasizing the individuality of each of the line's players, although their success came from the group nature of the game. But scoring a goal against an opponent meant something different for each of the Five: from "trying, once again, to show that the line was doing the thing it was most valued for" to "I scored, well that's glory for us [the line] and a plus for the whole team."[58] The players' individual traits are even defined by their differing relationships to food: while Larionov was "capable of giving a lecture on food as one of the most important restorative means for the athlete,"[59] for Kasatonov and Kurtov "the table [was one of] life's pleasures," which they never denied themselves. Makarov "knows the sense of moderation," and Fetisov was a "professional in every cell of his body, [who] subconsciously eats only as much as his organism needs after energy-intensive work on the ice."[60]

In terms of handling their immense popularity and renown, one person whom the Larionov Five themselves idolized stands out—Valerii Kharlamov, the Soviet ice hockey legend of the 1970s.[61] What Fetisov says in his memoirs about his great esteem for this figure with such a tragic fate reveals his search for his own position as a "hockey idol." Fetisov condensed Kharlamov's image into the exemplar of a "masculine character" who was able to define his relationship with the other members of the group and communicate effectively with the public and the regime: "Kharlamov was the personification of the Russian ice hockey style. He was fast, energetic, a virtuoso with the character of a real man. ... He never struggled to invent himself ... to adapt to circumstances or the team. Always and everywhere, Kharlamov remained Kharlamov. And he was accepted everywhere as theirs, as an equal."[62]

During *perestroika*, ice hockey players dared to look beyond the accepted limits of action. A "window of opportunity" opened wide for them, and a "fire escape" appeared, which they could use to save themselves if they needed to. Their protracted discussions and long-standing conflicts with Coach Viktor Vasil'evich Tikhonov and the Sports Committee came more and more often to the attention of a public that was already familiar with the terms "democracy" and "glasnost." Ice hockey players now felt they could express their opinions about how work was organized in the team. For instance, in the very widely read magazine *Ogonek*, an open letter from Larionov appeared in the 16 October 1988 issue.[63] On 13 January 1989, a critical article by Fetisov titled "I Don't Want to Play on Tikhonov's Team" was published in the newspaper *Moskovskii komsomolets*.[64]

It is not surprising that in conversations with their fellow players, ice hockey players no longer feared "Party" consequences. Reizer was a witness to these upheavals and, once again, he brought the players' voices together to create a single chronicle:

> Larionov: Our TsSKA officials got wind of my desire to leave the club. Not long ago they would drive up and say, "We'll make you a lieutenant colonel!" And I told them "I don't need your rank. You can't even make a decent apartment." Me, a lieutenant colonel! That's pathetic. What the hell kind of officers are we?! Yes, we fight. Yes, we work as a unit. But what do we have to do with it? We're hockey players. Professionals. Professional athletes, not professional soldiers. I've never shot anything in my life. Except shooting a puck into a goal.
>
> Fetisov: Yesterday the political administration called me in again. ... "Think about it," they say, "What are you doing?! You are a communist. What do you need this Canada, why do you want this NHL? Why do you need these dollars?!"[65]

Aware of their professional value, which their medals and state honors demonstrated, and understanding the commercial nature of the "new times," these athletes did not hesitate to enter into conflicts with the sports structures. Fetisov remembers that,

> when the Sportkom leadership got the feeling that there was a lot of demand for us and that hockey players have to be released from contracts sooner or later due to the new policy, then they decided to earn more money on our

contracts. At this very time, Sovintersport appeared. This was a firm that was the part of the Sportkom that dealt with Western contracts for Soviet athletes. None of the athletes asked how much they were [actually] going to be paid. They only wanted to know how much they would give us and the rest they were keeping for themselves. ... Sovintersport thought the hockey players were a good product.[66]

Although the Larionov line seemed like a single, indivisible entity and presented itself as a monolith to spectators at ice hockey matches, in the end it fell apart like many other things in the USSR at that time. However, the Five did not fall out of the ice hockey "box"; many of them signed contracts with "overseas" clubs and lived out their "athletic lifetime," becoming both "legends of Soviet hockey" and the idols of international sport known as the Russian Five. By an irony of fate, proximity to political power, which was one of the sources of ice hockey's popularity in the USSR, played a significant role in the final phase of the players' biographies. At present, as very wealthy people, they show their loyalty to the current regime by training on the ice with Vladimir Putin, which is duly chronicled by the new mass media.[67]

Conclusion: Heroes of the Ice at the Beginning of the Twenty-First Century

One goal dominated the era when the Soviet state and its people were conquering "the planet's white spot," the North Pole: to show the world the might and power of the Soviet state. Using the rhetoric of battle, ideologues involved in the project of mastering the North Pole, including the expedition of Papanin Four, set up a front line on the basis of the symbolic opposition of warmth and the cold. On one hand, there was the warmth of the Motherland's care for her sons, which Papanin emphasized in his published diary, *Life on the Ice Floe*. On the other hand, an unexplored region of cold and ice was a symbol of the enemy in terms of both natural forces and political opponents. Covering the struggles of the first Soviet drifting station, newspaper articles spoke of declaring war on the Arctic, battles with ice, human resilience in the most difficult circumstances, and how the "the Bolsheviks conquered the Pole" as the result of these battles. On 19 April 1934 *Pravda*'s front-page editorial declared that "the great war in the Arctic Ocean ended in a brilliant victory for the Bolsheviks." However, glorious pages were not the only ones in the history of struggles for the Arctic. Ill-considered decisions, haste in preparing expeditions, adventurism—all of this led to tragic consequences, the death of participants on expeditions, and rescue operations that propaganda portrayed as heroic victories. Therefore, it is not surprising that the ice continued to trouble people's hearts and minds. It awakened in them a thirst for victory and evoked a desire to test one's strength against the elements.

Ice hockey also has a long, interesting history. Here, as in the case of the polar explorers, the Soviet press, both the general press and sports journalism, actively helped to produce idols and heroes. The men acting on the ice were elevated above the masses. Thanks to influential fans, interest in ice hockey grew quickly. It was second in popularity to football as a spectator sport, incorporating all the best features of the Canadian version of the game. Before 1956 there were no rinks with artificial ice in the Soviet Union, which meant that the quality of the ice depended entirely on the ambient temperature. Therefore, a match had to be scheduled "according to the weather." In addition, snow and blizzards were rarely reasons to postpone an ice hockey game. Slogans like "Real men play hockey" and "Ice brigade" not only glorified the fight against nature but also proved once again that this type of sport was gendered. In fact, not only were ice hockey players surrounded by the "warmth of the Motherland" as they carried out their mission in the cold—which was also true of the polar explorers—but they also basked in the heat generated by their fans and supporters. The public and members of the press could watch ice hockey games in real time. In other words, people who were in the stadium saw, firsthand, what the players were actually doing (and those watching on television had a similar experience), and journalists reported from the perspective of seeing the games in person. In contrast, the polar explorers worked in isolation. The only way the public could "see" their work and their heroism was through its re-creation in the media at a distance, by journalists who did not see the polar explorers' work unfolding before their eyes.

As gendered images, polar explorers and ice hockey players are closely related. An approach that compares the professional activity of the polar explorers who carried out research on ice floes and ice hockey players, while also addressing the popularization of these figures in daily life, demonstrates how these two images of the "hero of the ice" helped shape different types of individual identity connected with both society and the regime. By looking at the images of "heroes of the ice" that have appeared in the mass media over the last few years, one could examine the multivalent potential that these scenarios of identity have in today's Russia. It is telling that both sports and polar motifs of male heroism figure in the masculine image of the leader of the country that is personified in the figure of V. V. Putin. In the spring of 2010 Putin visited Franz Joseph Land. The premier familiarized himself with studies of the local polar bear population being done on the archipelago by a scientific expedition from the A. N. Severtsov Institute of Ecology and Evolution of the Russian Academy of Sciences. With the scientists on hand, the head of state "helped to measure a polar bear from nose to tail" and put a satellite collar on him. During all the manipulations, the premier "gently stroked the bear and patted his ear, calming him," after which he shook the paw of the "master of the Arctic."[68]

When the images of "men of the ice" that have taken shape during the twentieth century in the USSR are seen through the prism of their current actualization, they take on new contours. The example discussed above of how these images are used in current Russian politics draws attention to both the political components of popular images of "heroes" associated with the meaning of "cold" and the relationship of these images to the regime in general as an interesting topic for future research.

Acknowledgments

This study was carried out at the University of Tübingen (Germany) as part of the French-German research project "Contemporary Environmental History of the Soviet Union and Its Successor States, 1970–2000: Ecological Globalization and Regional Dynamics," which was funded by the Agence Nationale de la Recherche (ANR, France) and the Deutsche Forschungsgemeinschaft (DFG, Germany) in 2014–17.

Translation by Jacqueline Friedlander

Alexander Ananyev is an associated researcher at the University of Tübingen. As a trained librarian he worked at the GHI Moscow and was engaged in a series of *digitalization projects*. As an environmental historian of Russia and the Soviet Union he has contributed several conference papers and articles internationally, including "Zhenshchiny v Arktike, ili mif ob odnom gendernom stereotipe," *Rodina* 5 (2013): 139–41. His first book deals with the state politics and environmental conditions in the Arctic: *Arktika—Territoriia bespredela: Rossiiskaia poliarnaia politika i ekologicheskie problemy 1990-ch.* (forthcoming).

Notes

1. In this study, heroism per se is not the focus of the analysis. The members of the DFG Collaborative Research Centre 948 "Heroes—Heroizations—Heroisms" at the University of Freiburg (Germany) have recently published a detailed overview and bibliography of new scholarship on heroism. See Ronald G. Asch et al., "Das Heroische in der neueren kulturhistorischen Forschung: Ein kritischer Bericht," H-Soz-Kult, 28 July 2015, retrieved 8 August 2018 from www.hsozkult.de/literaturereview/id/forschungsberichte-2216.
2. At one point there was a discussion about whether the staff at the polar stations could legitimately be called "winterers" (*zimovshchiki*). Many polar explorers objected to

such a definition, arguing that "only a bear spends the winter in its den, and a human differs from an animal because [the former] is active [and] works." For more detail on this, see Z. M. Kanevskii, *Borot'sia i iskat'! Razmyshleniia o professii poliarnika* (Leningrad, 1979). This article is about male polar explorers. On female participants in polar expeditions, see A. V. Ananyev, "Zhenshchiny v Arktike, ili Mif ob odnom gendernom stereotipe," *Rodina*, no. 5 (2013): 139–41.

3. B. Gromov, "Boitsy poliarnogo fronta," *Tekhnika-molodezhi*, no. 12 (1935): 106.
4. *Pravda*, 20 February 1938, 1.
5. *Stikhi o Papanintsakh*, Biblioteka zhurnala Ogonek, no. 31 (1090) (Moscow, 1938).
6. Ibid., 36.
7. I. D. Papanin, *Zhizn' na l'dine: Dnevnik* (Moscow, 1940); E. T. Krenkel', *Chetyre tovarishcha: Dnevnik* (Moscow, 1940).
8. The second edition of I. D. Papanin's *Life on the Ice: A Diary (Zhizn' na l'dine: Dnevnik)* had a print run of 27,500 copies. A copy cost fifteen rubles. E. T. Krenkel"s *Four Comrades: A Diary (Chetyre tovarishcha: Dnevnik)* had a print run of 20,000 copies; a copy cost twelve rubles.
9. Papanin, *Zhizn' na l'dine*, 15.
10. Ibid., 8.
11. Ibid., 142.
12. Ibid., 26.
13. Krenkel', *Chetyre tovarishcha*, 144.
14. Papanin, *Zhizn' na l'dine*, 24.
15. Ibid., 25. Papanin mentions the following works in his diary: *Peter I (Petr I)* by Aleksei Tolstoi; Chernyshevskii's *What Is to Be Done? (Chto delat'?)*; *In the East (Na vostoke)* by P. A. Pavlenko; and Gor'kii's *Mother (Mat')*.
16. Krenkel', *Chetyre tovarishcha*, 97.
17. Papanin, *Zhizn' na l'dine*, 25. *Valenki* are a traditional kind of Russian felt boots, and *malitsy* are fur-lined, caftan-like garments.
18. Ibid., 121.
19. Ibid., 81.
20. Ibid., 216.
21. Ibid.
22. Ibid., 160.
23. Ibid., 269.
24. Ibid., 274.
25. Krenkel', *Chetyre tovarishcha*, 141.
26. Because of censorship and for ideological reasons, discussion of interpersonal relationships in the published versions of the diaries was very limited: "We all lived together in a friendly fashion, we weren't moody, avoided unnecessary friction and helped each other. As Soviet people should. Of course, everyone has both his weaknesses and his individual human qualities, but nothing prevented us from carrying our extensive program of scientific work. Which was entrusted to us by Soviet science, the entire nation, our Government and personally by Comrade Stalin." Papanin, *Zhizn' na l'dine*, 19.
27. Ibid., 191: "In the evening I had an argument with Shirshov about the main areas of polar work. Eh, being in a bad mood affects everything. Our verbal scuffle was soon over. My mood improved after this."

28. Ibid., 178.
29. Krenkel', *Chetyre tovarishcha*, 240. Krenkel' tells the reader that the radio equipment was made in the radio laboratory of the Leningrad *Oblast'* NKVD Directorate.
30. Ibid., 61.
31. Papanin, *Zhizn' na l'dine*, 244.
32. Krenkel', *Chetyre tovarishcha*, 50.
33. Ibid., 84.
34. Ibid., 254.
35. "Headed by Stalin, the entire Politburo met the polar explorers [in the Kremlin's Georgievskii Hall]. Stalin sat me down beside him, 'Now let's drink to victory Comrade Papanin,' he said, raising his glass. 'The work was difficult, but all of us were confident that the four of you would carry it out honorably!'" Ivan D. Papanin, *Led i plamen'* (Moscow, 1977), 192.
36. Papanin received the title Hero of the Soviet Union after completing the North Air Expedition (22 March–25 June 1937) in June 1937.
37. Hans Ulrich Gumbrecht, *In Praise of Athletic Beauty* (Cambridge, MA, 2006), 8.
38. "Over the years, Soviet hockey players demonstrated that they could play on a level with the world's best. They brought a new and exciting style of play to the attention of the hockey world and revolutionized the game everywhere," Robert Edelman, *Serious Fun: A History of Spectator Sports in the USSR* (New York, 1993), 144. In the Russian translation, see R. Edel'man, *Ser"eznaia zabava: Istoriia zrelishchnogo sporta v SSSR* (Moscow, 2008), 218.
39. "In 1967, roughly 1,200,000 spectators watched domestic hockey games. The next year attendance rose to 1,346,000 spectators." Edelman, *Serious Fun*, 162; *Ser"eznaia zabava*, 243.
40. For an analysis of the relationship between a regime and sports (using football as an example), see Timm Beichelt, *Ersatzspielfelder—Zum Verhältnis von Fußball und Macht* (Berlin, 2018).
41. Edelman, *Serious Fun*, 182; *Ser"eznaia zabava*, 268.
42. L. Iu. Reizer, *Umnozhenie na piat'* (Moscow, 1992), 18.
43. Ibid., 7: "In this situation, when space and time are merged, so to speak, for the player, showing one's native wit is an exceptionally difficult, subtle technique. Where it's simpler to go head to head, like a battering ram. And only a few people keep a clear head and, without turning aside from the fight, they are eager to play hockey, replaying an opponent. There's more dependence on one's partner. In the science, it seems the epoch of brilliant loners has passed. In hockey, the same thing is definitely true. The heroes … were lucky: they were together, in one team. Five lines of human fate intersected at a single point."
44. Ibid., 18.
45. Ibid., 19.
46. V. A. Fetisov, *Overtaim* (Moscow, 1998), 73.
47. Reizer, *Umnozhenie*, 174.
48. Ibid., 176: "After games he is very upset. I look at my husband and somehow, I am feeling hurt for him, it seems to me that he alone is going through more than everyone else. Even if they won. … And I already know that he needs to be left alone. Don't ask him any questions. Just let him sit and think calmly."
49. Ibid., 177.

50. Ibid., 179.
51. Ibid., 180.
52. Ibid., 178.
53. Ibid., 172.
54. Ibid., 181.
55. Ibid., 171. The German *Burda Moden* was the first Western fashion magazine to be published in the USSR, and it had quite an impact on Soviet consumers in terms of the fashions featured in its issues.
56. Ibid., 194.
57. Fetisov, *Overtaim*, 38.
58. Ibid.
59. Reizer, *Umnozhenie na piat'*, 24.
60. Ibid.
61. It is interesting that Valerii Kharlamov's parents named him in honor of another Soviet legend, the polar pilot Valerii Chkalov. His father, Boris Kharlamov, said this in the documentary film *Valerii Kharlamov's Bullfight on the Ice* (*Ledovaia korrida Valerii Kharlamova*).
62. Fetisov, *Overtaim*, 38.
63. *Ogonek*, no. 42 (1988): "On 16 October 1988, 300,600,000 compatriots went behind the 'wings' of big sport and suddenly saw that all is not well in the holy of holies of Soviet hockey, in the TsSKA, [they saw] that honored master Igor Larionov has [made] serious charges against thrice-honored coach Viktor Vasil'evich Tikhonov."
64. Fetisov, *Overtaim*, 53. After the article was released, there was an altercation within the TsSKA team, and Viktor Tikhonov, the team's head coach, announced, "I always thought that I would work with hockey players who give themselves fully to the work that is dear to their hearts. And then it became clear that I was mistaken."
65. Reizer, *Umnozhenie*, 206.
66. Fetisov, *Overtaim*, 31.
67. "Prem'er-ministr Rossii Vladimir Putin provel segodnia trenirovku s legendami sovetskogo khokkea v sportivnom komplekse 'Megasport' v Moskve" [Today Prime Minister Vladimir Putin trained with the legends of Soviet hockey at the Megasport Complex in Moscow], *RIA NOVOSTI*, 18 November 2011, retrieved 8 August 2018 from http://ria.ru/society/20111118/492242858.html.
68. The polar bear on which Vladimir Putin put a tracking collar in the spring of 2010 got rid of the device in August of that year, which was reported by the prime minister's press service. "Belyi medved' sbrosil osheinik Putina" [The polar bear dropped Putin's collar], *Radio Business FM*, 18 November 2010, retrieved 8 August 2018 from https://www.bfm.ru/news/106514.

Bibliography

Ananyev, A. V. "Zhenshchiny v Arktike, ili Mif ob odnom gendernom stereotype." *Rodina*, no. 5 (2013): 139–41.

Asch, Ronald G., et al. "Das Heroische in der neueren kulturhistorischen Forschung: Ein kritischer Bericht." H-Soz-Kult, 28 July 2015. Retrieved 8 August 2018 from www.hsozkult.de/literaturereview/id/forschungsberichte-2216.

Beichelt, Timm. *Ersatzspielfelder—Zum Verhältnis von Fußball und Macht*. Berlin, 2018.

"'Belyi medved' sbrosil osheinik Putina" [The polar bear dropped Putin's collar]. *Radio Business FM*, 18 November 2010. Retrieved 8 August 2018 from https://www.bfm.ru/news/106514.

Edelman, Robert. *Serious Fun: A History of Spectator Sports in the USSR*. New York, 1993.

Edel'man, R. *Ser"eznaia zabava: Istoriia zrelishchnogo sporta v SSSR*. Moscow, 2008.

Fetisov, V. A. *Overtaim*. Moscow, 1998.

Gromov, B. "Boitsy poliarnogo fronta." *Tekhnika-molodezhi*, no. 12 (1935): 106–7.

Gumbrecht, Hans Ulrich. *In Praise of Athletic Beauty*. Cambridge, MA, 2006.

Kanevskii, Z. M. *Borot'sia i iskat'! Razmyshleniia o professii poliarnika*. Leningrad, 1979.

Krenkel', E. T. *Chetyre tovarishcha: Dnevnik*. Moscow, 1940.

Ogonek, no. 42 (1988).

Papanin, I. D. *Led i plamen'*. Moscow, 1977.

———. *Zhizn' na l'dine: Dnevnik*. Moscow, 1940.

Pravda, 20 February 1938, 1.

"Prem'er-ministr Rossii Vladimir Putin provel segodnia trenirovku s legendami sovetskogo khokkea v sportivnom komplekse 'Megasport' v Moskve" [Today Prime Minister Vladimir Putin trained with the legends of Soviet hockey at the Megasport Complex in Moscow]. *RIA NOVOSTI*, 18 November 2011. Retrieved 8 August 2018http://ria.ru/society/20111118/492242858.html.

Reizer, L. Iu. *Umnozhenie na piat'*. Moscow, 1992.

Stikhi o Papanintsakh, Biblioteka zhurnala Ogonek, no. 31 (1090) (Moscow, 1938).

Conclusion

Julia Herzberg, Andreas Renner, and Ingrid Schierle

In general, this book lacks heat and summers. They seem to be suspiciously absent in the imagination of travelers to and scholars of Russia, as if the country has been living through an eternal winter and has no southern provinces. Frost, ice, and snow, by contrast, are widely accepted to have shaped the course of Russian history and the identity of its peoples. Long a somewhat deterministic truism in popular histories of Russia, the cold has also recently attracted the interest of environmental historians.

But why, when, and how did this association develop? What makes the long Russian winters more fascinating than late springs or hot summers? Is cold really an omnipresent connotation that has been held by visitors and historians alike? And if so, what can we learn from studying Russian history from its cold side? Researchers have rarely posed these questions. In a first attempt to unravel the stereotyped conflation of coldness and Russianness, the contributors to this volume apply different tools in their exploration of Russian culture since the eighteenth century.

All authors assume a meta-perspective—this is not a volume about climate history (though this perspective on Russia still deserves more attention too).[1] The contributors are not interested in an exact reconstruction of climate change or bygone weather conditions or how agriculture, tsarist autocracy, or Soviet society have flourished in the proverbial Russian cold. Rather than focusing on human techniques for survival under severe climatic conditions, this book examines cultural techniques of interpretation and adaptation. However, the aim is neither to paint a picturesque panorama of associations and track clichés through the centuries nor to deconstruct myths of the Russian winter or Russian bleakness. Each chapter analyzes a particular strand of the production and/or application of knowledge about cold and its impact. As Julia Herzberg points out in chapter 1, the aim of this collection is to historicize cold in Russia—i.e., to consider it from the perspective of the historian (rather than the climatologist) and thus add a surprisingly neglected case study to the flourishing field of historical and cultural climate studies.[2] This collection paves the way for a history in which climate conditions are ascribed more agency than has been the case in historiography so far—yet it avoids the geographical determinism that undergirded many older monographs. The book proposes a dialectical approach to a Russian history of cold: frost, ice, and snow do not explain Russian history, but they help explain how people made their history. And one way to do so was to confront the climate and initiate ways to adapt to and even change it. Consequently, this volume understands climate as both a structuring and a structured condition of Russian history.

As with every edited volume, this one encompasses a whole gamut of questions. Researchers in the eighteenth century wondered about the very nature of cold, while the Soviet scientists, in turn, wanted to help conquer the "Red Arctic." To make Russia look more "European," liberal journalists of the late tsarist period tried to downplay the impact of cold on the history of Siberia, while World War II–era Soviet propagandists confronted the German invaders with the powerful "General Winter." Soviet cinematographers struggled with cold temperatures when filming winter scenes, while Soviet geographers of the subarctic struggled to bring their research in line with Marxism. Still, in this kaleidoscope of motifs, several repeating patterns can be discerned.

Following the structure of the book, the chapters analyze different fields of knowledge production: (scientific) explanations, (aesthetic) narratives, and (everyday) practices. One thing that they all have in common is that the authors challenge the above-cited clichés of the Russian cold that served as the point of departure for this book. Surprisingly, none of the chapters attempt to deconstruct—and compare—the travel and historiographic writing or the literary texts (Russian and foreign) that have popularized these clichés. Cultural studies have shown that foreign visitors tend to focus on what is unfamiliar and different from their homelands.[3] How does this apply to notions or connotations of cold, and how did Russian attitudes and representations differ from or react to the discovery of coldness in Russia by foreigners? This question runs, explicitly or implicitly, through all ten chapters of this collection.

Though the time frames overlap, the four parts of the book follow a chronological order. It was not poets and travelers who made the first systematic descriptions of the Russian cold but naturalists in the circles of the Academy of Sciences in Saint Petersburg. They not only surveyed the icy landscapes of the tsarist empire but also gauged the impact of cold climate and compared their findings and explanations with the results from other (warmer) countries. As many of these eighteenth-century scholars had a foreign background, they studied cold as a peculiarly Russian phenomenon. This was not only because of the stunningly low temperatures measured in Siberia but also because the rise of the Petrine empire in the age of the Enlightenment triggered discussion about Russia's position in or toward Europe. On the one hand, cold became a concept to measure and symbolize that difference, though, of course, not every meteorological study was undertaken in order to contribute to an image of the "coldness" of Russia. On the other hand, the exploration of Siberia and expeditions to the Arctic and Antarctica became a sign of the advancement of Russian and later Soviet science. Many studies have shown how in the 1930s scientists played a pivotal role both in the material conquest and the symbolic appropriation of the "Red" Arctic.[4] The authors of this volume focus on the less known yet ground-laying research of the tsarist era and on the less visible yet profound expertise of post-Stalinist Arctic science.

Scientific findings and especially scientific expeditions contributed to Russian and Soviet myths of Arctic nature and polar heroes who provided tools to control it. Under Stalinism, literary and visual images of these endeavors were transformed into propaganda stories and archetypal clichés of conquering nature. They stood in stark contrast to the foreign clichés of an inhospitably cold Russia. But, as chapters in the third section of this book emphasize, the motifs of coldness varied in different cultural discourses. Though snow and ice were particularly likely to be associated with masculine heroism and challenging nature, there was a considerable diversity with regard to context and, of course, the aesthetic means of expression. A simple antithesis of negative foreign and positive Russian (counter)images is clearly misleading. For example, prerevolutionary authors cast doubt on the very conflation of Russianness and coldness, while during Khrushchev's "Thaw" the frosty climate became loaded with negative connotations.

Looking beyond aesthetic discourses, the final three chapters address the tricky question of (collective) identity and cultural adaptation to frost, ice, and snow. But unlike some eighteenth-century theorists of cold climate who based their theories on the idea of a specifically Russian character or mentality, the authors of this volume avoid deterministic explanations. Rather, they study Soviet and post-Soviet everyday recreational practices. Over the years winter activities became less utilitarian (or militaristic) and more hedonistic. Though in this section the interplay between self-perception and the perception of others is limited to periods of war, it becomes clear that nature did not mechanically trigger certain attitudes and behavior. Rather, cultural practices were embedded into the social and political change.

The four sections of this book address different levels and elements of a cultural history of cold in Russia. However, this history of relations with the cold should not be understood as one of top-down dissemination from academic science to everyday cultural practices. Obviously, long before naturalists and writers took up this topic, people have given meaning to their natural environment, whether cold or hot. The case studies in this volume reflect the availability of sources and follow older research trends; inevitably, the result looks somewhat arbitrary. It would be unfair to blame the authors for their topics and the editors for producing a haphazard pattern. Still, the lack of some central and comparatively well-researched topics—like the Arctic research of the Russian Geographical Society or the meaning of the Northern Sea Route along Russia's Arctic coastline[5]—is surprising. Moreover, the study of non-Russian northern peoples[6] or the history of Arctic medicine[7] would have not only enriched the volume with interesting case studies but also added new disciplinary perspectives such as ethnography, which has given particular attention to the cultural interaction of human beings with the cold Russian North.[8]

However, shortcomings and all, this volume provides landmarks and lacunae for future research projects and thus lays the groundwork for writing a history of cold, whether in Russia or elsewhere. The contributions jointly make cold climate an object of cultural history, showing how it is shaped by the interaction of "objective" natural conditions and "subjective" representations. Human beings are studied not as separated from their environments but as living within them.

Julia Herzberg is professor for the history of East Central Europe and Russia in early modern times at LMU Munich. Her recent research has focused on, among other topics, the environmental history of Central Eastern Europe and Russia. She coedited *Ice and Snow in the Cold War: Histories of Extreme Climatic Environments* (2019) with Christian Kehrt and Franziska Torma, and *Umweltgeschichte(n): Ostmitteleuropa von der Industrialisierung bis zum Postsozialismus* (2013) with Martin Zückert and Horst Förster. She is currently working on an environmental history of "frost" in Russia that examines various social and cultural aspects of Russia's harsh climate.

Andreas Renner is a historian of Russia and professor of Russian-Asian studies at LMU Munich. His interest in the Russian cold stems from his research on the Northern Sea Route.

Ingrid Schierle is a lecturer at the University of Tübingen. Her research interests include the history of concepts, the Russian language in the eighteenth century, and provincial life in the Russian empire. She coedited *Dvorianstvo, vlast' and obshchestvo v provincial'noi Rossii XVIII veka* (2012) with Olga Glagoleva, and *"Poniatiia o Rossii": K istoricheskoi semantike imperskogo perioda* (2012) with Aleksei Miller and Denis Sdvizhkov.

Notes

1. Sam White, Christian Pfister, and Franz Mauelshagen, eds., *The Palgrave Handbook of Climate History* (London, 2018).
2. With a focus on discourses, cf. Marianna Poberezhskaya and Teresa Ashe, eds., *Climate Change Discourse in Russia: Past and Present* (London, 2019).

3. Cf. Arnd Bauernkämper, Hans Erich Bödeker, and Bernhard Struck, "Reisen als kulturelle Praxis," in *Die Welt erfahren: Reisen als kulturelle Begegnung von 1780 bis heute*, ed. Arnd Bauernkämper, Hans Erich Bödeker, and Bernhard Struck (Frankfurt/Main, 2004), 9–32.
4. John McCannon, *Red Arctic: Polar Exploration and the Myth of the North in the Soviet Union, 1932–1939* (Oxford, 1998).
5. D. A. Shirina, *Ekspeditsionnaia deiatel'nost' Akademii Nauk na Severovostoke Azii, 1861–1917* (Novosibirsk, 1993).
6. Yuri Slezkine, *Arctic Mirrors: Russia and the Small Peoples of the North* (Ithaca, 1994).
7. N. R. Deriapa, ed., *Voprosy meditsinskoi geografii Arktiki i Antarktiki* (Leningrad, 1971).
8. Joachim Otto Habeck, *Lifestyle in Siberia and the Russian North* (Cambridge, 2019).

Bibliography

Bauernkämper, Arnd, Hans Erich Bödeker, and Bernhard Struck. "Reisen als kulturelle Praxis." In *Die Welt erfahren: Reisen als kulturelle Begegnung von 1780 bis heute*, edited by Arnd Bauernkämper, Hans Erich Bödeker, and Bernhard Struck, 9–32. Frankfurt/Main, 2004.
Deriapa, N. R., ed. *Voprosy meditsinskoi geografii Arktiki i Antarktiki*. Leningrad, 1971.
Habeck, Joachim Otto. *Lifestyle in Siberia and the Russian North*. Cambridge, 2019.
McCannon, John. *Red Arctic: Polar Exploration and the Myth of the North in the Soviet Union, 1932–1939*. Oxford, 1998.
Poberezhskaya, Marianna, and Teresa Ashe, eds. *Climate Change Discourse in Russia: Past and Present*. London, 2019.
Shirina, D. A. *Ekspeditsionnaia deiatel'nost' Akademii Nauk na Severovostoke Azii, 1861–1917*. Novosibirsk, 1993.
Slezkine, Yuri. *Arctic Mirrors: Russia and the Small Peoples of the North*. Ithaca, 1994.
White, Sam, Christian Pfister, and Franz Mauelshagen, eds. *The Palgrave Handbook of Climate History*. London, 2018.

Index

Academy
    of Sciences in Saint Petersburg, 24, 47–65, 97, 250
    of Sciences of the Soviet Union (AS SU), 31, 74, 95–96, 104, 158
Adorno, Theodor, 137, 165n7
Æpinus, Franz Ulrich Theodor, 60–61, 65
aesthesis, 136
aesthetics of cold, 169–80
Agassiz, Louis, 25–26, 76
Agee, James, 149
Alaska, 5, 28
Alexander I Coast, 76–86
Alexander II, 114
All-Union Voluntary Society for Proletarian Tourism and Excursions (OPTE), 205–9, 211, 212, 214, 217, 220n10
Altai, 52, 123, 156, 212
Amur, 114–115, 129n5
Andreev, Aleksandr I., 80–83
Anisimov, K. V., 113
Anna, Empress, 53–55, 60–61
Antarctic continent, 10, 74–87, 90n33, 91n54, 154, 251
Antarctica
    discoverer of, 74–87
Anthropocene, 29–34, 164n4
Anuchin, V. A., 32
Arabov, Iurii, 152
Aranovich, Semen, 149–150
Arbuthnot, John, 20–21
Arctic
    Circle, 5, 157, 159–161, 179
Aristotle, 20, 57, 62

Arkhangel'sk, 197–198, 209, 212, 216
Asiatic Russia, 120. *See also* Siberia
Atlantic, 28
atmosphere, 25, 27, 33, 74, 96
Australia, 75, 85, 121

Bagalei, Dmitrii, 30
Bakuriani, 214
Balch, Edwin Swift, 79
Balleny, John, 76
Barents Sea, 26, 103
Batov, P. I., 193
Battle of Stalingrad, 155, 161, 169, 176, 178–179
Bauer, Josef Martin, 178
Bellingshausen, Fabian Gottlieb von, 10, 75–87, 90n33, 91n46, 91n59
Belomorsk, 216
Belov, Mikhail I., 83–84, 91n54
Berg, Lev, 79, 80, 82–83, 90n33
Bering Strait, 28, 227
Bering, Vitus Jonassen, 135, 155
Berman, M., 116
Betin, Vasilii, 31
Bilfinger, Georg Bernhard, 51
Biscoe, John, 76, 87
Black Sea, 217
Blumenbach, Johann Friedrich, 62
Boele, Otto, 8, 47
Bogner, Thomas, 174–75
Bogolepov, M. A., 33
Bol'shaia Zemlia, 232
Bondarchuk, Sergei, 135, 144
Borchgrevink, Carsten, 78
Borisov, Petr, 28

Boyle, Robert, 56–58, 62
Brain, Stephen, 28
Brandt, Helmut, 195
Bransfield, Edward, 79–80, 82, 86–87
Braun, Joseph Adam, 48, 60–65, 68n61
Brehm, Alfred, 122
Brezhnev, Leonid, 28, 234
  period, 212, 214
Brückner, Eduard, 26–27, 33
Bruegel, Pieter, 138
Budyko, Mikhail, 28, 98–101, 104, 106–7

California, 121
Canada, 5, 241
Cape Deschnev, 169
Carpathians, 212–14
Caspian Sea, 26, 76
Catherine II, 21
Caucasus, 206, 212–14, 217
Celsius, Anders, 53, 58, 69n64
Central Physical Observatory in Saint
  Petersburg, 25
Central Russia, 119, 138, 212
Charpentier, Jean de, 76
Cherepovets, 196, 198
Chiaureli, Mikheil, 144, 165n18
Chimbulak, 214
Chimgan, 214
China, 121
Chita, 188
Chizhevskii, Alexander, 30, 31
Chudnovskii, S. L., 127
cinematic atmosphere, 136, 147–49,
  169–80
climate
  change, 4–7, 13n9, 14n21, 25–30, 32–33,
    95, 164n4, 249
  diversity, 3, 53, 116
  factor, 6–8, 19–28, 30–33, 65, 98, 187–99
  history, 29–34
  limitations, 3–4, 20–22
  theories, 20–27, 33
climatology, 3, 5, 19, 24–30, 107
cold
  artificial, 48, 59–65
  causes of, 58

coldness, 11, 135–36, 169–70, 172–75,
  177–80, 249–51
  natural, 48, 59, 61–62, 64
Cold War, 3–5, 10, 28, 74–75, 86–87, 95,
  107, 176, 219
Columbus, Christopher, 85
Communist Party of the Soviet Union
  (CPSU), 75, 209
Consett, Thomas, 50
Cook, James, 76, 80, 85–86
Council for the Study of Productive Forces
  (KEPS), 96
Council of People's Commissars (SNK),
  227
Crimea, 196, 217
Crown Princess Martha Land, 79

Datsishina, M. V., 192
Davies, R. W., 188
Davos, 174
De l'Isle de la Croyère, Louis, 59, 61, 64
Debenham, Frank, 79–81
Degtev, Dmitrii, 187
Delisle, Joseph Nicolas, 53
  scale, 60–61, 69
Derham, William, 50, 56, 58
Descartes, 57
determinism, 7, 22–24
Deutsch, Leo, 127
Dezhnev, S.I., 135, 160
Diatlov, Igor, 210, 221n39
Diebold, Hans, 194
discourse analysis, 14n21, 113–28, 174–75,
  204–19
Dittlmann, Arthur, 180
Dokuchaev, V. V., 97–100, 108n20
Dombai, 213–14
Donskoi, Mark, 148, 151, 154, 159
Dostal', Nikolai, 149, 152
Dronin, N. M., 188
Droysen, Johann Gustav, 32
Drygalski, Erich von, 78
Dulov, A. V., 32

Eberson, John, 172
Edelman, Robert, 234

Eisenstein, S., 144, 146–47
Elbrus, 211, 213–14
Emmerich, Roland, 139
Engels, Friedrich, 96
Eniseisk, 59, 61
environmental history, 5–9, 14n23, 14n24
Ermler, Fridrikh, 144
Estonian SSR, 212
Euler, Leonhard, 56, 62–63
Europe, 20, 22, 25, 47–50, 53, 57–58, 61, 64, 116, 250
   Central, 50
   Eastern, 6–8, 21
   Western, 7, 20, 26, 30, 32, 143

Fahrenheit, Daniel, 53, 62
Fanck, Arnold, 139, 172–75, 180
Far East, 96, 104–5, 116, 129n5, 156, 159, 214–15
Fedorov, Evgenii, 228, 233
Ferenczi, Sándor, 138
Fetisov, Viacheslav, 235–36, 239–41
Fetisova, Lada, 238
Finsch, Otto, 122
France, 32, 75, 85
Franz Joseph Land, 243
frost
   frostbite, 190, 193–94, 196–98, 200n24
   hoarfrost, 151
   permafrost, 4, 26, 103
   Siberian frosts, 113–119, 122, 127–28
   summer frost, 30–31, 33

Gassendi, Pierre, 57
Gedeonov. *See* Tseitlin, A. G.
geographical determinism, 33, 96, 187, 250
geographical zonation, 95–107
Geomorphological Institute, 96
Gerasimov, Sergei, 142, 150–51, 157, 160
German army, 176–79, 189–94, 198–99
German postwar film, 176–80
German, Aleksei, 149, 161
Germany, 32, 98, 148, 169–70, 173–80, 187–94, 238
GilFillan, Seabury Colum, 22–23
global warming, 4, 7, 13n4, 29, 33, 134

Gmelin, Johann Georg, 52, 57, 59, 63–65
Golitsyn, Mikhail, 54–55
Goncharov, I. A., 120
Gorbachev, M. S., 5, 240
Great Britain, 50, 85
Greece
   ancient, 20
Greenland, 5, 8, 173–74, 228
Grigor'ev, A. A., 10, 80, 82–83, 95–97, 99–107, 108n20
Gumbrecht, Hans Ulrich, 233
Gumilev, Lev, 33, 188

Halder, Franz, 191
Hann, Julius, 25
Hansen, Joachim, 178
heat and moisture balance, 99–104
Heinrici, Gotthard, 193
Herder, Johann Gottfried, 24
Herodotus, 21, 23
Hettner, Alfred, 96
Hill, Aaron, 21
Hippocrates, 20–21, 23, 49
historiography, 30–32, 129n5, 187, 250
Hitler, 143, 169, 171, 174, 176–77, 179, 189–90
Horn, Eva, 24
Humboldt, Alexander von, 3, 25
Hume, David, 23
Huntington, Ellsworth, 22–24, 36n34

Iakhroma, 188, 217
Iakutiia, 96, 159–60
Iakutsk, 64, 120, 123
ice hockey, 226, 233–43
Ice Palace, 48, 53–59, 63–64, 67n30
icebreaker, 142, 151, 228, 233
   Sibiriak, 134
   Yermak, 233
Institute
   of Food Supply Engineers, 229
   of Geography in Moscow, 95–96, 99
Irkutsk, 64, 188
Isaev, A. A., 123
Iutkevich, Sergei, 144
Iuzhakov, S. N., 124

Janszoon, Wilhelm, 85
Jurin, James, 50–51

Kalatozov, Mikhail, 135, 140–42, 151, 159, 162
Kalesnik, Stanislav V., 80–83
Kalinin, 188
Kamchatka, 116, 156, 159, 214
Kandaksha, 152
Kant, Immanuel, 22, 36n28
Kapustin, S. Ia., 125
Karelia, 206, 212
Karelian-Finnish SSR, 195
Kasatonov, Aleksei, 235, 237–40
Kasatonova, Janna, 237–238
Kazakhstan, 214
Kennan, George, 116
Kharlamov, Valerii, 240–41, 247n61
Khibiny Mountains, 212
Khrushchev, N. S., 251
Kirilenko, A. P., 188
Kirov, 205
Kiselev, Egor, 82–83
Kliuchevskii, Vasilii, 7, 29, 188
Knipovich, Nikolai, 26
Kola Peninsula, 210
Kolyma, 152–53
Köppen, Wladimir, 19, 22
Korolenko, V.G., 127
Kosmodemianskaia, Zoia, 148, 163
Kozintsev, Grigorii, 144
Kracauer, Siegfried, 139–40, 171, 174
Krafft, Georg Wolfgang, 48, 50–51, 53–58, 65, 67n30
Kraft, Herbert, 191
Krasnoiarsk, 64
Krenkel', Ernst, 228–30, 233, 246n29
Krimskaia Oblast'. *See* Crimea
Kruglov, S. N., 198
Krutov, Vladimir, 235
Krutova, Nina, 238
Krylov, Vladimir, 192
Kursk, 142, 188

Ladoga, Lake, 19, 226

landscape, 96–97, 99, 104, 119–20, 134–39, 141–43, 147, 149–50, 152–53, 155, 164n4, 177, 179, 216, 230, 250
Larionov, I. N., 235–36, 240–42, 247n63
Larionova, Lena, 238
Latvian Republic, 216
Lawrence, T. E., 137
Laxmann, Erich, 52, 62
Lazarev, Mikhail P., 82–87, 91n46
Le Roy Ladurie, Emmanuel, 32
Lebedev, Vladimir, 83
Lebedev-Kumach, Vasilii, 228
leisure, 204–219
Lemberg, Hans, 47
Lenin, V. I., 143–46, 229
Leningrad, 19, 148, 188, 192, 226, 233. *See also* Saint Petersburg
Lepenies, Wolf, 58
Lethen, Helmut, 165n6
Levitov, I. S., 121
Lichkov, L. S., 122
Linke, Gerhardt, 190–91
Little Ice Age, 6, 47, 49
Lomonosov, Mikhail, 58, 60, 62–63, 65
London, 49–50
Luc, Jean André, 63
Lukács, Georg, 144
Lukin, Iurii, 228
Lund, Sweden, 50
Lydolph, Paul E., 3

Machtet, G. A., 126
Main Directorate of the Northern Sea Route (GUSMP), 227, 231–32
Main Geophysical Observatory in Leningrad, 99, 106
Makarov, Sergei, 235–36, 239–40
Makarova, Vera, 238
Malevich, Kazimir, 143
masculinity
  images of, 170, 173–80
Mediterranean, 76, 165, 172
Medvedev, D. A., 5
Meier, F. C., 50
mercury

freezing of, 3, 48, 59–64, 193
Mertsalov, A. N., 187
meteorological
   data, 49–50, 58, 99, 188
   instruments, 3, 20, 47–53, 58–61, 63, 193, 197
   network, 25, 50–52, 58, 64–65
   observation, 25, 48–53
   phenomenon, 9, 11, 19–20, 48, 74, 135, 170, 250
   station, 51, 157
   study, 6, 25–29, 251
meteorologist, 22, 25–27, 30, 32–33, 63–64, 105, 137
meteorology, 10, 19, 24–30
militarization, 207
Milov, Leonid, 7, 188
Ministry
   of Agriculture's Scientific Research Institute of Polar Agriculture, 106
   of Internal Affairs (MVD), 188, 198
Model, Johann Georg, 60
Monastyrskii, Boris, 148
Montesquieu, Charles Louis de Secondat, 21–24, 36n28, 65
Mordovian ASSR, 195
Moscow, 4, 47, 121, 158, 165n14, 187–91, 193, 199, 214, 216–17, 232–34
Mud'iug Island, 209
Mukachevo, 205
Müller, Gerhard Friedrich, 24
Murmansk, 104, 152, 161, 206, 212–13, 216

Nansen, Fridtjof Wedel-Jarlsberg, 135, 157
Napoleon, 8, 19, 143, 191–92
Nar'ian-Mar, 216
Narym, 124
national trauma, 169–80
Nechkina, M. V., 31
Nekrasov, N. A., 114–15
Neva, 47–48, 54, 56
Nevskii, Aleksandr, 19, 147, 226
Nietzsche, Friedrich, 174
Nikonov, A. P., 4
NKVD, 188, 194, 197–98

Nobile, Umberto, 135, 159
Nordenskiöld, Otto von, 78
North, 4, 8, 10, 15n28, 20–23, 26–29, 47, 64, 95–98, 103–5, 142, 153, 194, 209, 216, 252
North America, 50, 104, 107
North Polar Sea, 79
North Pole, 5, 76, 135, 156, 162, 210, 227–32, 234, 242
Northeast Passage, 4, 13n4. *See also* Northern Sea Route
Northern region, 7–8, 23, 64, 99, 155, 158, 188, 194–96
Northern Sea Route, 227, 231–32, 252
Novosibirsk, 212
Novosil'skii, Pavel M., 77–78, 82–84

Ob, 124
Oborina, Evgeniia, 205
Onufrowich, Bolesław, 127
Osipov, N. O., 124
Owen, Russell, 79

Pabst, G.W., 173
Pacific
   Coast, 227
   Northern, 103
   Ocean, 28, 216
Paglia, Camille, 143
Pakhta-Aral'skii, 194
Pallas, Peter Simon, 62
Palmer, Nathaniel, 79–80, 82, 86–87
Pamir, 140, 158, 163n2
Papanin, I. D., 135, 226–34, 239, 242, 246nn35–36
Paris, 47, 49
Pasternak, Boris, 146
Peipus, Lake, 3, 19, 148, 226
People's Commissariat (Narkomat), 227
permafrost, 4, 26, 103. *See also* frost
Peter I, 21, 30, 54, 97, 155, 165n14
Peter I Island, 76, 81, 84
Petrozavodsk, 204
Plekhanov, Georgii, 31
Pogosian, Elena, 54

polar history, 74–87, 91n54, 154, 157, 160, 227
polar ice, 5, 28, 75–77, 79–80, 82–86, 91n59, 228–34, 242–43
poles of cold, 64
Ponomarev, S. M., 125
popular imagination, 136–37
Preiss, Wolfgang, 178
Preobrazhenskii, Iurii, 31
Priamur region, 123
Prinzing, Robert, 196
Proust, Marcel, 171
Pudovkin, Vsevolod, 143–44
Putin, V.V., 5, 242–43, 247nn67–68

Réaumur, René-Antoine Ferchault de, 53
recreation, 11–12, 204, 211–19, 251
Reizer, Leonid, 235–36, 239, 241
Remnev, A. V., 113, 121
Riefenstahl, Leni, 139, 174, 192
Riiser-Larsen, Hjalmar, 79
Rodchenko, Alexander, 141
Rodoman, Boris, 209
Romm, Mikhail, 144
Rommel, Erwin, 176
Ross, James Clark, 76–77, 79, 86–87
Rou, Aleksandr, 150
Royal Society of London, 50–51, 53
Russian Academy of Sciences. *See* Academy: of Sciences in Saint Petersburg
Russian Antarctic Commission, 83
Russian Antarctic expedition 1819–1821, 75–87
Russian Geographical Society, 75, 80, 252
Russian Geographical Society's Meteorological Commission, 98
Russian Society for Tourists, 205

Saian mountains, 210
Saint Petersburg, 21, 47–62, 64–65, 98. *See also* Leningrad
Saint Petersburg Academy. *See under* Academy of Sciences in Saint Petersburg
Saint Petersburg University, 96–97
Sakhalin, 123, 154, 212, 214

Salamatov, Petr, 52
Sandomirskaia, Irina, 209, 215
Shmidt, O. Iu., 135, 227, 233
Schneeberger, Hans, 174
Scott Polar Research Institute, 79
Scott, Robert Falcon, 78
seasonal attractions, 204–19
Second World War. *See* World War II
Shalamov, Varlam, 151–53
Shaposhnikov, B. M., 188
Sharp, Dennis, 172
Shepit'ko, Larisa, 149–51
Shirshov, Petr, 228, 230, 233, 246n27
Shokal'skii, Iulii, 79
Sholokhov, Mikhail, 228
Shparo, Dmitrii, 210
Shvede, Evgenii E., 80–83
Siberia, 10–11, 20, 22, 24–25, 28, 47–48, 51, 53, 56–57, 59–60, 64–65, 97, 104–5, 113–28, 129n5, 130n25, 135, 155–57, 160–62, 169–70, 179–80, 188, 194, 250–51. *See also* Asiatic Russia
Simonov, Ivan M., 76, 82, 85, 91n59
skiing, 12, 148, 174, 204–19
Slutskii, Boris, 191
snow, 3, 6–8, 10–12, 19, 47, 52, 56–57, 60, 62, 65, 83, 99, 102, 104, 120, 134–43, 148–53, 155, 162, 165, 172–73, 175–77, 179–80, 189–93, 204–5, 207, 210–12, 216–17, 219, 229–32, 243, 249–51
Societas Meteorologica Palatina, 52. *See also* meteorological network
Society
 for Aid to Needy Settlers, 123
 for Assistance to Defense, Aviation, and Chemical Construction (OSOAVIAKhIM), 207, 217
 for Proletarian Tourism of the RSFSR, 205
Solov'ev, Sergei, 7, 29
South Pole, 76–80, 84–85
South Pole expedition, 10, 74–87, 90n33
Soviet POW camps, 162, 169, 178–80, 194–98
Spielberg, Steven, 139

Stalin, J. V., 27–28, 30–31, 75, 145–47, 165n14, 165n18, 169, 229, 245n26, 246n35
Stalin era, 97, 97, 100, 136, 140–42, 164, 205, 207–11, 215, 217, 219, 221n26, 233, 251
Stalingrad, 155, 161, 169–70, 176–80, 187, 193–94, 199
Staniukovich, K. M., 121, 126, 130n22
Stiller, Mauritz, 139
Stolper, Aleksandr, 142, 151, 156, 161, 178
Strohmeyer, Ernst August, 63
subarctic, 95, 101–7, 250

Takov, 214
Tarasov-Kaslinskii, A., 204, 207–208
Tarkovsky, Andrei, 138–39, 153
Tazhikistan, 214
temperature per capita, 47, 66n3
thick journals, 113–14, 123, 128
Tian-Shan, 140, 212
Tikhonov, V. V., 241, 247n63, 247n64
Tiumen, 118, 160, 212, 222n52
Tiupa, V. I., 113
Tobol'sk, Province, 126
Tolstoi, L. N., 135
Tomsk, 52, 121
tourism, 12, 204–19, 220n6, 221n26, 221n30, 223n77
Trauberg, Leonid, 144
Traversay, Marquis de, 84–85
Trenker, Luis, 139, 173
Tret'iakov, Sergei, 140
Trinity Land, 80
Troianovskii, Vitalii, 149
Tseitlin, A. G., 126–27
tundra, 95–106, 154

Ukrainian SSR, 159, 213
Umgelter, Fritz, 169, 178–80
United States, 4, 19, 28, 75, 85–86, 172, 176
Urals, 116, 121, 156–57, 194, 206, 210, 212
US Weather Bureau, 107

USSR, 95, 97, 103–104, 155, 158, 160, 178, 187–99, 204–19, 221n30, 226–44, 247n55
Uzbekistan, 195–96, 214

Vasil'ev, Sergei, 144, 156, 164n4
Velikii Ustiug, 64
Vernadskii, V. I., 96
Vertov, Dziga, 140–41, 144–47, 164n4
Viazemskii, Konstantin, 120
Victoria Land, 76
visual imagination, 134–53
Voeikov, Alexander, 26–27, 98–99
Volga, 120
Vrangel, Ferdinand, 26
Vyborg, 120, 144

weather, 4–7, 9, 11, 19–20, 22–29, 32, 34, 48–53, 58–59, 62, 65, 80, 82, 126, 190–91, 196–98, 230, 232, 243, 249
Weimar Republic, 171, 173–75, 180
Weiss, Heinz, 169, 178
Werrett, Simon, 54
Wheatcroft, Stephen, 188
White Sea, 227
Wieder, Joachim, 193–94
Wild, Heinrich, 25, 27
Wilkes, Charles, 76–77, 79, 86–87
winter tourism, 12, 204–19, 223n77
Wisbar, Frank, 169, 176, 178, 180
Wolf, Rudolf, 26–27, 33
Wolff, Larry, 47
World War II, 3, 11, 29, 74, 156–57, 160–61, 163, 171, 176, 180, 187–99, 210, 226, 250

Yalta, 239

Zarusky, Jürgen, 180
Zefirov, Mikhail, 187
Zeiher, Johann Ernst, 60
Ziemann, Sonja, 178
Zoshchenko, Mikhail, 147

www.ingramcontent.com/pod-product-compliance
Lightning Source LLC
Chambersburg PA
CBHW071337080526
44587CB00017B/2863